CAREER OPPORTUNITIES IN THE RETAIL AND WHOLESALE INDUSTRY

Sʜᴇʟʟʏ Fɪᴇʟᴅ

Facts On File, Inc.

This book is dedicated to my parents Ed and Selma Field who were always there to cheer me on through every step and every milestone. Thank you for believing in my dreams and helping me along the way.

CAREER OPPORTUNITIES IN THE RETAIL AND WHOLESALE INDUSTRY

Copyright © 2001 by Shelly Field

Checkmark Books
An imprint of Facts On File, Inc.
11 Penn Plaza
New York, NY 10001

Library of Congress Cataloging-in-Publication Data

Field, Shelly.
     Career opportunities in the retail and wholesale industry / Shelly Field.
          p.   cm.—(Career opportunities series)
     Includes bibliographical references and index.
     ISBN 0-8160-4315-9 (alk.paper)—ISBN 0-8160-4316-7 (pbk : alk.paper)
     1. Retail trade—Vocational guidance. I. Title. II. Facts on File's career opportunities series.

HF5429 .F434 2001
381′.023′73—dc21   00-053524

Checkmark Books are available at special discounts when purchased in bulk quantities for businesses, associations, institutions or sales promotions. Please call our Special Sales Department in New York at (212) 967-8800 or (800) 322-8755.

You can find Facts On File on the World Wide Web at http://www.factsonfile.com

Cover design by Nora Wertz

Printed in the United States of America

VB Hermitage 10 9 8 7 6 5 4 3 2 1
          (pbk) 10 9 8 7 6 5 4 3 2 1

This book is printed on acid-free paper.

CONTENTS

E-COMMERCE, MAIL ORDER, AND DIRECT RESPONSE SHOPPING

WHOLESALE

APPENDIXES

HOW TO USE THIS BOOK

Over the past few years, the retail and wholesale industries have expanded tremendously. Department stores, chains, and specialty stores are abundant in this country. Developers build new malls and shopping centers. There are superstores and mini-marts to shop in as well as large supermarkets, small groceries and more.

Catalogs sell every conceivable item. Infomercials fill the airwaves every night into the early morning hours. Televised shopping channels sell everything except homes and cars and that will probably happen in the future. With the use of the Internet, individuals and large companies alike can open on-line stores where customers can come from virtually anyplace in the world.

The retail and wholesale industries offer a wide array of career options. No matter your interest or your experience level, opportunities exist. Retail and wholesale jobs may be located anywhere. There are full-time positions and part-time jobs. There are often openings for young people still in high school, those who want to make retailing and wholesaling a career choice, and people retired and seeking to augment a fixed income.

This book is designed to help you prepare for interesting, exciting, fun, and rewarding jobs. If you are interested in working in retail, you can always find employment. A dedicated, hardworking employee can quickly move up the career ladder often without higher education.

Thousands are currently working in the retail and wholesale industries. Many more are eager to enter but have no concept of what career opportunities are available, where to find them, or what training and qualifications are required.

Career Opportunities in Retail and Wholesale is the single most comprehensive source for learning about job opportunities in this growing field. This book was written for everyone who aspires to work in retail and wholesale. It will give you an edge over other applicants. The jobs discussed in this book include careers not only in selling, but also in the business, administration, marketing, creative, and management areas.

The retail and wholesale industries offers an array of opportunities and requires people with a variety of different skills and talents. It needs salespeople, secretaries, bookkeepers, property managers, webmasters, artists, leasing people, security employees, administrative assistants, special events coordinators, advertising directors, customer service representatives, store managers, buyers, mystery shoppers, executives, car salespeople, copywriters, call center representatives, trade show representatives, and more. The trick to locating the job you want is developing your skills and using them to enter these exciting and expanding industries. Once you have your foot in the door, you can climb the career ladder to success.

Sources of Information

Information for this book was obtained through interviews, questionnaires, and a variety of books, magazines, newsletters, other literature, and television and radio programs. Some information was a result of fourteen years of personal experience as a marketing, public relations, and mall management consultant. Other data were obtained from friends and business associates in various areas of the retail and wholesale industries.

Among the people interviewed were men and women in all aspects of retailing and wholesaling. These include individuals working in the business, administration, and management end of the industries as well as frontline employees and support personnel.

Also interviewed were human resources directors and staff, training managers, publicists, marketing managers, property managers, salespeople, store managers, leasing directors, district managers, security people, maintenance supervisors, mall management personnel, marketing coordinators, public relations directors, benefit coordinators, sales associates, secretaries, administrative assistants, and others.

Interviews included personnel from large and small malls and shopping centers, manufacturers, specialty stores, discount stores, chains, department stores, car dealerships, groceries and supermarkets, distributors, schools, colleges, unions, and trade associations.

Organization of Material

Career Opportunities in the Retail and Wholesale Industry is divided into five general employment sections. These sections are: Malls and Shopping Centers; Department Stores; Stores, Chains, Shops, and Boutiques; E-Commerce, Mail

Order, and Direct Response Shopping; and Wholesale. Within each of these sections are descriptions of individual careers.

There are two parts to each job classification. The first part offers job information in a chart form. The second part presents information in a narrative text. In addition to the basic career description, you will find additional information on unions and associations as well as tips for entry.

Ten appendixes are offered to help locate information you might want or need to get started looking for a job in the field. These appendixes include two- and four-year college and university degree programs in retail management, public relations, and advertising; trade associations and unions and other organizations; a bibliography of retail and wholesale industry books and periodicals; directory of chain stores; directory of department stores; directory of supermarkets and groceries; directory of catalog companies; tele-

vision shopping channels; directory of manufacturers and other companies; and a glossary.

This book will help you take the first step toward preparing for a great career. Job opportunities exist throughout the country and the world and are increasing. Opportunities exist in malls, shopping centers, discount stores, chains, department stores, specialty shops, auto dealerships, television shopping channels, catalogs, manufacturers, wholesalers, and more.

No matter which facet of the retail or wholesale job market you choose to enter, you can find a career that is rewarding, exciting, challenging, and fun. The jobs are out there waiting for you. You just have to go after them. Persevere. I know you will have a great career!

—Shelly Field
www.shellyfield.com

ACKNOWLEDGMENTS

I would like to thank every individual, company, union, and association that provided information, assistance, and encouragement for this book.

I acknowledge with appreciation my editor, James Chambers, for his continuous help and encouragement. I gratefully acknowledge the assistance of Ed and Selma Field for their ongoing support in this and every other of my projects.

Others whose help was invaluable include Ellen Ackerman; Advertising Club of New York; Advertising Council; Advertising Research Foundation; Advertising Women of New York, Inc.; Harrison Allen; Julie Allen; American Association of Advertising Agencies; Dan Barrett; Lloyd Barriger, Barriger and Barriger; Allan Barrish; Steve Blackman; Joyce Blackman; Theresa Bull; Earl "Speedo" Carroll; Eileen Casey, Superintendent, Monticello Central Schools; Catskill Development; Anthony Cellini, Town of Thompson Supervisor; Brandi Cesario, Nevada Society of Certified Public Accountants; Patricia Claghorn; Dr. Jessica L. Cohen; Lorraine Cohen; Norman Cohen; Jan Cornelius; Crawford Library Staff; Margaret Crossley, Nevada Society of Certified Public Accountants; Meike Cryan; Daniel Dayton; W. Lynne Dayton; Carrie Dean; Charlie Devine, Devine Realty, Inc.; Direct Mail/Marketing Association, Inc.; Direct Marketing Educational Foundation, Inc.; Joseph Doucette, General Sales Manager, Middletown Honda; Dress Barn; Scott Edwards; Michelle Edwards; Dan England, UNLV; Ernest Evans; Julie Evans; Sara Feldberg; Field Associates, Ltd.; Deborah K. Field, Esq.; Greg Field; Edwin M. Field; Lillian (Cookie) Field; Mike Field; Robert Field; Selma G. Field; Finkelstein Memorial Library Staff; David Garthe, CEO, Graveyware.com; John Gatto; Sheila Gatto; Morris Gerber; Kaytee Glantzis; Larry Goldsmith; Sam Goldych; Alex Goldman; Gail Haberle; Hermann Memorial Library Staff;

Hank Hershey; Joan Howard; International Brotherhood of Electrical Workers; International Council of Shopping Centers; Linda Joslin; Jimmy "Handyman" Jones; K-LITE Radio; Dave Kleinman; Janice Kleinman; Bruce Kohl, Boston Herald.com; Crystal Lauter; Karen Leever; Liberty Central School; Liberty Public Library Staff; Judy McCoy; June E. McDonald; Phillip Mestman; Rima Mestman; Beverly Michaels, Esq.; Martin Michaels, Esq.; Monticello Central School High School Library Staff; Monticello Central School Middle School Library Staff; Jennifer Morganti, Nevada Society of Certified Public Accountants; Middletown Honda, Middletown, N.Y.; David Morris; National Association of Music Merchants; National Association of Recording Merchandisers; National Music Publishers Association; National Retail Federation; Earl Nesmith; Newburgh Free Library; New York State Employment Service; Nikkodo, U.S.A., Inc.; Ellis Norman, UNLV; Heather Dawn O'Keefe; Ivy Pass; Ed Pearson, Nokkodo, USA; Outlet Bound; Barbara Pezzella; Herb Perry; Public Relations Society of America; Doug Puppel; QVC; Harvey Rachlin; Ramapo Catskill Library System; John Riegler; Doug Richards; Diane Ruud, Nevada Society of Certified Public Accountants; Joy Shaffer; Raun Smith, Casino Career Center; Smith Employment Agency; Laura Solomon; Debbie Springfield; Matthew E. Strong; Sullivan County Community College; The Teenagers; United States Department of Labor; Brian Vargas; Pat Varriale; Carol Williams; John Williams; Ann Williamson; John Wolfe, General Manager, WTZA-Television; WSUL Radio, WVOS Radio and WTZA.

My thanks also to the many people, associations, companies, and organizations that provided material for this book who wish to remain anonymous.

FOREWORD

As Senior Vice President of Marketing and Administration for Belz Enterprises and as President of the Belz Factory Outlet division, I relish the opportunity to contribute to an ever-evolving industry that is continually offering new career opportunities and challenges. I have witnessed firsthand revolutions in all sectors of retail, wholesale, and discount merchandising, so I was especially pleased when Shelly Field asked me to write the foreword to *Career Opportunities in the Retail and Wholesale Industry.*

As multibillion-dollar industries, the retail and wholesale fields are closely intertwined, with the success of each depending largely upon that of the other. Together they are huge economic forces offering vast employment opportunities.

Every day hundreds of thousands of employees in all facets of the retail industry go to work. These jobs would not be possible without the wholesale sector manufacturing and selling the product to the retail industry. There are myriad employment opportunities for individuals with varying talents and skills in both the wholesale and retail sectors. What you do depends on your dreams and desires.

Until now, there has been no comprehensive guide describing career opportunities in these industries. Shelly Field,

a fourteen-year veteran consultant to shopping centers nationwide and national SAVVY Marketing Award recipient, has done a remarkable job of researching these opportunities and detailing them in this volume.

Career Opportunities in the Retail and Wholesale Industry is a great source for those just starting out as well as for veterans aspiring to move into other aspects of either field. This book offers people at all levels of career achievement the information they need to match their skills, talents, and interests to the vast opportunities available. If you're looking for a career with few limits as well as one offering a variety of future growth opportunities, consider a career in the wholesale or retail industries. If you are willing to work hard, you will have no trouble climbing the career ladder. I invite everyone looking for an exciting, rewarding, and gratifying career to read this book so you too can learn more about becoming part of the retail/wholesale world and explore the possibilities.

—Andrew J. Groveman
President, Belz Factory Outlet Division,
Belz Enterprises, pioneer of the
Factory Outlet Mall

INTRODUCTION

As far back as anyone can remember, trade has existed. It may not always have taken the sophisticated form that we know today, but it was trade just the same. Throughout history, people traded with each other first to get necessities such as food and clothing, and then to obtain luxuries as well.

Barter may have preceded the exchange of money in trading and still exists to some extent in some circles. However, today, money is the medium of exchange.

Before there were marketplaces there were peddlers, traveling salespeople and trading caravans. Then people traveled to marketplaces in towns where small stalls sold specialty items and wares. As time went on towns had general stores where almost anything could be purchased. Today there are department stores, specialty stores, supermarkets, malls, and shopping centers for people to buy everything they want and need. Catalogs, televised shopping, and on-line options also exist.

Over the years, retail and wholesale has evolved into a multibillion-dollar business. Today, thousands and thousands of people work in these industries. We all reap the benefits and pleasures of trade.

As you read the various sections in this book, searching to find the "perfect" job, keep in mind every job can be a learning experience and a stepping stone to the next level. I have given you the guidelines. You have to do the rest.

Within each section of this book you will find all of the information necessary to acquaint you with most of the important jobs in the industry. A key to the organization of each entry follows:

Alternate Titles

Many jobs in retail and wholesale, as in all industries, are known by alternate titles. The duties of these jobs are the same; only the name is different. Titles vary from company to company.

Career Ladder

The career ladder illustrates a normal job progression. Remember that in many parts of retail and wholesale there are no hard-and-fast rules. Job progression may not necessarily follow a precise order.

Position Description

Every effort has been made to give well-rounded job descriptions. Keep in mind that no two companies are structured exactly the same. Therefore, no two jobs will be exactly alike.

Salary Ranges

Salary ranges for the job titles in this book are as accurate as possible. Salaries for a job will depend on how big a company is, where it is located, and the applicant's experience.

Employment Prospects

If you choose a job that has an EXCELLENT, GOOD, or FAIR rating, you are lucky. You will have an easier time finding a job. If, however, you would like to work at a job that has a POOR rating, don't despair. The rating means that it is difficult to obtain a job—not totally impossible.

Advancement Prospects

Try to be as cooperative and helpful as possible in the workplace. Don't try to see how little work you can do. Be enthusiastic, energetic, and outgoing. Do that little extra that no one asked you to do. When a job advancement possibility opens up, make sure that you're prepared for it.

Education and Training

Although the book only gives the minimum training and educational requirements, this doesn't mean that is all you should have. Try to get the best training and education possible. A college degree does not guarantee a job, but it might help prepare a person for life in the workplace. Education and training also encompass courses, seminars, programs, on-the-job training, and learning from others. Volunteer work, internships, and even helping out in family businesses can look good on your resume.

Experience, Skills, and Personality Traits

These will differ from job to job. However, whichever job you want, you will probably need a lot of perseverance. Being an outgoing individual also helps. Networking is essential to success. Contacts are important in all facets of the business. Make as many as you can. These people will be helpful in advancing your career.

Best Geographical Location

Most jobs in retail can be located throughout the country. Wholesale jobs may be easier to locate in large cities or areas where there is more industry. If you are creative in your job hunting, opportunities may be found most anywhere in the country.

Unions/Associations

Unions and trade associations offer valuable help in getting into the business, obtaining jobs, and making contacts. They may also offer scholarships, fellowships, seminars, and other programs.

Tips for Entry

Use this section for ideas on how to get a job and gain entry into the area of the business in which you are interested. When applying for any job always be as professional as possible. Dress neatly. Don't wear sneakers. Don't chew gum. Don't smoke. Always have a few copies of your resume with you. These, too, should look neat. Have them typed and well presented.

Use *every* contact you have. Don't get hung up on the idea that you want to get a job by yourself. If you are lucky enough to know someone who can help you obtain a job you want, take him or her up on it. You'll have to prove yourself at the interview and on the job. Nobody can do that for you. (Remember to send a thank-you note to the person who helped you as well as to the interviewer after the interview.)

Once you get your foot in the door, learn as much as you can. Do that little extra bit of work that is not expected of you. Be cooperative. Be a team player. Don't burn bridges; it will hurt your career. Ask for help. Network. Find a mentor.

Remember that customer service is very important in every part of retail and wholesale. Even if you feel the customer is wrong, try to make him or her feel important and valued. The ability to provide excellent customer service will help you excel in your career no matter the area in which you work.

The last piece of advice in this section is to *be on time* for everything. This includes job interviews, phone calls, work, and meetings. People will remember when you're habitually late and it will work against you in advancing your career.

Have faith and confidence in yourself. You *will* make it to the top eventually, but you must persevere. In many instances the individual who didn't make it in the career they wanted is the one who gave up too soon and didn't wait that extra day.

Have fun reading this book. Use it. It will help you find a career that is rewarding and exciting. When you do get the job of your dreams, do someone else a favor and pass along the benefit of your knowledge. Help them too.

We love to hear success stories. If this book helped you in your quest for a job and you would like to share your story, go to www.shellyfield.com and let us know.

Good luck!

MALLS AND
SHOPPING CENTERS

PROPERTY MANAGER— SHOPPING CENTER/MALL

CAREER PROFILE

Duties: Overseeing one or more shopping center properties; handling the day-to-day management of shopping center properties; acting as owner's agent; negotiating leases and rental agreements

Alternate Titles: Real Estate Manager

Salary Range: $35,000 to $125,000,000+

Employment Prospects: Fair

Advancement Prospects: Fair

Best Geographical Location(s) for Position: Jobs may be located throughout the country

Prerequisites:

Education and Training—Educational requirements vary
Experience—Experience in mall management, real estate management, or related fields necessary
Special Skills and Personality Traits—Problem solving skills; negotiation skills; communication skills; ability to deal well with people; administrative skills

CAREER LADDER

```
┌─────────────────────────────────┐
│   Property Manager for Larger,   │
│  More Prestigious Malls, Shopping │
│      Centers, Management         │
│    or Development Companies       │
└─────────────────────────────────┘

┌─────────────────────────────────┐
│   Property Manager—Shopping      │
│         Center/Mall              │
└─────────────────────────────────┘

┌─────────────────────────────────┐
│   Assistant Property Manager     │
│        or Mall Manager           │
└─────────────────────────────────┘
```

Position Description

The retail Property Manager is responsible for overseeing one or more shopping center properties. The individual acts as the owner's agent representing landlords, owners, and investors of shopping centers and malls. In some situations, the Property Manager also oversees additional income producing properties such as office buildings, residential buildings, and commercial properties.

The responsibilities of Property Managers vary depending on the specific situation and structure of the company with which he or she works. In smaller companies, the Property Manager may have more general duties. In larger companies, the individual may handle more specific responsibilities. The Property Manager at one company may, for example, oversee mall managers at various malls. Another company may not employ on-site managers and the Property Manager must float from center to center making frequent visits to each.

This job involves a great deal of bookkeeping and paperwork. The Property Manager may do this alone or it may be handled by an on-site manager, bookkeeper, and/or secretaries. While tenants are supposed to pay rents and other fees on a timely basis, this doesn't always happen without some prompting. The Property Manager is expected to make sure all the rents and fees are collected and credited properly. He or she must also pay all bills, mortgages, taxes, insurance premiums, and payrolls and account for all expenditures.

The Property Manager must be adept at tenant relations. It is essential that the individual deal well with people and keep tenants as happy as possible. Tenants need to feel that their problems and concerns are taken seriously. If they feel otherwise, they will not renew their leases.

One of the most important functions of Property Managers is problem solving. A leaky roof, a lack of customers, a negative story about the mall in the media, a snow covered parking lot, a flood in one of the stores, or a new store which is not ready on time can all turn into disasters if not handled quickly and efficiently. A successful Property Manager will know what to do and who to call to resolve every situation.

Property Managers lease empty stores and other vacant space. They may do this alone or with the help of leasing managers, leasing agents, or leasing consultants. As part of the job, they negotiate leases and other rental agreements under the direction of the mall owners, developers, or landlords.

An important responsibility of Property Managers is bidding and negotiating contracts for services. These might include grounds keeping, snow removal, security, janitorial, maintenance, and other services. Managers might also bid on and negotiate for equipment and supplies including cleaning supplies, paper products, landscaping, or office products.

Additional duties of Property Managers might include:

- Overseeing construction
- Dealing with governmental officials, community and public interest groups, and public utilities
- Overseeing consultants
- Hiring and supervising on-site personnel

Salaries

Annual earnings for Property Managers working in shopping centers can range from approximately $35,000 to $125,000 or more. Compensation is determined by the size, prestige, geographic location, and number of properties the Manager oversees as well as the experience, responsibilities, and education of the individual. Property Managers in some situations may receive bonuses or a small percentage of ownership in projects.

Employment Prospects

Employment prospects for Property Managers are fair. Property Managers may find employment throughout the country. Individuals may be employed by malls or work for real estate developers, development companies, or property management companies. It should be noted that relocation may be necessary to take advantage of job openings.

Advancement Prospects

Property Managers can climb the career ladder in a number of ways. More experience, additional training, and certification help individuals obtain better paying jobs. One of the most common methods of career advancement in this field is locating similar positions with larger, more prestigious real estate development companies and property management firms.

Education and Training

Much of the training Property Managers receive is on the job. However, whether the individual works directly for malls, shopping centers, real estate developers, or property management companies, most employers require or prefer applicants with a college degree. Relevant majors might include real estate, business administration, liberal arts, retail management, public administration, finance, or communications.

Professional and trade associations often offer helpful seminars and courses in all aspects of construction, finance, marketing, human resources, and retail management.

The International Council of Shopping Centers (ICSC) offers a voluntary certification program for shopping center management.

Experience, Skills, and Personality Traits

Experience is essential in order to become a Property Manager. Some individuals begin their careers as on-site mall managers, promotion, marketing, or public relations managers or in some aspect of real estate.

Property Managers should be energetic, detail-oriented and highly motivated. Individuals need to know a great deal about many different areas. To begin with, Property Managers should have a basic understanding and knowledge of maintenance, construction, human resources, tenant relations, community relations, leasing, budgets, advertising, and marketing.

One of the most important skills that a good Property Manager should have is the ability to solve problems while remaining calm. Communication skills, both written and verbal, are essential. The ability to work with and get along with a variety of people on all levels is necessary.

Unions/Associations

Property Managers may be members of a number of trade associations. These include the International Council of Shopping Centers (ICSC), the Building Owners and Managers Institute International (BOMII) and the Institute of Real Estate Management (IREM).

Tips for Entry

1. Many larger property management and real estate development companies have internships and training programs.
2. There are a number of search firms dealing exclusively with jobs in shopping centers and malls.
3. Send your resume and a cover letter to retail property management companies, real estate development companies, and large malls.
4. Positions are often advertised in the classified sections of newspapers. Look under classifications including "Property Management," "Property Manager," or "Retail Real Estate Management."

5. Jobs in this field, might also be located on-line. Begin your search on some of the more popular job search sites such as the Monster board (www.monster.com) and Hot Jobs (www.hotjobs.com).

6. Positions may also be advertised in trade journals such as *Value Retail News.*

7. Attend seminars and classes to hone skills and make professional contacts.

MALL MANAGER

CAREER PROFILE

Duties: Overseeing the day-to-day management of mall or shopping center; negotiating leases and rental agreements; acting as owner's agent

Alternate Titles: Shopping Center Manager

Salary Range: $29,000 to $100,000+

Employment Prospects: Fair

Advancement Prospects: Good

Best Geographical Location(s) for Position: Jobs may be located throughout the country

Prerequisites:

Education and Training—Educational requirements vary

Experience—Experience in mall management, marketing and/or promotions preferred

Special Skills and Personality Traits—Problem solving skills; negotiation skills; communication skills; public relations skills; ability to deal well with people; administrative skills

CAREER LADDER

```
┌─────────────────────────────────┐
│        Mall Manager for Larger,  │
│   More Prestigious Mall or Shopping │
│   Center or Property Manager     │
└─────────────────────────────────┘

┌─────────────────────────────────┐
│          Mall Manager            │
└─────────────────────────────────┘

┌─────────────────────────────────┐
│     Assistant Mall Manager       │
│      or Marketing Director       │
└─────────────────────────────────┘
```

Position Description

The Mall Manager has a great deal of responsibility. He or she is responsible for overseeing everything that occurs in the mall or shopping center. Some duties may vary depending on the specific structure of the mall, while others are common to all shopping centers.

Mall Managers represent the mall's owner. In this capacity, the individual meets with a variety of people for a wide array of reasons. For example, the Mall Manager might meet with government officials or city or county representatives or attend city or town council meetings to work on changes in zoning, explore grant possibilities, or lobby for tax abatements.

Malls and shopping centers must meet state and local building code requirements. The Mall Manager may meet with state or local building inspectors to learn how to obtain certificates of occupancy for the mall or its individual stores.

Every mall has tenants with problems and concerns that need to be dealt with on a timely basis. Good tenant relations are essential in this job. The Mall Manager is expected to meet with local and corporate tenants, store managers, and owners, and address these concerns. Tenants may, for

example, be worried about security issues, increased rents, heavy shoplifting, mall hours, or mall maintenance. Successful Mall Managers listen to concerns and try to deal with them effectively. It is essential that tenants feel that they are important and are being listened to or they will not be eager to renew their lease. In many centers, Mall Managers also facilitate regular tenant meetings.

The Mall Manager may be in charge of leasing space or may oversee a leasing agent, director, or consultant. He or she may show stores to potential tenants, discuss the pros of the specific mall and negotiate leases. When negotiating, the individual must know the parameters regarding rents and extra charges.

Customers do not enjoy shopping in unkempt, dirty, or poorly maintained malls. One of the most important functions of the Mall Manager is the maintenance of the mall and its property. The most successful malls are clean and well maintained. To do this, Mall Managers must make sure rest rooms are kept clean and working; roofs are not leaking; floors are clean; and carpeting is free of debris, mold, and mildew. In addition the Mall Manager must attend to the outside of the property. This means making sure parking lots are free of potholes, snow and ice are cleaned during the winter months, the building is cared for, and the grounds are neat and clean. The Mall Manager usually oversees a maintenance and janitorial staff who handle these functions.

The Mall Manager works with members of the mall management staff. Depending on the size and structure of the specific property, these might include a promotions director, marketing director, advertising manager, public relations director, construction manager, leasing director, bookkeepers, and secretaries.

There is a great deal of paperwork in this job. The Mall Manager must make sure accurate records are kept of rents received and all expenditures. A bookkeeper may or may not assist with this. The individual is also responsible for keeping records of accidents or incidents involving customers or employees occurring in the mall. He or she might interview customers who slipped and fell in the mall, people who had accidents in the parking lot, or store managers who had shoplifting incidents. It is imperative that every incident be documented for insurance purposes and in case of lawsuits.

A great deal of what the Mall Manager does is solve problems. He or she must constantly try to keep tenants, customers, and the landlord happy.

Additional duties of Mall Managers might include:

- Developing the mall's annual budget
- Attending local community, civic, and not-for-profit meetings on behalf of the mall
- Overseeing construction
- Bidding and negotiating contracts for services, equipment, and supplies
- Hiring and supervising on-site personnel

Salaries

Earnings for Mall Managers can range from approximately $29,000 to $100,000 or more. Earnings are affected by the size, prestige, and geographic location of the mall, as well as the experience, responsibilities, and education of the individual.

Mall Managers in some situations may receive bonuses based on increases of sales, rentals, or the handling of extra projects.

Employment Prospects

Employment prospects for Mall Managers are fair. Individuals may find employment throughout the country. Mall Managers may be employed by malls directly or might work for real estate developers, development companies, or property management companies.

Advancement Prospects

Advancement prospects for Mall Managers are good. As individuals gain experience, they can climb the career ladder by locating similar positions with larger, more prestigious malls or by becoming property managers for larger real estate developers.

Education and Training

Educational requirements vary from mall to mall. While much of the training individuals receive is on the job, most employers prefer their Mall Managers to have a college degree. Others require it. Good majors might include business, real estate, liberal arts, retail management, public administration, finance, communications, public relations, marketing, or related fields.

Professional and trade associations often offer helpful seminars and courses in all aspects of construction, finance, marketing, human resources, and retail management.

The International Council of Shopping Centers (ICSC) offers a voluntary certification program for shopping center management.

Experience, Skills, and Personality Traits

Mall Managers begin their careers in a variety of ways. Some start out as promotion or marketing directors. Others work in some aspect of real estate, manage stores, or work as assistant mall managers.

The ability to deal with and work well with people is essential for Mall Managers. Individuals need to be good problem solvers, energetic, detail oriented, and highly motivated.

A basic understanding and knowledge of maintenance, construction, security, tenant relations, community relations, leasing, budgets, advertising, and marketing is necessary.

Unions/Associations

Mall Managers do not usually belong to a bargaining union. They may, however, be members of a number of trade associations. These include The International Council of Shopping Centers (ICSC), the Building Owners and Managers Institute International (BOMII) and the Institute of Real Estate Management (IREM).

Tips for Entry

1. There are a number of executive search firms dealing exclusively with jobs in shopping centers and malls.
2. Contact larger property management and real estate development companies to find out what internship and training programs they have available in this area.
3. Consider sending your resume and a cover letter to retail property management companies, real estate development companies, and large malls.
4. Positions are often advertised in the classified sections of newspapers. Look under classifications including "Mall Management," or "Mall Manager," or "Shopping Center Manager."

5. Openings are also advertised in trade journals such as *Value Retail News.*
6. Jobs in this field, may be located on-line. Begin your search on some of the more popular job search sites such as the Monster board (www.monster.com) and Hot Jobs (www.hotjobs.com).

PUBLIC RELATIONS DIRECTOR— SHOPPING CENTER/MALL

CAREER PROFILE

Duties: Develop and implement shopping center and mall public relations and marketing campaigns; handle day-to-day public relations functions; create goodwill between the center and the community; plan and implement special events

Alternate Titles: Mall P.R. Manager; P.R. Director

Salary Range: $23,000 to $65,000+

Employment Prospects: Fair

Advancement Prospects: Fair

Best Geographical Location(s) for Position: Jobs may be located throughout the country

Prerequisites:

Education and Training—Bachelor's degree in public relations, advertising, business, journalism, marketing, liberal arts, English, communications, or business

Experience—Publicity or public relations experience or training necessary

Special Skills and Personality Traits—Creativity; good verbal and written communication skills; knowledge of retail industry

CAREER LADDER

```
┌─────────────────────────────────────┐
│  Shopping Center/Mall Marketing     │
│  Director or Public Relations       │
│  Director for Larger, More          │
│  Prestigious Center                 │
└─────────────────────────────────────┘

┌─────────────────────────────────────┐
│  Public Relations Director—Shopping │
│  Center/Mall                        │
└─────────────────────────────────────┘

┌─────────────────────────────────────┐
│  Assistant Public Relations         │
│  Director, P.R. Assistant or        │
│  Publicist                          │
└─────────────────────────────────────┘
```

Position Description

All malls and shopping centers have some type of public relations and marketing campaign. The Mall Public Relations Director develops these campaigns. He or she works with the mall marketing or advertising department and the advertising directors of various shops to promote the mall and its image and events. The main goal of the P.R. Director is to get as much positive publicity and exposure for the center as possible.

Depending on the size and structure of the specific center, the Public Relations Director may be referred to as the Public Relations Manager. In certain centers, the Public Relations Director also handles the responsibilities of the marketing director. In others, the P.R. Director works under the direction of the marketing director.

The Public Relations Director is expected to handle the day-to-day public relations functions at the mall. These might include developing and writing a variety of press releases, calendars, newsletters, special interest stories, and feature stories about mall events and special promotions. The P.R. Director must write clearly and concisely in a factual and interesting manner. He or she must develop "hooks" or angles to make stories and releases interesting to the media.

The individual may be responsible for producing both internal and external communications, booklets, pamphlets, posters, or newsletters. He or she may do all the actual writing and layout or work with assistants, publicists, graphic artists, copywriters, or printers, to complete projects.

The P.R. Director may take photographs of special events occurring in the mall or may assign the project to an assistant or professional photographer. Photos may then be used with captions to send to the press or used in other communications.

An important function of the P.R. Director is handling any problems which develop with mall customers, store owners, or managers. He or she might make phone calls to people who have had problems or write letters to try to resolve complaints and situations.

The Public Relations Director keeps in contact with the media to let them know about special events occurring at the mall and must answer calls from the media seeking information.

Often, the P.R. Director is asked to be the spokesperson for the center. He or she must speak on radio and television and to reporters. It is therefore imperative that the individual feels comfortable handling these tasks. It is also essential that the P.R. Director maintains a good business relationship with all media to help ensure that press releases get placed in papers and special events are covered by news people.

The Mall P.R. Director is often responsible for developing, planning, and implementing unique special events and promotions that draw people into the mall. These might include contests, weddings in the mall, taste tests, petting zoos, craft shows, antiques shows, classic car shows, or karaoke competitions. In some malls, these tasks may also be handled by an event coordinator.

The individual also is expected to create goodwill between the shopping center and the local community. He or she might, for example, invite local or civic groups such as hospitals, 4-H, schools, Red Cross, American Heart Association, Girl Scouts, or Boy Scouts into the mall to demonstrate activities, pass out literature, or raise money. These groups often hold bake sales, craft sales, or other events to help achieve their goals.

Additional duties of the Shopping Center P.R. Director may include:

- Helping mall stores promote their special events
- Developing media lists
- Attracting bus tours, shopping tours, or other group events
- Designing and developing promotional material

Salaries

Earnings for the Director of Public Relations working in shopping centers or malls can vary greatly depending on a number of variables. These include the size, location, and prestige of the mall as well as the experience and responsibilities of the individual. Annual salaries can range from $23,000 to $65,000 or more. Individuals with experience working in larger, more prestigious malls will earn the highest salaries.

Employment Prospects

Employment prospects are fair for individuals seeking this position. Jobs can be located in malls and shopping centers throughout the country. While smaller centers may have this position, the responsibilities of the P.R. Director may be picked up by the mall manager or marketing director.

There is a fair amount of turnover in this job due to advancement and the general mobility of people in today's job market.

Advancement Prospects

Prospects for career advancement for Public Relations Directors working in malls and shopping centers are fair. Individuals have a number of different options for moving up the career ladder.

One possibility is to move into a similar position in a larger or more prestigious center resulting in increased responsibilities and earnings. Another option is to move into the position of mall marketing director. Some Public Relations Directors move into mall management. Still others advance their careers by striking out on their own and starting P.R. consulting firms.

Education and Training

Most malls and shopping centers either require or prefer the person in this position to hold a minimum of a four-year college degree. Good choices for majors include public relations, advertising, business, journalism, marketing, liberal arts, English, communications, and business.

Courses and seminars in public relations, marketing, publicity, promotion, and the retail industry help give individuals an edge in both obtaining jobs and career advancement.

Experience, Skills, and Personality Traits

Public Relations Directors working in malls and shopping centers should be very creative people who can communicate effectively both verbally and on paper. The ability to deal well with people is essential.

P.R. Directors need to handle many tasks at the same time without getting flustered. Knowledge of publicity, promotion, public relations, and the retail industry will help the Public Relations Director working in this industry excel in his or her job and move up the career ladder.

Unions/Associations

Public Relations Directors working in malls and shopping centers do not usually belong to any union. Individuals may belong to a number of trade associations providing support and guidance. The most prevalent is the Public Relations Society of America (PRSA). This organization provides educational guidance, support, seminars, and important information to members. Mall P.R. Directors may also be members of the International Council of Shopping Centers (ICSC).

Tips for Entry

1. Join the student group of the Public Relations Society of America (PRSA). This association provides many services to help you cultivate your skills as well as offering an opportunity to make valuable contacts.

2. There is quite a bit of turnover in these positions. Consider sending your resume and a cover letter to a number of malls and shopping centers in the area in which you are interested. Ask that your resume be kept on file. Send your letter and resume to the mall owner, developer, or manager. Call each mall's management office to get correct names.

3. You might want to gain some experience in publicity or promotions by volunteering to handle publicity for a local civic or not-for-profit group or a school play or project.

4. Positions are advertised in display ads in newspapers. Look under classifications including "Public Relations," "Promotion," "Malls," "Shopping Center," or "Retail."

5. Larger malls and shopping centers often have internships in the management office. Others may have summer jobs as assistants. Contact malls in your area to check into the possibilities.

6. Take seminars and courses in promotion, public relations, marketing, and publicity.

7. Other seminars in retail management, mall management, and shopping center development will also give you added knowledge in the field as well as helping you make contacts.

8. There are employment agencies dealing specifically with finding employment position in public relations. Check ahead of time to see who pays the fee if you get a job.

PUBLICIST—SHOPPING CENTER/MALL

CAREER PROFILE

Duties: Publicize mall or shopping center; write press releases and compile press kits; deal with customer service problems

Alternate Titles: Public Relations Specialist; P.R. Rep; P.R. Representative

Salary Range: $18,000 to $40,000+

Employment Prospects: Fair

Advancement Prospects: Fair

Best Geographical Location(s) for Position: Jobs may be located throughout the country

Prerequisites:

Education and Training—Bachelor's degree in public relations, advertising, business, journalism, marketing, liberal arts, English, communications, or business

Experience—Publicity or public relations experience helpful

Special Skills and Personality Traits—Creativity; good verbal and written communication skills; pleasant personality; knowledge of retail industry

CAREER LADDER

```
┌─────────────────────────────────────┐
│   Mall Public Relations Director     │
│   or P.R. Director in Other Industry │
└─────────────────────────────────────┘

┌─────────────────────────────────────┐
│             Publicist                │
└─────────────────────────────────────┘

┌─────────────────────────────────────┐
│  Publicist in Other Industry or Intern │
└─────────────────────────────────────┘
```

Position Description

The main function of Publicists who work in malls is to publicize the center. Depending on the structure of the mall, individuals may have varied responsibilities. Some malls may employ P.R. directors and one or more Publicists. In these cases, the Publicist will work under the direction of the P.R. director. Other malls might not hire a P.R. director, opting instead to hire only a Publicist. In these cases the individual usually will handle more general duties.

The Publicist is expected to write stock press releases on the center, as well as news releases on special events and promotions the mall is holding. For example, the mall may be having a "Safe Trick or Treat" night for local children or a "Soap Opera Festival" hosting national television personalities. In order to get the most publicity from the event, the Publicist must develop press releases specific to the events and distribute them to the media. The Publicist also takes photographs of special events and promotions or finds someone else to handle the task.

Publicists develop and put together press kits on the shopping center. These might include stock press releases, the history of the center, fact sheets, mall brochures containing a list of stores, photographs, schedules of special events, and other interesting and pertinent information. The Publicist sends these press kits and press releases to the various media, and must compile media lists for the general trade as well as those specific to the retail and shopping center industry.

It is essential that the Publicist have a good working relationship with news editors for print, television, cable, and radio. The individual must also develop a good working relationship with television and radio producers, guest coordinators, and print feature editors, so he or she will be in a better position to have stories placed in print. The Publicist also answers calls from the media seeking information.

Publicists also handle customer relations problems. He or she might make phone calls to people who have had problems at the mall or write letters to resolve complaints and other situations.

If there is no P.R. director, the Publicist will be expected to act as the spokesperson for the center. This may include speaking on radio and television and to reporters.

Additional duties of the Publicist may include:

- Helping mall stores promote their special events
- Developing, planning, and implementing unique special events to draw people into the mall
- Designing and developing promotional material
- Creating goodwill between the shopping center and the local community

Salaries

Annual earnings for Mall Publicists may range from approximately $18,000 to $40,000. Salaries vary greatly depending on a number of factors. These may include the size, location, and prestige of the center as well as the responsibilities and experience of the individual.

Employment Prospects

Employment prospects are fair for individuals seeking this position. Jobs can be located in malls and shopping centers throughout the country. Larger malls may hire a P.R. director and one or more publicists. Smaller centers may hire one or the other.

There is a fair amount of turnover in this job due to advancement and the general mobility of people in today's job market.

Advancement Prospects

Publicists working in malls may advance their careers in a number of ways. After obtaining some experience, some individuals may climb the career ladder by landing jobs as either the assistant P.R. director or a full-fledged P.R. director. Others move into P.R. positions in other industries, some related, some not.

Education and Training

Generally, malls and shopping centers require or prefer the person in this position to hold a four-year college degree. Good choices for majors include public relations, advertising, business, journalism, marketing, liberal arts, English, communications, and business.

Courses and seminars in public relations, marketing, publicity, promotion, and the retail industry help give individuals an edge in both obtaining jobs and career advancement.

Experience, Skills, and Personality Traits

Publicists should enjoy working with people. Individuals should be outgoing, assertive, articulate, and personable. Publicists need to be creative enough to come up with catchy angles for press releases, media events, and feature stores. An excellent writing style is essential in this job. Verbal communications skills are mandatory.

Unions/Associations

Publicists working in malls and shopping centers do not usually belong to any union. Individuals may belong to a number of trade associations providing support and guidance. The most prevalent is the Public Relations Society of America (PRSA). This organization provides educational guidance, support, seminars, and important information to members. Individuals may also take advantage of activities of the International Council of Shopping Centers (ICSC).

Tips for Entry

1. Join the student group of the Public Relations Society of America (PRSA). This association provides many services to help you hone your skills as well offering an opportunity to make valuable contacts.
2. Send your resume and a cover letter to a number of malls and shopping centers in the area in which you are interested. Ask that your resume be kept on file if there are no current openings.
3. Obtain experience in publicity or promotions by volunteering to handle publicity for a local civic or not-for-profit group or a school play or project.
4. Job openings are often advertised in display ads in newspapers. Look under classifications including "Publicists," "Publicity," "Public Relations," "Promotion," "Malls," "Shopping Center," or "Retail."
5. Larger malls and shopping centers often have internships in the management office. Others may have summer jobs as assistants. Contact malls in your area to check into the possibilities.
6. Take seminars and courses in promotion, public relations, marketing, and publicity.

MARKETING DIRECTOR— SHOPPING CENTER/MALL

CAREER PROFILE

Duties: Develop and implement a mall's marketing plans and campaigns; handle day-to-day marketing functions; plan and implement special events; oversee advertising and public relations program

Alternate Titles: Mall Marketing Manager; Director of Marketing; Director of Mall Marketing

Salary Range: $24,000 to $70,000+

Employment Prospects: Good

Advancement Prospects: Good

Best Geographical Location(s) for Position: Jobs may be located throughout the country; areas hosting multiple malls and shopping centers will have more opportunities.

Prerequisites:

Education and Training—Bachelor's degree in marketing, public relations, advertising, business, journalism, liberal arts, English, communications, or business

Experience—Marketing, publicity, public relations, and advertising experience necessary

Special Skills and Personality Traits—Creativity; good verbal and written communications skills; people skills; knowledge of retail industry

CAREER LADDER

```
┌─────────────────────────────┐
│  Marketing Director at Larger, │
│    More Prestigious Mall       │
│      or Mall Manager           │
└─────────────────────────────┘

┌─────────────────────────────┐
│  Marketing Director—Shopping   │
│        Center/Mall             │
└─────────────────────────────┘

┌─────────────────────────────┐
│  Assistant Marketing Director— │
│     Shopping Center/Mall       │
└─────────────────────────────┘
```

Position Description

The Marketing Director of a mall or shopping center is responsible for developing the concepts and campaigns for marketing the center to potential shoppers. The Director is expected to determine the most effective techniques and programs for the mall and its tenants, and as part of the job, must plan and coordinate all of the centers marketing goals and objectives.

Shopping Centers may utilize a variety of programs and services to attract shoppers. The Marketing Director must select the most viable programs and services for his or her specific center.

For example, does the mall want to market to young families or senior citizens? Does the mall want to attract upscale shoppers or bargain hunters? The Marketing Director will base some of his or her marketing efforts on the answers to questions such as this.

To get this information, the Marketing Director does research by utilizing surveys, questionnaires, focus groups, and comments from shoppers.

Mall Marketing Directors must come up with new and innovative ideas to attract new visitors. These may cover a wide array of promotions, special events, and attractions, and might include exhibits, art shows, craft shows, carnivals, health fairs, and community fairs. Other promotions might run the gamut from cooking and craft demonstrations, antiques shows, career expos, and computer shows to sidewalk sales, wine and cheese tasting, beauty contests, weddings, and bridal shows.

Promotions are designed to bring people in to browse and hopefully buy. Marketing Directors often utilize traditional marketing efforts such as coupon books. Holidays and other annual events might feature Safe Trick or Treating, the Arrival of Santa Claus, the Easter Bunny, or

Mother's Day Make-Over Contests. The most successful Mall Marketing Directors are those who devise the most innovative and creative ideas.

Once the ideas are developed, the Marketing Director will work with the public relations and advertising directors to publicize and advertise the promotions. In smaller malls, the Marketing Director may also be responsible for handling the public relations and advertising functions.

Depending on the specific center, the Mall Marketing Director often will work in conjunction with local or corporate tenants on copromotions. For example, the mall may put together a shopping guide showcasing all the tenants, coupon books, or a bus program. Sometimes, the Marketing Director may work with tenants on co-op ads or billboards.

Additional duties of the Mall Marketing Director might include:

- Overseeing the marketing, public relations, and advertising programs
- Supervising the marketing, public relations, and advertising staff
- Developing bus tours, shopping tours, or other group events
- Designing and developing marketing materials
- Conducting marketing research

Salaries

Annual salaries for Marketing Directors of malls and shopping centers can range from approximately $24,000 to $70,000 or more, based on the size, prestige, and geographic location of the specific center as well as the experience and responsibilities of the individual. Generally, those working in larger, more prestigious malls have the highest salaries.

Many malls also have bonus plans for their Marketing Directors, where the individuals receive bonuses for annual or bi-annual increases in sales.

Employment Prospects

Most malls employ Marketing Directors. Employment prospects are fair for this position and getting better every day. Jobs can be located in malls and shopping centers throughout the country. The greatest number of opportunities will be located in areas hosting a large number of malls.

Advancement Prospects

Marketing Directors have a number of options in career advancement. The most common method of climbing the career ladder is locating a similar position with increased responsibilities and earnings in a larger, more prestigious mall.

Another possibility for career advancement is to become a mall manager. Some Marketing Directors move into marketing positions in other industries, while others strike out on their own and start their own marketing firms.

Education and Training

Mall Marketing Directors are usually required to hold a four-year college degree. Good choices for majors include public relations, advertising, business, journalism, marketing, liberal arts, English, communications, and business. Courses and seminars in marketing, public relations, publicity, promotion, and the retail industry are also helpful.

Experience, Skills, and Personality Traits

Communications skills, both written and verbal, are essential for Marketing Directors. Individuals should be creative, innovative, ambitious, articulate, and highly motivated. Marketing Directors also need to be energetic, with the ability to handle many details and projects at one time without getting flustered.

A knowledge of publicity, promotion, public relations, and advertising as well as research techniques is also necessary.

Unions/Associations

Marketing Directors working in malls and shopping centers do not usually belong to any union. Individuals may belong to a number of trade associations providing support and guidance. These might include International Council of Shopping Centers (ICSC), the American Marketing Association (AMA), the Marketing Research Association (MRA), and the Public Relations Society of America (PRSA).

Tips for Entry

1. Send your resume and a cover letter to a number of malls and shopping centers in the area in which you are interested. Ask that your resume be kept on file. Send your letter and resume to the mall owner, developer, or manager. Call the mall's management office to get correct names.
2. Positions are advertised in display ads in newspapers. Look under classifications including "Marketing," "Marketing Director," "Malls," "Shopping Center," or "Retail."
3. Join trade associations. These will help you in searching for internships, scholarships, and training programs. Jobs may also be advertised in trade journals.
4. Larger malls and shopping centers often have internships in the management office. Others may have summer jobs as assistants. Contact malls in your area to check into the possibilities.
5. Take seminars and courses in marketing, promotion, public relations, publicity, retail management, mall management, and shopping center development. These will give you an edge over other applicants as well as helping you hone your skills and make valuable contacts.

SHOPPING CENTER/MALL ADVERTISING DIRECTOR

CAREER PROFILE

Duties: Plan, develop, and implement advertising campaigns for a shopping center or mall

Alternate Titles: Ad Manager; Advertising Manager; Director of Advertising

Salary Range: $24,000 to $48,000+

Employment Prospects: Fair

Advancement Prospects: Fair

Best Geographical Location(s) for Position: Jobs may be located throughout the country

Prerequisites:

Education and Training—Bachelor's degree in advertising, business, journalism, public relations, marketing, liberal arts, English, communications, or business

Experience—Experience in some facet of advertising necessary

Special Skills and Personality Traits—Creativity; ability to handle details; knowledge of retail industry; knowledge of copywriting, graphics, and layout; ability to meet deadlines

CAREER LADDER

```
┌─────────────────────────────────────┐
│   Shopping Center/Mall Marketing     │
│   Director or Advertising Director   │
│   of Larger, More Prestigious Center │
└─────────────────────────────────────┘

┌─────────────────────────────────────┐
│      Shopping Center/Mall            │
│      Advertising Director            │
└─────────────────────────────────────┘

┌─────────────────────────────────────┐
│   Assistant Advertising Director     │
│   or Advertising Assistant           │
└─────────────────────────────────────┘
```

Position Description

Some communities feature a number of large malls and shopping centers, while others only have one or two small strip centers. In order to attract potential shoppers, malls and shopping centers must advertise.

The Advertising Director working in a shopping center or mall setting is responsible for planning, developing, and implementing advertising campaigns and individual ads for the facility. He or she may work with the center's private shop owners, corporate tenants, store managers, mall owner, and developers.

The Advertising Director is responsible for planning and developing the annual advertising budget for the center. The Advertising Director must develop campaigns for the entire year, including special plans for individual holidays, promotions, special events and sales programs. He or she will call, write, and meet with representatives of various media to get rate sheets, demographics, information sheets, and other useful material. The individual also meets with various representatives of the advertising media to learn more about their publications or broadcast stations.

Customers may come from local areas as well as long distances to shop, so the Mall Advertising Director must decide where his or her advertising dollars would best be spent. Choices might include local or regional newspapers, magazines and other publications, television stations, radio stations, cable stations, billboards, and the Internet.

After the Ad Director has developed the budget, he or she takes it either to the mall marketing director (if there is one), mall management, or the mall owners for review. If the budget is acceptable, the Ad Director then implements it. If it comes in too high, he or she must make adjustments.

In some instances, mall tenants pay an annual advertising fee to a community marketing fund, and these tenants may have more input into the way money is spent on advertising.

Shopping centers and stores often feel that as long as they have people walking and browsing, they will have shoppers. While these people may not make immediate purchases, they may buy at some later date. The Advertising Director works with the marketing, promotional, and public relations departments to come up with ads and campaigns to inform as many people as possible of what the mall offers. The objective for Mall Advertising Directors is to attract shoppers and browsers.

Mall Advertising Directors often work with the corporate headquarters of stores and private shops in the mall to put together group or cooperative ads. These are advertisements in which a number of mall stores advertise special sales together at a given time. This might also encompass placing ads advertising all of a mall's stores, shops, and food outlets in publications.

The Advertising Director is responsible for advertising all special events and promotions the mall is hosting. These might include craft, antique and home shows, petting zoos, circuses, celebrity appearances, soap opera festivals, performers, demonstrations, and other events. An Ad Director may develop personally such promotions or may just advertise events developed by the promotion or public relations departments.

The Advertising Director may be required to do actual copywriting, graphics, layout, and production for advertisements or may work with freelance copywriters, graphic artists, and producers. He or she might also sketch out rough ideas for advertisements and have the publication's or broadcast station's advertising department put the final ad together. In some instances, the Advertising Director may also work with advertising agencies which handle some of these functions.

As part of the job, the Advertising Director is expected to decide the best media in which to place ads, specific sections of publications in which to have ads inserted, and when to schedule broadcast commercials. He or she is responsible for making sure all advertisements and commercials have accurate copy and graphics and are mailed or delivered to the correct media before deadline.

Additional duties of the Mall Advertising Director may include:

- Developing and putting together shopper's guides
- Tracking tear sheets, clippings, visual cuts, and audiotapes
- Checking bills for ad placement
- Sending or authorizing payment for ads

Salaries

Salaries for Advertising Directors working in malls and shopping centers range from approximately $24,000 to $48,000 or more annually. Compensation varies according to the size and prestige of the specific mall, its geographic location, size of the advertising budget, and the responsibilities and experience of the individual. Advertising Managers also often receive bonuses when there are sales increases in given periods.

Generally, the smaller the mall or the less experience the Advertising Director has, the lower the salary. Larger shopping centers with bigger annual advertising budgets usually offer higher earnings. Malls hosting more prestigious stores and shops may offer salaries on the higher end of the scale.

Employment Prospects

Employment prospects are fair for Advertising Directors in shopping centers. Malls are located throughout the country and more are springing up. Almost every center of any size has someone on staff to fill this advertising function. They may, however, delegate the advertising responsibilities to someone in mall management, public relations or marketing.

Advancement Prospects

Career advancement for Advertising Directors working in malls and shopping centers are fair. Individuals may move up the career ladder in a number of ways.

Some individuals find similar positions in larger or more prestigious centers resulting in increased responsibilities and earnings. Others become mall public relations, marketing, or promotions managers. Some move into mall management positions.

Education and Training

Most malls and shopping centers either require or prefer a four-year college degree. Good choices for majors include advertising, business, journalism, public relations, marketing, liberal arts, English, communications, and business.

Courses and seminars in advertising, copywriting, business, or retail management are also helpful.

Experience, Skills, and Personality Traits

Advertising Directors need to be creative with the ability to communicate both verbally and on paper. Experience working in advertising is usually necessary. This might include knowledge of creating and placing ads, or of copywriting, graphics, and layout.

An understanding of the inner workings of the retail industry is helpful in order to plan successful, effective ads and campaigns. The ability to work on multiple projects at one time and to meet deadlines is essential.

Unions/Associations

Advertising Directors working in malls and shopping centers do not usually belong to any union. Individuals may belong to a number of trade associations providing support and guidance. These may include the American Advertising Federation (AAF) and the Business/Professional Advertising Association (B/PAA).

Tips for Entry

1. There is quite a bit of turnover in these positions. Consider sending your resume and a cover letter to a number of malls and shopping centers in the area in which you are interested. Ask that your resume be kept on file. (Send your letter and resume to the mall owner or developer.)

2. Positions are advertised in display ads in newspapers. Look under classifications including "Advertising," "Promotion," "Malls," "Shopping Center," "Advertising Director," "Advertising Manager," or "Retail."

3. Larger malls and shopping centers often have internships in the management office. Others may have summer jobs as assistants. Contact malls in your area to check into the possibilities.

4. Take seminars and courses in advertising, promotion, public relations, marketing, and publicity.

5. Other seminars in retail management, mall management, and shopping center development will also give you added knowledge in the field as well as helping you make contacts.

6. A good way to gain experience in advertising is to work for a local newspaper, magazine, television, or radio station in the advertising department.

ADVERTISING ASSISTANT— SHOPPING CENTER/MALL

CAREER PROFILE

Duties: Assist in the development and implementation of advertising campaigns and individual promotional ads; assist in creating advertisements and commercials

Alternate Titles: Ad Assistant; Mall Advertising Coordinator; Advertising Trainee

Salary Range: $18,000 to $30,000+

Employment Prospects: Fair

Advancement Prospects: Good

Best Geographical Location(s) for Position: Jobs may be located throughout the country

Prerequisites:
   Education and Training—College degree preferred
   Experience—Experience in some facet of advertising helpful, but not always necessary
   Special Skills and Personality Traits—Creativity; detail oriented; knowledge of copywriting, graphics, and layout; good writing skills

CAREER LADDER

```
┌─────────────────────────────────────┐
│     Assistant Advertising Manager     │
└─────────────────────────────────────┘

┌─────────────────────────────────────┐
│    Advertising Assistant—Shopping     │
│             Center/Mall               │
└─────────────────────────────────────┘

┌─────────────────────────────────────┐
│  Entry Level, Intern, Secretarial Position,  │
│          or College Student           │
└─────────────────────────────────────┘
```

Position Description

The Advertising Assistant working in a mall or shopping center is responsible for helping the advertising director. The individual will assist in the development and implementation of the mall's advertising campaign and develop individual ads as well.

Duties of the Advertising Assistant will vary among malls and according to individual experience. The Ad Assistant might be expected to fulfill secretarial duties such as typing letters, updating the returns from mail or ad campaigns, returning phone calls, keeping records of the cost of ad space, checking media prices, etc.

The Ad Assistant may learn how to read and use a book called *Advertising Rate and Data.* This publication lists advertising rates for television, radio, magazines, and newspapers throughout the country. The individual must also become familiar with rate cards which give the prices of ads in various media.

The advertising director might call on the Assistant to write ad copy, create graphics, layout print ads, or develop copy for sales letters, circulars, direct-mail, or other marketing pieces. The individual might be asked to help create storyboards and scripts for broadcast commercials.

The Advertising Assistant may be expected to place ads in publications, purchase space on radio and television and deliver ads and commercials to the media on deadline. He or she will also be responsible for checking billings, authorizing payments, and keeping accurate records. While the individual may be required to check ad copy for accuracy, he or she will usually be expected to have ads reviewed by the advertising director.

An important function of the Advertising Assistant is helping the Advertising Director plan and develop the annual advertising budget for the center. In this position, the Ad Assistant works with the advertising director and learns how to budget the amount of money to be spent on promotions, the various types of media, and cost-effective places to advertise.

In malls or shopping centers where there is no advertising director, the Advertising Assistant may work with the director of marketing.

Additional duties of the Advertising Assistant working in a mall or shopping center may include:

- Tracking tear sheets, press clippings, visual cuts from broadcasts, and audiotapes
- Overseeing television and radio commercial production and filming
- Conducting research
- Acting as buffer for the advertising director

Salaries

Salaries for Advertising Assistants working in malls and shopping centers range from approximately $18,000 to $30,000 or more annually. Variables that affect compensation include the size, prestige, and geographic location of the specific mall as well as the responsibilities and experience of the individual.

Employment Prospects

Employment prospects are fair for Advertising Assistants in shopping centers. Individuals may find job opportunities located throughout the country. There is a great deal of turnover in these positions due to promotion and the general mobility of today's population.

Advancement Prospects

Career advancement for Advertising Assistants working in malls and shopping centers are good. Aggressive and enthusiastic individuals may move up the career ladder in a number of ways.

After obtaining experience, some Ad Assistants find similar positions in larger or more prestigious centers resulting in increased responsibilities and earnings. Others become assistant advertising managers or locate other positions in the malls's marketing department.

Education and Training

Educational requirements for this position vary. Some malls and shopping centers may prefer the person in this position to hold a four-year college degree. Others have no educational requirement. For individuals aspiring to advance their career, a college degree is essential. Good choices for majors include advertising, business, journalism, public relations, marketing, liberal arts, English, communications, and business.

Courses and seminars in advertising, copywriting, business, or retail management are also helpful.

Experience, Skills, and Personality Traits

Experience requirements vary from mall to mall. Advertising Assistant is an entry-level position in many malls, but others may prefer candidates with some experience. Internships and training programs are useful.

Advertising Assistants need to be extremely detail-oriented, articulate, personable, and persuasive. Copywriting skills and a knowledge of graphics and layout are helpful. The ability to use computer graphic design programs is necessary.

Unions/Associations

Advertising Assistants working in malls and shopping centers do not usually belong to any union. Individuals may belong to a number of trade associations providing support and guidance. These may include the American Advertising Federation (AAF), the Business/Professional Advertising Association (B/PAA), and the International Council of Shopping Centers (ICSC).

Tips for Entry

1. There is quite a bit of turnover in these positions. Consider sending your resume and a cover letter to a number of malls and shopping centers in the area in which you are interested. Ask that your resume be kept on file. (Send your letter and resume to the mall owner, developer, or human resources director.)
2. Positions are advertised in display ads in newspapers. Look under classifications including "Advertising," "Advertising Assistant," "Promotion," "Malls," "Shopping Center," "Retail," etc.
3. Attend seminars in all phases of advertising and retail management. These are useful to hone skills and make professional contacts.
4. Larger malls and shopping centers often have internships in the management office. Others may have summer jobs as assistants. Contact malls in your area to check into the possibilities.
5. A good way to gain experience in advertising is to work for a local newspaper, magazine, television, or radio station in the advertising department.
6. Read the trades. These periodicals often advertise job openings and keep you up on current trends in advertising and mall management. If you can't find them in your local library or magazine store, write to the publisher to see if you can get a short-term subscription.

TENANT RELATIONS MANAGER

CAREER PROFILE

Duties: Attending to needs of tenants in shopping center; keeping tenants happy; acting as liaison between mall management and tenants

Alternate Titles: Tenant Relations Director

Salary Range: $25,000 to $48,000+

Employment Prospects: Poor

Advancement Prospects: Fair

Best Geographical Location(s) for Position: Jobs may be located throughout the country; areas hosting more large malls will provide more opportunities

Prerequisites:

Education and Training—College degree preferred

Experience—Experience in retail, mall management, or marketing

Special Skills and Personality Traits—Problem solving skills; negotiation skills; communication skills; ability to deal well with people; administrative skills

CAREER LADDER

```
┌─────────────────────────────────┐
│  Tenant Relations Manager for Larger, │
│  More Prestigious Mall or Shopping    │
│  Center, Mall Manager,                │
│  or Property Manager                  │
└─────────────────────────────────┘

┌─────────────────────────────────┐
│     Tenant Relations Manager     │
└─────────────────────────────────┘

┌─────────────────────────────────┐
│      Assistant Mall Manager      │
└─────────────────────────────────┘
```

Position Description

It is essential to malls and shopping centers to keep tenants happy. The Tenant Relations Manager is responsible for making sure this happens. He or she walks the line trying to satisfy the tenants while competently representing the mall or mall management company.

The Tenant Relations Manager is expected to promote tenant relations, and stay in close contact with tenants. He or she may call, visit, or send correspondence on a regular basis, and may for example, visit stores to see if everything is going well or if they are experiencing any problems. The Tenant Relations Manager may also schedule meetings with local store managers, real estate agents, corporate managers, or store owners.

The Tenant Relations Manager acts as the liaison between the tenants and mall management. When tenants report a problem, the Manager must see how it can be resolved as quickly as possible.

Problems may be easily solved or may be more complex. Tenants may feel the mall is not making repairs which were promised. The Tenant Relations Manager must determine if the repairs were actually promised and if so, why they weren't carried out. A tenant might dispute a charge on his or her CAM (common area maintenance) bill. In this case, the Tenant Relations Manager might speak to the accounting department to straighten it out.

One of the most important functions of the Tenant Relations Manager is making sure that tenants feel that management hears their concerns and cares about them. He or she must establish a good working relationship between the tenant and the mall management.

The individual may deal with various members of the mall management staff including the leasing director, mall manager, marketing, public relations and advertising departments, maintenance department, and management company.

Tenant Relations Managers working for real estate developers or mall management companies may handle the tenant relations of more than one mall.

Additional duties of Tenant Relations Managers might include:

- Discussing tenant problems with mall owners
- Scheduling meetings between mall management and tenants
- Arranging for credits on tenants bills when necessary
- Attending mall meetings
- Handling crises

Salaries

Earnings for Tenant Relations Managers can range from approximately $25,000 to $48,000 or more annually. Variables affecting earnings include the size, prestige, and geographic location of the property and the number of properties for which the individual is responsible. Other variables include the experience, responsibilities, and education of the individual.

Employment Prospects

Employment prospects are poor for Tenant Relations Managers, since not every mall employs a Tenant Relations Manager. Generally, this position can only be found in larger malls or working for a mall management company. In smaller malls the mall manager will be responsible for handling the tenant relations functions.

Advancement Prospects

The most common method of career advancement for Tenant Relations Managers is to find similar positions in larger, more prestigious malls or mall management companies. Depending on career aspirations, some individuals climb the career ladder by becoming mall managers or property managers.

Education and Training

Educational requirements vary from mall to mall. While much of the training individuals receive is on the job, many employers prefer that Tenant Relations Managers have a college degree. Others require it.

Good majors might include business, public administration, marketing, public relations, communications, finance, or related fields.

Professional and trade associations often offer helpful seminars and courses in retail management, mall management, and related subjects.

Experience, Skills, and Personality Traits

Experience requirements vary. Some Tenant Relations Managers start out in marketing, public relations, or community relations. Others may work in mall management.

Tenant Relations Managers need to be diplomatic. The ability to solve problems while remaining calm is essential. The ability to see both sides of a problem also is necessary.

Individuals should be detail oriented and have a basic understanding of everything that goes on in a mall. This includes maintenance, construction, human resources, tenant relations, community relations, leasing, budgets, advertising, and marketing.

Communication skills, both written and verbal are essential. The ability to work with and get along with people is mandatory.

Unions/Associations

Mall or shopping center Tenant Relations Managers may get additional career information by contacting the International Council of Shopping Centers (ICSC) and the Institute of Real Estate Management (IREM).

Tips for Entry

1. Contact larger property management and real estate development companies to find out what internship and training programs they have available in this area.
2. There are a number of executive search firms dealing exclusively with jobs in shopping centers and malls.
3. Send your resume and a cover letter to retail property management companies, real estate development companies, and large malls.
4. Contact the International Council of Shopping Centers (ICSC) to check out what courses they are offering. These will provide valuable training as well as an opportunity to network.
5. Positions may be advertised in the classified sections of newspapers. Look under classifications including "Tenant Relations Manager," or "Mall/Shopping Center Opportunities," or "Retail Opportunities."
6. Openings are also advertised in trade journals.
7. Jobs in this field may be located on-line. Begin your search on some of the more popular job search sites such as the Monster board (www.monster.com) and Hot Jobs (www.hotjobs.com).

INFORMATION REPRESENTATIVE—MALL/SHOPPING CENTER

CAREER PROFILE

Duties: Provide information regarding mall, mall stores, and mall services to customers

Alternate Titles: Information Clerk

Salary Range: $5.50 to $8.50+ per hour

Employment Prospects: Fair

Advancement Prospects: Fair

Best Geographical Location(s) for Position: Jobs may be located throughout the country

Prerequisites:

Education and Training—High school diploma or equivalent preferred

Experience—No experience necessary

Special Skills and Personality Traits—Pleasant personality; outgoing; interpersonal skills; people skills; communications skills

CAREER LADDER

```
┌────────────────────────────────┐
│   Customer Service Director     │
└────────────────────────────────┘

┌────────────────────────────────┐
│   Information Representative     │
└────────────────────────────────┘

┌────────────────────────────────┐
│         Entry Level             │
└────────────────────────────────┘
```

Position Description

Many malls and shopping centers host information centers for the convenience of their customers. These centers are usually found in a central location in the mall for the convenience of shoppers and may be a storefront, a counter, or a kiosk.

The Information Representative is the individual who mans the mall's information center. He or she is responsible for answering the questions of mall customers. These might include simple things such as where specific stores are or the location of the closest rest room. The Information Representative may be asked the names of stores in the mall which sell certain merchandise such as children's shoes or electronics.

The Information Representative often will give directions to locations within the mall. In very large malls the individual might use a mall floor plan to help direct shoppers to specific stores as well as verbal instructions. He or she might also give customers directions to places outside the mall such as roads, highways, restaurants, or even other retail establishments.

The Information Representative may answer patron's inquiries about activities, special events, and promotions going on in the mall or mall stores. He or she may, for example, give dates, times, and locations of where a special event is taking place.

The Information Representative will often be asked about mall hours. He or she is expected to know the correct hours that the mall is open daily, as well as holidays. Depending on the specific mall, the Information Representative may also handle the duties of a customer service representative such as wrapping gifts, selling gift certificates, renting baby strollers, or wheelchairs.

This is an ideal job for those who enjoy meeting new people and dealing with and helping others.

Additional duties of the Information Representatives may include:

- Selling gift certificates
- Assisting lost children
- Assisting people who are looking for each other in the mall
- Making announcements in the mall on the public announcement system
- Answering phone inquiries regarding mall questions
- Giving phone numbers of mall stores

Salaries

Information Representatives working in malls or shopping centers may earn between $5.50 and $8.50 per hour or more. Variables affecting earnings include the geographic location, size, and prestige of the shopping center as well as the experience and responsibilities of the individual.

Employment Prospects

Employment prospects are fair for individuals seeking this position. Jobs can be located in malls and shopping centers throughout the country. While every mall does not employ an Information Representative, those who do usually hire more than one.

There is a great deal of turnover in these positions. This may be a result of a number of situations including other career aspirations, advancement, the general mobility of today's society and "Mall Hopping." Many malls and shopping centers have "Mall Hoppers." This means that employees move from store to store and job to job within the mall in hopes of earning more money, better working conditions, increased benefits, or career advancement.

Information Representatives may work full time or part time depending on the specific position.

Advancement Prospects

There are not generally a lot of career advancement possibilities in this area. However, advancement prospects for Information Representatives are dependent to a great extent on the career aspirations of the individual.

Those who are in this position to earn money while in school will probably move to different types of careers as they continue their education. Some individuals may move into administrative assistant positions in the mall management office. Others who are interested in moving up the career ladder in this field might become the mall's customer service manager if the mall has this position.

Education and Training

Most malls prefer their Information Representatives to have a minimum of a high school diploma or the equivalent. The mall provides on-the-job training for this position.

Experience, Skills, and Personality Traits

Generally, this is an entry-level position. Interpersonal and customer relations skills are essential. Communications skills are mandatory.

To be successful at their job, Information Representatives should have a pleasant personality, be outgoing, and enjoy dealing with people.

Unions/Associations

There is no association specific to Information Representatives working in malls or shopping centers. However, individuals may obtain information about this type of career by contacting the International Council of Shopping Centers (ICSC) or mall management offices.

Tips for Entry

1. Jobs may be advertised in the classified sections of newspapers. Look under classifications such as "Information Representative," "Information Clerk," or "Mall/Shopping Center Opportunities."
2. Stop in the mall's management office and ask to fill in an employment application. Ask that your application be kept on file if there are no current openings.
3. Some malls also have a job board posted somewhere in the center. Call the mall management office and ask if they have one.
4. Many local chambers of commerce or community colleges offer hospitality and customer service seminars. These may be helpful in giving you the edge over another applicant.

ASSISTANT MARKETING DIRECTOR—SHOPPING CENTER/MALL

CAREER PROFILE

Duties: Assist the mall's marketing director with plans and campaigns; handle day-to-day marketing functions; assist in the planning and implementation of special events

Alternate Titles: Assistant Marketing Manager; Assistant Mall Marketing Director

Salary Range: $23,000 to $40,000+

Employment Prospects: Fair

Advancement Prospects: Good

Best Geographical Location(s) for Position: Jobs may be located throughout the country

Prerequisites:

Education and Training—Bachelor's degree in marketing, public relations, advertising, business, journalism, liberal arts, English, communications, or business

Experience—Marketing experience or training necessary

Special Skills and Personality Traits—Creativity; marketing skills; good graphic sense; good verbal and written communication skills; people skills; knowledge of retail industry

CAREER LADDER

```
┌─────────────────────────────┐
│   Shopping Center/Mall       │
│   Marketing Director         │
└─────────────────────────────┘

┌─────────────────────────────┐
│  Assistant Marketing Director—│
│   Shopping Center/Mall       │
└─────────────────────────────┘

┌─────────────────────────────┐
│   Public Relations, Marketing│
│  or Advertising Assistant or Publicist │
└─────────────────────────────┘
```

Position Description

The Assistant Mall Marketing Director is responsible for helping the mall's marketing director develop concepts and campaigns to market the center to potential shoppers. The individual works with the marketing director coordinating the marketing goals and objectives.

The Assistant Marketing Director may perform research to see what types of programs and services will bring in the most shoppers and where customers are coming from. For example, are all customers local or are they driving distances to reach the center? The individual will work with the marketing director to determine how far customers will travel so they know where to market the mall.

The individual may also help to develop surveys or promotions to identify the most effective media in which to advertise. For example the Assistant Marketing Director might help develop a sweepstakes, where in order to enter, shoppers must

write down the newspapers they read, television stations they watch, and radio stations they listen to most frequently. In this manner, the marketing department will know which media is most effective to market the mall. They can then make recommendations to the advertising director.

The Assistant Director of Marketing will often brainstorm with the marketing director to come up with unique and innovative ideas and promotions to market the center. Once ideas are finalized, the individual is expected to assist the marketing director in their implementation. Depending on the structure of the center, he or she may work with the public relations and advertising director, promotions coordinator, community relations manager, and mall manager to bring the promotion or program to fruition.

The Assistant Mall Marketing Director is expected to be on hand for special events and promotions when they are taking place. This might mean working on weekends or during the evening.

The most successful Assistant Marketing Directors are detail-oriented. They can keep track of everything that needs to be taken care of for specific promotions. Depending on the project, tables may need to be rented, ads designed, press releases developed, the media notified, and extra security retained.

If the mall does not have a public relations or advertising director, the Assistant Marketing Director may handle many of their functions. He or she may be expected to write press releases, develop ads, handle publicity, and work with the media.

The Assistant Marketing Director will work with the marketing director in dealing with local and corporate tenants on any copromotions. He or she may handle correspondence with the tenants regarding co-op ads, billboards, or promotions. The individual might also set up and attend meetings on behalf of the marketing director.

Additional duties of Assistant Mall Marketing Directors may include:

- Helping mall stores promote their special events
- Assisting in market research
- Tabulating data
- Attracting bus tours, shopping tours, or other group events
- Designing and developing promotional marketing material

Salaries

Earnings for Assistant Mall Marketing Directors can vary greatly depending on a number of variables. These include the size, location, and prestige of the mall as well as the experience and responsibilities of the individual. Annual salaries can range from $23,000 to $40,000 or more.

Many malls also have bonus plans for the marketing director and Assistant Marketing Director, in which individuals receive bonuses for annual or biannual increases in sales.

Employment Prospects

While every mall does not employ an Assistant Marketing Director, there are opportunities in many mid-size and larger malls throughout the country. There is also a fair amount of turnover in this job due to advancement and the general mobility of people in today's job market.

Advancement Prospects

Prospects for career advancement for the Assistant Mall Marketing Director are good. Individuals can find similar positions in larger or more prestigious malls. However, the more common path to climbing the career ladder is for individuals to become a full fledged mall marketing director. This may be in the same mall already employing the individual or might be in a different center completely.

Education and Training

As a rule, individuals seeking this position must hold a four-year college degree. Good choices for majors include marketing, public relations, advertising, business, journalism, liberal arts, English, communications, and business.

Courses and seminars in marketing, public relations, publicity, advertising, promotion, and the retail industry help give individuals an edge in both obtaining jobs and career advancement.

Experience, Skills, and Personality Traits

Assistant Mall Marketing Directors, like individuals working in other aspects of marketing, need excellent verbal and written communications skills. Knowledge of the fundamentals of marketing are necessary in order to be successful in this job.

Assistant Mall Marketing Directors should be creative and innovative with the ability to come up with unique ideas and angles to market the mall.

There are often deadlines which must be met and projects which need to be completed. Individuals need the ability to handle multiple tasks at the same time without getting flustered.

Unions/Associations

Assistant Mall Marketing Directors working in malls and shopping centers may belong to a number of trade associations. These might include the International Council of Shopping Centers (ICSC), the American Marketing Association (AMA), the Marketing Research Association (MRA), and the Public Relations Society of America (PRSA).

These associations provide members with educational opportunities, support, and career guidance.

Tips for Entry

1. Joining trade associations and attending their meetings and conferences will give you an opportunity to make valuable contacts.
2. Send your resume and a cover letter to a number of malls and shopping centers. Ask that your resume be kept on file if there are no current openings.
3. Positions are often advertised in display ads in newspapers. Look under classifications including "Marketing," "Assistant Marketing Director," "Malls," and "Shopping Center."
4. Openings may also be advertised in trade journals such as *Value Retail News*.
5. Larger malls and shopping centers often have internships in the management office. Others may have summer jobs as assistants. Contact malls in your area to check into the possibilities.
6. Take seminars and courses in marketing, publicity, and public relations to help you hone skills.
7. Other seminars in retail management, mall management, and shopping center development will also give you added knowledge in the field.

COMMUNITY RELATIONS DIRECTOR— MALL/SHOPPING CENTER

CAREER PROFILE

Duties: Cultivate and coordinate relationships between corporation and local agencies and civic and community groups; represent mall in beneficial community activities

Alternate Titles: Community Relations Manager; Community Affairs Coordinator; Community Affairs Manager

Salary Range: $20,000 to $48,000+

Employment Prospects: Poor

Advancement Prospects: Fair

Best Geographical Location(s) for Position: Positions may be located throughout the country. Areas hosting large malls, shopping centers, and department stores will have more opportunities

Prerequisites:
Education and Training—Four-year degree preferred, but not always required
Experience—Experience working with community and not-for-profit groups helpful
Special Skills and Personality Traits—People skills; creativity; good written and verbal communications skills; public speaking ability; organization

CAREER LADDER

```
┌─────────────────────────────────────┐
│        Public Relations Director     │
│    or Community Relations Director    │
│     in Larger, More Prestigious Mall  │
└─────────────────────────────────────┘

┌─────────────────────────────────────┐
│      Community Relations Director     │
└─────────────────────────────────────┘

┌─────────────────────────────────────┐
│    Community Relations Assistant,     │
│       Public Relations Assistant,     │
│        or Journalism Position         │
└─────────────────────────────────────┘
```

Position Description

The Community Relations Director of a mall or shopping center is a great job for anyone who enjoys working with people. The individual coordinates community activities between the mall or shopping center and local agencies, civic groups, schools, community groups, political entities, and governmental agencies. In addition, the Community Relations Director cultivates relationships with these groups.

In smaller areas, the local shopping center is often the gathering place of the community. In larger areas, malls may be utilized for the activities of not-for-profit and civic groups. The Community Relations Director helps coordinate these efforts.

The Community Relations Director plans and designs programs to help the local community and promote the image of the shopping center in a positive manner. While performing these functions, the Director must remain sensitive to the local community and its needs.

The Community Relations Director represents the corporation in beneficial community activities, including the sponsorship of programs such as sporting events, cultural events, and community related programs. For example, the Community Relations Director may arrange to have the shopping center sponsor a Little League team, concert, or local sports team.

The Mall Community Relations Director may develop programs with local community groups such as the United Way or Red Cross to address specific issues, such as a Red Cross program for employees of the mall to volunteer to donate blood.

The Mall Community Relations Director must develop new and innovative community relations programs in which the mall can take leadership. These might include marathons, fairs, art auctions, or parades. These events keep the mall favorably in the public eye and market the mall's name and services to the public. Though sponsored by a single chain of stores rather than a mall, Macy's Thanksgiving Day Parade, which airs on television every year, is an example of this type of event.

The Community Relations Director acts as the mall's representative on not-for-profit organization boards and committees, and is often expected to be an active member of many civic and community groups.

The Community Relations Director should have a good working relationship with the media. In this way, when the mall is sponsoring a local team, helping to raise money for a worthwhile cause, or working on any other community event, the center will reap the benefits of good press coverage.

Additional duties of Community Relations Directors working in malls or shopping centers include:

- Giving speeches on behalf of the mall to local community groups
- Representing the mall at community events
- Appearing on local public service television and radio interview shows to promote the mall's community projects
- Making sure the mall maintains a good public image

Salaries

Earnings for Community Relations Directors working in malls or shopping centers can range from approximately $20,000 to $48,000 or more. Factors affecting earnings include the size, prestige, and geographic location of the mall as well as the responsibilities and experience of the individual. Generally, the larger the mall, the higher the earnings.

Employment Prospects

Employment prospects are poor for individuals seeking this position. Even though there are thousands of malls and shopping centers throughout the country, many do not hire someone specifically for this job. Instead many malls expect someone from the public relations or marketing department to handle the community relations functions.

Advancement Prospects

Advancement prospects are fair in this position. There are a number of different possibilities for climbing the career ladder depending on career aspirations. Some individuals locate similar positions in larger, more prestigious malls. Others move on to similar positions in large corporations. Many land jobs as a mall's director of public relations.

If the individual has developed a good working relationship with a not-for-profit organization that is seeking a director, the individual may be considered for the position.

Education and Training

Most malls and shopping centers require their Community Relations Directors to hold a minimum of a four-year college degree. While majors vary, emphasis should be placed on courses in publicity, public relations, marketing, advertising, journalism, English, communications, writing, psychology, and sociology.

There are many seminars related to working with not-for-profit groups, community relations, public relations, and publicity that are useful in obtaining a job and excelling in it.

Experience, Skills, and Personality Traits

It is essential in this type of position to enjoy working with people. Individuals should be community minded and have an understanding of non-for-profit civic and community groups.

Community Relations Directors should be outgoing, personable, assertive, and articulate. Good writing, organization, and planning skills are necessary. The ability to speak in front of groups is necessary.

Community Relations Directors working in malls usually have had experience working with not-for-profit or civic groups or as publicity or community relations assistants.

Unions/Associations

Community Relations Directors working in malls and shopping centers may be members of local civic groups, not-for-profit organizations, and service clubs. Individuals may also take advantage of opportunities offered by the Public Relations Society of America (PRSA) or the International Council of Shopping Centers (ICSC).

Tips for Entry

1. Send your resume and a short cover letter to shopping centers and malls in the area in which you are interested in working.
2. Openings may be advertised in the classified section of the newspaper. Look under classifications including "Retail," "Shopping Centers," "Mall," "Community Relations," and "Community Affairs."
3. Jobs may also be advertised on-line at specific shopping center and mall websites as well as job sites such as the Monster Board (www.monster.com) or Hot Jobs (www.hotjobs.com) among others.
4. Jobs may also be advertised in trade journals such as *Value Retail News.*
5. Join civic and not-for-profit groups and volunteer to be on committees. This will give you hands-on experience working with these groups.
6. Many large malls offer internships and training programs. Contact them to check out availability.

CUSTOMER SERVICE REPRESENTATIVE— MALL/SHOPPING CENTER

CAREER PROFILE

Duties: Provide special services to mall customers; sell gift certificates; wrap gifts; rent strollers and wheelchairs; give information regarding the mall, mall stores and mall services

Alternate Titles: Customer Service Clerk

Salary Range: $5.50 to $8.50+ per hour

Employment Prospects: Fair

Advancement Prospects: Fair

Best Geographical Location(s) for Position: Jobs may be located throughout the country

Prerequisites:

Education and Training—High school diploma or equivalent preferred

Experience—No experience necessary

Special Skills and Personality Traits—Pleasant personality; outgoing; interpersonal skills; people skills; communications skills

CAREER LADDER

```
┌─────────────────────────────────┐
│   Customer Service Director      │
└─────────────────────────────────┘


┌─────────────────────────────────┐
│ Customer Service Representative  │
└─────────────────────────────────┘


┌─────────────────────────────────┐
│          Entry Level             │
└─────────────────────────────────┘
```

Position Description

Today, there are many places for people to shop. Stand-alone stores, department stores, strip malls, small, mid-sized and large indoor malls, catalogs, television shopping channels, and the Internet are all possibilities. With all these choices, many malls feel that the more services they provide, the easier it will be for people to shop there. As a result, many malls host a variety of special services designed to make shopping easier and more convenient. These services are provided by Customer Service Representatives.

The customer service area of a mall is usually centrally located to make it easy for shoppers to find. The area may be a kiosk, store, or customer service counter in the mall.

The Customer Service Representative's duties vary depending on the specific center, its structure, and the services they provide. In some centers, the Customer Service Representative will also be expected to act as an information representative. This means the individual will be expected to answer mall customers' questions. These might include things like where specific stores are located in the mall, the location of the closest rest rooms, or which stores in the mall sell certain merchandise.

Many malls rent strollers and wheelchairs for customer use in the mall for a small fee or deposit. The Customer Service Representative is responsible for helping customers get the stroller or wheelchair, explaining the conditions of use, taking payment, and keeping records of rentals and deposits. He or she must also check in strollers and wheelchairs which are returned.

Certain malls offer gift wrapping services which are offered either gratis or for a small fee. The Customer Service Representative would be responsible for wrapping packages in a neat and attractive manner.

Other malls offer shipping services for the convenience of customers. In these instances, the Customer Service Representative may weigh items, package them for shipping, collect monies, and get the correct shipping information.

The more time a customer spends in a mall, the better the chance he or she will purchase something. With this in mind, many malls feel that customers will be more comfortable shopping without carrying around their other purchases, heavy outerwear, or packages. Therefore, they have areas where customers can store their belongings, outerwear, and purchases while they shop. The Customer Service Representative usually takes the customer's belongings and gives the customer one half of a ticket to use to retrieve their merchandise when they are done shopping. The other half of the ticket is kept with the customer's items.

If a shopper has a problem in the mall, he or she will usually go to the customer service counter or area and speak to a Customer Service Representative. It is the responsibility of the individual to help the customer as much as possible. Problems can vary tremendously in a mall and the Customer Service Representative must be adept at handling an array of situations in a calm and helpful manner.

People lose their wallets, leave their handbags in dressing rooms or rest rooms, and put bags of merchandise down and forget to pick them up again every day in malls. Customers may find large sums of money or jewelry that others have dropped or misplaced or bags of merchandise that someone else has lost.

Some situations are more stressful than others and need more understanding. Children often wander away from parents, customers slip or fall, or accidents occur. The Customer Service Representative must keep everyone calm while following the mall's procedures. Depending on the situation, he or she may be expected to call mall management, security, or even the police when needed.

The Customer Service Representative will answer patron's questions about mall hours and special events and promotions. He or she will give out brochures, coupons, or other materials provided by the mall.

The Customer Service Representative may be responsible for selling mall gift certificates and explaining any conditions and limitations. In some malls, gift certificates may be sold by the mall management office or specific stores in the mall instead.

Additional duties of Customer Service Representatives working in malls may include:

- Assisting lost children
- Assisting people who are looking for each other in the mall
- Making announcements in the mall on the public address system
- Answering phone inquiries regarding mall questions
- Giving phone numbers of mall stores

Salaries

Customer Service Representatives working in malls earn between $5.50 and $8.50 per hour or more. Variables affecting earnings include the geographic location, size, and prestige of the shopping center as well as the experience and responsibilities of the individual.

Employment Prospects

Employment prospects are fair for individuals seeking this position. Jobs can be located in malls and shopping centers throughout the country. While every mall does not employ a Customer Service Representative, those who do usually hire more than one.

There is a great deal of turnover in these positions. This may be a result of a number of situations including other career aspirations, advancement, the general mobility of today's society and a phenomenon called "Mall Hopping."

Many malls and shopping centers have "Mall Hoppers." This means that employees move from store to store and job to job within the mall in hopes of making more money, better working conditions, increased benefits, or career advancement.

Customer Service Representatives may work full time or part time depending on the specific position.

Advancement Prospects

Advancement prospects for Customer Service Representatives working in malls are dependent to a great extent on the career aspirations of the individual. Generally, advancement prospects for Customer Service Representatives working in malls are limited. Individuals may move up to become customer service managers, but these jobs are few and far between. Usually these jobs can only be found at larger malls.

Individuals who want to work in customer service and advance their career may move into customer service positions in other industries. Those who want to stay in a mall environment may move into administrative assistant positions in the mall management office.

Education and Training

Customer Service Representatives working in malls generally are required to have a minimum of a high school diploma or the equivalent. Many malls, however, also hire individuals who are still attending school. The mall provides informal on-the-job training for this position.

A college degree or background is helpful for those aspiring to move up the career ladder in customer service. There are also many seminars, courses, and workshops in the area of customer service which will be useful in honing skills and may give one applicant an edge over another.

Experience, Skills, and Personality Traits

This is usually an entry-level position. Interpersonal and customer relations skills are essential. Individuals should be articulate with good communications skills.

Customer Service Representatives working in malls should be outgoing with a pleasant personality. They should enjoy dealing with the public.

Unions/Associations

There is no association specific to Customer Service Representatives working in malls or shopping centers. However, individuals may obtain information about this type of career by contacting the International Council of Shopping Centers (ICSC) or mall management offices.

Tips for Entry

1. Jobs may be advertised in the classified sections of newspapers. Look under classifications such as "Customer Service Representative," "Customer Service Clerk," "Customer Service," or "Mall/Shopping Center Opportunities."

2. Visit the mall management office to fill out an employment application. Ask that your application be kept on file if there are no current openings.

3. Some malls also have a job board posted somewhere in the center. Call the mall management office and ask if they have one; if so, check it regularly.

4. Many local chambers of commerce or community colleges offer hospitality and customer service seminars. These may be helpful in giving you the edge over another applicant.

5. Malls often have websites where they advertise employment opportunities. Look in the newspaper for ads to find the website addresses of the mall you're interested in working in.

ADMINISTRATIVE ASSISTANT—
SHOPPING CENTER OR MALL OFFICE

CAREER PROFILE

Duties: Assist mall executives in their functions; screen phone calls for executive; return phone calls; compose correspondence; schedule meetings; coordinate office services

Alternate Titles: Executive Assistant

Salary Range: $8.00 to $30.00+ per hour

Employment Prospects: Fair

Advancement Prospects: Fair

Best Geographical Location(s) for Position: Jobs may be located throughout the country

Prerequisites:

Education and Training—High school diploma or equivalent; on-the-job training; additional training may be required

Experience—Experience requirements vary

Special Skills and Personality Traits—Good judgment; communications skills; detail oriented; office skills; computer skills; phone skills; people skills

CAREER LADDER

```
┌─────────────────────────────────────┐
│ Administrative Assistant in Larger,  │
│ More Prestigious Center or Assistant │
│ Marketing Director, Assistant P.R.   │
│ Director, or Assistant Mall Manager  │
└─────────────────────────────────────┘

┌─────────────────────────────────────┐
│       Administrative Assistant       │
└─────────────────────────────────────┘

┌─────────────────────────────────────┐
│              Secretary               │
└─────────────────────────────────────┘
```

Position Description

A mall office may have an array of support personnel helping the mall or shopping center run smoothly. Depending on the size and structure of the center, there may be one or more Administrative Assistants helping the mall management staff.

The Administrative Assistant may be assigned to work with the mall manager or one of the other directors, managers, or departments. These might include marketing, advertising, leasing, or tenant relations. In some malls, the Administrative Assistant may work with the entire administrative staff.

The Administrative Assistant has varied duties. His or her main function is to assist the mall management executives. The individual might coordinate the office staff and services. He or she may schedule the work of the office personnel. The Administrative Assistant might assign specific projects to staff on behalf of the mall manager or other department managers. The individual may, for example, assign secretaries to type correspondence or to put together leasing packages.

If the Administrative Assistant is working with a specific department in the management office, he or she might have more specialized duties. Working in this capacity, the individual has the opportunity to obtain experience and learn more about the functions of a department.

The Assistant working in the advertising department, for example, might be asked to call the media to get rate cards or check space availabilities and prices. The individual might be responsible for proofing ads for accuracy and correcting any errors. As the individual gains experience, he or she might even begin to develop simple ads or layouts. Everything, of course, will be done under the director's supervision.

The Administrative Assistant working with the public relations director might have other duties. He or she might be expected to proof press releases, check information for accuracy, or put together press packages. The individual might be asked to schedule meetings with members of the media, help the P.R. director put together a press conference, or coordinate a special event.

In some situations, he or she may act in the capacity of secretary. The individual might screen, take, and return phone calls on behalf of the mall executive. He or she might also prepare, compose, and type correspondence or check correspondence done by secretary.

Administrative Assistants are often called upon to type or handle confidential documents. Individuals might also be expected to handle confidential phone calls or schedule important meetings. It is essential the Administrative Assistant keep information learned in the mall office confidential and be discrete at all times.

In many mall offices, one of the major projects of the year is preparing the annual budget. The Administrative Assistant may help collect information for the budget as well as assist in its preparation.

Other duties of an Administrative Assistant working in a mall office may include:

- Reviewing reports
- Training office staff
- Screening visitors
- Dealing with emergencies

Salaries

Earnings for Administrative Assistants working in shopping centers and malls can range from approximately $8.00 to $30.00 or more per hour. Variables affecting earnings include the geographic location, size, and prestige of the shopping center as well as the experience and responsibilities of the individual.

One of the perks for Administrative Assistants working in malls is that individuals often receive an employee discount from many of the mall stores.

Employment Prospects

Employment prospects are fair for individuals seeking this position. Jobs can be located in malls and shopping centers throughout the country. As noted previously, malls may hire one or more Administrative Assistants.

Advancement Prospects

Administrative Assistants working in mall offices may advance their career in a number of ways. Some find similar positions in larger malls resulting in increased responsibilities and earnings.

Depending on the individual's education and the area he or she has worked in, after obtaining experience the Administrative Assistant might advance to positions such as assistant director of marketing, public relations, advertising, leasing, or even assistant mall manager.

Education and Training

Education and training requirements vary from mall to mall. Generally, most malls prefer their Administrative Assistants to hold a minimum of a high school diploma. Some prefer a college background. This will be especially important for individuals seeking to advance their careers in this field. Depending on the aspirations of the Administrative Assistant, good choices for majors might include retail management, communications, marketing, advertising, public relations, English, liberal arts, or a related field.

Experience, Skills, and Personality Traits

Experience working in an office environment may be required or preferred. However, some malls will hire Administrative Assistants with experience in public relations, marketing, advertising, or leasing instead.

Administrative Assistants need excellent communications skills. Individuals should be dependable, detail oriented, and extremely organized. Interpersonal and customer relations skills are essential. Good judgment is mandatory.

Unions/Associations

Individuals interested in working as Administrative Assistants in mall offices may learn more by contacting the International Council of Shopping Centers (ICSC). Those working in specific departments aspiring to move up may belong to more industry specific organizations. For example, those working in the public relations department, might belong to the Public Relations Society of America (PRSA).

Tips for Entry

1. Jobs may be advertised in the classified sections of newspapers. Look under classifications such as "Administrative Assistant," "Mall Office," "Retail Opportunities," or "Executive Assistant."
2. Stop by the mall management office to fill out an application. Ask that your application be kept on file if there are no current openings.
3. You can also send a short cover letter and your resume to the mall management office.
4. Many malls now have websites listing their openings. Check out on line the malls in which you are interested in working. If you don't know their web address, you can either call the mall office or see if the address is in advertisements.
5. Some malls have internship programs. Call or write to check the possibilities.

SECRETARY—SHOPPING CENTER OR MALL OFFICE

CAREER PROFILE

Duties: Answering telephones in mall office; returning phone calls; filing; typing; routing mail; greeting people

Alternate Titles: None

Salary Range: $6.00 to $20.00+ per hour

Employment Prospects: Fair

Advancement Prospects: Fair

Best Geographical Location(s) for Position: Jobs may be located throughout the country

Prerequisites:

Education and Training—High school diploma or equivalent; on-the-job training; additional training may be required

Experience—Secretarial or office experience preferred, but not always required

Special Skills and Personality Traits—Office skills; computer skills; phone skills; typing skills; communication skills; good judgment; people skills

CAREER LADDER

```
┌─────────────────────────────────────┐
│  Secretary in Larger, More Prestigious │
│     Center, Executive Secretary,      │
│     or Administrative Assistant       │
└─────────────────────────────────────┘

┌─────────────────────────────────────┐
│              Secretary                │
└─────────────────────────────────────┘

┌─────────────────────────────────────┐
│       Entry Level or Secretary        │
│          in Other Industry            │
└─────────────────────────────────────┘
```

Position Description

Most malls and shopping centers have mall offices. These require the services of an array of support personnel including Secretaries, executive secretaries, administrative assistants, receptionists, and more. Each of these individuals help the mall management office run smoothly.

Depending on the size and structure of the mall, there may be one or more Secretaries employed by the center. The size and structure of each center will also determine the exact functions of each individual.

Secretaries handle a wide variety of clerical duties. They are expected to type a variety of correspondence, envelopes, and reports. Typing may be done on a typewriter, word processor, or computer.

Individuals might additionally use various software programs to accomplish different tasks necessary to the mall on the computer. These might include more common programs such as Microsoft Word, Excel, or Word Perfect. Many malls also utilize specific mall management software programs to keep track of tenancies, rents, and leases.

The Mall Secretary might be asked to take and transcribe dictation or may be required to take shorthand. Depending on the situation, he or she may be expected to assist the mall manager, leasing agent, marketing director, public relations director, or advertising director with their clerical work.

The Mall Secretary may photocopy documents such as leases, contracts, letters, or reports. He or she will also be responsible for filing, maintaining files, collating reports, sorting mail, and sending faxes.

An important function of the Mall Secretary is greeting in a courteous manner people who visit the mall office. Visitors might include tenants, mall employees, contractors, potential tenants, and customers.

The Secretary must answer the phones and return phone calls in a professional and polite manner. The individual may also be responsible for screening calls and scheduling meetings and appointments.

On occasion, the Mall Secretary may deal with emergencies, finding the correct people to handle the problem.

Other duties of the Mall Secretary may include:

- Answering letters and other correspondence
- Handling accounts payable and receivable
- Screening visitors
- Answering customer's questions regarding the mall
- Giving directions to stores within the mall

Salaries

Earnings for Secretaries working in shopping centers and malls can range from approximately $6.00 to $20 or more per hour. Variables affecting earnings include the geographic location, size, and prestige of the shopping center as well as the experience and responsibilities of the individual.

One of the perks for Secretaries working in malls is that individuals often receive an employee discount from mall stores.

Employment Prospects

Employment prospects are fair for individuals seeking this position. Jobs can be located in malls and shopping centers throughout the country. As noted previously, malls may hire one or more Secretaries.

Advancement Prospects

Secretaries working in mall offices may advance their career in a number of ways. After obtaining experience, some individuals find similar positions in larger, more prestigious malls. Others may climb the career ladder by becoming executive secretaries or administrative assistants.

Education and Training

Education and training requirements vary from mall to mall. Generally, most malls prefer their Secretaries to hold a minimum of a high school diploma or the equivalent. Some prefer some college or secretarial school. Secretarial courses as well as instruction in computers and various software packages are helpful.

Experience, Skills, and Personality Traits

Entry-level positions may be open in some malls. Experience, working in an office environment is usually required or preferred.

Secretaries should have excellent typing skills, with the ability to type accurately between 55 and 65 words per minute. Word processing and computer skills are usually necessary. The ability to take dictation is often required or preferred.

Successful Mall Secretaries are pleasant to be around. Interpersonal and customer relations skills are essential. Communications skills are mandatory.

Unions/Associations

Individuals may obtain information about a career in this field by contacting Professional Secretaries International (PSI). Secretaries working in malls and shopping centers may also want to contact the International Council of Shopping Centers (ICSC) for additional career information.

Tips for Entry

1. There are community colleges, secretarial schools, and vocational and technical schools that offer courses in various aspects of office work, computers, and software. These courses give you the working knowledge which may be useful in giving you the edge over other applicants.
2. Jobs may be advertised in the classified sections of newspapers. Look under classifications such as "Secretary," "Mall Office," "Retail," "Executive Secretary," or "Administrative Assistant," "Office Workers."
3. Stop by the mall management office to see if you can fill out an application. Ask that your application be kept on file if there are no current openings.

BOOKKEEPER—SHOPPING CENTER OR MALL OFFICE

CAREER PROFILE

Duties: Recording accounts receivable and accounts payable

Alternate Titles: Accounting Clerk, Bookkeeping Clerk

Salary Range: $7.00 to $25.00+ per hour

Employment Prospects: Fair

Advancement Prospects: Fair

Best Geographical Location(s) for Position: Jobs may be located throughout the country

Prerequisites:

Education and Training—High school diploma or equivalent; on-the-job training; additional training may be required

Experience—Bookkeeping or accounting experience preferred, but not always required

Special Skills and Personality Traits—Aptitude for numbers; orderly; detail oriented; office skills; computer skills; communication skills; good judgment

CAREER LADDER

```
┌─────────────────────────────────┐
│   Bookkeeper in Larger, More    │
│ Prestigious Center or Accountant │
└─────────────────────────────────┘

┌─────────────────────────────────┐
│           Bookkeeper            │
└─────────────────────────────────┘

┌─────────────────────────────────┐
│   Entry Level Bookkeeping       │
│     or Accounting Clerk         │
└─────────────────────────────────┘
```

Position Description

A great deal of money is involved in running malls. Rents and other charges are paid to the mall owner in exchange for a location in the center. Other monies are paid out to run the center. The Mall Bookkeeper is responsible for accurately recording all money received and spent. This information is invaluable in running the mall. As in all businesses, it will reflect the profit and losses of the mall.

Depending on the size and structure of the mall office, there may be one or more Bookkeepers. In centers where there is only one Bookkeeper, the individual will be responsible for all of the accounting duties. Centers with more than one individual in the department may have more specialized duties.

For example, in some centers the Mall Bookkeeper may be solely responsible for accounts receivable or conversely just the accounts payable. In other centers, one Bookkeeper may handle everything. Large malls may also have head Bookkeepers as well as entry-level clerks.

A major function of the Mall Bookkeeper is recording tenant rents. In addition to monthly rents, malls charge vari-ous other monies to tenants. These might include taxes, CAM (common area maintenance) fees, advertising, or mar-keting. These various charges must be billed to tenants on a regular basis. The Mall Bookkeeper is responsible for preparing and sending out these bills on a monthly basis.

The individual may also be expected to monitor pay-ments to ensure they are up to date. In some malls, the Bookkeeper may be required to call tenants when bills are not paid by tenants on time.

Running a mall is expensive. There are a wide array of expenses which are paid out. These might include payroll, consultants, advertising, taxes, loans, equipment, and sup-plies. It is the responsibility of the Mall Bookkeeper to han-dle these account payables. He or she is expected to review invoices and statements for accuracy and completeness, cut checks, have them signed by the correct party, and send them out. Bills must be paid in a timely manner in order to avoid the mall being charged late fees.

Mall Bookkeepers must post the details of each financial transaction. This may be done manually (by hand on paper), with adding machines, or with the help of a computer. Special accounting or bookkeeping software or mall management programs are commonly used.

Malls may have one or more bank accounts. Individuals are responsible for totaling, balancing, and reconciling each account to ensure accuracy.

Many malls have codes for various categories of incomes and expenses. The Bookkeeper must code each invoice properly. This makes it easier to prepare reports detailing transactions and for annual budgeting purposes.

The Mall Bookkeeper may be responsible for printing out and reviewing monthly management reports detailing accounts receivable, expenses, or budget comparisons.

Mall Bookkeepers in many centers may also be responsible for handling payroll functions. In these cases individuals may collect time cards, and tabulate hours worked and pay due to each employee.

Other duties of the Mall Bookkeeper may include:

• Performing secretarial functions
• Writing letters and other correspondence regarding accounts payable and/or receivable
• Answering tenants questions regarding billings
• Preparing reports for auditors

Salaries

Earnings for Bookkeepers working in shopping centers and malls can range from approximately $7.00 to $25 or more per hour. Variables affecting earnings include the geographic location, size, and prestige of the shopping center as well as the experience and responsibilities of the individual.

One of the perks for Bookkeepers working in malls is that individuals often receive employee discounts from mall stores.

Employment Prospects

Employment prospects are fair for individuals seeking this position. Jobs may be located in malls and shopping centers throughout the country. Management companies and developers may also employ Bookkeepers for malls they manage. Depending on the size and structure of the center, there may be one or more Bookkeepers on staff.

Advancement Prospects

Bookkeepers in mall offices may advance their career in a number of ways. After obtaining experience, individuals may take on additional duties or find similar positions in larger, more prestigious malls. Others may climb the career ladder by taking additional training and becoming an accountant.

Education and Training

Education and training requirements vary from mall to mall. Generally, malls require their Bookkeepers to hold a minimum of a high school diploma or the equivalent. Many prefer a college background or some business courses. Classes in bookkeeping, accounting, computers, and accounting software are helpful.

In some properties, the mall will provide in-service training in the use of the software programs or the specific bookkeeping procedures used in the center.

Experience, Skills, and Personality Traits

Bookkeepers should have a strong aptitude for numbers. Individuals need to be careful, orderly, and detail oriented. Mall Bookkeepers should be comfortable using computers and able to use accounting software packages.

Unions/Associations

There is no association specific to Mall Bookkeepers. Individuals working toward becoming an accountant might get additional information from the National Society of Public Accountants (NSPA) or the American Institute of Certified Public Accountants (AICP).

Tips for Entry

1. Courses and workshops in accounting and bookkeeping techniques as well as bookkeeping and accounting software are helpful in making you more marketable.
2. Jobs may be advertised in the classified sections of newspapers. Look under classifications such as "Bookkeeper," "Accounting Clerk," "Bookkeeping Clerk," and "Mall Office Personnel."
3. Stop by the mall management office to see if you can fill out an application. Ask that your application be kept on file if there are no current openings.

JANITORIAL SUPERVISOR— SHOPPING CENTER/MALL

CAREER PROFILE

Duties: Overseeing center's janitorial staff; keeping mall and property clean and well maintained

Alternate Titles: Building Custodian Supervisor

Salary Range: $20,000 to $45,000+

Employment Prospects: Fair

Advancement Prospects: Poor

Best Geographical Location(s) for Position: Jobs may be located throughout the country

Prerequisites:

Education and Training—Educational requirements vary
Experience—Supervision experience
Special Skills and Personality Traits—Supervisory skills; ability to deal well with people; knowledge of use of cleaning supplies and equipment

CAREER LADDER

```
┌─────────────────────────────────────┐
│ Janitorial Supervisor for Larger, More │
│ Prestigious Malls/Shopping Centers   │
│ or Maintenance Supervisor            │
└─────────────────────────────────────┘

┌─────────────────────────────────────┐
│ Janitorial Supervisor—Shopping       │
│ Center/Mall                          │
└─────────────────────────────────────┘

┌─────────────────────────────────────┐
│ Assistant Janitorial Supervisor      │
│ or Janitor                           │
└─────────────────────────────────────┘
```

Position Description

It is essential to their success that malls be clean and well maintained. The Janitorial Supervisor is responsible for overseeing the janitors and cleaning people. In some situations, he or she may also function as the maintenance supervisor. In others, the individual must work in conjunction with the maintenance department.

The Janitorial Supervisor coordinates and schedules the other janitors, cleaners, and custodians. Depending on the mall hours, janitors may work various shifts including morning, afternoon, evening, or overnight. The individual may also schedule and oversee independent contractors for special projects such as cleaning windows, skylights, fountains, or carpets.

The Janitorial Supervisor assigns tasks on a daily basis for the mall's janitors to accomplish. Some of these tasks may need to be done on a daily basis, while others may be done on a weekly or monthly basis. For example daily tasks may include emptying ashtrays and trash receptacles, cleaning rest rooms, checking and replenishing rest room paper products, and cleaning and vacuuming floors and food court areas. Weekly tasks might include washing inside mall windows, shampooing carpets, and washing down walls.

Monthly tasks might include cleaning vents and major cleaning projects on the property.

Not only must the Janitorial Supervisor assign the tasks, he or she must make sure they are completed correctly. Not every assigned job must be inspected, but the supervisor must see that tasks are executed in a timely manner.

The Janitorial Supervisor also trains new employees. He or she must explain all pertinent procedures, rules, and regulations to employees. The supervisor issues cleaning supplies and equipment to employees and shows them how each is used properly.

Janitorial Supervisors often meet with salespeople from companies selling paper products or cleaning supplies. They may sample cleaning supplies and products for possible use in the mall, and they must inventory cleaning supplies and paper products on a regular basis to be sure supplies and paper products are available when needed. They must also maintain cleaning equipment in good working condition.

Additional duties of Janitorial Supervisors might include:

- Screening, interviewing, and hiring janitors
- Recommending promotions and dismissals
- Preparing reports for budgets and expenses and schedules
- Performing cleaning duties

Salaries

Annual earnings for Janitorial Supervisors working in malls and shopping centers ranges from approximately $20,000 to $45,000 depending on a number of variables. These include the size, prestige, and geographic location of the specific mall or shopping center as well as the experience, responsibilities, and education of the individual.

Employment Prospects

Employment prospects for Janitorial Supervisors are fair. Individuals may find employment in malls throughout the country. As noted previously, in some malls there is a maintenance supervisor who handles the functions of the Janitorial Supervisor. Additionally, some malls contract outside janitorial companies to clean the center.

Advancement Prospects

Advancement is difficult for Janitorial Supervisors. Individuals may find similar positions in larger, more prestigious properties to advance their careers. They might also become Maintenance Supervisors.

Education and Training

Generally, most employers prefer to hire individuals who have completed high school. A great deal of the training Janitorial Supervisors receive is usually on the job. Many malls have in-service training programs to hone skills. Technical schools and trade programs may also offer training.

Experience, Skills, and Personality Traits

Experience handling janitorial work is necessary. Most Janitorial Supervisors were once janitors or custodians. Supervisory skills are essential. A basic understanding and knowledge of the use of cleaning products and equipment as well as maintenance is helpful. The ability to work well with others is also needed.

Unions/Associations

There is no association specific to Shopping Center Janitorial Supervisors. Some Supervisors may take advantage of educational programs of the International Council of Shopping Centers (ICSC).

Tips for Entry

1. Many larger property management and real estate development companies have internships and training programs.
2. Get your foot in the door by stopping in to the mall management office and a filling out an application.
3. Positions are often advertised in the classified sections of newspapers. Look under classifications including "Janitorial Supervisor," "Custodian Supervisor," "Malls," or "Shopping Centers."

MAINTENANCE SUPERVISOR— SHOPPING CENTER/MALL

CAREER PROFILE

Duties: Overseeing center's maintenance staff; making sure mall and property are well maintained and in good working order; doing routine preventative maintenance

Alternate Titles: Maintenance Mechanic Supervisor

Salary Range: $20,000 to $45,000+

Employment Prospects: Fair

Advancement Prospects: Fair

Best Geographical Location(s) for Position: Jobs may be located throughout the country

Prerequisites:

Education and Training—Training requirements vary

Experience—Experience in mall or property maintenance

Special Skills and Personality Traits—Basic knowledge of woodworking, electricity, and plumbing; problem solving skills; time management skills; communication skills; ability to deal well with people

CAREER LADDER

```
┌─────────────────────────────────┐
│ Maintenance Supervisor for Larger │
│     Malls/Shopping Centers        │
└─────────────────────────────────┘

┌─────────────────────────────────┐
│ Maintenance Supervisor—Shopping   │
│          Center/Mall              │
└─────────────────────────────────┘

┌─────────────────────────────────┐
│  Assistant Maintenance Supervisor │
│     or Maintenance Mechanic       │
└─────────────────────────────────┘
```

Position Description

The mall's Maintenance Supervisor cares for the physical appearance of the mall. Depending on the size of the mall, he or she may work with and supervise one or more maintenance people. In some malls, the individual also oversees the janitorial staff.

People generally don't enjoy shopping in an unkempt and dirty mall. Every building has things that break, and malls are no exception. The Maintenance Supervisor must constantly look out for things that are not working are in or need of repair or replacement, so that he or she can quickly correct the situation.

Maintenance Supervisor's look for an array of things. These might include stained ceiling tiles, broken paper towel dispensers, nonworking toilets, chipped paint, cracked benches, broken food court chairs, and bulbs that are burned out.

Broken or damaged fixtures of furniture might also be a liability. For example, a big pothole in the parking lot might cause an accident. Cracked blacktop or sidewalks might result in a trip or fall. A leaky roof might allow water to damage tenants' goods and result in insurance claims.

In addition to fixing things, Maintenance Supervisors also do routine preventative work to ensure that things are kept in working order. Individuals may, for example, do routine checks on ballasts, heating and air conditioning vents, and other equipment.

The Maintenance Supervisor is expected to oversee the repair and maintenance of the mall, its property, machinery, and equipment. This might include working on plumbing, electrical, and air conditioning and heating systems. A successful Maintenance Supervisor needs to be a jack-of-all-trades. Generally, the smaller the property, the more the Maintenance Supervisor and his or her staff must know how to do. While the services of outside contractors such as HVAC (heating, ventilation, and air-conditioning) mechanics, certified electricians, and roofers may be utilized, individuals must know the basics. The Supervisor must know how to evaluate a situation and when to call in a professional.

The Maintenance Supervisor and his or her staff are often expected to handle plaster and drywall repairs or putting up walls to cover empty stores. Other responsibilities might include checking and repairing the roof, painting the building, clearing clogged toilets and leaky faucets, and doing work within the building structure to bring it in compliance with local building codes. The Maintenance Supervisor and his or her staff additionally might be expected to repair air conditioning and heating problems. In many malls, each maintenance man or woman has a specialty. In that manner, a Supervisor can then assign the correct person to handle each job.

The Maintenance Supervisor is expected to coordinate and schedule the maintenance staff. He or she assigns tasks on a daily basis to the maintenance staff. The individual may also schedule and oversee the work of independent contractors.

Additional duties of Maintenance Supervisor might include:

• Screening, interviewing, and hiring the maintenance staff
• Recommending promotions and dismissals
• Preparing reports for budgets and expenses and schedules
• Performing maintenance
• Making sure maintenance jobs are performed correctly and on a timely basis

Salaries

Annual earnings for Maintenance Supervisors working in malls and shopping centers can range from approximately $20,000 to $45,000 depending on a number of variables. These include the size, prestige, and geographic location of the specific mall or shopping center as well as the experience, responsibilities, and education of the individual.

Employment Prospects

Employment prospects for Maintenance Supervisors are fair. Individuals may find employment in malls throughout the country. The more skilled the individual, the more employable he or she will be.

Advancement Prospects

Maintenance Supervisors may advance their careers by locating similar positions in larger, more prestigious proper-

ties. Others climb the career ladder by finding employment with large real estate developers or management companies.

Education and Training

Maintenance Supervisors obtain their training in different ways. Some train informally, learning new skills by watching others. Apprenticeships are an excellent training opportunity in this field. Many individuals also attend trade, technical, or vocational schools to learn various skills.

Experience, Skills, and Personality Traits

Experience working in maintenance is necessary for this job. Most Maintenance Supervisors worked in maintenance prior to their current job. Supervisory skills and the ability to work well with others are needed. An understanding and knowledge of all aspects of maintenance is essential.

Unions/Associations

There is no association specific to Shopping Center Maintenance Supervisors.

Tips for Entry

1. Stop in to the mall management office and fill out an application. Ask that it be kept on file if there are no current openings.
2. Many larger property management and real estate development companies have internships and training programs.
3. Positions are often advertised in the classified sections of newspapers. Look under classifications including "Maintenance Supervisor," "Maintenance," "Malls," or "Shopping Centers."
4. Many malls have websites featuring job opportunities. Check advertisements in newspapers or mall brochures for mall website addresses.

SECURITY DIRECTOR— SHOPPING CENTER/MALL

CAREER PROFILE

Duties: Develop security plan for mall; hire, train, and supervise security officers; patrol, inspect, and protect shopping center and center property; enforce regulations; supervise loss prevention plan

Alternate Titles: Director of Security

Salary Range: $24,000 to $48,000+

Employment Prospects: Poor

Advancement Prospects: Fair

Best Geographical Location(s) for Position: Jobs may be located throughout the country; areas hosting large malls will offer more opportunities

Prerequisites:

Education and Training—High school diploma or equivalent; on-the-job training; additional training may be required

Experience—Experience requirements vary

Special Skills and Personality Traits—Supervisory skills; good judgment, responsible; interpersonal skills; communications skills; good moral character; clean police record

CAREER LADDER

```
┌─────────────────────────────────┐
│  Security Director in Larger, More │
│   Prestigious Center or Owner    │
│      of Security Company         │
└─────────────────────────────────┘

┌─────────────────────────────────┐
│        Security Director         │
└─────────────────────────────────┘

┌─────────────────────────────────┐
│   Security Officer or Assistant  │
│        Security Director         │
└─────────────────────────────────┘
```

Position Description

Today more than ever, security in malls is of the utmost importance. In order for customers to feel comfortable, mall owners try to provide as safe an environment as possible.

The Security Director in a mall or shopping center is responsible for overseeing the safety of the mall, its employees, and customers. The Director develops and implements a mall safety and security plan. Some centers employ their own security department. Others contract out for the services of a security company.

The mall Security Director is expected to protect the mall and the mall's property. The individual hires security officers and trains and supervises them. He or she must explain the mall's policies and procedures to each officer.

Every mall has different days and times in which the center is busiest. The Security Director is in charge of scheduling the security staff in the most effective manner possible,

and monitoring the activities in the mall to make sure the schedule is working properly.

While tenants are generally responsible for handling shoplifting incidents in their own store, the mall is expected to provide a security presence which will deter this crime. If there is a great deal of shoplifting occurring in the mall on Friday nights, for example, the Security Director may put more officers on duty that night.

Shrinkage is a big problem to stores in malls. Shrinkage is the loss of merchandise due to various means, the most prominent being shoplifting. Loss prevention is important. Shoplifters often go from store to store in a mall taking merchandise. The Security Director often develops seminars for mall employees to help them find ways to cut their shrinkage. He or she may also put together various classes on safety.

In some instances, the shrinkage in mall stores involves employees. The mall Security Director may be asked to hire undercover officers or involve the police in the investigation.

The mall Security Director usually has a good working relationship with the local law enforcement agencies. Usually, the mall security calls local law enforcement to arrest people for infractions as they themselves have very limited authority.

The mall Security Director is in charge of keeping the entire mall property safe. He or she may assign officers to patrol the inside of the mall as well as the outside of the property including the parking lot.

Shrinkage is not the only problem that might occur in a mall. There are a variety of potential disturbances and problems that might need to be addressed. The Security Director is in charge of handling these situations or assigning a security officer to take care of the problem. These problems might include calming loud or boisterous customers, evicting customers who are acting in a disorderly fashion, or helping in a medical emergency. Individuals must be able to handle emergency situations such as power outages, weather problems, and medical emergencies.

The Security Director often uses a two-way radio system to keep in contact with officers.

Additional duties of the Security Directors working in shopping centers or malls may include:

- Assuming duties of security officers
- Checking to make sure daily shift reports detailing occurrences are complete
- Handling traffic concerns going in and out of the mall
- Preparing reports for mall management on security and safety
- Making recommendations to mall management about security and safety concerns
- Formulating policies regarding safety
- Determining need for special safety programs

Salaries
Annual earnings for Security Directors working in shopping centers and malls can range from approximately $24,000 to $48,000 or more. Variables affecting earnings include the geographic location, size, and prestige of the shopping center as well as the experience, training, and responsibilities of the individual.

Employment Prospects
Employment prospects are poor for individuals seeking this position. As noted previously, many malls employ outside security firms instead of in-house people. The best prospects for employment in this area will be at large malls.

Advancement Prospects
Security Directors working in malls may advance their career in a number of ways. The most common is landing similar positions in larger, more prestigious malls. Others may climb the career ladder by striking out and starting their own security firms.

Education and Training
Education and training requirements vary for this type of position. While some malls require their Security Directors to have a minimum of a high school diploma or the equivalent, most malls will prefer or require individuals to have a college background or degree.

Certain states may require individuals working in security to go through specified training programs. Some states may also require an annual in-service course to refresh or update officers in changes in the security field.

Any armed officer must go through a firearms training course. These usually involve both classroom instruction and a specified number of hours on the firing range.

Experience, Skills, and Personality Traits
The Security Director is required to have a great deal of experience. Many Security Directors started out in police work. Some are retired police officers. Others have experience in the military or other areas of civil service. There are also some individuals who obtained experience and worked themselves up to the top position from security departments in malls or working with outside security companies.

The Security Director working in a mall should have an array of skills. First and foremost, individuals need to be responsible people with good judgment. Leadership skills are vital. Interpersonal and customer relations skills are essential. Communications skills are mandatory.

A clean record and good moral character are essential. As previously noted, those who are armed usually also must be registered with their specific state to carry firearms.

Unions/Associations
Individuals may obtain information about possible licensing requirements from their state or local licensing commission.

Tips for Entry
1. Openings may be advertised in the classified sections of newspapers. Look under heading classifications such as "Malls," "Shopping Centers," "Security Directors," or "Mall/Shopping Center Security."
2. Check out openings on the Internet. Many malls have their own websites listing employment opportunities.
3. You might also find openings on the World Wide Web job sites. Start with the more popular ones such as www.hotjobs.com and www.monster.com. A new site, www.abracat.com, is easy to use and has many job openings in all industries by geographical area.
4. Contact mall management companies. As they usually handle more than one center, they may be aware of openings.

SECURITY OFFICER— SHOPPING CENTER/MALL

CAREER PROFILE

Duties: Patrol, inspect, and protect the shopping center and center property; enforce regulations; handle loss prevention

Alternate Titles: Guard

Salary Range: $6.50 to $14.00+ per hour

Employment Prospects: Fair

Advancement Prospects: Fair

Best Geographical Location(s) for Position: Jobs may be located throughout the country

Prerequisites:

Education and Training—High school diploma or equivalent; on-the-job training; additional training may be required

Experience—Experience requirements vary

Special Skills and Personality Traits—Good judgment, responsible; interpersonal skills; leadership; people skills; communications skills; good moral character

CAREER LADDER

```
┌─────────────────────────────────────┐
│  Security Director or Security Officer │
│   in Larger, More Prestigious Center  │
└─────────────────────────────────────┘

┌─────────────────────────────────────┐
│           Security Officer            │
└─────────────────────────────────────┘

┌─────────────────────────────────────┐
│     Entry Level, Security Officer     │
│          in Other Industry            │
└─────────────────────────────────────┘
```

Position Description

It is essential that malls be as safe as possible. Security Officers are responsible for helping to keep malls safe for customers and mall tenants. Some centers employ their own security department. Others contract out for the services of a security company.

Security Officers are expected to protect the mall and the mall's property. Generally, Security Officers are uniformed and can be identified. On occasion, Security Officers may work "undercover." In these instances, they will not wear uniforms and will dress in plain clothes to blend in with the other shoppers.

Security Officers patrol the mall. They walk around the center and maintain a presence. Some Security Officers may also drive around the property to assure the safety of customers and mall employees in the parking lot. Security Officers may be assigned designated areas to patrol or may move around the mall during their shift. It is up to them to identify potentially dangerous situations and act in an effective manner. It is important to note that unless the Security Officer is also a licensed police officer he or she usually has limited legal authority.

Security Officers are expected to keep the peace. Individuals handle any disturbances within the shopping center, such as calming situations if customers become loud or boisterous. They may also be required to evict a customer who is acting in a disorderly fashion.

Loss prevention is a major problem in many malls. Security Officers are responsible for protecting against theft and vandalism. Individuals must be alert to everything going on around them. They must observe the actions and activities of both customers and employees. If they see a potential problem, they are expected to contact the police or other local law enforcement agency to handle the arrest.

Security Officers often use two-way radios to keep in contact with their supervisor. Individuals must be able to handle emergency situations such as power outages, weather problems, and medical emergencies which may occur.

Security officers are expected to file daily shift reports detailing occurrences and logging any incidents or accidents during their shifts. All unusual activities within the mall must be documented.

Additional duties of the Security Officers working in shopping centers or malls may include:

- Assisting lost children
- Checking to make sure store gates are down, doors are closed and locked
- Escorting mall employees to their vehicles after hours
- Answering customers' questions regarding the mall
- Giving directions to stores within the mall

Salaries

Earnings for Security Officers working in shopping centers and malls can range from approximately $6.00 to $14.00 or more per hour. Variables affecting earnings include the geographic location, size, and prestige of the shopping center as well as the experience, training, and responsibilities of the individual. Salaries may also differ depending on whether the individual is employed directly by the mall or working for a security company which is contracted by the mall.

In some cases, off-duty police officers work as Security Officers in their off hours. These individuals may earn upward of $30 or more per hour.

Employment Prospects

Employment prospects are fair for individuals seeking this position. Jobs can be located in malls and shopping centers throughout the country. As noted previously, individuals may be employed by malls directly or by security companies.

Advancement Prospects

Security Officers may advance their career in a number of ways. After obtaining experience, some individuals find similar positions in larger, more prestigious malls or with larger security companies. Others may climb the career ladder by becoming security supervisors or directors. Still others decide they enjoy security work and become trained police officers.

Education and Training

Education and training requirements vary from mall to mall. Generally, most malls prefer their Security Officers to have a minimum of a high school diploma or the equivalent. Depending on the situation, the mall may provide on-the-job training. Those working for security companies may go through similar training programs.

Certain states may require individuals working as Security Officers to go through a specified training program offered in the area. Some states may also require an annual in-service course to refresh or update officers in changes in the security field.

Armed officers must go through a firearms training course. These usually involve both classroom instruction and a specified number of hours on the firing range.

Experience, Skills, and Personality Traits

Entry-level positions may be open in some malls. Experience, however, working in private security, the military, or civil service police is useful. Security Officers need a multitude of skills. Individuals should be responsible people with good judgment. Interpersonal and customer relations skills are essential. Communications skills are mandatory.

A clean record and good moral character are essential. Security officers who are armed usually also must be registered with the state in which the mall is located to carry firearms.

Unions/Associations

There is no association specific to Security Officers working in malls or shopping centers. However, individuals may obtain information about possible licensing requirements from their state or local licensing commission.

Tips for Entry

1. There are some community colleges, vocational, and technical schools offering courses for security officers. These courses may be useful in career advancement.
2. Jobs may be advertised in the classified sections of newspapers. Look under classifications such as "Security Officer," "Security," "Guard," or "Mall/Shopping Center Security."
3. Stop in the mall's management office to see if you can fill out an employment application. Ask that your application be kept on file if there are no current openings.
4. Look in the yellow pages to check the names and addresses of security companies.
5. If your local mall utilizes the services of a security company, ask one of the officers to give you a contact name and phone number. Then call the company and make an appointment for an interview.

LEASING DIRECTOR— MALL/SHOPPING CENTER

CAREER PROFILE

Duties: Leasing the stores in mall or shopping center; negotiating leases and rental agreements; acting as owner's agent

Alternate Titles: Real Estate Director

Salary Range: $30,000 to $125,000+

Employment Prospects: Fair

Advancement Prospects: Fair

Best Geographical Location(s) for Position: Jobs may be located throughout the country

Prerequisites:

Education and Training—Educational requirements vary

Experience—Experience working in real estate and leasing necessary

Special Skills and Personality Traits—Negotiating skills; problem solving skills; communication skills; ability to deal well with people; pleasantly aggressive

CAREER LADDER

```
┌─────────────────────────────────────┐
│   Leasing Director for Larger, More  │
│   Prestigious Mall or Shopping Center│
└─────────────────────────────────────┘

┌─────────────────────────────────────┐
│          Leasing Director            │
└─────────────────────────────────────┘

┌─────────────────────────────────────┐
│     Assistant Leasing Director,      │
│        Real Estate Agent             │
│       or Real Estate Broker          │
└─────────────────────────────────────┘
```

Position Description

The way mall and shopping center owners and management make money is by renting space to tenants. The person responsible for this function is the Leasing Director, but in some malls, the mall manager may handle the duties. Leasing Directors act as the mall owner's representative or agent.

Prospective tenants often contact malls to find out about rents, other charges, and availabilities. The Leasing Director may send out leasing packages to these individuals or may set up meetings to discuss pertinent information. If individuals are interested, the Director is expected to show spaces in the mall.

The Leasing Director must also seek out tenants who might be beneficial to the mall's tenant mix. The success of malls often depends on this. Just filling up stores does not always work, because people like to visit malls where they have a variety of shopping options. Having ten shoe stores, for example, with little else might not be the best mix to bring in the most shoppers.

In this position, the individual may be required to meet frequently with prospective tenants. He or she will answer questions and emphasize the selling points about the mall that are likely to be the most important to the tenant. For example, the Director may show sales figures, foot traffic reports, or advertising budgets.

Once tenants decide they might be interested in leasing space in the mall, the Leasing Director must negotiate a lease. There are a variety of areas to consider including rents, taxes, CAM (common area maintenance) charges, advertising charges, prepping of the space, length of the lease, options, and kick-out clauses. (A kick-out clause allows a tenant to leave without penalty if certain conditions are not met. For example, not meeting a specified amount of sales.) The Leasing Director usually has a degree of leeway to negotiate terms.

The Leasing Director is often the individual responsible for dealing with tenants after a lease has been executed when the tenants have a major complaint. Continual roof leaks, constantly dirty rest rooms, unkempt mall property, low foot traffic, or lack of mall advertising and promotion might all cause tenants to complain bitterly. The Leasing Director is expected to calm the tenants and deal with the problems. He or she may contact the mall manager, tenant relations director, marketing director, or public relations director to look into the problems and solve them. In some instances, the Leasing Director may authorize abatements to appease irate tenants.

The Leasing Director is in charge of tracking tenant leases and handling renewals. He or she may write letters, call, or personally visit tenants when leases are close to completion and need to be renewed. At times, the Leasing Director may renegotiate the lease. In other situations, the Director may just make sure the tenant picks up his or her option.

There is a great deal of paperwork connected with this job. The Leasing Director must make sure accurate records are kept. It is essential that the individual remember what was said at meetings, promised during phone calls, and negotiated. The Leasing Director must be sure leases are executed and signed by all parties.

Leasing Directors working for real estate developers or mall management companies may be responsible for handling the leasing of more than one mall.

Additional duties of Leasing Directors might include:

- Developing leasing packages
- Working with outside real estate agents
- Dealing with corporate leasing directors and agents
- Attending conventions and other leasing events
- Visiting other malls to seek out potential tenants

Salaries
Earnings for mall Leasing Directors can vary greatly starting at approximately $30,000 and going up to $125,000 or more. Earnings depend on the size, prestige, and geographic location of the property and number of properties the individual is responsible for leasing. Other variables include the experience, responsibilities, and education of the individual.

Leasing Directors often receive a salary plus commissions or percentages on the gross terms of the leases they write. In some situations individuals may receive bonuses based on increased rentals or the handling of extra projects.

Employment Prospects
Aggressive and effective Leasing Directors are always in demand. However it should be noted that every mall does not employ a Leasing Director. In smaller malls the mall manager often handles the leasing functions.

Individuals seeking this position may find employment throughout the country. Leasing Directors may be directly employed by malls or work for real estate developers, development companies, or property management companies.

Advancement Prospects
The most common method of career advancement for Leasing Directors is to find similar positions in larger, more prestigious malls, mall management companies, or real estate developers. Some individuals strike out on their own and form leasing companies.

Education and Training
Educational requirements vary from mall to mall. While much of the training individuals receive is on the job, many employers prefer that individuals have some sort of real estate training. Others require it.

Most positions will also prefer or require the Leasing Director to hold a real estate agent or brokers license. In order to obtain this licensing, individuals must usually take and pass a written test as well as go through at least 30 hours of classroom instruction to become an agent or 90 hours of training to become a broker.

For those interested in a college degree, relevant majors might include real estate, business, public administration, finance, or related fields.

Professional and trade associations often offer helpful seminars and courses in all aspects of real estate.

Experience, Skills, and Personality Traits
Leasing Directors may begin their careers in a variety of ways. Some work as assistant leasing directors or in real estate in other industries. Others work in various aspects of mall administration either directly for a mall, a mall management company, or a real estate management company.

Leasing Directors should be assertive with an ability to deal with and work well with others. Individuals need to be good problem solvers who are energetic, detail oriented, and highly motivated.

Successful Leasing Directors have developed many contacts. This is helpful in bringing people to the table when looking for new tenants. The ability to negotiate well is essential.

Unions/Associations
Mall or shopping center Leasing Directors may be members of a number of associations providing career guidance and support. These include the National Association of Realtors (NAR), a local state real estate association, the International Council of Shopping Centers (ICSC), and the Institute of Real Estate Management (IREM).

Tips for Entry
1. Contact larger property management and real estate development companies to find out what internship and training programs they have available in this area.
2. There are a number of executive search firms dealing exclusively with jobs in shopping centers and malls.
3. Send your resume and a cover letter to retail property management companies, real estate development companies, and large malls.

4. Positions are often advertised in the classified sections of newspapers. Look under classifications including "Leasing Director," or "Mall Leasing Director," or "Shopping Center Leasing Director," and "Retail Leasing Director."

5. Openings are also advertised in trade journals such as *Value Retail News.*

6. Jobs in this field may be located on-line. Begin your search on some of the more popular job search sites such as the Monster board (www.monster.com) and Hot Jobs (www.hotjobs.com).

SPECIAL EVENTS COORDINATOR— MALL/SHOPPING CENTER

CAREER PROFILE

Duties: Plan, develop, and implement special events and promotions for mall or shopping center

Alternate Titles: Special Events Manager; Events Coordinator

Salary Range: $22,000 to $35,000+

Employment Prospects: Fair

Advancement Prospects: Fair

Best Geographical Location(s) for Position: Jobs may be located throughout the country

Prerequisites:

Education and Training—Bachelor's degree preferred

Experience—Experience in special events, publicity, and/or public relations preferred

Special Skills and Personality Traits—Creativity; detail oriented; imagination; innovation; communications skills; understanding of shopping center industry

CAREER LADDER

```
┌─────────────────────────────┐
│   Public Relations Director  │
│    or Marketing Director     │
└─────────────────────────────┘

┌─────────────────────────────┐
│  Special Events Coordinator  │
└─────────────────────────────┘

┌─────────────────────────────┐
│   Special Events Assistant   │
│  or Public Relations Assistant │
└─────────────────────────────┘
```

Position Description

Most malls and shopping centers sponsor a variety of special events and promotions throughout the year in order to bring in potential shoppers, attract the attention of the media, and create goodwill in the community.

The Special Events Coordinator is responsible for helping to develop, create, and implement the special events and promotions in the mall. The individual is often expected to develop an annual calendar of events. This contains all the events and promotions planned for the coming year. While the calendar is subject to change, it gives tenants the opportunity to plan copromotions if they wish, and also helps them plan to have more staff when traffic may be busiest. For example, if the mall schedules a Washington's Birthday Sidewalk Sale, the stores must make sure they have merchandise marked down. If the mall is sponsoring a safe trick-or-treating night, store managers may need to put on more staff to deal with the crowds of children and their parents.

Promotions and events may be routine or may be more complex. Routine events might include things such as sidewalk sales, health fairs, community fairs, Santa's arrival, crafts shows, antiques shows, a safe Trick or Treat night, or fashion shows. More complex events might include how-to days, wine and cheese tastings, soap opera festivals, concerts in the parking lot, museum exhibits, mall anniversary celebrations, or weddings in the mall.

Some events are developed and executed by the Special Events Coordinator, but others may require outside contractors. For example, the Coordinator may hire a carnival or circus promoter to set up in the mall or parking lot. He or she might put together crafts shows, antiques shows, or computer shows, or work with a promoter or agent to bring in events like puppet shows, beauty pageants, or petting zoos.

Many Special Events Coordinators work on events and promotions with cosponsors. These may include stores within the mall, car dealerships, radio or television stations, or newspapers. Some promotions may feature contests or sweepstakes giving away big prizes such as cars, jewelry, or money.

Depending on the structure of the mall, the Special Events Coordinator may be responsible for dealing with the community organizations. In many centers, mall management allows not-for-profit groups to set up in the hallways to raise funds, have bake sales, or recruit new members. In this case the individual may be expected to coordinate the groups, show them where to set up, and take care of any necessary paperwork.

When developing events and promotions the Special Events Coordinator takes a number of things into account. These include what events will bring the most shoppers into the mall, what it takes to execute the event, and how it figures into the budget.

Foot traffic is essential to malls. The more people walking around, the better the chance they will make purchases. Sometimes the purchases may not be immediate. In some cases, once an event brings in people to the mall, they see what is available and return when they need items.

The number of events the individual will be responsible for annually depends to a great extent on the size and structure of the center as well as its promotional budget. Events and promotions can be inexpensive or they might be very expensive. The best ideas in malls are sometimes the tried and true ones. However, the successful Special Events Coordinator must initiate innovative and creative events to supplement the standard routine events.

The Special Events Coordinator is expected to create a basic plan for the event, and develop and stick to a budget to complete the project. In some cases, the Special Events Coordinator may be responsible for handling the promotion and publicity for the events. In other cases, the individual will work with the public relations and advertising departments on these functions.

Generally, the mall Special Events Coordinator must be on hand for special events and promotions. This means, the individual may work on weekends or during evening hours.

Other duties of a mall Special Events Coordinator may include:

- Developing special events for mall employees
- Working on off-site events such as mall sponsorship of runs or marathons
- Obtaining proposals from outside vendors
- Supervising staff

Salaries

Earnings for Special Events Coordinators working in a retail environment range from approximately $22,000 to $35,000 or more. Factors affecting earnings include the specific retail store as well as its size, prestige, and location. Other variables include the education, experience, and responsibilities of the individual.

Employment Prospects

Employment prospects are fair for Special Events Coordinators, however, every mall does not have such a position. In some centers, the public relations director, marketing director, or community relations director, or a combination of the three, may be responsible for handling these functions.

Advancement Prospects

Advancement prospects are fair for Special Events Coordinators. Individuals might climb the career ladder by finding similar positions in larger or more prestigious malls. With education, experience, and training, individuals might also advance to become mall public relations or marketing directors.

Education and Training

While there are exceptions, individuals seeking positions in mall special event coordination are usually required to hold a bachelor's degree. Good majors include communications, public relations, English, liberal arts, advertising, business, journalism, or retail management.

Seminars and workshops in special events, promotions, public relations, publicity, and advertising are helpful.

Experience, Skills, and Personality Traits

Special Events Coordinators working in malls often receive experience as interns or assistants in the marketing, public relations, or special events office prior to their current position.

Successful Special Events Coordinators are creative, innovative, and have excellent communications skills. Individuals need to be extremely organized and detail oriented with the ability to deal calmly with stressful situations.

Unions/Associations

Special Events Coordinators working in malls might be associated with a number of associations and organizations providing professional support and educational guidance. These might include the Public Relations Society of America (PRSA), the International Council of Shopping Centers (ICSC), the National Retail Merchants Association (NRMA), or the National Retail Federation (NRF).

Tips for Entry

1. Contact the International Council of Shopping Centers and other organizations to see when and where they hold seminars or workshops in mall promotion and special events.
2. Look for an internship or a position as a special events assistant in a mall. This will give you great experience and get your foot in the door.
3. Positions may be located in the newspaper help wanted section. The Sunday classified section is usually the largest of the week. Look under headings such as "Special Events," "Special Events Coordinator," "Retail Opportunities," "Public Relations," "Marketing," "Promotion," or "Malls."
4. Job openings may also be listed in trade publications such as *Value Retail News*.
5. Jobs may also be located via the Internet. Start by checking out some of the more popular sites such as www.hotjobs.com.

DEPARTMENT STORES

STORE MANAGER—DEPARTMENT STORE

CAREER PROFILE

Duties: Handle day-to-day management of department store; oversee staffing needs of store; deal with customer service issues; make sure store is in compliance with safety issues; work with staff to help store meet sales and profit goals

Alternate Titles: Manager

Salary Range: $33,000 to $150,000+

Employment Prospects: Good

Advancement Prospects: Fair

Best Geographical Location(s) for Position: Jobs may be located throughout the country

Prerequisites:
Education and Training—Training requirements vary
Experience—Experience in retail management
Special Skills and Personality Traits—Problem solving skills; negotiation skills; communications skills; ability to deal well with people; management skills; administrative skills

CAREER LADDER

```
┌─────────────────────────────────┐
│  Department Store Manager for   │
│  Larger or More Prestigious Store │
│        or Area Manager          │
└─────────────────────────────────┘

┌─────────────────────────────────┐
│        Store Manager            │
└─────────────────────────────────┘

┌─────────────────────────────────┐
│     Assistant Store Manager     │
└─────────────────────────────────┘
```

Position Description

Department stores encompass a variety of sizes and types. Some are huge stores covering three floors or more. Others are smaller. Department stores may cater to average consumers offering discount merchandise or they may cater to upscale shoppers. No matter what type of store, each has a Store Manager.

The Department Store Manager has a great deal of responsibility. He or she is ultimately responsible for everything that happens within the store. The individual handles the day-to-day management of the department store. Within the scope of the job, the Manager has many different duties.

One of the main functions of the Store Manager is working with his or her staff to meet corporate sales and profit goals. Stores generally keep accurate records of sales figures on a daily, weekly, monthly, and annual basis. This information is used to help project profits. Based on these figures along with various other information, the corporate offices set sales goals. It is up to the Manager to try to find ways to meet these goals. This might include working with

assistant managers, merchandise managers, buyers, operations people, and the corporate office as well as other store employees.

The Store Manager oversees the staffing needs of the store. In large department stores there may be a human resources department or manager handling these functions. However, the Store Manager will still usually oversee the hiring or termination of key executives within the store. In smaller department stores, the Manager may be responsible for staffing the store with the help of assistant managers. He or she may schedule job fairs or write and place help wanted ads for the newspaper or other media.

The working and customer climate of department stores often depends on the Store Manager. Those who can make a store a pleasant shopping environment for customers and a pleasant workplace for employees will be most successful.

The Department Store Manager also oversees a staff of assistant managers, department managers, merchandise managers, and other employees who help fulfill the duties of running the store. The Store Manager must be familiar with the workings of every department.

There are an array of laws, rules, and regulations which must be followed for health, legal, and safety reasons. It is the responsibility of the Store Manager to make sure all of these are adhered to. These may include making sure aisles are wide enough for wheelchairs to get through, merchandise isn't blocking exits, and fire extinguishers are inspected.

The Store Manager is also expected to make sure that all employment regulations are followed within the store. These might include things like following labor rules, making sure teenagers don't work more hours than their allotted time, or forms are filled out for tax purposes. While the individual may have others handling these tasks, the Manager still is responsible for overseeing the function.

Many department stores, especially chains, have weekly promotions and sales advertised in the local paper and fliers. These promotions, ads, and fliers are used to attract customers. While these are often handled by the corporate office of a chain, it is up to the Manager to make sure the specials and items advertised are on the shelves. The Manager is expected to make sure the merchandise is moved from the stockroom to the shelves so it is available. In instances where merchandise wasn't delivered to the store, the Manager must determine how to best handle the situation. In some stores, the Manager may decide to give rain checks to customers. In others, Store Managers may offer the customer comparable merchandise when items aren't available.

The Store Manager sets the tone for customer service in the store. Customer service is of utmost importance to keeping customers happy and satisfied. The Store Manager is expected to make sure the customer service of the store is up to par. While most department stores have customer service representatives and managers, there are always customers and situations that need extra special care and attention.

The Manager will usually be the one called when a customer has a problem no one else can handle or wants to handle. He or she is responsible for dealing with emergencies, crises, and any problems which crop up in the store during the day. He or she is expected to write reports on accidents or other incidents such as when employees or customers are hurt within the store or in the parking lot.

Most department stores have accounting departments or cash offices. As the Department Store Manager is ultimately responsible for overseeing all monies in the store, he or she usually works closely with the managers of these departments. He or she may go over reports of the day's receipts as well as weekly and monthly reports.

In some department stores the Manager may also be responsible for depositing the day's receipts in the bank or may accompany an assistant manager or other employee in this task. The Manager also may be expected to analyze other data as well to help determine what direction the store might take to increase profits.

Many chain department stores have similar layouts in each store. That means that the floorplans are much the same whether you are in a store in New York or Los Angeles. In many department stores, the Manager is responsible for making sure that the store layout is handled in accordance with corporate layout designs.

Additional duties of Department Store Managers may include:

- Representing the store at community events
- Handling emergencies and crises
- Handling loss prevention
- Terminating employees
- Recommending raises and promotions for employees

Salaries
Earnings for Department Store Managers can range from approximately $33,000 to $150,000 or more. Variables affecting earnings include the size, prestige, and geographic location of the department store. Other variables include the experience, responsibilities, and education of the individual. Generally, those with the highest salaries will have a great deal of responsibility and manage large stores. Some Store Managers may also receive bonuses when sales meet or exceed goals.

Employment Prospects
Employment prospects are good for Department Store Managers. Positions are located throughout the country. Possibilities include large chains stores like Ames, Wal-Mart, K-Mart, Target, Kohls, J.C. Penney, Sears, Macy's, Dillards, Bloomingdales, Nordstroms, and Sterns. Individuals may also find employment working in smaller department stores that are locally owned.

Advancement Prospects
The most common method of career advancement for Store Managers working in department stores is locating similar jobs in larger or more prestigious stores. Those working in chains may climb the career ladder by promotion to larger stores within the chain. Individuals may also advance their careers by becoming area managers or moving into other areas of corporate management.

Education and Training
Educational and training requirements vary from store to store. Generally larger stores and chains require their Managers to go through formal training programs which include both classroom and in-store training. Many of the larger department store chains send their management recruits to these training programs which are often located at the company's corporate offices. Some stores will hire individuals who have no formal training, but who have worked their way up obtaining on-the-job training along the way.

Educational backgrounds of Department Store Managers vary too. While stores may not require individuals to hold anything above a high school diploma, they may prefer Managers with college backgrounds or degrees. Good majors include business, management, marketing, retailing, merchandising, communications, advertising, liberal arts, or related fields.

Experience, Skills, and Personality Traits

Department Store Managers are required to have experience in retail and management. Generally, individuals have worked the sales floor and have been department managers, group department managers, and assistant store managers prior to becoming Store Managers.

Managers must have a knowledge of management principles as well as a total understanding of the retail industry. Leadership skills, self-confidence, and decisiveness are essential. The ability to deal with and work well with people is mandatory. Individuals need to be good problem solvers who are energetic, detail oriented, and highly motivated.

Communication skills, both written and verbal, are necessary as well.

Unions/Associations

Individuals interested in learning more about careers in this field should contact the American Collegiate Retailing Association (ACRA), National Retail Federation (NRF) and the National Retail Merchants Association (NRMA).

Tips for Entry

1. Many larger department and chain stores offer management training programs. Contact the headquarters of these stores to find out about requirements.
2. Positions may be advertised in the classified sections of newspapers. Look under classifications including "Store Manager," "Retail Opportunities," "Department Stores," "Store Management," or "Management Opportunities."
3. Openings are also advertised in trade journals.
4. Jobs in this field may be located on the Internet. Begin your search on some of the more popular job search sites such as Monster board (www.monster.com) and Hot Jobs (www.hotjobs.com).
5. Check out the websites of retail chains. Many list openings.
6. Contact recruiters and executive search firms specializing in retail management positions.
7. Send your resume and a short cover letter to the corporate offices of chain and department stores.

ASSISTANT STORE MANAGER— DEPARTMENT STORE

CAREER PROFILE

Duties: Assist department store manager in day-to-day management of store; deal with customer service issues; work with manager to assure store is in compliance with safety issues; work with staff to help store meet sales and profit goals

Alternate Titles: None

Salary Range: $25,000 to $50,000+

Employment Prospects: Good

Advancement Prospects: Good

Best Geographical Location(s) for Position: Jobs may be located throughout the country

Prerequisites:

Education and Training—Training requirements vary

Experience—Experience in retail management

Special Skills and Personality Traits—Problem solving skills; leadership skills; negotiation skills; communication skills; ability to deal well with people; management skills; administrative skills

CAREER LADDER

```
┌─────────────────────────────────────┐
│           Store Manager             │
└─────────────────────────────────────┘


┌─────────────────────────────────────┐
│       Assistant Store Manager       │
└─────────────────────────────────────┘


┌─────────────────────────────────────┐
│       Department Manager            │
│       or Management Trainee         │
└─────────────────────────────────────┘
```

Position Description

No matter the size of a department store or the clientele they hope to attract, most employ not only a manager, but one or more Assistant Managers. These individuals assist the store manager with the day-to-day management of the store. Specific responsibilities depend on the size and structure of the store.

The Assistant Manager works with the store manager to find ways to meet corporate sales and profit goals. He or she may work with the manager in reviewing daily, weekly, monthly, and annual sales figures. This information is often used to determine which days of the week generally require more sales staff, which promotions and special events work and which do not. The information is also used to help the corporate office set sales goals for the coming year.

The Assistant Store Manager will act in the capacity of the store manager when that individual is off duty. He or she may also work when the manager is on duty assisting with the various functions of the store.

The Assistant Manager is on the front line with both the customers and the staff. He or she may assist in the staffing needs of the store working with the manager or the human resources department. He or she may assist with the decisions concerning hiring key employees. The Assistant Manager may also be expected to terminate employees when required.

The individual is responsible for helping to make a pleasant workplace. He or she may assist in training programs or supervising trainers. Successful Assistant Managers know how to motivate employees to do their job well and provide excellent customer service.

Depending on the size and structure of the department store, the Assistant Manager may oversee department managers, merchandise managers, sales associates, cashiers, or stock people. He or she may offer suggestions to department managers regarding how to improve their departments and productivity.

The Assistant Manager often will be on the frontline checking to see if more cashiers are needed, if customers need help, or if any problems need to be solved. He or she will work with other store management in assuring health, legal, and safety rules, regulations, and laws are followed precisely. The individual will routinely check to see if aisles or entrances are blocked, spills are cleaned, and fire exits are free.

The Assistant Manager must also make sure the store and its rest rooms and parking lot are safe, clean, and orderly. In the event there are accidents, slips, and falls or other incidents, the individual will be expected to make written reports.

The Assistant Manager helps assure customer service in the store. In the event a customer isn't happy, the Assistant Manager may be called in to help resolve the problem. As he or she has more authority, the individual may offer customers solutions that more directly resolve their problem with the store.

The Assistant Manager and manager may share responsibility for going over reports of the day's receipts. They may work with the accounting department or cash office on this task. The individual may also accompany another employee when depositing the day's receipts in the bank.

Additional duties of Department Store Assistant Managers may include:

- Analyzing data to help determine what direction the store might take to increase profits
- Representing store at community events
- Handling emergencies and crises
- Handling loss prevention
- Helping set up the store according to corporate floorplans

Salaries
Annual earnings for Department Store Assistant Managers can range from approximately $25,000 to $50,000 or more. Variables affecting earnings include the size, prestige, and geographic location of the department store as well as the experience, responsibilities, and education of the individual.

Employment Prospects
Employment prospects are good for Department Store Assistant Managers. Many department stores may have two or more Assistant Managers on staff.

Positions are located throughout the country. Possibilities include large chains stores like Ames, Wal-Mart, K-Mart, Target, Kohls, J.C. Penney, Sears, Macy's, Dillards, Bloomingdales, and Sterns. Individuals may also find employment working in smaller department stores owned by local merchants.

Advancement Prospects
The most common method of career advancement for Department Store Assistant Managers is promotion to store manager. Another way individuals climb the career ladder is to locate similar positions in larger or more prestigious department stores.

Education and Training
There are no hard-and-fast rules regarding education and training requirements for Department Store Assistant Managers. While not always required, a college degree or background is usually preferred and may give one applicant an edge over another. College may also provide opportunities and experiences which the individual may not otherwise have. Good choices for majors might include retailing, merchandising, business, management, marketing, communications, advertising, liberal arts, or related fields.

Generally, larger department stores and chains have formal training programs for their key executives including managers and Assistant Managers. These programs include both classroom and in-store training. Smaller stores may have informal and on-the-job training.

Some stores will hire individuals who have no formal training, but have worked their way up obtaining on-the-job training along the way.

Experience, Skills, and Personality Traits
Department Store Assistant Managers are required to have experience both in retail and management. Prior to becoming Assistant Managers, most individuals will have worked on the sales floor as sales associates, as department managers, or group department managers. Some Department Store Assistant Managers have already managed smaller specialty stores or other retail outlets.

Assistant Managers should be self-confident individuals with an understanding of management principles. The ability to deal with and work well with people is mandatory. Individuals need to be good problem solvers who are energetic, detail oriented, and highly motivated.

Communications skills, both written and verbal, are necessary as well. An understanding and knowledge of the retail industry is also needed.

Unions/Associations
Individuals interested in learning more about careers in this field should contact the American Collegiate Retailing Association (ACRA), National Retail Federation (NRF) and the National Retail Merchants Association (NRMA).

Tips for Entry
1. One of the best ways to get into store management is by going through an executive training program. Many larger department and chain stores offer these management training programs. Contact the headquarters of stores to find out about requirements.

2. Many department stores post signs and posters touting their management career opportunities. Look for these at store entrances and in the customer service department. Don't forget to check out the human resources department.

3. Positions may be advertised in the classified sections of newspapers. Look under classifications including "Assistant Store Manager," "Retail Opportunities," "Department Stores," "Store Management," or "Management Opportunities."

4. Openings are also advertised in trade journals.

5. Contact recruiters and executive search firms specializing in management positions in retail.

6. Send your resume and a short cover letter to the corporate offices of chain and department stores.

7. Jobs in this field may be located on the Internet. Begin your search on some of the more popular job search sites such as Monster board (www.monster.com) and Hot Jobs (www.hotjobs.com).

DEPARTMENT MANAGER— DEPARTMENT STORE

CAREER PROFILE

Duties: Supervise and coordinate activities of employees working in a department; assign duties to employees; train department workers; handle customer service within the department; prepare sales and inventory reports

Alternate Titles: Toy Department Manager; Clothing Department Manager; Housewares Department Manager; Electronics Department Manager

Salary Range: $23,000 to $50,000+

Employment Prospects: Good

Advancement Prospects: Fair

Best Geographical Location(s) for Position: Jobs may be located throughout the country

Prerequisites:
   Education and Training—Training requirements vary
   Experience—Experience in retail management
   Special Skills and Personality Traits—Leadership skills; communication skills; ability to deal well with people; management skills; administrative skills

CAREER LADDER

```
┌─────────────────────────────────────┐
│   Department Manager of Larger       │
│   Department, Group Department        │
│ Manager, or Assistant Store Manager  │
└─────────────────────────────────────┘

┌─────────────────────────────────────┐
│        Department Manager            │
└─────────────────────────────────────┘

┌─────────────────────────────────────┐
│    Department Manager Trainee        │
│       or Floor Supervisor            │
└─────────────────────────────────────┘
```

Position Description

Department stores are made up of a number of departments, each selling different types of merchandise. Each of these departments has an individual called the Department Manager overseeing the area.

Depending on the specific store, departments might include: health and beauty; housewares; women's clothing; junior's clothing; children's clothing; men's clothing; boy's clothing; infants; small appliances; large appliances; electronics; books; office supplies; toys; jewelry; cards; gifts; bed and bath; cd's, tapes, videos; automotive; hardware; and house and garden. Different stores have different departments. They may also call departments by different names.

The Department Manager supervises and coordinates the activities of the employees in his or her department. He or she will assign tasks and duties to each individual so that the department is kept clean, well stocked, and orderly. For example, the Department Manager may assign one employee the task of putting out new merchandise. He or

she may assign another the task of making sure that displays of merchandise are straightened at regular intervals during the day. Another may work at the register. One or all may work on the sales floor helping customers.

The Department Manager schedules lunch and dinner breaks for each employee in the department. This must be done so that the sales floor is always covered. Depending on the specific store, the individual may also be responsible for scheduling the work hours and vacations for employees in the department.

Another function of the Department Manager is training the employees. He or she may suggest more effective methods of selling or displaying merchandise. The individual also must explain store and department policies to employees.

The Department Manager may assist employees in completing difficult transactions. He or she also is expected to listen to customer complaints and try to resolve them. A successful Department Manager will know how to restore and promote goodwill by offering the best customer service possible to each customer.

When customers are returning merchandise, the Department Manager will often be the individual who examines it. The individual must determine if the merchandise is defective, used, or new and can be put back on the selling floor.

The Department Manager must keep track of merchandise that is selling. He or she may then be expected to order needed merchandise or give an order to the main office. The individual will also be responsible for preparing sales and inventory reports.

As merchandise comes in, the Department Manager will make sure that it is priced correctly and displayed in an attractive manner. Often, customers come in and ask for a product that the store doesn't carry. Other times the individual may see merchandise in other stores that his or her store doesn't have. The individual may then suggest to the buyer that the merchandise be added to the department's line.

Additional duties of Department Managers may include:

- Working on the sales floor
- Evaluating performance of department employees
- Handling loss prevention
- Helping set up the department displays

Salaries

Annual earnings for Department Managers working in department stores can range from approximately $23,000 to $50,000 or more. Variables affecting earnings include the size, prestige, and geographic location of the department store as well as the experience, responsibilities, and education of the individual. Some Department Managers may also receive bonuses when sales meet or exceed goals.

Employment Prospects

Employment prospects are good for Department Managers. Positions are located throughout the country. Possibilities include large chains stores like Ames, Wal-Mart, K-Mart, Target, Kohls, J.C. Penney, Sears, Macy's, Dillards, Nordstroms, Bloomingdales, and Sterns. Individuals may also find employment working in smaller department stores.

Advancement Prospects

Department Managers may climb the career ladder in a number of ways. The most common method of career advancement is to land a job as a Department Manager of a larger department or in a larger, more prestigious department store. This will result in increased responsibilities and earnings. Other Department Managers become group department managers.

After obtaining experience or training, some individuals may also land positions as assistant store managers.

Education and Training

There are no hard-and-fast rules regarding education and training requirements for Department Managers. There are many Department Managers who hold just a high school diploma. However, a college background or degree may give one applicant an edge over another and is often helpful in career advancement. College may also provide opportunities and experiences which the individual may not otherwise have. Good choices for majors might include retailing, merchandising, business, management, marketing, communications, advertising, liberal arts, or related fields.

As far as training is concerned, larger department stores and chains generally have formal training programs for their management personnel. These programs include both classroom and in-store training. Smaller stores may have informal and on-the-job training.

Experience, Skills, and Personality Traits

Some stores hire individuals who have no formal training, but have worked their way up obtaining on-the-job training along the way. Others recruit people who are graduating from college. Whichever way individuals are hired, they usually must have had retail and supervisory experience.

Department Managers should have a complete understanding of the workings of the retail industry as well as management principles. They should be self-confident individuals with the ability to deal with and work well with others.

Department Managers need the ability to work on multiple projects at one time without getting flustered. They should be detail oriented and highly motivated individuals with a great deal of energy. Customer service skills are mandatory. Communication skills are imperative.

Unions/Associations

Individuals interested in learning more about careers in this field should contact the American Collegiate Retailing Association (ACRA), National Retail Federation (NRF) and the National Retail Merchants Association (NRMA).

Tips for Entry

1. Most department stores promote from within. Get your foot in the door, learn everything you can, and move up the career ladder.
2. One of the best ways to get into a management position is by going through an executive training program. Many larger department and chain stores offer these management training programs. Contact the headquarters of stores to find out about requirements.
3. Many department stores post signs and posters touting their management career opportunities. Look for these at store entrances and in the customer service department. Don't forget to check out the human resources department.

4. Positions may be advertised in the classified sections of newspapers. Look under classifications including "Department Manager," "Department Store," or "Retail Opportunities." Jobs may also be advertised in ads for specific department stores.

5. Stop in to department stores and ask to fill out an application. Ask that it be kept on file if there are no current openings.

COMPENSATION AND BENEFITS MANAGER—DEPARTMENT STORE

CAREER PROFILE

Duties: Oversee and coordinate employee wage, salary, and benefit programs in department store; supervise payroll and benefits office employees

Alternate Titles: Payroll Manager; Benefits Manager; Compensation Manager

Salary Range: $30,000 to $53,000+

Employment Prospects: Fair

Advancement Prospects: Fair

Best Geographical Location(s) for Position: Jobs may be located throughout the country; large cities hosting more department stores offer more possibilities

Prerequisites:

Education and Training—Educational requirements vary

Experience—Experience in human resources, benefits, or labor relations

Special Skills and Personality Traits—Communications skills; people skills; interpersonal skills; computer skills; patience; familiarity and understanding of compensation and benefits programs utilized in the industry

CAREER LADDER

```
┌─────────────────────────────────────┐
│  Compensation and Benefits Manager   │
│    in Larger, More Prestigious Store, │
│  Director of Compensation and Benefits,│
│     or Human Resources Manager       │
└─────────────────────────────────────┘

┌─────────────────────────────────────┐
│  Compensation and Benefits Manager   │
└─────────────────────────────────────┘

┌─────────────────────────────────────┐
│  Payroll Clerk or Benefits Coordinator │
└─────────────────────────────────────┘
```

Position Description

Department stores generally have many employees working in an array of areas. Depending on their type of work, experience, and responsibilities, individual employees may receive various compensation packages. In order to recruit and retain employees many department stores also offer a variety of benefits in addition to earnings. The individual in charge of overseeing and directing the various compensation and benefit plans at a department store is called the Compensation Manager.

He or she may also be called the Compensation and Benefits Manager or Payroll Manager. The Manager oversees the employees in the compensation and benefits or payroll office. Depending on the size and structure of the specific department store, the Compensation Manager may supervise benefits coordinators, payroll clerks, compensation and benefits analysts, and benefit clerks.

In some stores, the Compensation Manager may administer the health insurance and other benefit plans personally. In others, this task may be handled by a benefits coordinator.

Generally, department store employees meet with the Compensation Manager during the hiring process. The Manager discusses the type of compensation the employee will receive for the job. Some employees are paid on an hourly basis. Others are compensated with a set salary. The Compensation Manager will explain to each employee whether he or she will be paid on a weekly or biweekly basis.

The Compensation Manager also explains the benefits which are offered as part of the job to each employee. Depending on the store, benefits may include health insurance, life insurance, pension plans, profit sharing, child care, educational reimbursement, paid holidays, sick days, and vacations.

In many cases, employees may have questions regarding compensation or benefits. The Compensation Manager may answer these questions him or herself or may refer employees to other employees working in the department for answers and assistance.

An important function of the Compensation Manager is tracking employee evaluations, promotions, length of time they are in service, additional education, and training information. These factors are often used to determine employee raises. Raises are usually within the policy previously set by the department store.

Additional duties of the department store Compensation Manager may include:

- Gathering information regarding salaries, wages, and benefits offered within the industry as well as the geographic area in which the department store is located
- Analyzing the store's compensation and benefits programs and making recommendations for new ones
- Assuring that employees meet the proper employment requirements
- Maintaining accurate files on employees and the compensation and benefits they receive

Salaries

Earnings for Compensation Managers working in department stores range from approximately $30,000 to $53,000 or more annually. Factors affecting earnings include the size, structure, prestige, and geographic location of the specific department store. Other variables include the education, experience, and responsibilities of the individual.

Employment Prospects

Employment prospects for Compensation Managers aspiring to work in department stores are fair. Positions may be located throughout the country. Areas hosting greater numbers of large department stores will offer the most opportunities.

Advancement Prospects

Compensation Managers may climb the career ladder in a number of ways. Individuals may land similar positions in larger, more prestigious stores resulting in increased responsibilities and earnings. Compensation Managers may also be promoted to directors of payroll and benefits. Those who have the education and experience may even become assistant directors or directors of human resources.

Education and Training

Educational requirements for Compensation Managers vary from store to store. Many stores require or prefer individuals hold a degree in human resources, personnel management, labor relations, compensation and benefits, business management, or economics.

In some stores, experience is accepted in lieu of education. This is often the case when an individual has moved up the ranks in the compensation and benefits area.

Experience, Skills, and Personality Traits

Compensation Managers should have experience in various areas of human resources, personnel administration, insurance administration, labor relations, benefits, and compensation. Individuals should have an understanding of insurance programs, retirement plans, labor relations, and wage and benefit trends.

Individuals should have excellent communications and interpersonal skills. Management, administrative, and supervisory skills are also needed. The ability to handle multiple projects at one time without becoming flustered is necessary.

Unions/Associations

Those interested in learning more about careers in this field should contact the International Foundation of Employee Benefit Plans (IFEBP) and the American Compensation Association (ACA). Individuals might also contact the National Retail Federation (NRF).

Tips for Entry

1. Jobs may be advertised in the classified sections of newspapers. Look under classifications such as "Compensation Manager," "Payroll Manager," "Retail Opportunities," "Department Stores," "Benefits and Compensation," "Benefits and Compensation Manager."
2. You might also look for jobs on the Internet. Many department stores now have websites listing their employment opportunities.
3. Send your resume and a short cover letter to department stores. Ask that your resume be kept on file if there are no current openings.
4. Contact the corporate offices of large chains and department stores to see who you might contact for this position in their local stores.
5. Department stores often promote from within. Get your foot in the door and move up the ranks.

PAYROLL CLERK—DEPARTMENT STORE

CAREER PROFILE

Duties: Ensure that department store employee paychecks are correct; calculate earnings and deductions; compute pay; maintain backup files; research payroll records

Alternate Titles: Payroll Specialist; Payroll Technician; Compensation Clerk

Salary Range: $6.00 to $15.00+ or more per hour

Employment Prospects: Good

Advancement Prospects: Fair

Best Geographical Location(s) for Position: Jobs may be located throughout the country; large cities will offer more possibilities

Prerequisites:

Education and Training—Educational requirements vary
Experience—Accounting or payroll background preferred, but not always required
Special Skills and Personality Traits—Detail oriented; organized; ability to work accurately with numbers; data entry skills

CAREER LADDER

```
┌─────────────────────────────────┐
│  Payroll Supervisor, Payroll    │
│  Manager, or Compensation       │
│  Manager                        │
└─────────────────────────────────┘

┌─────────────────────────────────┐
│         Payroll Clerk           │
└─────────────────────────────────┘

┌─────────────────────────────────┐
│  Payroll Clerk in other         │
│  industry, Payroll Trainee or   │
│  Entry Level                    │
└─────────────────────────────────┘
```

Position Description

Department stores employ large numbers of workers. Each expects his or her paycheck to be correct. Payroll Clerks, who may also be referred to as Payroll Specialists, Payroll Technicians, or Compensation Clerks, help ensure that this happens.

Specific responsibilities of Payroll Clerks depend on the specific department store and the manner in which payroll is handled. Generally, Payroll Clerks input data regarding employees' pay, as well as maintaining and researching these records.

Payroll Clerks are responsible for calculating the earnings of the employee. This includes regular and overtime hours. They must also calculate deductions such as income tax withholding, social security, credit union payments, and insurance. This task is usually accomplished using computers.

Generally hourly employees in department stores punch time cards. At the end of the pay period, Payroll Clerks screen the time cards to make sure there are no calculating, coding, or other errors. Pay is then computed by subtracting allotments such as retirement, federal and state taxes, or insurance from the employee's gross earnings.

When a computer is used to perform these calculations, it will alert the payroll clerk to problems or errors in data. The individual can then adjust the errors.

In some situations, the department store utilizes the services of a payroll service. In these circumstances the Clerk still must give the service the correct information.

Payroll Clerks may be expected to enter the correct data on checks, check stubs, and master payroll sheets or more commonly on forms for computer preparation of checks. Individuals are also expected to prepare and distribute pay envelopes.

Payroll Clerks may be called on by employees to correct problems in their checks or to explain calculations. These may include adjusting monetary errors or incorrect amounts of vacation time.

Other responsibilities of Payroll Clerks working in department stores may include:

- Performing additional clerical tasks
- Maintaining records of employee sick leave pay and non-taxable wages

- Typing, checking, and filing wage information forms
- Keeping wage and fringe benefit information on employees

Salaries

Earnings for Payroll Clerks working in department stores range from approximately $6.00 to $15.00 per hour or more. Factors affecting earnings include the experience, level of training, and responsibilities of the individual as well as the geographic location, size, and prestige of the specific department store.

Employment Prospects

Employment prospects for Payroll Clerks are good. Large department stores may employ one or more people in this position. As noted previously, even department stores utilizing payroll services usually have at least one individual working in payroll.

Advancement Prospects

Advancement prospects for Payroll Clerks are fair. After obtaining additional experience and or training individuals may climb the career ladder by becoming payroll supervisors, payroll managers, or compensation managers.

Education and Training

Educational requirements for Payroll Clerks can vary from employer to employer. While some employers prefer a college or business school background, many employers will hire those with a high school diploma. While no specific training may be necessary, Payroll Clerks must have the ability to use adding machines, calculators, computers, and word processors. The ability to use office machinery may be self taught or learned in high school or business courses at vocational-technical schools, community colleges, or adult education.

Many department stores also offer on-the-job training, including payroll trainee positions.

Experience, Skills, and Personality Traits

Experience requirements vary from employer to employer. In many situations this is an entry-level position. Some employers, however, prefer or require experience or background in payroll.

Clerks should be detail oriented and organized. The most successful Payroll Clerks enjoy working with numbers. The ability to work accurately, and find and correct math errors is essential. Data entry skills are mandatory. Communications skills are helpful as well.

Unions/Associations

Individuals interested in pursuing a career in this field might also obtain additional information from the National Retail Federation (NRF) and the American Collegiate Retailing Association (ACRA).

Tips for Entry

1. Jobs may be advertised in the newspaper classified section under headings including "Payroll," "Payroll Specialist," "Payroll Clerk," "Payroll Technician," "Retail Opportunities," or "Department Store."
2. Send your resume and a short cover letter to department stores.
3. Many department stores also list openings on their website.
4. Contact the corporate offices of large chains and department stores to see who you might contact for this position in their local stores.

DIRECTOR OF HUMAN RESOURCES— DEPARTMENT STORE

CAREER PROFILE

Duties: Direct operations of human resources department; supervise and monitor department employees; develop and administer policies; recruitment; oversee employee relations

Alternate Titles: Human Resources Manager; Human Resources Director

Salary Range: $32,000 to 65,000+

Employment Prospects: Fair

Advancement Prospects: Fair

Best Geographical Location(s) for Position: Jobs may be located throughout the country; large cities will offer more opportunities

Prerequisites:

Education and Training—Bachelor's degree required or preferred

Experience—Extensive experience in human resources

Special Skills and Personality Traits—Interpersonal skills; communications skills; management skills; knowledge of federal and state employment laws; detail oriented; organized

CAREER LADDER

```
┌─────────────────────────────────────┐
│   Director of Human Resources in     │
│ Larger, More Prestigious Department   │
│  Store, or VP of Human Resources     │
└─────────────────────────────────────┘

┌─────────────────────────────────────┐
│     Director of Human Resources      │
└─────────────────────────────────────┘

┌─────────────────────────────────────┐
│ Assistant Director of Human Resources │
│       or Personnel Manager           │
└─────────────────────────────────────┘
```

Position Description

Without employees, department stores couldn't function. Attracting, training, and retaining the best employees available is essential to the success of every department store.

The department handling a store's employees is called human resources. Depending on the specific store, it may also be referred to as the personnel or employment department.

At one time or another, everyone who is hired must go through the human resources department. The individual in charge of the department is called the Director of Human Resources. He or she has a very important position.

The Director controls the operation of the department, and is responsible for planning, organizing, and managing everything that happens within it.

In large stores, the Human Resources Director may oversee several areas. Each of these is headed by a manager specializing in a specific human resource activity. These might include employment, compensation, benefits, employee relations, and training and development. In smaller department stores, the Human Resources Director may be responsible for handling all these on his or her own or with the help of one or more assistants.

The Director of Human Resources develops, writes, and administers policies. These policies have a direct impact on the employees who are hired and the manner in which they are expected to work. They also have a great impact on the store atmosphere and the way the department store functions.

The Human Resources Director is responsible for strategic planning as it relates to human resources. The individual may develop programs designed to enhance training, provide internship opportunities, and create career development for employees within the department store or any of its sister stores.

Other duties of the Director of Human Resources working in a department store may include:

- Developing employee relations programs
- Working with negotiators during contract negotiations
- Overseeing special projects and promotional events such as job fairs to stimulate recruitment of potential employees
- Developing and coordinating personnel programs

Salaries

The Director of Human Resources working in department stores may earn between $32,000 and $65,000 or more annually. Factors affecting earnings include the geographic location, size, and prestige of the specific store as well as the education, experience, and responsibilities of the individual. Generally, those with the most education and experience working in larger stores will earn the highest salaries.

Employment Prospects

Employment prospects are fair for a qualified Human Resources Director seeking employment in department stores. Those seeking jobs in this field may have to relocate to areas hosting great numbers of large department stores.

Advancement Prospects

Advancement prospects for the Director of Human Resources working in department stores are fair. Individuals might climb the career ladder by locating a similar position in a larger or more prestigious department store. Some find similar jobs in other industries. After obtaining a great deal of experience, some individuals move into positions as the vice president of Human Resources.

Education and Training

Most department stores today either require or prefer their Directors of Human Resources hold a minimum of a bachelor's degree. The best major is human resources. However, majors in other areas are often acceptable with work experience.

Additional courses, workshops, and seminars in human resources, labor relations, personnel, compensation, employee relations, and the retailing industry are very helpful. A graduate degree may give one applicant an edge over another.

Experience, Skills, and Personality Traits

A great deal of experience working in human resources and related areas is usually necessary for this type of position. Human Resources Directors usually have worked in the Human Resources department in various other positions. Many have been personnel directors or the director of human resources in areas other than retail.

Human Resources Directors should have supervisory and administrative skills. Writing and communications skills are also necessary. Individuals must have in-depth knowledge of all federal and state employment laws.

Unions/Associations

Those interested in learning more about careers in this field should contact the Society for Human Resources Management (SHRM). This organization provides professional guidance and support to its members.

Tips for Entry

1. Jobs may be advertised in the newspaper classified section under headings including "Human Resources," "Human Resources Director," "H.R. Director," "Retail Opportunities," or "Retail/Human Resources Director."
2. Send your resume and a short cover letter to department stores.
3. Many department stores have websites listing their openings.
4. Contact the corporate offices of large chains and department stores to see who you might contact for this position.
5. Contact an executive search firm specializing in retail and/or human resources.

HUMAN RESOURCES GENERALIST— DEPARTMENT STORE

CAREER PROFILE

Duties: Schedule preemployment job interviews; screen applicants; check references; evaluate applicants

Alternate Titles: Human Resources Interviewer; Human Resources Coordinator

Salary Range: $7.00 to $18.00 + per hour

Employment Prospects: Fair

Advancement Prospects: Fair

Best Geographical Location(s) for Position: Jobs may be located throughout the country; large cities will offer more opportunities

Prerequisites:

Education and Training—Bachelor's degree required or preferred

Experience—Experience in recruiting, counseling, interviewing, or retail helpful

Special Skills and Personality Traits—Interpersonal skills; people skills; communications skills; interviewing skills; personable; objective; detail oriented

CAREER LADDER

```
┌─────────────────────────────────┐
│       Personnel Manager         │
└─────────────────────────────────┘

┌─────────────────────────────────┐
│   Human Resources Generalist    │
└─────────────────────────────────┘

┌─────────────────────────────────┐
│     Human Resources Clerk       │
└─────────────────────────────────┘
```

Position Description

Department stores employ many people. Prior to becoming employed, each individual must be recruited, screened, and interviewed. The Human Resources Generalist may have an array of duties depending on the specific job.

The Generalist, who also may be called an Interviewer or Human Resources Coordinator, greets applicants upon arrival at the department store's human resources department for the initial interview. He or she schedules and conducts preemployment job interviews with potential applicants. This determines their qualifications as well as if they match those of the job openings. The individual ascertains the skills, personality traits, education, and training of applicants. In this manner, the Human Resources Generalist determines other jobs for which the potential employee may be qualified.

There may be a number of people for each job opening. The Human Resources Generalist may be responsible for screening applicants to weed out those who do not have the proper qualifications or might not fit into the department store environment.

Other duties of the Human Resources Generalist may include:

- Assisting applicants with applications
- Checking references
- Handling administrative functions
- Developing and placing ads for employees in newspapers and magazines
- Assisting the human resources department with special projects

Salaries

Human Resources Generalists may earn between $7.00 and $18.00 or more per hour. Factors affecting earnings include the geographic location, size, and prestige of the specific department store as well as the experience, education, and responsibilities of the individual. Generally, those with the most education and experience working in larger stores will earn the highest salaries.

Employment Prospects

Employment prospects are fair for qualified Human Resources Generalists seeking employment in department stores. The most opportunities will be in areas hosting large numbers of department stores.

Advancement Prospects

Advancement prospects for Human Resources Generalists working in department stores are fair. Individuals may climb the career ladder in a number of ways. Some Human Resources Generalists obtain experience and locate similar positions in larger or more prestigious department stores. Others who have the proper education and training eventually may be promoted to different positions in the human resources department.

Education and Training

Department stores may prefer, but not always require, their Human Resources Generalists hold a college degree. Good majors include human resources, liberal arts, marketing, communications, and retail. However, majors in other areas are often acceptable with work experience.

Courses, workshops, and seminars in human resources, labor relations, personnel, compensation, employee relations, and the retailing industry are also helpful.

Experience, Skills, and Personality Traits

Experience working in human resources, recruiting, or vocational counseling is usually required. Prior to getting their job in the department store, many Human Resources Generalists have worked in public or private personnel offices or departments. Some have moved up the ranks in the human resources department of the store.

A knowledge and understanding of the retailing industry is necessary. Human Resources Generalists should be objective and articulate. Good communications skills and interviewing skills are essential. The ability to make people comfortable is useful.

Unions/Associations

Those interested in learning more about careers in this field might be members of the Society for Human Resources Management (SHRM). This organization provides professional support and guidance.

Tips for Entry

1. Jobs may be advertised in the newspaper classified section under headings including "Human Resources," "Human Resources Generalist," "H.R. Interviewer," "Retail Opportunities," or "Retail/Human Resources Generalist."
2. Send your resume and a short cover letter to department stores.
3. Many department stores have websites listing their openings.
4. Contact the corporate offices of large chains and department stores to see who you might contact for this position.
5. Get experience in this department by starting out as a secretary or administrative assistant.

TRAINING MANAGER— DEPARTMENT STORE

CAREER PROFILE

Duties: Develop and facilitate classes, seminars, workshops, and other training programs for employees; develop key management programs

Alternate Titles: Training and Development Manager; Training Director

Salary Range: $24,000 to $55,000+

Employment Prospects: Fair

Advancement Prospects: Fair

Best Geographical Location(s) for Position: Areas hosting large numbers of department stores and chains

Prerequisites:
    Education and Training—College degree preferred
    Experience—Experience in training and development
    Special Skills and Personality Traits—Communications skills; interpersonal skills; employee relations skills; writing skills; ability to speak in public; creative; organized

CAREER LADDER

```
┌─────────────────────────────────┐
│  Training Manager for More       │
│  Prestigious Store or Company    │
└─────────────────────────────────┘

┌─────────────────────────────────┐
│       Training Manager           │
└─────────────────────────────────┘

┌─────────────────────────────────┐
│           Trainer                │
└─────────────────────────────────┘
```

Position Description

Department stores employ large numbers of employees. Training Managers are employed to develop programs for employees in a multitude of areas and a variety of subjects depending on the needs of the specific department store.

The Training Manager has a great deal of responsibility. The Manager may facilitate all classes personally or work with a staff which may include a training coordinator and other trainers to handle this task.

The Training Manager works with the human resources director who writes and administers policies. These policies have a direct impact on the way employees are expected to work. The human resources director may, at his or her discretion, ask the Training Manager to develop programs designed to enhance training as well as providing internship opportunities within the store.

The Training Manager may develop and facilitate orientation programs for new employees. During orientation, employees will learn the policies of the department store, and the way they are expected to act on the job and react to difficult situations.

In some situations, the department store Training Manager may be expected to develop and put together an employee handbook discussing workplace policies and regulations. In others, the individual may work with other members of the human resources department on this task.

As department stores learn that success can be built on customer service, it is essential that each and every employee be trained to treat customers in a courteous and gracious manner. An important function of Training Managers in department stores is teaching employees what good customer service is and how it should be provided.

The Training Manager may offer classes for management in learning how to communicate with their employees. Other subjects covered in this type of class may include acceptable methods for disciplining employees and how to speak to subordinates without coming across abruptly. The individual may also develop classes for employees dealing with sexual harassment in the workplace and avoiding this problem.

The Training Manager may develop classes specific to certain jobs in the department store such as cashiers, salespeople, or customer service.

Other duties of the Training Manager may include:

- Creating and directing programs to teach department directors, managers, and supervisors methods of conducting training within their department
- Teaching department directors, managers, and supervisors proper procedures for interview techniques and handling employment reviews
- Training employees in team building so that managers, supervisors, and subordinates all work together

Salaries

Annual earnings for Training Managers working in department stores can range from approximately $24,000 and $55,000 or more. Factors affecting earnings include the geographic location, size, and prestige of the specific department store as well as the education, experience, and responsibilities of the individual.

Employment Prospects

Employment prospects for department store Training Managers are fair. The greatest number of opportunities will be in areas hosting large numbers of department stores. Certain department store chains employ a Training Manager in their main store or corporate office instead of one in each store. Note that not every department store employs a Training Manager. Some facilities utilize the services of the human resources director to handle the training functions as well.

Advancement Prospects

Training Managers working in department stores may advance their careers by locating a similar position in larger or more prestigious facilities. Individuals might also climb the career ladder by becoming an assistant director of human resources or director of human resources. These promotions usually require additional experience, training, and education.

Education and Training

Educational requirements vary from employer to employer. Generally department stores require or prefer individuals to hold a minimum of a bachelor's degree in human resources, communications, retail, or a related field. There are some department stores, however, which may accept individuals with a high school diploma and a background and experience in training, human resources, or the retail industry.

Experience, Skills, and Personality Traits

Experience working in training and development is almost always required. Additional experience in retailing may also be needed.

Training Managers must have excellent people and employee relations skills. They must also have both good verbal and written communication skills. The ability to speak effectively in front of groups of people is essential to success in this position.

Unions/Associations

Those interested in learning more about careers in this field should contact the American Society of Training Developers (ASTD) and the Society for Human Resources Management (SHRM).

Tips for Entry

1. Become either an active or affiliate member of the ASTD. This may give you the edge over another applicant with the same qualifications.
2. If you have experience in training, see if a position exists as a trainer. Get your foot in the door of the department store, obtain some experience, and climb the career ladder.
3. Openings are often advertised on the Internet. They may be located via the home pages of department stores. They may also be found by doing a search of department store job opportunities.
4. Positions may be advertised in the classified sections of newspapers. Look under classifications such as "Department Store Training Manager," "Training and Development Manager," "Retail Opportunities," or "Human Resources."
5. You may be asked to conduct an impromptu training presentation as part of your interview process. Develop a sample program ahead of time and rehearse before the interview.

STOCK ROOM MANAGER

CAREER PROFILE

Duties: Oversee stock room; supervise and coordinate activities of stock room workers

Alternate Titles: Stock Room Supervisor

Salary Range: $22,000 to $35,000+

Employment Prospects: Good

Advancement Prospects: Fair

Best Geographical Location(s) for Position: Jobs may be located throughout the country

Prerequisites:

Education and Training—On-the-job training

Experience—Experience working in stock room

Special Skills and Personality Traits—Supervisory skills; organized; ability to lift cartons of various weights and sizes

CAREER LADDER

```
┌─────────────────────────────────┐
│  Warehouse Manager or Stock Room │
│     Manager in Larger Store      │
└─────────────────────────────────┘

┌─────────────────────────────────┐
│       Stock Room Manager         │
└─────────────────────────────────┘

┌─────────────────────────────────┐
│   Assistant Stock Room Manager   │
└─────────────────────────────────┘
```

Position Description

Department stores are filled with great amounts of merchandise. When merchandise is received it is unloaded and brought into the stock room. The stock room of a store is the area in which merchandise is checked in, priced, and stored until it is put out on the selling floor. The individual responsible for the stock room is called the Stock Room Manager.

The Stock Room Manager supervises and coordinates the activities of the stock room workers. He or she will assign duties to each worker so that the stock room is run effectively and efficiently.

The Stock Room Manager assigns workers to receive merchandise as well as inventory control. In many stores today, this is accomplished with the help of hand-held scanners and computers. UPCs (Universal Product Codes) which look like lines or bars are found on merchandise or merchandise tags and tickets. Once these bars are scanned, employees of the store or the Stock Room Manager can instantly find out what is and is not in stock.

The individual keeps records of merchandise received and merchandise returned. He or she is responsible for reviewing these records and determining any discrepancies. The Stock Room Manager must also be sure that procedures regarding returning defective merchandise are followed.

The Stock Room Manager is expected to organize the stock room. He or she may plan the layout of the stockroom, warehouse, and other storage areas. This is important so that merchandise can be stored both safely and so it can be located easily. When doing this, the Stock Room Manager must take certain factors into account, such as the amount of merchandise needed to be stored, the size and weight of the items, and the expected turnover time.

Additional duties of Stock Room Managers might include:

• Unpacking and repacking cartons of merchandise
• Checking inventory for specific items
• Scheduling workers for inventories
• Handling loss prevention in the storeroom area

Salaries

Annual earnings of Stock Room Managers can range from approximately $22,000 to $35,000 or more. Variables affecting earnings include the size and geographic location of the store and the experience and responsibilities of the individual.

Employment Prospects

Employment prospects for Stock Room Managers are good. Positions may be located throughout the country. The greatest number of openings are located in large areas hosting a great number of stores.

Advancement Prospects

The most common method of career advancement for Stock Room Managers is locating similar positions in larger department stores. This will result in increased responsibilities and earnings. Individuals may also find jobs as warehouse supervisors or managers.

Education and Training

Generally, Stock Room Managers have moved up the ranks and obtained their experience through the on-the-job training necessary to perform their job. Some stores might also provide more formal training programs.

Experience, Skills, and Personality Traits

Prior experience working in stock rooms is necessary. Supervisory experience is helpful. Stock Room Managers should be very organized people. Communications skills are useful as are computer skills.

Unions/Associations

Individuals may get additional career information by contacting the National Retail Federation (NRF).

Tips for Entry

1. Jobs are often advertised in the classified section of the newspaper. Look under headings such as "Stock Room Manager," "Stock Room," "Department Store," or "Retail Opportunities," Specific stores may also advertise a number of job opportunities.
2. There is often turnover in these positions. Stop in stores and ask the manager if you can fill out an application.
3. Remember to bring the names, addresses, and phone numbers of a few people you can use as references with you when applying for jobs. Make sure you ask people if you can use them as references BEFORE you use them.
4. Stores often call local labor offices to post these jobs. Remember to stop by your state employment office.
5. Stores often promote from within. Get your foot in the door, do a little bit extra, and climb the career ladder.

LOSS PREVENTION MANAGER—RETAIL

CAREER PROFILE

Duties: Develop loss prevention plan for store; hire, train, and supervise loss prevention associates for store; oversee loss prevention plan

Alternate Titles: Shrinkage Control Manager; Shrinkage Control Director; Security Manager

Salary Range: $26,000 to $65,000+

Employment Prospects: Fair

Advancement Prospects: Fair

Best Geographical Location(s) for Position: Jobs may be located throughout the country

Prerequisites:

Education and Training—High school diploma or equivalent; on-the-job training; additional training may be required

Experience—Experience in retail security and loss prevention

Special Skills and Personality Traits—Supervisory skills; good judgment, responsibility; interpersonal skills; people skills; communications skills; computer skills; good moral character; clean police record

CAREER LADDER

```
┌─────────────────────────────────────┐
│ Loss Prevention Manager in Larger,   │
│ More Prestigious Store, or Loss      │
│ Prevention Director at Corporate Level│
└─────────────────────────────────────┘

┌─────────────────────────────────────┐
│      Loss Prevention Manager         │
└─────────────────────────────────────┘

┌─────────────────────────────────────┐
│ Assistant Loss Prevention Manager    │
│ or Assistant Security Director       │
└─────────────────────────────────────┘
```

Position Description

Loss prevention is an important part of the retail industry and every store takes it seriously. While most people are honest, a great deal of theft still occurs in stores. This may encompass shoplifting by shoppers, as well as inside theft by store employees and others.

The Loss Prevention Manager is the individual responsible for developing a plan to control the shrinkage of store's inventory. Shrinkage is a tremendous problem to stores. Shrinkage is the loss of merchandise from various means, the most prominent being shoplifting. Loss prevention is very important to the bottom line of a store. Depending on the specific employment situation, the Loss Prevention Manager may have varied responsibilities.

The Loss Prevention Manager in a retail environment is responsible for overseeing the safety of the store, its employees, and customers. The individual is in charge of developing and implementing the store's safety and security plan. In some situations, the Loss Prevention Manager works for the corporate office of a chain or department store. In these cases, he or she will develop plans for all the stores in the chain.

It should be noted that some retail stores employ their own security department while others contract it out utilizing the services of a security company. However, one way or the other, most larger stores will still hire their own Loss Prevention Manager to oversee the security department.

The Loss Prevention Manager is responsible for recruiting, hiring, training, and supervising security guards for the store. It is essential that each guard know and understand the store's policies and procedures and is instructed in the ways to carry them out.

The Loss Prevention Manager is expected to recommend the type of security devices the store should utilize. These may include closed-circuit cameras, electronic security devices, security tags, and mirrors. The individual must also determine how many security guards are needed as well as if they should be undercover or uniformed. Undercover officers are often used to catch shoplifters as well as watching out for internal theft by store employees. Security guards are used to provide a security presence within the store.

The Loss Prevention Manager must develop procedures for handling shoplifting incidents within the store. These must follow legal procedures for stopping, searching, and holding suspected shoplifters. Generally, once a suspect is stopped, the local law enforcement agency is called in to make an arrest.

The Loss Prevention Manager may develop seminars for store employees to help them find ways to cut their shrinkage. However, in some instances, the shrinkage in retail stores is internal (involving employees). In these cases, the Loss Prevention Manager must utilize undercover officers or involve the police in the investigation. Internal shrinkage is often more difficult to find until stores conduct their inventory.

The Loss Prevention Manager may work with others in store management scheduling inventories and going over results. A large shrinkage, no matter what the reason, means people are not doing their jobs correctly.

The Loss Prevention Manager in many situations is also responsible for safety issues within the store. He or she may recommend policies regarding safety of employees, customers, and the handling of emergencies. The Manager may also develop and run seminars for store employees to help them find ways to make the store safer and more pleasant in which to shop.

The Loss Prevention Manager needs to develop policies on dealing with potential disturbances and problems such as calming loud or boisterous customers, evicting customers who are acting in a disorderly fashion, helping in a medical emergency, or dealing with lost children. The individual must be sure store employees know how to handle emergency situations such power outages, weather problems, and medical emergencies.

Additional duties of Retail Loss Prevention Managers may include:

- Assuming duties of security guards
- Checking to make sure daily shift reports detailing occurrences in stores are complete
- Preparing reports for management on security and safety in store
- Making recommendations to store management about store security and safety concerns
- Formulating policies regarding safety and determining needs for safety programs

Salaries

Annual earnings for Loss Prevention Managers working in retail can range from approximately $26,000 to $65,000 or more. Variables affecting earnings include the geographic location, size, and prestige of the specific store as well as the number of stores for which the Loss Prevention Manager is responsible. Other factors affecting earnings include the experience, training, and responsibilities of the individual.

Employment Prospects

Employment prospects are fair for Loss Prevention Managers in the retail industry. Individuals may find employment in department stores and chain stores as well as specialty shops selling big ticket items. Positions may also be located with the corporate office of chains and department stores. The best prospects for employment will be in areas hosting a large number of retail stores.

Advancement Prospects

Loss Prevention Managers working in retail may advance their career in a number of ways. The most common method is finding similar positions in larger, more prestigious retail stores. This results in increased responsibilities and earnings. Individuals may also be promoted to the position of loss prevention director. Some might advance to positions such as vice president of Loss Prevention and Security. This type of position, however, is usually only found in the corporate office of chains and department stores. Others may climb the career ladder by striking out and starting their own security firms.

Education and Training

Education and training requirements vary for this type of position. While some retail stores require their Loss Prevention Managers to hold a minimum of a high school diploma, most stores will prefer or require individuals to have a college background or degree.

Certain states may require individuals working in security to go through specified training programs offered in the area. Some states may also require an annual in-service course to refresh or update officers in changes in the security field. The Loss Prevention Manager may fall into this category.

If the Loss Prevention Manager is armed when working, he or she must go through a firearms training course. These usually involve both classroom instruction and a specified number of hours on the firing range.

Classes, seminars, and workshops in loss prevention and retail loss prevention are helpful in keeping abreast of new techniques and strategies in this field.

Experience, Skills, and Personality Traits

The Loss Prevention Manager working in retail is required to have a great deal of experience in security, loss prevention, and retail. Some have worked as police officers or mall security directors prior to their current appointment. Others have experience in the military or other areas of civil service. There are also some individuals who obtained experience working in security and loss prevention and moved up the career ladder.

The Retail Loss Prevention Manager should have an array of skills. As in all other security and loss prevention positions, individuals should be responsible with good judgment. Leadership skills are important. Interpersonal and customer relations skills are essential. Communications skills are mandatory.

A clean record and good moral character are essential. As noted, those who are armed usually also must be registered with their specific state to carry firearms.

An understanding of the retail industry is necessary.

Unions/Associations

Retail Loss Prevention Managers may obtain additional information by contacting the National Retail Federation (NRF). Individuals may also obtain information about possible licensing requirements from their state or local licensing commission.

Tips for Entry

1. Openings may be advertised in the classified sections of newspapers. Look under heading classifications such as "Loss Prevention Manager," "Director of Loss Prevention," "Retail Opportunities," "Retail Security Director," "Retail Security Manager," or "Shrinkage Control Manager." Also look under specific store listings for job opportunities.

2. Jobs may be located on the Internet. Many retail stores have their own websites which list employment opportunities.

3. Don't forget to look on some of the World Wide Web job sites. Start with some of the more popular ones such as Monster board (www.monster.com) and Hot Jobs (www.hotjobs.com). A new site, www.abracat.com, is easy to use and offers many job openings in all industries by geographical area.

4. Contact the corporate office of chains and department stores. Send a short cover letter and your resume inquiring about openings.

RECEIVING CLERK—DEPARTMENT STORE

CAREER PROFILE

Duties: Receive, unpack, and check in merchandise

Alternate Titles: Stock Clerk

Salary Range: $5.50 to $9.50+ per hour

Employment Prospects: Good

Advancement Prospects: Fair

Best Geographical Location(s) for Position: Jobs may be located throughout the country

Prerequisites:
Education and Training—On-the-job training
Experience—No experience required
Special Skills and Personality Traits—Organized; ability to lift cartons of various weights and sizes

CAREER LADDER

```
┌─────────────────────────────────────┐
│  Receiving Clerk in Larger Store     │
│  or Stock Room Assistant Manager     │
└─────────────────────────────────────┘

┌─────────────────────────────────────┐
│          Receiving Clerk             │
└─────────────────────────────────────┘

┌─────────────────────────────────────┐
│           Entry Level                │
└─────────────────────────────────────┘
```

Position Description

Department stores, by definition, sell many different types of merchandise. This merchandise is delivered by trucks on a regular basis. Some stores have daily deliveries, others weekly or biweekly.

Deliveries of merchandise are received and put into the stock room until they can be inventoried and ticketed. While smaller stores may just employ stock clerks to handle stock room functions, larger department stores may have a number of different employees working in the stock room. These may include a stock room manager, ticketers, stock clerks, inventory clerks, and Receiving Clerks.

Receiving Clerks work in the stock room of the department store, unloading the merchandise off the truck. In some situations the truck driver will take the merchandise off the truck and place it on a loading dock. The Receiving Clerk must then move the merchandise from the loading dock to the store's stock room. Generally, when merchandise is delivered it comes with a delivery or shipping list, indicating exactly what merchandise is supposed to be in the delivery.

For example, the delivery might include 18 boxes. The Receiving Clerk must check to be sure each box is accounted for. Sometimes the delivery doesn't come in boxes. Clothing might come on racks. The Receiving Clerk must then count the dresses or jackets against the list. No matter what the merchandise or container, the individual must account for its delivery before a final acceptance. The

Receiving Clerk will then sign the slip indicating that the merchandise has been delivered and accepted.

Boxes of merchandise usually come with packing lists telling what should be in each box. Packing lists may include information such as the number of items, the color, and the size. The list will also include the identification numbers corresponding to each piece of merchandise.

When unpacking each box, the Receiving Clerk is responsible for checking to see if any of the items are damaged or broken. The store is usually not responsible for paying for damaged merchandise. If the Receiving Clerk finds damaged goods, he or she will record the information. This will then be used when the store does a final accounting for payment.

Depending on the specific department store and its size and structure, Receiving Clerks may also fulfill some duties handled by others in the stock room of smaller stores. For example, individuals may scan incoming merchandise into the store's computer systems. Additionally, they may be responsible for ticketing or putting prices on merchandise. In other stockrooms this may be done by a ticketer or a stock clerk.

Additional duties of Receiving Clerks might include:

- Repacking merchandise and returning it to manufacturer
- Keeping records of merchandise which must be sent back
- Checking inventory for specific items
- Storing merchandise in correct area of store room
- Stocking shelves

Salaries

Receiving Clerks working in department stores earn between $5.50 and $9.50 per hour or more. Variables affecting earnings include the size and geographic location of the store and the experience and responsibilities of the individual.

Employment Prospects

Employment prospects for Receiving Clerks are good. Jobs may be located throughout the country. The greatest number of openings are located in areas hosting large department stores.

Advancement Prospects

This is an entry-level position. Advancement prospects are based, to a great extent, on individual career aspirations. Some Receiving Clerks may find similar positions at larger department stores resulting in increased responsibilities and higher earnings. With additional experience and training, the Receiving Clerk may climb the career ladder by becoming an inventory or stock room assistant manager.

Education and Training

Receiving Clerks generally do not need any specialized training. On-the-job training is often provided by the stock room manager or other stock room employees.

Most employers prefer to hire those who hold a high school diploma or the equivalent, or individuals who are still in school. However, there are many who will hire able people who are eager to work no matter what their educational background.

Experience, Skills, and Personality Traits

As noted previously, this is an entry-level position. No prior experience is needed. Receiving Clerks should be organized with the ability to keep good records. The ability to lift large boxes or heavy merchandise is necessary.

Unions/Associations

Individuals may get additional career information by contacting the National Retail Federation (NRF). Depending on the specific department store, Receiving Clerks may belong to house unions.

Tips for Entry

1. Jobs are located in the classified section of newspapers under headings such as "Receiving Clerk," "Stock Room," or "Retail Opportunities."
2. There is a great deal of turnover in these positions. Visit the human resources department of stores and ask to fill out an application.
3. Remember to bring with you the names, addresses, and phone numbers of a few people you can use as references on your applications. Make sure you ask people if you can use them as references. BEFORE you use them.
4. Stores often call local labor offices to post these jobs. Remember to stop by your state employment office.

CUSTOMER SERVICE MANAGER— DEPARTMENT STORE

CAREER PROFILE

Duties: Supervise customer service desk; oversee customer service department; handle returns and other problems for customers; handle difficult customers; provide information regarding the store to customers

Alternate Titles: Customer Service Director

Salary Range: $24,000 to $48,000+

Employment Prospects: Fair

Advancement Prospects: Fair

Best Geographical Location(s) for Position: Jobs may be located throughout the country

Prerequisites:

Education and Training—Educational requirements vary
Experience—Experience in retail, customer service, and management
Special Skills and Personality Traits—Pleasant personality; supervisory skills; outgoing; interpersonal skills; people skills; communications skills

CAREER LADDER

```
┌─────────────────────────────────┐
│  Customer Service Manager in     │
│  Larger, More Prestigious Store  │
│  or Assistant Store Manager      │
└─────────────────────────────────┘

┌─────────────────────────────────┐
│     Customer Service Manager     │
└─────────────────────────────────┘

┌─────────────────────────────────┐
│  Customer Service Representative │
└─────────────────────────────────┘
```

Position Description

Most department stores have customer service desks. These areas are set up so the store can handle various services for customers. The individual responsible for overseeing this area in the department store is called the Customer Service Manager.

It is the main function of the Customer Service Manager to make the shopping experience as pleasant as possible for every customer. He or she may offer suggestions to the store management regarding steps that can be taken to accomplish this goal. For example, customers may approach the Customer Service Manager to complain about dirty rest rooms. The individual will bring this to the attention of the store manager who will see that the situation is corrected.

The Customer Service Manager oversees the customer service department. He or she will not only determine how many individuals are needed at particular times in order to adequately cover the desk, but schedule them as well.

As part of the job, the Customer Service Manager is expected to train his or her staff. The individual may develop programs or work with the department store's training department.

The customer service area will usually handle returns and exchanges. The Customer Service Manager sets policies for returns and exchanges. While many department store chains have policies set by the corporate office, the Customer Service Manager often has the authority to make exceptions. For example, even if the store has a 30-day return policy, the Customer Service Manager may override the policy for a customer if the merchandise has not been used and the individual has a receipt.

Many department stores offer an array of other customer services including gift wrapping, shipping, layaways, gift certificates, and personal shopping. The Customer Service Manager may oversee all of these areas.

Problems can vary tremendously in department stores. The Customer Service Manager must be adept at handling an array of situations in a calm and helpful manner. It is not uncommon in department stores for customers to lose their wallets, leave their purses in dressing rooms or rest rooms, and put bags of merchandise down and forget to take them. Customers may find large sums of money or jewelry that others have dropped by mistake or bags of merchandise that someone else has lost. The Customer Service Manager generally has a policy for handling these situations so customer service representatives know what to do.

Some situations are more stressful than others and need more understanding. Children often wander away from parents, husbands can't find wives, customers slip or fall, or other accidents may occur. The Customer Service Manager may assist the store manager or others in keeping everyone calm while following the store's procedures. Depending on the situation, he or she may be expected to call store management, security, or even the police when needed.

Additional duties of Customer Service Manager working in department stores may include:

- Handling special orders for customers
- Answering customers questions regarding store policies
- Calling other stores in the chain to look for merchandise for customers that may not be available in their specific store
- Answering phone inquiries regarding merchandise in the store

Salaries

Department Store Customer Service Managers can have annual earnings ranging from approximately $24,000 to $48,000 or more. Variables affecting earnings include the size, prestige, and geographic location of the specific store as well as the experience, education, and responsibilities of the individual.

Employment Prospects

Employment prospects are fair for individuals seeking positions as Customer Service Managers in department stores. Jobs can be located throughout the country in a variety of types of stores ranging from discount chains to upscale department stores.

The greatest number of opportunities will be located in areas hosting large number of department stores.

Advancement Prospects

Department Store Customer Service Managers climb the career ladder by locating similar position in larger or more prestigious stores. Depending on experience and training, some individuals advance their career by becoming either an assistant or full-fledged store manager.

Education and Training

Educational requirements vary from store to store. While a college background or degree is usually preferred, it is not always required. College gives individuals the opportunity to gain experience and may be useful in career advancement. It may also give one applicant an edge over another who doesn't have a college degree. There are also many seminars, courses, and workshops in the area of customer service that will be useful in honing skills and may give one applicant an edge over another.

Experience, Skills, and Personality Traits

Customer Service Managers must possess the ability to make decisions quickly and effectively. Individuals should enjoy dealing with the public and have a pleasant personality. Interpersonal and customer relations skills are essential. The ability to lead others is necessary as well.

Customer Service Managers should have excellent written and oral communications skills. In addition to dealing with the public, individuals may be responsible for developing written policies, writing reports, and handling other paperwork.

Unions/Associations

Individuals interested in becoming department store Customer Service Managers can obtain additional information by contacting the National Retail Merchants Association (NRMA) and the National Retail Federation (NRF).

Tips for Entry

1. There are many seminars, workshops, and courses offered throughout the country in customer service. These are useful to hone skills, obtain new ideas, and make useful contacts.
2. Jobs may be advertised in the classified sections of newspapers. Look under classifications such as "Customer Service Manager," "Customer Service," "Retail Opportunities," or specific department store ads advertising multiple positions.
3. Many department stores today have websites where they advertise employment opportunities.
4. Trade journals also may advertise openings.
5. Stop by the human resources office of department stores to fill out an application.

CUSTOMER SERVICE REPRESENTATIVE— DEPARTMENT STORE

CAREER PROFILE

Duties: Handle returns and exchanges for customers; sell gift certificates; wrap gifts; provide information regarding stores and merchandise

Alternate Titles: Customer Service Clerk

Salary Range: $5.50 to $10.00+ per hour

Employment Prospects: Good

Advancement Prospects: Fair

Best Geographical Location(s) for Position: Jobs may be located throughout the country

Prerequisites:

Education and Training—High school diploma or equivalent preferred

Experience—No experience necessary

Special Skills and Personality Traits—Pleasant personality; outgoing; interpersonal skills; people skills; communications skills

CAREER LADDER

```
┌─────────────────────────────────┐
│   Customer Service Director      │
└─────────────────────────────────┘

┌─────────────────────────────────┐
│ Customer Service Representative  │
└─────────────────────────────────┘

┌─────────────────────────────────┐
│         Entry Level              │
└─────────────────────────────────┘
```

Position Description

Most Department Stores have customer service areas where special services are provided for customers. These areas are usually centrally located in the store so customers can find them easily. The customer service area is staffed by Customer Service Representatives.

The Customer Service Representative's duties vary depending on the specific store, its structure, and the services provided. One of the main responsibilities of Customer Service Representatives is handling returns and exchanges for customers. The individual is expected to follow the store's policies regarding returns. He or she may issue a credit, return cash, or do an exchange depending on the customer's wishes. If there is a problem, the Representative must call the customer service manager or store manager to see if he or she can handle the difficulty.

The Customer Service Representative may answer customers' questions about store merchandise either in person or on the phone. He or she may direct individuals to a specific department to find merchandise they are seeking or give directions to the store's rest rooms, restaurants, elevators, or escalators.

Many department stores have special promotions to attract shoppers such as frequent buyer's clubs or senior citizen discounts. The Customer Service Representative may give out applications and prepare cards for customers so they can take advantage of these discounts and promotions. The individual might also offer customers sale flyers and advertised coupons.

Some department stores provide gift wrapping services either free or for a small fee. The Representative may be expected to wrap customers' gifts in a neat and attractive manner.

Other stores offer shipping or delivery services for the convenience of customers. In these instances, the Customer Service Representative may be responsible for weighing items, packaging them for shipping, collecting monies, and getting the correct shipping information.

If a customer has a problem in the store, he or she usually will go to the customer service counter and speak to a Customer Service Representative. It is the responsibility of the individual to help the customer as much as possible. Problems can vary tremendously in department stores. Whether it is customers losing their wallets, someone finding a handbag in a dressing room, an angry shopper, or a child who has wandered away from his or her parents, the Customer Service Representative must be adept at handling any situation in a calm and helpful manner.

The Customer Service Representative may also sell gift certificates or gift cards and explain how they may be used and any conditions and limitations.

Additional duties of Customer Service Representatives may include:

- Holding merchandise for customers until they pick it up
- Checking with a department manager to see if specific merchandise is in stock
- Assisting lost children and others looking for each other in the store
- Making announcements on the public address system
- Answering phone inquiries regarding store hours or availability of merchandise

Salaries

Customer Service Representatives working in department stores can earn between $5.50 and $10.00 per hour or more. Variables affecting earnings include the geographic location, size, and prestige of the store as well as the experience and responsibilities of the individual.

One of the added perks of working in a department store is often an employee discount.

Employment Prospects

Employment prospects are good for Customer Service Representatives seeking employment in department stores. Almost every department store employs Customer Service Representatives. Most employ more than one.

Jobs can be located throughout the country. Possibilities include large chains stores like Ames, Wal-Mart, K-Mart, Target, Kohls, J.C. Penney, Sears, Macy's, Dillards, Bloomingdales, and Sterns. Individuals may also find employment working in smaller department stores.

Customer Service Representatives may work full time or part time depending on the specific position.

Advancement Prospects

Advancement prospects for Customer Service Representatives working in department stores are fair. After obtaining experience, motivated individuals may move up to positions as assistant customer service managers or full-fledged customer service managers. They may, however, need to find positions in other stores.

Education and Training

Most stores prefer to hire Customer Service Representatives with a minimum of a high school diploma or the equivalent. However, there are also many stores that hire individuals who are still attending school.

Informal on-the-job training is usually provided for this position. Those seeking to advance their careers in retail may want to consider college.

Experience, Skills, and Personality Traits

This is usually an entry-level position. Most stores do not require experience.

The Customer Service Representative working in a department store should be an outgoing individual with a pleasant personality. He or she should be articulate with good customer service skills. Interpersonal and customer relations skills are essential. The ability to empathize with a customer who has a problem is a plus.

Unions/Associations

Individuals interested in learning more about careers in retail customer service can obtain additional information by contacting the National Retail Merchants Association (NRMA) and the National Retail Federation (NRF).

Tips for Entry

1. Jobs may be advertised in the classified sections of newspapers. Look under classifications such as "Customer Service Representative," "Customer Service Clerk," "Customer Service," or "Retail Opportunities." Specific stores may also advertise multiple jobs in an advertisement.
2. Stop in stores and ask to fill out an application. Request that it be kept on file if there are no current openings.
3. Local chambers of commerce or community colleges often offer hospitality and customer service seminars. These may be helpful in giving you the edge over another applicant.
4. There are also many seminars, courses, and workshops in the area of customer service which will be useful in honing skills and may give one applicant an edge over another.
5. Many department stores now have websites where they list employment opportunities. Some even allow you the opportunity to fill out an application on line.

GREETER

CAREER PROFILE

Duties: Welcome customers entering store; check receipts of customers leaving to ensure merchandise has been paid for; say good-bye to customers; answer customers' questions

Alternate Titles: None

Salary Range: $5.50 to $9.50+ per hour

Employment Prospects: Good

Advancement Prospects: Fair

Best Geographical Location(s) for Position: Jobs may be located throughout the country

Prerequisites:
Education and Training—On-the-job training
Experience—No experience necessary
Special Skills and Personality Traits—People skills; communications skills; pleasant smile

CAREER LADDER

```
┌─────────────────────────────────┐
│   Cashier or Sales Associate    │
└─────────────────────────────────┘

┌─────────────────────────────────┐
│            Greeter              │
└─────────────────────────────────┘

┌─────────────────────────────────┐
│          Entry Level            │
└─────────────────────────────────┘
```

Position Description

Customers like to feel valued by the stores in which they shop. Many department stores employ people called Greeters to welcome customers as they enter a store.

The main function of Greeters is to make customers feel important when they walk into the store. They accomplish this by warmly welcoming customers, saying hello as the people walk through the door, and smiling.

Greeters may help customers get shopping carts to make shopping easier. They may also assist customers in getting wheelchairs or mobile shopping carts.

In some department stores, Greeters give children little toys, balloons, stickers, or coloring books. These products may be emblazoned with the store's logo. Greeters may also hand out flyers or store coupons to shoppers.

Greeters answer customers' questions as they enter the store. Customers may ask the Greeter the location of specific items in the store or where specific departments are located within the store. Customers may ask where rest rooms are or if the store has a baby changing area. Sometimes customers need to know where extra flyers or shopping baskets can be found. Others may be looking for the customer service or lay-a-way desk.

Depending on the department store, the Greeter may be responsible for tagging merchandise customers come into the store to return. The Greeter may stamp or tag the merchandise and then direct the individual to the customer service area for returns.

Additional duties of Greeters may include:

- Informing management when shopping carts are needed
- Thanking customers for visiting and wishing them well when they leave the store
- Keeping an eye out for people leaving the store without paying for merchandise

Salaries

Earnings for Greeters working in department stores can range from approximately $5.50 to $9.50 or more per hour. Variables affecting earnings include the geographic location, size, and prestige of the store, the specific days and hours the individual works, as well the experience and responsibilities of the individual. Earnings for Greeters are also dependent on the demand for employees in a given area.

Employment Prospects

Employment prospects are good for Greeters. Individuals may find work throughout the country.

One of the selling points for many people seeking this job is the flexibility of working hours. Individuals may work full time, part time, mornings, afternoons, evenings, weekdays, weekends, or holidays.

Advancement Prospects

Advancement prospects for Greeters are dependent to a great extent on the individual's career aspirations. Some people take jobs as Greeters while in school or on a part-time basis to augment other income. These individuals usually move on to other types of jobs depending on their training. Others may start out as Greeters and move into positions as sales associates or cashiers.

Education and Training

Generally, there are no educational requirements for Greeters. Most employers prefer people who have either a minimum of a high school diploma or are still in school. Individuals are trained on the job.

Experience, Skills, and Personality Traits

This is an entry-level position. No experience is required. Good interpersonal and customer relations skills are essential, as is a pleasant personality. Greeters are on their feet a good portion of the workday.

Unions/Associations

Greeters may get additional career information by contacting the National Retail Federation (NRF). Depending on the place of the employment, Greeters may belong to house unions.

Tips for Entry

1. There is a great deal of turnover in these positions. Stop in stores in which you are interested in working and ask to fill out an application.
2. Openings may be posted in store windows. Look for announcements stating "Greeters Wanted."
3. Jobs may be advertised in the classified sections of newspapers. Look under classifications such as "Greeters" or "Retail Opportunities," "Department Stores," or see the ads of specific department stores.
4. Remember to bring with you the names, addresses, and phone numbers of a few people you can use as references when filling out applications. Make sure you ask people if you can use them as references BEFORE you use them.
5. Stores often call local labor offices to post these jobs. Remember to stop by your state employment office.

STORES, CHAINS, SHOPS, AND BOUTIQUES

DISTRICT MANAGER

CAREER PROFILE

Duties: Oversee stores in district; oversee transfer of merchandise; assure stores in district are running properly; oversee key staffing positions; oversee merchandising in stores; work with staff to help store meet sales and profit goals

Alternate Titles: District

Salary Range: $35,000 to $75,000+

Employment Prospects: Good

Advancement Prospects: Good

Best Geographical Location(s) for Position: Jobs may be located throughout the country

Prerequisites:

Education and Training—Training requirements vary

Experience—Experience in retail management

Special Skills and Personality Traits—Management skills; problem solving skills; communications skills; ability to deal well with people; administrative skills

CAREER LADDER

```
┌─────────────────────────────┐
│      Regional Manager       │
└─────────────────────────────┘

┌─────────────────────────────┐
│      District Manager       │
└─────────────────────────────┘

┌─────────────────────────────┐
│       Store Manager         │
└─────────────────────────────┘
```

Position Description

Chain and department stores often have multiple outlets in locations from one end of the country to the other. To assure that all the stores are run properly, corporations divide the areas in which they are located into regions. Regions are overseen by regional managers. These regions are then divided into districts. Depending on the specific company, a district may have eight to 15 stores or more. Each district is overseen by an individual called a District Manager.

District Managers are responsible for overseeing all of the stores in a specific area or district. They are expected to make sure each store in the district is running properly.

The District Manager is ultimately responsible for everything that happens within the stores in the district. The individual communicates with each store on a regular basis. Many District Managers speak to their store managers daily. During these conversations, they check to see if there are any problems in the stores and make sure the day-to-day management is going well.

He or she will usually ask how sales are, about store traffic, and what merchandise is moving and what is not. The District, as he or she may be referred to, may ask about per-

sonnel issues or possible problems with the landlord or mall management.

If there are problems in any of the stores, the District Manager will offer suggestions to effectively deal with them. This may be handled on the phone or the individual may visit the store to help deal with the situation.

The District Manager is the liaison between the corporate office and the store. He or she is responsible for communicating routine corporate policies to store managers as well as letting them know of any policy changes. For example, the corporate office may want customer returns handled in a certain manner. The District Manager must make sure all store managers are familiar with the policy and make sure they follow it. The individual may either send a written letter or fax or make a call to each store manager.

One of the main functions of the District Manager is working with his or her stores to make sure they meet corporate sales and profit goals. He or she may visit the store to motivate employees as well as to give them product information helpful in making sales. The individual may make suggestions about displays, merchandising, and other visual opportunities designed to attract the attention of potential customers.

What sells in one store may not sell in another. In many stores, the District Manager will supervise the transfer of merchandise that is not moving to a store where it might.

Stores generally keep accurate records of sales figures on a daily, weekly, monthly, and annual basis. This information is used to help project profits. Based on these figures, along with various other information, the corporate offices set sales goals. In many stores, the store manager is expected to call in or fax the daily figures to the District Manager.

The District Manager is often responsible for recruiting managers and assistant managers for his or her stores. He or she may write and place ads for the newspaper or other media, schedule interviews, and hire qualified individuals.

Many stores, especially chains, have weekly promotions and sales advertised in the local paper and flyers. These promotions, ads, and flyers are used to attract customers. The District Manager will make sure the store management in his or her district knows about the promotions so they can be run effectively.

The District Manager is often required to step in to handle a customer service problem when it can't be handled on the store level. A customer, for example, may have had a problem with a store manager and wants to deal with a person on a higher level. The District Manager, as everyone else in retail, constantly strives to make sure his or her store excels in customer service.

There is a great deal of traveling involved in this job. District Managers may work out of an office or one of the stores in their area. They may travel to visit stores three or four times a week. This is essential to make sure stores are merchandised properly, everything is going well, and all problems are taken care of immediately.

Additional duties of District Managers may include:

- Preparing new stores for opening
- Handling loss prevention
- Terminating key employees
- Recommending raises and promotions for key employees

Salaries

Earnings for District Managers can range from approximately $35,000 to $75,000 or more. Variables affecting earnings include the number of stores in the specific district, as well as the size, prestige, and geographic locations of each. Other variables include the experience, responsibilities, and education of the individual. Generally, those with the highest salaries will have a great deal of responsibility and oversee large districts.

Employment Prospects

Employment prospects are good for District Managers. Positions are located throughout the country. Employers may include chain and department stores, convenience stores, supermarkets, drug stores, and stores in specialty chains.

Advancement Prospects

District Managers may climb the career ladder in a number of ways. Some individuals find similar jobs with larger or more prestigious chains or retail outlets. Others are promoted to positions overseeing larger districts. Another common method of career advancement for District Managers is landing a job as a regional manager. These individuals oversee a number of districts.

Education and Training

Educational backgrounds of District Managers vary. There are many District Managers who hold a high school diploma and no higher education. There are others who have college backgrounds and degrees.

While stores may not require individuals to hold anything above a high school diploma, some may prefer District Managers with college backgrounds or degrees. Good majors include retailing, merchandising, business, management, marketing, communications, advertising, liberal arts, or related fields.

Training requirements vary from store to store. Some stores provide formal training programs. Others have on-the-job training.

Experience, Skills, and Personality Traits

District Managers usually have gone through the ranks getting experience as sales associates, assistant managers, and then store managers prior to their placement in current positions. Individuals need a complete knowledge of management principles as well as a total understanding of the retail industry. Leadership skills, self-confidence, and the ability to make decisions are essential. The ability to deal with and work well with others is necessary. Individuals need to be good problem solvers who are energetic, detail oriented, and highly motivated. Communications skills, both written and verbal, are necessary as well.

Unions/Associations

Individuals interested in learning more about careers in this field should contact the American Collegiate Retailing Association (ACRA), National Retail Federation (NRF), and the National Retail Merchants Association (NRMA).

Tips for Entry

1. Stores often promote from within. Get your foot in the door, learn everything you can, and move up the career ladder.
2. Many chains and department stores offer management training programs. Contact the headquarters of these stores to find out about requirements.

3. Positions may be advertised in the classified sections of newspapers. Look under classifications including "District Manager," "Retail Opportunities," or "Management Opportunities." Look also in the ads of specific stores.

4. Jobs in this field, may be located on the Internet. Begin your search on some of the more popular job search sites such as Monster board (www.monster.com) and Hot Jobs (www.hotjobs.com).

5. You might also check specific store websites. Many post job openings.

6. Contact recruiters and executive search firms specializing in management positions in retail.

7. Send your resume and a short cover letter to the corporate offices of chain and department stores.

REGIONAL MANAGER—RETAIL

CAREER PROFILE

Duties: Oversee stores in region, coordinate the activities of district managers; assure stores in region are running properly; recruit and train district managers; work with key employees to help store meet sales and profit goals

Alternate Titles: Regional

Salary Range: $45,000 to $100,000+

Employment Prospects: Good

Advancement Prospects: Good

Best Geographical Location(s) for Position: Jobs may be located throughout the country

Prerequisites:

Education and Training—Training requirements vary

Experience—Extensive experience in retail management

Special Skills and Personality Traits—Management skills; problem solving skills; communications skills; ability to work well with people; administrative skills; leadership skills

CAREER LADDER

```
┌─────────────────────────────┐
│  Regional Manager for Larger │
│ or More Prestigious Company  │
│     or Director of Stores    │
└─────────────────────────────┘

┌─────────────────────────────┐
│      Regional Manager        │
└─────────────────────────────┘

┌─────────────────────────────┐
│      District Manager        │
└─────────────────────────────┘
```

Position Description

The day-to-day management of a single retail store is handled by a store manager. Many retail stores have multiple outlets in locations from one end of the country to the other. In order to assure all the stores are run properly, corporate management divides the areas in which stores are located into regions. These regions are overseen by individuals called Regional Managers.

The Regional Manager oversees all the stores in the region. The Regional Manager is expected to coordinate the activities of the district managers in his or her region. The Regional Manager provides leadership and motivation and works with district managers and their stores to help each meet sales and profit goals.

The Regional Manager works with the corporate office to set both long- and short-term sales goals and strategies. These are based on a number of factors and information including prior sales figures. Stores generally keep accurate records of sales figures on a daily, weekly, monthly, and annual basis. These figures are usually called in or faxed to the district manager who in turn gets them to the Regional Manager.

The Regional Manager tracks the sales figures. If he or she sees sales slipping in one or more stores, the individual will call the district manager to see what the problem is and how it can be remedied.

Sales can decline for numerous reasons. For example, sales may be off for a simple reason such as bad weather, which may keep people off the roads. This will resolve itself as soon as the weather gets better. Sometimes, if there has been a big storm during a storewide scheduled promotion, the Regional Manager will suggest to corporate that the promotion be extended.

Sales may be off because a new competitor has just opened a store in the area. In this case, the Regional Manager may call the marketing department and recommend additional advertising, coupons, or promotions for a short period of time. On the other hand, sales may be off because a store in the region is not being managed properly or customer service is poor. The Regional Manager will work with the district manager straightening out the situation.

Regional Managers are responsible for overseeing all of the stores in his or her region. They are expected to make sure each store in the region is running properly. To do this, the individual communicates with each district manager on a regular basis.

The Regional Manager also works closely with district managers to identify and correct general management problems within stores in the region. This may include things such as improving traffic and merchandising matters, dealing with personnel issues, and handling any possible problems with the landlord or mall management.

The Regional Manager may visit stores with the district manager to deal with specific problems or to see firsthand how things are going. The individual is the liaison between upper corporate management and the district managers. He or she is responsible for communicating routine corporate policies and policy changes to district managers so they, in turn, can inform store managers.

In many cases, the Regional Manager will assist upper corporate management in the development of policies and policy changes. The Regional Manager often recruits district managers, and he or she may also assist the district managers in recruiting and hiring key personnel such as managers or assistant managers for stores in the region.

The Regional Manager may work with others in upper corporate management recommending merchandise, sales, or marketing programs.

Regional Managers travel a great deal in their job. Depending on the specific company and its structure, they may work out of a corporate office or out of one of the stores in their region. Regional Managers often travel to meet with their district managers as well as to visit stores in their region.

Additional duties of Regional Managers may include:

- Preparing new stores for opening
- Helping close stores in the chain
- Meeting or calling the landlord or mall management to discuss problems and complaints
- Terminating district managers or other key employees
- Recommending raises and promotions for district managers or other key employees

Salaries

Earnings for Regional Managers can range from approximately $45,000 to $100,000 or more. Variables affecting earnings include the number of districts and number of stores in the specific region, as well as the size, prestige, and geographic locations of each. Other variables include the experience, responsibilities, and education of the individual. Generally, those with the highest salaries will have a great deal of responsibility and oversee large regions.

Employment Prospects

Employment prospects are good for Regional Managers. Positions are located throughout the country. Employers may include chain and department stores, convenience stores, supermarkets, drug stores, and stores in specialty chains.

Advancement Prospects

Regional Managers may climb the career ladder in a number of ways. Some individuals find similar jobs with larger or more prestigious stores. Others are promoted to positions overseeing larger regions. Another method of career advancement for Regional Managers is landing a job as a director of stores.

Education and Training

Educational backgrounds of Regional Managers vary. There are many Regional Managers who hold a high school diploma and no higher education. There are others who have college backgrounds and degrees.

While some companies may not require individuals to hold anything above a high school diploma, some may prefer Regional Managers with college backgrounds or degrees. Relevant majors include retailing, merchandising, business, management, marketing, communications, advertising, liberal arts, or other related fields.

Training requirements also vary from company to company. Some companies provide formal training programs, while others have on-the-job training.

Experience, Skills, and Personality Traits

Regional Managers are required to have a great deal of experience in retail management. Most have gone through the ranks getting experience as sales associates, assistant managers, store managers, and regional managers prior to their current positions. Individuals need a complete knowledge of management principles as well as a total understanding of the retail industry. Leadership skills, self-confidence, and decisiveness are essential. The ability to deal with and work well with others is necessary. Individuals need to be good problem solvers who are energetic, detail oriented, and highly motivated. Communications skills, both written and verbal, are necessary as well.

Unions/Associations

Individuals interested in learning more about careers in this field should contact the American Collegiate Retailing Association (ACRA), National Retail Federation (NRF) and the National Retail Merchants Association (NRMA).

Tips for Entry

1. Contact recruiters and executive search firms specializing in management positions in retail.

2. Trade journals often advertise openings.

3. Retail companies like to promote from within. Get your foot in the door, learn everything you can, and move up the career ladder.

4. Many chains and department stores offer management training programs. Contact the headquarters of these stores to find out about requirements.

5. Positions may be advertised in the classified sections of newspapers. Look under classifications including "Regional Manager," "Retail Opportunities," or "Management Opportunities." Look also in the ads of specific stores.

6. Jobs in this field may be located on the Internet. Begin your search on some of the more popular job search sites such as Monster board (www.monster.com) and Hot Jobs (www.hotjobs.com).

7. You might also check specific store websites. Many post job openings.

8. Send your resume and a short cover letter to the corporate offices of chain and department stores. Ask that your resume be kept on file if there are no current openings.

STORE MANAGER—SPECIALTY OR CHAIN STORE

CAREER PROFILE

Duties: Handle day-to-day management of store; oversee staffing needs of store; deal with customer service issues; assist customers; prevent theft; work with staff to help store meet sales and profit goals; handle advertising and promotional needs of store

Alternate Titles: Manager

Salary Range: $25,000 to $70,000+

Employment Prospects: Good

Advancement Prospects: Fair

Best Geographical Location(s) for Position: Jobs may be located throughout the country

Prerequisites:

Education and Training—Training requirements vary
Experience—Experience in retail management
Special Skills and Personality Traits—Problem solving skills; negotiation skills; communications skills; ability to deal well with people; management skills; administrative skills

CAREER LADDER

```
┌─────────────────────────────────┐
│   Store Manager for Larger or   │
│     More Prestigious Store      │
│      or Regional Manager        │
└─────────────────────────────────┘

┌─────────────────────────────────┐
│         Store Manager           │
└─────────────────────────────────┘

┌─────────────────────────────────┐
│     Assistant Store Manager     │
└─────────────────────────────────┘
```

Position Description

While department stores are prevalent in this country, there are an array of other types of stores where people shop. These include specialty stores selling merchandise such as toys, fabrics, clothing, hardware, jewelry, luggage, electronics, books, plants, cosmetics, and gourmet foods, among other items. Each of these stores needs a Manager. In some stores, the owner may act as the Manager.

The Store Manager handles the day-to-day management of the store. His or her management techniques will have a direct impact on the success of the store.

Specific responsibilities will depend, of course, on the type of store the individual is managing. However, there are general duties all Store Managers must fulfill. As in all retail outlets, the Store Manager is expected to work with his or her staff to meet sales and profit goals.

The Store Manager is responsible for opening the store each day. This responsibility may be shared with other key holders such as the assistant manager or third key. Before the gates or doors are opened to the public, the Manager makes sure the store is ready. If the carpet or floor wasn't cleaned the night before, the Manager or his or her staff may vacuum. The individual must be sure the shelves, displays, and racks are stocked and neat. The Store Manager will also go to the safe and take out cash to fill cash drawers with change for the day.

The Manager is expected to make sure all scheduled employees are present. If employees call in sick, the Manager is responsible for calling in replacement staff.

The Manager is responsible for the recruiting and training needs of the staff for the store. He or she may place ads, conduct interviews, and hire needed employees. The Store Manager is also expected to make sure that all employment regulations are followed within the store. These might include things like following labor rules, making sure teenagers don't work more hours than their allotted time, and forms are filled out for tax purposes. The Manager will recommend raises and promotions and is also expected to terminate employees.

The Store Manager must constantly strive to keep customers happy. The climate of the store is often dependent, to a great extent, on the Store Manager. Those who can make a store a pleasant shopping experience for customers and a pleasant workplace for employees will be most successful.

To accomplish these goals, the Manager must provide the best customer service possible. It is the responsibility of the Manager to train the rest of the staff to provide excellent customer service as well.

The Manager will usually be the individual called upon when a customer has a problem no one else can or wants to handle. He or she will always try to resolve customer complaints to the customer's satisfaction.

The Manager must make sure that the store is stocked with merchandise that customers want. If the store has sales and promotions, the Manager must be sure stock is available, and must keep abreast of what is selling and what is needed. When merchandise is low, the Manager may place an order personally or may inform the store's buyer or owner.

The individual is often responsible for accepting merchandise shipped to the store. He or she may also supervise its unpacking. At times, the Manager will also supervise the repacking of merchandise to send back to a manufacturer or to another store.

The Manager may design store windows and displays so that merchandise is attractively shown. In other cases, the individual may assign this duty to the assistant manager or another member of the staff.

The individual is expected to deal with any emergencies or problems within the store. These might include accidents or incidents in which either customers or employees are hurt. The individual may call paramedics or ambulances when needed. He or she will also be expected to file reports detailing incidents for store owners or insurance purposes.

The Manager is responsible for loss prevention. He or she must key an eye out for shoplifters as well as employee theft, and may work with local police agencies or private investigators.

The Store Manager is ultimately responsible for overseeing all monies in the store. He or she may go over the day's receipts as well as weekly and monthly reports. In many stores, the Manager must report daily figures to the corporate office or store owner.

At the end of the day, the Store Manager, an assistant, or key holder will be responsible for cashing out registers and counting the day's receipts. Depending on the specific store, the individual may either put the day's receipts in the store's safe or deposit it in the bank.

Some Store Managers develop and implement advertising campaigns, promotions, and special events. He or she may also write advertising copy, design ads, and place them in various media.

Additional duties of Store Managers may include:

- Assisting customers
- Representing the store at community events and organizations
- Handling emergencies and crises after hours
- Closing the store after hours
- Scheduling employees work hours
- Approving customers' returns

Salaries

Annual earnings for Store Managers can range from approximately $25,000 to $70,000 or more. Variables affecting earnings include the size, prestige, and geographic location of the specific store. Other variables include the experience, responsibilities, and education of the individual. Some Store Managers may also receive bonuses when sales meet or exceed goals.

Employment Prospects

Employment prospects are excellent for Store Managers seeking to work in retail. Positions are located throughout the country. There are an array of possibilities ranging from small boutiques to larger specialty stores, chains, franchises, and everything in between. Stores like Dress Barn, J. Crew, Petco, Eckerd, Rite Aid, Victoria's Secret, The Gap, Borders, and Barnes and Noble have locations nationwide.

Advancement Prospects

The most common method of climbing the career ladder for Store Managers is locating similar jobs in larger or more prestigious stores. Those working in chains may climb the career ladder by promotion to larger stores within the chain. Individuals also may advance their careers by becoming area managers or moving into other areas of corporate management.

Education and Training

Educational backgrounds of Store Managers vary. While stores may not require individuals to hold anything above a high school diploma, they may prefer Managers with college backgrounds or degrees. Good majors include retailing, merchandising, business, management, marketing, communications, advertising, liberal arts, or other related fields.

Chain stores often require their management recruits to go through their own formal training programs. These may be necessary even if a Manager has worked in the same position in a store outside of the specific chain. These programs train the individual in store policies and management techniques necessary to running the store effectively.

Experience, Skills, and Personality Traits

The most successful Store Managers work in stores where they have some knowledge or interest in the products or merchandise being sold. Most Managers have had experience on the selling floor as well as third keys and assistant managers prior to their current position.

Store Managers must be self-confident, enthusiastic leaders who are energetic, detail oriented, and highly motivated. They must know a great deal about the products and merchandise the store carries in order to be able to assist customers effectively. The ability to solve problems and make quick decisions is essential.

Customer service skills are vital for store management. The ability to deal with and work well with people is mandatory. Store Managers should also be articulate with good communications skills.

Unions/Associations

Individuals interested in learning more about careers in this field should contact the American Collegiate Retailing Association (ACRA), National Retail Federation (NRF) and the National Retail Merchants Association (NRMA).

Tips for Entry

1. Positions may be advertised in the classified sections of newspapers. Look under classifications including "Store Manager," "Retail Opportunities," "Store Management," or "Management Opportunities." Other positions may be advertised under specific store names.

2. Many chain stores offer management training programs. Contact the headquarters of these stores to find out about requirements.

3. Many stores now have websites where they also list employment opportunities.

4. Jobs may also be located on the Internet. Begin your search on some of the more popular job search sites such as Monster board (www.monster.com) and Hot Jobs (www.hotjobs.com).

5. Contact recruiters and executive search firms specializing in management retail positions.

6. Send your resume and a short cover letter to the corporate offices of chain stores.

ASSISTANT STORE MANAGER— SPECIALTY OR CHAIN STORE

CAREER PROFILE

Duties: Assist manager in daily operations; deal with customer service issues; assist customers; assist with loss prevention; work with staff to help store meet sales and profit goals

Alternate Titles: None

Salary Range: $22,000 to $48,000+

Employment Prospects: Good

Advancement Prospects: Good

Best Geographical Location(s) for Position: Jobs may be located throughout the country

Prerequisites:

Education and Training—Training requirements vary
Experience—Experience in retail management
Special Skills and Personality Traits—Problem solving skills; negotiation skills; communications skills; ability to deal well with people; management skills; administrative skills

CAREER LADDER

```
┌─────────────────────────────┐
│       Store Manager         │
└─────────────────────────────┘

┌─────────────────────────────┐
│   Assistant Store Manager   │
└─────────────────────────────┘

┌─────────────────────────────┐
│         Third Key           │
└─────────────────────────────┘
```

Position Description

There are many different types of stores. Some might specialize in selling clothing, toys, accessories, fabrics, luggage, pet products, or gifts, among other things. Some may specialize in more niche markets such as gourmet teas, hair pieces, antique clothing, or music boxes. Some stores may be a part of chains or franchises. Others may be privately owned. Each of these stores has a manager. Most also have Assistant Managers.

These individuals are second in command in the store. They assist the store manager with day-to-day store operations. Assistant Managers also step in and assume the duties of the manager when he or she is off.

While there are similarities between the management of department stores and other types of stores, there are also differences. In smaller independent stores, for example, the Assistant Manager may have more generalized duties. He or she may work with the manager to buy merchandise. The individual may also assist with the store's accounting and bookkeeping functions.

Depending on the store, the Assistant Manager may be expected to help develop and implement advertising campaigns, writing copy, designing ads, and placing them. The individual might also help the manager develop promotions and special events to attract customers to the store.

In order for stores to stay in business they need to sell merchandise. Assistant Managers are expected to help motivate the staff to work to meet sales and profit goals.

The Assistant Manager may take turns with the store manager and the third key opening the store. Before the gates or doors are opened to the public, the individual works with other employees making sure the store is ready for customers. This might include checking to see if shelves, displays, and racks are neat and fully stocked, the floor is clean, and the registers have change.

The Assistant Manager may be required to fill in when other employees call in sick and replacement staff can't be located. The individual may assist the store manager in recruiting and training staff. He or she will work with the manager assuring that all employment regulations are followed within the store. These might include things like following labor rules, making sure teenagers don't work more hours than their allotted time, or filling out forms for tax purposes.

One of the main responsibilities of the Assistant Manager is making sure the store employees provide excellent customer service, and that shopping in the store is a pleasant experience. In the event a customer does have a problem or complaint, the Assistant Manager may be called to resolve it.

The Assistant Manager makes sure that merchandise sold during the day is replaced from the stock room at regular intervals. In this way displays always look filled and appear inviting to customers.

The individual is expected to deal with any emergencies or problems within the store when the manager is not available. These might include accidents or incidents in which either customers or employees are hurt. He or she will also be expected to file reports detailing incidents for store owners or insurance purposes.

The Assistant Manager works with others in the store on loss prevention. He or she must keep an eye out for shoplifters as well as employee theft. The Assistant Manager and the manager may work with local police agencies or private investigators.

Depending on who is working at the close of business, the Assistant Manager, manager, or third key will be responsible for cashing out registers and counting the day's receipts. One or more of these individuals may put the day's receipts in the store's safe or deposit it at a bank.

Additional duties of Assistant Store Managers may include:

- Assisting customers
- Handling emergencies and crises after hours when the manager is not available
- Closing the store after hours when manager is not on duty
- Assisting with the scheduling of employees work hours
- Approving customers' returns

Salaries

Annual earnings for Assistant Store Managers can range from approximately $22,000 to $48,000 or more. Variables affecting earnings include the size, prestige, and geographic location of the specific store. Other variables include the experience, responsibilities, and education of the individual. Some Store Managers may also receive bonuses when sales meet or exceed goals.

Employment Prospects

Employment prospects are good for Assistant Managers. Positions may be located throughout the country. There are an array of possibilities ranging from small boutiques to larger specialty stores, chains, franchises, and everything in between. Chain stores such as Dress Barn, J. Crew, Petco,

Eckerd, Rite Aid, Victoria's Secret, The Gap, Borders, and Barnes and Noble have locations nationwide.

Advancement Prospects

Some Assistant Store Managers advance their careers by landing similar positions in larger or more prestigious stores. This results in increased responsibilities and earnings.

Another common method of career advancement for Assistant Managers is promotion to store manager. Those working in chains may climb the career ladder by promotion to larger stores within the chain.

Education and Training

Educational backgrounds of Assistant Managers vary. While stores may not require individuals to hold anything above a high school diploma, they may prefer Assistant Managers with college backgrounds or degrees. Good majors include retailing, merchandising, business, management, marketing, communications, advertising, liberal arts, or related fields. College is especially helpful for individuals seeking to advance their careers.

Chain stores often require their management recruits to go through their own formal training programs. These may be necessary even if the individual has worked as an Assistant Manager in a store outside of the specific chain. These programs train the individual in store policies and management techniques necessary to running the store effectively.

Experience, Skills, and Personality Traits

Assistant Managers are required to have experience working in a retail environment. Most have worked on the selling floor as well as been in third key positions.

Assistant Store Managers should be highly motivated, self-confident, and enthusiastic individuals. They should be detail oriented and have the ability to do multiple projects at one time. Customer service skills are essential. Good communications skills are mandatory.

Unions/Associations

Individuals interested in learning more about careers in this field should contact the American Collegiate Retailing Association (ACRA), the National Retail Federation (NRF) and the National Retail Merchants Association (NRMA).

Tips for Entry

1. Stores often post signs in their windows advertising openings for management positions.
2. You might also stop in stores and ask to fill out an application. Ask that your resume be kept on file if there are no current positions.
3. Positions may be advertised in the classified sections of newspapers. Look under classifications including "Assistant Store Manager," "Retail Opportunities,"

"Store Management," or "Management Opportunities." Other positions may be advertised under specific store names.

4. Many chain stores offer management training programs. Contact the headquarters of these stores to find out about requirements.

5. Many stores now have websites where they also list employment opportunities.

6. Remember to check out corporate websites of chain stores as well.

THIRD KEY

CAREER PROFILE

Duties: Oversee small staff; assist customers; sell merchandise; open store; close store; cash out registers; handle deposits

Alternative Titles(s): Junior Assistant Manager

Salary Range: $7.00 to $18.00+ per hour

Employment Prospects: Excellent

Advancement Prospects: Excellent

Best Geographical Location(s) for Position: Positions located throughout the country

Prerequisites:

Education and Training—On-the-job training

Experience and Qualifications—Retail sales experience required

Special Skills and Personality Traits—Management skills; customer service skills; sales ability; communications skills; pleasant attitude; money handling skills

CAREER LADDER

```
┌─────────────────────────────┐
│   Assistant Store Manager   │
└─────────────────────────────┘

┌─────────────────────────────┐
│         Third Key           │
└─────────────────────────────┘

┌─────────────────────────────┐
│       Sales Associate       │
└─────────────────────────────┘
```

Position Description

Retail establishments may have an array of supervisors and managers running the store. Depending on the size and structure of the establishment these might include managers, assistant managers, department managers, supervisors, and Third Keys.

The Third Key is an entry-level management position with varied duties depending on the organization. The Third Key may be in charge of overseeing staff. A Third Key may often work either on weekends or evenings when a manager or assistant manager is not on duty. During this time, the Third Key will supervise the staff. In this position, the Third Key may handle problems which might occur within the store. These might include unhappy or irate customers, accidents with customers or employees, shoplifters, or difficult merchandise returns.

The Third Key reports to the assistant manager and manager of the store. He or she may work full time or part time and usually will be expected to work evenings or weekends.

Depending on the store, managers, assistant managers, and Third Keys may hold the keys to the store. One of the responsibilities of the Third Key may be opening the store for business in the morning. To do this the individual unlocks the door, makes sure the store is straightened and ready to open, puts cash in the registers for change, and makes sure all scheduled employees are accounted for.

Conversely, the Third Key may be scheduled to close the store at the end of business hours. When doing this he or she must first make sure all customers are out of the store and then close the doors or pull the gate for the evening. The Third Key may be expected to cash out the registers, do cash counts and then prepare a deposit. Some stores may have safes where money is kept until a morning deposit. In other stores, only monies designated for change will be kept in a safe at night. The rest of the day's receipts must be dropped in a night deposit by the Third Key or another member of the management staff.

Before the Third Key leaves, he or she must make sure the store is ready to open the next day. He or she will work with other members of the staff putting back merchandise, vacuuming the store, and straightening displays in preparation for the next day's business.

Some Third Keys may be assigned to specific parts of the store or departments. The individual may, for example, be in charge of keeping display tables stocked and arranged attractively. This may need to be done a number of times a day as customers rifle through stock looking for merchandise.

Third Keys are also expected to assist customers. Like sales associates, they must determine the needs of customers to make each person feel comfortable whether they come in the store to browse or buy. Third Keys often take payment when customers decide on purchases.

The Third Key job is a stepping stone to a management position in retail. Other duties of Third Keys include:

- Stocking, pricing, and ticketing merchandise
- Displaying merchandise
- Training new employees
- Handling loss prevention
- Accounting for sales
- Handling returns

Salaries

Earnings for Third Keys range from approximately $7.00 to $18.00 or more per hour. Factors affecting earnings include the geographic location, size, prestige, and specific type of retail establishment. Other variables include the experience and responsibilities of the individual. A perk of the job for many individuals is often an employee discount in the store in which they work.

Employment Prospects

Employment prospects are excellent for Third Keys. Individuals may find positions throughout the country in a variety of retail establishments. Third Keys may work full time or part time, as well as various shifts.

Most stores employ Third Keys or the equivalent. Many employ more than one person in this position. As noted, this is an entry-level management position. There is a great deal of turnover as individuals climb the career ladder or move to other jobs.

Advancement Prospects

Advancement prospects are excellent for Third Keys. With experience or additional training, Third Keys often advance to positions as assistant store managers.

Education and Training

The Third Key usually receives on-the-job training at the store in which he or she works. Many stores also provide formal training programs.

Experience, Skills, and Personality Traits

Third Keys need retail sales experience. They usually start out as sales associates. Individuals should be reliable with management skills and the ability to supervise others.

They should be courteous, pleasant people with good customer service skills. Sales ability and money handling skills are essential.

Unions/Associations

Those interested in learning more about careers as sales associates can obtain information from the National Retail Merchants Association (NRMA) or the American Collegiate Retailing Association (ACRA).

Tips for Entry

1. Larger stores often have management training programs. If you are aspiring to a career in retail seek these out.
2. Jobs are often advertised in the classified sections of newspapers. Look under classifications such as "Retail," "Retail Opportunities," "Third Key," or "Management—Retail."
3. Many larger stores have job hotlines. These are frequently recorded updated messages listing job availability. Call stores directly to obtain their job hotline phone numbers, or check their ads.
4. Stop by the human resources department of larger stores to learn about job openings.
5. Stop in smaller stores and ask the manager if there are any openings or if you can fill out an application.
6. Many stores post "help wanted" signs in their store's windows.

SALES ASSOCIATE

CAREER PROFILE

Duties: Assist customers; sell merchandise; handle cashier duties

Alternate Titles(s): Salesclerk, Salesperson, Saleswoman, Salesman

Salary Range: $6.00 to $15.00+ per hour

Employment Prospects: Excellent

Advancement Prospects: Excellent

Best Geographical Location(s) for Position: Positions located throughout the country

Prerequisites:

Education and Training—High school diploma or equivalent; on-the-job training

Experience and Qualifications—Sales experience helpful, but not always required

Special Skills and Personality Traits—Customer service skills; sales ability; communications skills; pleasant; money handling skills

CAREER LADDER

```
┌─────────────────────────────┐
│   Third Key, Floor Supervisor, │
│   or Assistant Store Manager  │
└─────────────────────────────┘

┌─────────────────────────────┐
│       Sales Associate        │
└─────────────────────────────┘

┌─────────────────────────────┐
│        Entry Level           │
└─────────────────────────────┘
```

Position Description

There are a variety of retail establishments of every size and type. These include department stores, specialty shops, grocery stores, convenience stores, newspaper and sundry shops, souvenir stores, kiosks, clothing stores, and boutiques and gift shops to name a few. No matter what they sell, every store and shop needs Sales Associates, also referred to as Salesclerks.

Sales Associates assist customers, and determine the needs of each customer. Sales Associates must make every person who comes into the retail establishment feel comfortable whether they are just browsing or they want to buy. Customer service is extremely important in this job.

Sales Associates must know the stock in their store and be able to answer questions regarding merchandise. Individuals may offer suggestions to customers regarding purchase possibilities.

Once patrons decide what they want to purchase, Sales Associates may be responsible for taking payment. Individuals must know how to ring up purchases and make correct change if people are paying with cash. They also must know the proper procedure for accepting checks or processing credit card charges.

Sales Associates in some stores stock, price, and ticket merchandise. They are responsible for putting merchandise out in displays. Individuals also are expected to clean and to organize shelves as well as keep the shop or store neat and orderly.

Other duties of Sales Associates include:

- Handling loss prevention
- Accounting for sales
- Handling returns

Salaries

Salaries for Sales Associates may vary greatly. Many Associates earn minimum wage. Others may be paid between $6.00 and $15.00 or more per hour. Factors affecting earnings include the geographic location, size, prestige, and specific type of retail establishment. Other variables include the experience and responsibilities of the individual. In some stores, Sales Associates may be paid a commission in addition to their hourly wage boosting their earnings.

One of the perks many Sales Associates enjoy is an employee discount in the store in which they work.

Employment Prospects

Employment prospects are excellent for Sales Associates throughout the country. One of the great things about working as a Sales Associate is the flexibility it affords. Sales Associates might work full time, part time, nights, weekends, or holidays. In addition to being a good career choice for those interested in retail, it is often an excellent opportunity for students or people looking for a second income.

Advancement Prospects

With experience and/or additional training, Sales Associates are often promoted to supervisory or managerial positions. Depending on career aspirations individuals might be promoted to third key, floor supervisor, or even assistant store manager.

Education and Training

Generally, Sales Associates receive on-the-job training. Depending on the specific employer, training might include how to help customers with sales, as well as how to use the cash register and credit card machines properly.

Experience, Skills, and Personality Traits

Experience requirements for Sales Associates vary. There are many entry-level positions in sales requiring no experience. Others may prefer or require some type of retail sales experience.

Sales Associates must be courteous, pleasant, and have good customer service skills. Sales ability and money handling skills are essential. The most successful Sales Associates enjoy being around people.

Unions/Associations

Those interested in learning more about careers as sales associates can obtain information from the National Retail Merchants Association (NRMA) or the National Retail Federation (NRF).

Tips for Entry

1. While retail experience is not always needed, it may be preferred. Include any prior retail experience on your job application or resume.
2. Jobs are often advertised in the classified sections of newspapers in areas hosting large department stores. Look under classifications such as "Retail," "Retail Opportunities," "Sales Associates," or "Salesclerks."
3. Many larger stores have job hotlines. These are frequently recorded updated messages listing job availability. Call stores directly to obtain their job hotline phone numbers, or check their ads.
4. Stop by the human resources department of larger stores to learn about job openings.
5. Feel free to stop in smaller stores to ask the manager if there are any openings or if you can fill out an application.
6. Look for help wanted signs in store windows.

BUYER

CAREER PROFILE

Duties: Determine which products are best; find suppliers and vendors; negotiate lowest prices; award contracts

Alternate Titles: Purchasing Professional

Salary Range: $23,000 to $75,000+

Employment Prospects: Good

Advancement Prospects: Good

Best Geographical Location(s) for Position: Jobs may be located throughout the country; large cities will offer more possibilities

Prerequisites:

Education and Training—College degree preferred

Experience—Experience in buying or merchandising

Special Skills and Personality Traits—Self-confidence; leadership; communications skills; organization; ability to foresee trends

CAREER LADDER

```
┌─────────────────────────────────────┐
│  Head Buyer or Merchandise Manager   │
└─────────────────────────────────────┘

┌─────────────────────────────────────┐
│              Buyer                   │
└─────────────────────────────────────┘

┌─────────────────────────────────────┐
│   Junior Buyer or Assistant Buyer    │
└─────────────────────────────────────┘
```

Position Description

Every time you walk into a store full of merchandise, you are seeing the work of a Buyer. The Buyer is the individual responsible for choosing the merchandise that is sold in the store. In some stores, especially smaller ones, the owner or manager assumes the responsibilities of the Buyer.

Responsibilities of Buyers can vary depending on the specific employment situation. Buyers may be responsible for buying the merchandise for an entire store or may be responsible for buying for one or more specific departments. A large department store may, for example, have a toy buyer, a women's clothing buyer, and a small appliance buyer. In large chains, Buyers of specific departments often are expected to buy merchandise for all of the chain's stores.

Buyers usually have a number of different vendors to choose from when selecting merchandise. They must evaluate and select vendors or suppliers based on a number of criteria. While price is important, it can not be used solely in choosing suppliers of merchandise. Other factors to be considered when choosing suppliers include the quality of the merchandise, availability, selection, and reliability of the vendor.

One of the Buyers most important functions is finding the correct merchandise. The individual may look for merchandise which is currently in demand as well as predict trends and seek out new merchandise which may be in demand in the future.

Depending on the situation, the individual may look for suppliers and vendors both domestically and internationally. Buyers find merchandise in a variety of ways. They may meet with vendors to look at merchandise in their own offices or may visit showrooms or factories. Individuals might review listings in catalogs, industry periodicals, directories, and trade journals. Buyers often research the reputation and history of suppliers to assure that they are reliable.

Buyers often must travel a great deal. Individuals may go on buying trips as well as attend meetings, trade shows, and conferences. Individuals also may visit vendors' plants and distribution centers, so they can examine products as well as assess the vendor's production and distribution capabilities.

The Buyer solicits bids from vendors to obtain the best prices for the merchandise. He or she must then price the merchandise so that it sells at the best markup possible. The Buyer must keep abreast of changes affecting the supply and demand for products. If products aren't selling he or she must mark down prices in an effort to move them and improve sales. The bottom line is to keep the store or department as profitable as possible.

Additional duties of Buyers might include:

- Studying sales record and inventory levels of current stock
- Working with the advertising department to create ad campaigns for specific merchandise
- Visiting the selling floor to assure products are displayed properly
- Meeting with sales staff to discuss new merchandise or trends in the marketplace
- Developing good working relationships with vendors
- Overseeing assistant buyers

Salaries

Annual earnings for Buyers can range from approximately $23,000 to $75,000 or more depending on a number of variables. These include the size, prestige, and geographic location of the specific employers as well as the experience, responsibilities, and education of the individual.

Employment Prospects

Employment prospects for Buyers are good. Individuals may find employment in a variety of retail or wholesale outlets throughout the country. These might include large retail organizations, small stores, department stores, specialty stores, or chain stores. The greatest opportunities will exist in areas hosting large numbers of retail and wholesale outlets.

Advancement Prospects

Advancement prospects for Buyers are good. After obtaining experience, Buyers may climb the career ladder by moving to a department managing a larger volume of merchandise resulting in increased responsibilities and earnings. An individual might also become a senior buyer, purchasing manager, or merchandising manager.

Education and Training

Educational requirements vary depending on the specific employer. While there are exceptions, most employers prefer to hire Buyers holding college degrees. Depending on the size of the organization, employers usually prefer to hire individuals with a minimum of an associate's or bachelor's degree.

Good majors for this type of career include business, retailing, merchandising, and marketing, among others. These are useful because many schools with majors in these fields work with employers on internship and placement programs. Once on the job, individuals often go through either formal or informal training programs.

Experience, Skills, and Personality Traits

Generally Buyers begin their careers as trainees, junior buyers, and assistant buyers. Some companies promote qualified employees to assistant buyer positions. Others recruit and train college graduates as assistant buyers. One way or the other, individuals must have experience for this position.

Buyers should be motivated, confident individuals with an interest in merchandising. They should be good at planning and decision making. Good judgment is essential. Successful Buyers need the ability to predict sales trends and anticipate consumer preferences.

Buyers should have good communications skills. The ability to deal with stress and pressure is necessary.

Unions/Associations

Buyers might belong to a number of associations including the American Collegiate Retailing Association (ACRA), American Purchasing Society, Inc. (APS) or the National Association of Purchasing Management, Inc. (NAPM). Individuals might also obtain additional career information from the National Retail Federation (NRF).

Tips for Entry

1. Make sure that you register with the placement office at your college. Retail recruiters often work with these placement offices.
2. Check out the websites of stores in which you're interested in working. Many have employment opportunities on the site.
3. Jobs can often be located on-line too. Look at some of the major sites such as www.hotjobs.com.
4. Positions are often advertised in the classified sections of newspapers under headings including "Retail Opportunities," "Retail," "Buyer," and "Purchasing Professional."

ASSISTANT BUYER

CAREER PROFILE

Duties: Assist buyer in determining which products are best; handle clerical duties; help buyer in locating suppliers and vendors; handle customer service

Alternate Titles: Junior Buyer

Salary Range: $19,000 to $29,000+

Employment Prospects: Good

Advancement Prospects: Good

Best Geographical Location(s) for Position: Jobs may be located throughout the country; large cities will offer more possibilities

Prerequisites:

Education and Training—College degree and/or executive training program

Experience—Experience requirements vary

Special Skills and Personality Traits—Clerical skills; leadership; self-confidence; communication skills; organization; ability to foresee trends

CAREER LADDER

```
┌─────────────────────────────┐
│           Buyer             │
└─────────────────────────────┘

┌─────────────────────────────┐
│       Assistant Buyer       │
└─────────────────────────────┘

┌─────────────────────────────┐
│  College Student or Trainee │
└─────────────────────────────┘
```

Position Description

The job of buyers can be tremendous. Generally, they have one or more Assistant Buyers to help them handle their responsibilities. The Assistant Buyer may have varied depending on the specific employer and the structure of the company.

One of the best things about a job as an Assistant Buyer is the opportunity for the individual to watch the buyer do his or her job. From this experience, the Assistant learns the ropes. The individual starts out handling routine functions. He or she might, for example handle records and do clerical work. As part of that function, the Assistant might check that orders go out and verify that shipments come in.

As the individual gains more experience, he or she will be assigned projects with more responsibilities. The buyer may ask the Assistant to write special orders or reorders of merchandise which is selling well. As part of the job, the individual might also check on stock and keep the buyer appraised of the status of that stock. If something is selling particularly well, the Assistant must alert the buyer so more can be ordered. On the other hand, if something isn't moving, an alert by the Assistant can help the buyer decide to do price markdowns so the merchandise moves.

Gradually, the Assistant will learn more about dealing with vendors. He or she might sit in on meetings with vendors or accompany the Buyer on buying trips. The individual may also attend other meetings, trade shows, and conferences as well as visit vendors' plants and distribution centers. In this manner he or she can learn about examining products as well as assessing the vendor's production and distribution capabilities. It's essential at this point that the Assistant become familiar with consumer trends so he or she will begin to understand what types of merchandise will sell and what won't.

Depending on the situation, the Assistant may work with a buyer responsible for the merchandise for an entire store or may work with a buyer responsible for one or more specific departments. An individual working in a large department store may, for example, work as the Assistant Toy Buyer, Assistant Children's Clothing Buyer, or Assistant Domestics Buyer.

Sometimes the difference between merchandise selling and not selling is the way it is presented. Assistant Buyers often work closely with the store's salespeople to make sure merchandise is displayed attractively. Individuals may help the sales staff choose which merchandise should be presented in windows or on wall or stand-alone displays.

Additional duties of Assistant Buyers might include:

- Studying sales record and inventory levels of current stock to see what is selling and what is not
- Handling special orders for customers
- Visiting the selling floor to assure products are displayed properly
- Overseeing inventory counts

Salaries

Annual earnings for Assistant Buyers can range from approximately $19,000 to $29,000 or more depending on a number of variables. These include the size, prestige, and geographic location of the specific employer as well as the experience, responsibilities, and education of the individual.

Employment Prospects

Employment prospects for Assistant Buyers are good. Individuals may find employment in a variety of retail or wholesale outlets throughout the country. These might include large retail organizations, small stores, department stores, specialty stores, or chain stores. The greatest opportunities will exist in areas hosting large numbers of retail and wholesale outlets.

Advancement Prospects

Advancement prospects are good for motivated individuals. After obtaining experience, Assistant Buyers may climb the career ladder by becoming full-fledged buyers.

Education and Training

Educational requirements vary depending on the specific employer. While there are exceptions, most employers prefer to hire Assistant Buyers holding college degrees. Based on the size or the organization, employers usually prefer to hire individuals with a minimum of an associate's or bachelor's degree.

Appropriate majors for this type of career include business, retailing, merchandising, and marketing. These are useful because many schools with majors in these fields work with employers on internships and placement programs. Generally, once on the job, individuals go through either formal or informal training programs.

Experience, Skills, and Personality Traits

Assistant Buyers often start their careers on the sales floor. Many individuals have been recruited from colleges.

Assistant Buyers should be eager to learn. Individuals need to be motivated and confident with an interest in merchandising. Clerical skills are often necessary when assisting the buyer. Good communications skills are essential, as is the ability to deal with stress and pressure.

Unions/Associations

Assistant buyers might belong to a number of associations including the American Collegiate Retailing Association (ACRA), American Purchasing Society, Inc. (APS) or the National Association of Purchasing Management, Inc. (NAPM). Individuals might also obtain additional career information from the National Retail Federation (NRF).

Tips for Entry

1. Contact stores you are interested in working at to find out if they offer executive training programs.
2. Make sure that you register with the placement office at your college. Retail recruiters often work with these placement offices.
3. Check out the websites of stores where you're interested in working. Many have employment opportunities on the site.
4. Jobs can often be located on-line too. Look at some of the major sites such as www.hotjobs.com.
5. Positions are often advertised in the classified sections of newspapers under headings including "Retail Opportunities," "Retail," "Assistant Buyer," and "Junior Buyer."
6. Contact executive recruiters specializing in the retail industry. Make sure you check ahead of time to see who pays the fee when you get the job—you or the employer.

ADVERTISING DIRECTOR—RETAIL STORE

CAREER PROFILE

Duties: Plan, develop, and implement print, broadcast, or Internet advertising campaigns for retail store

Alternate Titles: Ad Manager; Advertising Manager; Director of Advertising

Salary Range: $24,000 to $75,000+

Employment Prospects: Fair

Advancement Prospects: Fair

Best Geographical Location(s) for Position: Jobs may be located throughout the country

Prerequisites:

Education and Training—Bachelor's degree in advertising, business, journalism, public relations, marketing, liberal arts, English, communications, or business

Experience—Experience in retail advertising necessary

Special Skills and Personality Traits—Creativity; ability to handle details; knowledge of retail industry; knowledge of copywriting, graphics, and layout

CAREER LADDER

```
┌─────────────────────────────────────┐
│   Advertising Director in Larger     │
│ or More Prestigious Store, Marketing │
│    Director, or V.P. of Advertising  │
└─────────────────────────────────────┘

┌─────────────────────────────────────┐
│  Advertising Director—Retail Store   │
└─────────────────────────────────────┘

┌─────────────────────────────────────┐
│    Assistant Advertising Director    │
│     or Advertising Assistant         │
└─────────────────────────────────────┘
```

Position Description

In any given area, there are an array of stores from which customers can choose to shop. In order to attract potential shoppers, most retail stores advertise in some manner. The individual responsible for the advertising is called the Advertising Director.

Retail stores utilize advertising for a number of reasons. It helps people learn what a specific store carries. Advertising also lets customers know when products are on sale. Additionally, advertising helps put the name of a store in the public's mind and eye.

A retail store can carry just the right product that everyone wants at a lower price than their competitors. However, if no one knows it's available and few people are familiar with the store, the product will not sell. One of the functions of the Retail Advertising Director is making sure this doesn't happen.

The Retail Advertising Director plans, develops, and implements the advertising campaigns and individual ads for the store. Those working in the corporate offices of retail chains will be responsible for handling the advertising for the entire chain.

In smaller stores the Advertising Director may work alone or with the help of an assistant and perhaps a graphic designer. In larger stores or in the corporate office, the Advertising Director will work with a staff. This might include an assistant advertising director, advertising assistants, graphic artists, art directors, copywriters, or producers.

The Advertising Director works closely with the store's marketing director. Together they plan the direction of the store's marketing and advertising campaigns.

The Advertising Director develops and plans the store's annual advertising budget. Depending on the store or chain, this may encompass weekly sales flyers, inserts in newspapers, print ads in newspapers and magazines, radio and television commercials, and billboards. Advertising may also include promotions, promotional merchandise, and other items used to draw attention to the store and its merchandise.

Today, many retail stores advertise on the World Wide Web utilizing banner ads and other advertisements. Additionally, many traditional retail stores now also have on-line stores. The Advertising Director must be able to advertise both effectively.

The Advertising Director must develop ad campaigns and single ads which are memorable and effective. Many stores such as K-Mart, Wal-Mart, and Target have continuing advertising themes carried through in their print, television, and Internet ads. This helps keep the name of the store in the public's mind. In many circumstances, the individual will develop ads and campaigns for the entire year. These may include advertising for holidays, promotions, special events, and sales programs.

Most stores feel that as long as they have people walking through and browsing, they will have shoppers. While these people may not make immediate purchases, they may buy at a later date. The Advertising Director works with the marketing, promotional, and public relations departments to develop ads and campaigns that will help make as many people as possible aware of what the store offers.

Depending on the size and structure of the specific retail store, the Advertising Director may be required to do copywriting, graphics, layout, and production for advertisements and commercials or may work with copywriters, graphic artists, and producers. He or she might also lay out rough ideas for advertisements and have the publication's or broadcast station's advertising department put the ad together. In some instances, the Advertising Director may also work with advertising agencies that handle some of these functions.

As part of the job, the Advertising Director is expected to decide what media to place ads in or on, specific sections of publications to have ads inserted and when to schedule broadcast commercials. He or she is responsible for making sure all advertisements and commercials have accurate copy and graphics and are mailed or delivered to the correct media before deadline.

Additional duties of the Retail Advertising Directors may include:

- Developing and putting together weekly advertising flyers
- Tracking tear sheets, clippings, visual cuts, and audiotapes
- Checking bills for ad placement and authorizing payment
- Advertising special events and promotions store is hosting
- Working on cooperative ads or billboards with malls in which their stores are located

Salaries

Salaries for Advertising Directors can range from approximately $24,000 to $75,000 or more annually. Factors affecting earnings include the size and prestige of the specific store, as well as its geographic location. Other factors include the store's advertising budget and whether the individual is responsible for the advertising for one store or an entire retail chain. Other variables include the responsibilities, experience, and education of the individual.

In addition to a salary, some Retail Advertising Directors also receive bonuses when there are sales increases in given sales periods.

Employment Prospects

Employment prospects are fair for Retail Advertising Directors. Individuals may find employment throughout the country in a variety of retail outlets. These include small, midsized, and large stores, chain and department stores, supermarkets, convenience stores, and more.

Advancement Prospects

Retail Advertising Directors may climb the career ladder in a number of ways. Some individuals find similar positions in larger or more prestigious stores. Others may become directors of retail marketing. Still others may be promoted to the vice president of Advertising. There are also individuals who find positions in advertising agencies or become advertising directors in other industries.

Education and Training

Most employers require or prefer their Retail Advertising Directors hold a minimum of a four-year college degree. Good choices for majors include advertising, business, journalism, public relations, retail, marketing, liberal arts, English, communications, and business.

Courses and seminars in advertising, copywriting, business, or retail management are also helpful.

Experience, Skills, and Personality Traits

Retail Advertising Directors should be creative people with an understanding of both advertising and the retail industry. Individuals are often asked to show their portfolio of ads and campaigns prior to being hired. These are used to illustrate talent to potential employers.

Advertising Directors working in retail need the ability to communicate well, both verbally and on paper. Experience working in advertising in the retail industry is usually required.

Individuals need the knowledge to develop both single ads and entire advertising campaigns which are successful and effective. The ability to work on multiple projects at one time and meet deadlines is essential.

Unions/Associations

Retail Advertising Directors may belong to a number of trade associations providing support and guidance. These may include the American Advertising Federation (AAF), the Business/Professional Advertising Association (B/PAA) and the American Marketing Association (AMA). Individuals interested in this type of career might also contact the National Retail Federation (NRF) and the American Collegiate Retailing Association (ACRA) for additional information.

Tips for Entry

1. Join trade associations and attend their meetings and conventions. These are invaluable sources of information and networking opportunities.

2. Positions are often advertised in the classified sections of newspapers. Keep in mind the Sunday paper usually has the largest classified section. Look under headings including "Advertising," "Marketing," "Advertising Director," or "Retail Opportunities." Stores also often advertise a number of opportunities in a boxed classified ad.

3. Send your resume and a cover letter to specific retail stores as well as to their corporate offices. Ask that your resume be kept on file.

4. Larger chain stores often offer internship or summer jobs as assistants. Contact both stores in your area and corporate offices of chains to check into the possibilities.

5. Take seminars and courses in advertising, promotion, public relations, marketing, and publicity.

6. A good way to gain experience in advertising is to work in the advertising department of a local newspaper, magazine, or television or radio station.

7. Start working on your portfolio now. Make it diverse and full of your best work. As noted, a good portfolio can get you a job.

DIRECTOR OF REAL ESTATE—STORE

CAREER PROFILE

Duties: Find properties to locate stores; visit properties and sites to make appraisals and evaluations; do selections of stores within shopping centers; negotiate business terms and conditions

Alternate Titles: Real Estate Director; Leasing Director

Salary Range: $35,000 to $150,000+

Employment Prospects: Fair

Advancement Prospects: Fair

Best Geographical Location(s) for Position: Jobs may be located throughout the country

Prerequisites:

Education and Training—Educational requirements vary

Experience—Experience working in real estate and leasing necessary

Special Skills and Personality Traits—Negotiating skills; problem solving skills; communications skills; ability to deal well with people; assertive

CAREER LADDER

```
┌─────────────────────────────────────┐
│         V.P. of Real Estate          │
└─────────────────────────────────────┘

┌─────────────────────────────────────┐
│        Director of Real Estate        │
└─────────────────────────────────────┘

┌─────────────────────────────────────┐
│         Real Estate Manager           │
│    or Assistant Real Estate Manager   │
└─────────────────────────────────────┘
```

Position Description

There are many places retail stores can be located. These include indoor malls and shopping centers, outdoor strip centers, stand alone stores, and more. Many retail stores, most notably chains, employ Directors of Real Estate. These individuals, also known as Leasing Directors, are the people who are responsible for finding just the right locations for retail stores.

Within the scope of the job, the Director of Real Estate may have varied duties. His or her main function is to find the perfect location for the retail chain's stores. Depending on the size and structure of the real estate department, the individual may be assisted by one or more managers, assistants, and other staff members.

The Director of Real Estate is often contacted by the corporate office when they determine that they are interested in opening new stores in one or more geographic areas. The individual may also be responsible for scouting out new locations where stores might be viable. In some situations a leasing director from a mall may contact the store's Director of Real Estate.

The Director of Real Estate is expected to do extensive research on various locations. He or she often must go to look at properties and sites. The individual may visit malls or other centers to make an evaluation.

The Director of Real Estate may check out things such as the foot traffic, the condition of the mall, and how the management company cares for the property. While at a mall, the Director of Real Estate may stop into mall stores and listen to comments by customers or employees. All this information helps him or her make an informed decision about the viability of a property for a new store.

Once the decision has been made that a store would be viable in a mall, the Real Estate Director is responsible for selecting the specific store within the center.

The Director of Real Estate may contact mall leasing directors or real estate agents representing available properties, or management companies to find out about rents, other charges, and availabilities. The individual may ask for leasing packages or may set up meetings to discuss pertinent information. The Real Estate Director may also visit the various locations to see the physical spaces.

Sometimes the Director of Real Estate may be contacted by malls which are interested in having the Director's stores in the mall. The Director of Real Estate may meet with mall management or other real estate people a number of times before a lease is signed. He or she may ask to see sales figures of other stores, foot traffic reports, or advertising budgets.

The Director of Real Estate negotiates leases. The business terms of the lease may include rents, taxes, CAM (common area maintenance) charges, advertising charges, preparation of the space, length of the lease, options, and kick-out clauses. (A kick-out clause is a clause in a lease whereby a tenant may leave without penalty if certain conditions are not met. For example, not meeting a specified amount of sales.) The Director is expected to make the best deal possible for the store.

The individual may also negotiate for any necessary construction costs before the store can move in. This is especially important with chain stores which often have similar layouts in every location.

The Director of Leasing must keep track of when leases are up for all his or her stores. In this way the individual can handle renewals or exercise any options available according to the lease agreement.

There is a great deal of paperwork in this job. The Director of Leasing must keep immaculate records. He or she must make sure leases incorporate all negotiated points. The individual must also be sure all leases are executed and signed by all parties.

Additional duties of the Director of Leasing for retail stores might include:

- Handling lease administration
- Working with real estate agents
- Dealing with mall management or landlords regarding problems in the mall or on the property
- Attending conventions and other leasing events

Salaries

Real Estate Directors working in retail stores and chains can earn between $35,000 and $150,000 or more. The tremendous range is dependent on a number of factors. Variables affecting earnings include the size, prestige, and geographic location of the property and number of properties the individual is responsible for leasing. Other variables include the experience, responsibilities, and education of the individual.

Employment Prospects

Employment prospects are fair for Directors of Real Estate in a retail chain environment. Individuals may find employment in the corporate offices of a variety of chain and other retail stores. These might include drug stores, department stores, supermarkets, clothing stores, furniture stores, or toy stores.

While jobs may be located throughout the country, individuals may need to relocate for specific positions.

Advancement Prospects

The most common method of career advancement for Directors of Real Estate is to find similar positions in larger, more prestigious companies. Another way an individual may climb the career ladder is to land a position as a vice president of real estate in the retail company. Many Directors of Real Estate strike out on their own and become leasing consultants or form their own leasing companies.

Education and Training

Educational requirements for Directors of Real Estate vary from store to store. Most retail chains today prefer individuals have a college background and degree. There are individuals in this position who hold law degrees or have majors in accounting, retail management, business, marketing, real estate, public administration, finance, liberal arts, or related fields.

While experience is the best teacher, many employers also prefer that individuals have some sort of real estate training. Others require it. Most positions will also prefer or require the Director of Real Estate to hold a real estate agent or broker's license. In order to obtain this licensing, individuals must usually take and pass a written test as well as go through at least 30 hours of classroom instruction to become an agent or 90 hours of training to become a broker.

Professional and trade associations often offer helpful seminars and courses in all aspects of real estate.

Experience, Skills, and Personality Traits

The Director of Real Estate needs a great deal of experience for this position. Many individuals started out in real estate first as salespeople and then as brokers. Others have gone through training programs in retail environments. Some started out as assistant leasing administrators and obtained experience moving up the ranks.

Directors of Real Estate need to be highly motivated, energetic individuals. They should be pleasantly aggressive with the ability to deal with and work well with others. Individuals need to be good problem solvers and negotiators.

Unions/Associations

Directors of Real Estate working in retail chains may be members of a number of associations providing career guidance and support. These include the National Association of Realtors (NAR), local state real estate associations, the Outlet Retail Manufacturers Association (ORMA), the International Council of Shopping Centers (ICSC) and the Institute of Real Estate Management (IREM).

Tips for Entry

1. Many large chain stores offer internship and training programs in this area.

2. There are a number of executive search firms dealing exclusively with jobs in retail.

3. Send your resume and a cover letter to the corporate offices of large chain stores.

4. Positions are often advertised in the classified sections of newspapers. Look under classifications including "Leasing Director," or "Store Leasing Director," or "Retail Leasing Director," "Director of Leasing," or "Real Estate Director-Retail."

5. Openings are also advertised in trade journals.

6. Jobs in this field may be located on-line. Begin your search on some of the more popular job search sites such as Monster board (www.monster.com) and Hot Jobs (www.hotjobs.com).

CASHIER

CAREER PROFILE

Duties: Take payment from customers for purchases; ring up sales; complete credit card transactions; give change to customers

Alternate Titles: Clerk

Salary Range: $5.50 to $10.00+ per hour

Employment Prospects: Excellent

Advancement Prospects: Excellent

Best Geographical Location(s) for Position: Jobs may be located throughout the country

Prerequisites:

Education and Training—On-the-job training

Experience—Experience requirements vary

Special Skills and Personality Traits—Ability to use cash register; basic math skills; people skills; communications skills; good moral character

CAREER LADDER

```
┌─────────────────────────────┐
│     Cashier Supervisor      │
└─────────────────────────────┘

┌─────────────────────────────┐
│          Cashier            │
└─────────────────────────────┘

┌─────────────────────────────┐
│        Entry Level          │
└─────────────────────────────┘
```

Position Description

Cashiers are the individuals responsible for taking the payment from customers for their purchases. Within the scope of the job, Cashiers may perform varied duties.

After customers choose the items they are interested in purchasing they bring them to a Cashier. The individual is expected to ring up the merchandise. This may be done in a variety of ways depending on the situation. Cashiers in grocery stores, for example, might scan the selected items over a special scanning device. Those working in other stores may scan the pricing label or manually punch in prices on a cash register. In some situations, the Cashier may ring up a price from a sales slip prepared by a salesperson. In performing this function, the individual may need to punch in certain codes to make sure correct taxes are charged.

After the Cashier rings up the customer's purchases, he or she informs the customer the amount that is due. The customer may pay the amount due in a number of different methods. These include cash, check, or a credit card.

If the customer chooses to pay in cash, the Cashier must make sure he or she gives the individual the correct amount of change. In the event the customer is paying by check, the Cashier is expected to follow the correct procedures. For example, the individual may need to take down identifying information from the customer's license or may need to get approval from a supervisor for accepting the check.

Many people pay with credit cards or debit cards. In these cases, the Cashier must complete the transactions according to procedures. This may include getting approval from the credit card company for putting through the charge. The Cashier must also be sure the customer signs the credit card slip and that he or she gets a copy of the transaction.

At the end of his or her shift, the individual compares the totals on the cash register with the amount of currency in the register to verify balances. In doing this, he or she must take into account checks and charge slips.

Additional duties of the Cashiers may include:

• Processing refunds
• Taking layaways
• Performing the duties of a salesperson
• Packing merchandise

Salaries

Earnings for Cashiers working in retail environments can range from approximately $5.50 to $10.00 or more per hour. Variables affecting earnings include the geographic location, size, and prestige of the store as well as the experience and responsibilities of the individual. Earnings for Cashiers are also dependent on the demand for employees in a given area.

Employment Prospects

Employment prospects are excellent for Cashiers. Individuals may find work throughout the country in a variety of retail situations including department stores, convenience stores, grocery stores, boutiques, and stores selling every conceivable type of merchandise.

One of the perks for many people seeking this job is the flexibility of working hours. Individuals may work full time, part time, mornings, afternoons, evenings, weekdays, weekends, or holidays.

Advancement Prospects

Advancement prospects for Cashiers depend to a great extent on the individual's career aspirations. Some people take jobs as Cashiers while in school or on a part-time basis to augment other incomes. These individuals usually move on to other types of jobs depending on their training. Others interested in a full-time career in retail, may start out as Cashiers and move into sales positions or cashier supervisors.

Education and Training

Generally, Cashiers are trained on the job. Individuals will learn how to run cash registers and use charge card systems. Most employers prefer people who have a minimum of a high school diploma.

Experience, Skills, and Personality Traits

There are many entry-level positions available as Cashiers as well as those for experienced people. Individuals must have basic math skills with the ability to make change correctly. The ability to handle large sums of money is mandatory. Good interpersonal and customer relations skills are essential as is a pleasant personality. Cashiers are on their feet a good portion of the workday.

Unions/Associations

Cashiers may get additional career information by contacting the National Retail Federation (NRF). Depending on the place of the employment and the specific type of store, Cashiers may be members of unions.

Tips for Entry

1. There is a great deal of turnover in these positions. Stop in stores in which you are interested in working and ask to fill out applications.
2. Openings may be posted in store windows. Look for announcements stating "Cashier Wanted."
3. Jobs may be advertised in the classified sections of newspapers. Look under classifications such as "Cashiers," "Retail Opportunities," "Department Stores," or "Grocery Stores."
4. Remember to bring with you the names, addresses, and phone numbers of a few people you can use as references when filling out applications. Make sure you ask people if you can use them as references BEFORE you use them.
5. Stores often call local labor offices to post these jobs. Remember to stop by your state employment office.

TAILOR—CLOTHING STORE, DEPARTMENT STORE/BOUTIQUE

CAREER PROFILE

Duties: Alter clothing purchased in store to fit individual customers

Alternate Title(s): Seamstress; Alteration Tailor

Salary Range: $23,000 to $50,000+

Employment Prospects: Good

Advancement Prospects: Good

Best Geographical Location(s) for Position: Positions located throughout the country

Prerequisites:

Education and Training—Training requirements vary

Experience and Qualifications—Experience in tailoring, dressmaking, sewing

Special Skills and Personality Traits—Fitting skills; tailoring skills; alteration skills; hand-sewing skills; machine-sewing skills; customer service skills; pleasant; communication skills

CAREER LADDER

```
┌─────────────────────────────────┐
│  Tailor at Larger, More Prestigious │
│   Store or Boutique or Supervisor   │
│      of Alteration Workroom        │
└─────────────────────────────────┘

┌─────────────────────────────────┐
│             Tailor              │
└─────────────────────────────────┘

┌─────────────────────────────────┐
│         Tailor Apprentice        │
└─────────────────────────────────┘
```

Position Description

Off-the-rack clothing often does not fit every body perfectly. Sometimes parts of an article of clothing may be too big, too small, too long, too short, or too tight. While there are some people who alter their own clothing and others who may use tailors off-site, many people prefer their clothing to fit correctly when they take it home from a store after a purchase. To handle this function, stores often employ Tailors.

An on-site Tailor is a customer service many customers appreciate. Tailors are coveted employees. A talented on-site Tailor can mean the difference between a customer shopping at one store or shopping at another with similar merchandise. Depending on the store, the service may be offered for a fee or free of charge to customers purchasing the store's clothing.

The main function of Tailors employed by stores is to alter clothing purchased at the store to fit the individual customer. When a customer decides to purchase an item, he or she will either go to the Tailor's office or the Tailor will go to the dressing room. He or she will then have the customer try on the garment. The Tailor may be asked perform a vari-

ety of alterations depending on what is needed and what the customer wants done.

For example, a woman may be purchasing a suit and need the skirt shortened and tapered, and the jacket's sleeves shortened. A man purchasing a suit may need the pants hemmed and buttons moved on the jacket. Individuals may need waistlines expanded or narrowed, collars or shoulders raised or lowered, or buttons changed.

Sometimes alterations are simple. Often they may be more complex. The Tailor must be capable of handling both. Some alterations are done using hand sewing. Others may be accomplished better by machines.

Once the individuals try on the articles of clothing, the Tailor will mark the alterations needed with tailor's chalk and pins. He or she may need to remove stitching from clothing by using a seam ripper or razor. In many instances, the individual will need to cut excess fabric, make the alterations, and resew the garment making sure the drape, style, and proportions are maintained.

A good Tailor knows and uses correct pressing techniques to finish his or her work. In this manner, the garment will appear fresh and finished. In some cases, the Tailor may work with an apprentice, supervising his or her work.

Customers may have an idea of what they want done or may ask the advice of the Tailor. Some people like things looser or tighter. The individual must be able to be communicate with customers so they know what the customer is looking for in fit. It is essential that the customer be pleased when the garment is done.

Other duties of on-site Tailors include:

- Repairing defective garments
- Repairing garments altered by people trying them on
- Replacing buttons or zippers
- Shortening or pressing drapes or other household accessories sold in the store
- Creating headpieces or accessories to go with clothing

Salaries
Salaries for Tailors can vary greatly. Full-time Tailors may have annual earnings ranging from $23,000 to $50,000 or more. Factors affecting earnings include the specific store size, prestige, and geographic location in which the individual is working. Other variables include the experience, responsibilities, and talent of the Tailor. If the individual is in an area with a shortage of Tailors, he or she can also command a higher salary.

In some stores, individuals may be paid a base salary plus a commission on fees charged to customers for tailoring.

Employment Prospects
Employment prospects are good for Tailors. The need for talented Tailors is greater than the number of qualified people available to handle the jobs. Individuals may find employment throughout the country both full time or part time.

Possible employment includes department stores, specialty clothing stores, and boutiques for men and women.

Advancement Prospects
Tailors generally climb the career ladder by locating similar positions at either larger, more exclusive, or more prestigious stores. Some Tailors advance their careers by becoming supervisors of alteration workrooms in large stores. Still others strike out on their own.

Education and Training
Many Tailors are self-taught. Others have attended classes, courses, and workshops or have gone through certificate programs in tailoring from vocational-technical schools. Some Tailors apprentice with experienced Tailors to learn the tricks of the trade. As a rule, if an individual can prove he or she can handle the job skillfully, there are no education or training requirements.

Experience, Skills, and Personality Traits
Tailors need experience handling a variety of alterations. No retail store wants a Tailor coming in and ruining an article of clothing a customer has purchased.

Tailors need a full working knowledge of hand- and machine-sewing techniques. They must be experts at tailoring, fitting techniques, and alterations. Customer service skills and communications skills are essential.

Unions/Associations
Those interested in learning more about careers as Tailors can obtain information from the National Retail Federation (NRF).

Tips for Entry
1. Try to find an experienced Tailor with whom you can apprentice. This will give you the best experience.
2. Jobs are often advertised in the classified sections of newspapers. Look under classifications such as "Retail," "Retail Opportunities," "Tailor," or "Seamstress."
3. Take as many classes, workshops, and seminars as you can. Each one will give you the opportunity to learn a new technique.
4. Contact the human resources manager of department stores to find if you can fill out an employment application. Ask that your application be kept on file. Check back frequently.
5. Don't forget to check out boutiques, men's clothing stores, wedding boutiques, and specialty stores for job possibilities.
6. Look for help wanted signs in store windows.

BILLING MANAGER—DEPARTMENT OR SPECIALTY STORE

CAREER PROFILE

Duties: Oversee billing department; supervise billing clerks; look into errors and discrepancies on customer bills; handle customer service

Alternate Titles: Billing Supervisor

Salary Range: $24,000 to $45,000+

Employment Prospects: Fair

Advancement Prospects: Fair

Best Geographical Location(s) for Position: Jobs may be located throughout the country; areas hosting many large department stores will offer more opportunities

Prerequisites:

Education and Training—Training requirements vary
Experience—Experience working in retail billing office necessary
Special Skills and Personality Traits—Aptitude for numbers; orderly; detail oriented; office skills; computer skills; communication skills; good judgment; customer relations skills

CAREER LADDER

```
┌─────────────────────────────┐
│   Billing Manager in Larger │
│   or More Prestigious Store │
└─────────────────────────────┘

┌─────────────────────────────┐
│      Billing Manager        │
└─────────────────────────────┘

┌─────────────────────────────┐
│   Entry Level or Bookkeeping│
│   or Accounting Clerk       │
└─────────────────────────────┘
```

Position Description

Depending on a store's policies there are a number of methods customers can use to pay for merchandise. These include cash, checks, major credit cards, and store charge cards among others. Stores that have their own charge cards or allow customers to charge merchandise usually employ a Billing Manager.

When customers use store credit cards, they sign a slip promising to pay for their purchases. Some stores may not utilize store credit cards for charges. Instead, customers may just sign charge slips when making a purchase. Whatever the method of charges, the store must keep track of customer purchases and monies owed.

The Billing Manager has a number of different responsibilities depending on the size and structure of the store and the setup of the billing department. His or her main function is to oversee the billing department.

The Billing Manager coordinates and supervises the activities of the other employees in the department. These may include an assistant billing manager or supervisor, billing clerks, and sometimes credit clerks.

The Billing Manager trains each employee so he or she can accomplish assigned tasks. Today, most billing statements are computer generated. Some stores also utilize billing machines or special billing software to help prepare monthly statements. The individual may show employees how to run computer or billing machines as well as explain how to use the software effectively.

The Billing Manager must make sure billing clerks fully understand everything about monthly statements. This includes purchases, late charges, finance charges, and unpaid balances. It also includes customer discounts and credits of payments previously made. In some stores there are special codes for each charge. The Manager also must be sure the staff knows what each of these codes represents. This is essential when customers call to complain about errors on a bill. Sometimes there truly is an error. Other times, the customer may not understand how to read the monthly statement.

The Billing Manager assists billing clerks when they can not fully explain statements to customers. He or she is also called in when dealing with angry or irate customers. The Billing Manager often has the authority to take off a late charge or a finance charge on a customer's bill. He or she is always trying to find ways to keep the customer satisfied.

The Billing Manager is responsible for setting the tone for customer service in the billing department. It is essential to a store's success for everyone working there to make a customer feel that he or she is appreciated. This is especially important in the billing department where customers usually call when there is a problem. The Manager tries to teach the staff how to maintain a good relationship with each customer.

In some stores, the Billing Manager may be expected to supervise the monitoring of customers' payments to make sure they are updated. In other stores, this may be handled by the collection department.

Other duties of the Billing Manager may include:

- Writing letters and other correspondence regarding customers' bills
- Answering customers' questions regarding billings
- Developing policies for the billing department
- Recommending salary increases for department employees
- Recommending termination of employees

Salaries

Annual earnings for Billing Managers working in retail stores can range from approximately $24,000 to $45,000 or more. Variables affecting earnings include the geographic location, size, and prestige of the specific store as well as the experience, education, and responsibilities of the individual.

Employment Prospects

Employment prospects are fair for Billing Managers. Individuals may find jobs in both larger department stores and smaller local stores throughout the country.

Advancement Prospects

Billing Managers working in retail environments can climb the career ladder by landing similar jobs in larger or more prestigious stores. This results in increased responsibilities and earnings.

Education and Training

Educational requirements vary. Some stores require or prefer their Billing Managers to hold a college degree or at least have some college background. Other stores may hire individuals with a minimum of a high school diploma if they have experience and can illustrate that they can handle the job effectively.

Courses in bookkeeping, accounting, computers, and accounting software are helpful.

Experience, Skills, and Personality Traits

Billing Managers should like working with numbers. The ability to solve problems is needed. Individuals should be organized and detail oriented. Customer service skills and the ability to calm irate customers is necessary. Supervisory and leadership skills are also needed.

Unions/Associations

Billing Managers interested in working in retail environment may get additional career information by contacting the National Retail Federation (NRF).

Tips for Entry

1. Jobs may be advertised in the classified sections of newspapers. Look under headings such as "Billing Manager," "Retail Opportunities," "Billing Department," "Billing Supervisor," and "Department Store Opportunities." Positions may also be located in the ads of specific stores.
2. Visit the human resources office of larger stores to fill out an application. In smaller stores, ask to see the manager. Ask that your application be kept on file if there are no current openings.
3. Many larger chain stores have internship and training programs. Contact the corporate offices to find out about opportunities.
4. Department stores often promote from within. Get your foot in the door in the billing department, learn what you can, and climb the career ladder.

BILLING CLERK—DEPARTMENT STORE OR SPECIALTY STORE

CAREER PROFILE

Duties: Produce bills used to settle customer accounts; send bills to customers; correct errors on customer's bills

Alternate Titles: Billing Representative

Salary Range: $7.00 to $25.00+ per hour

Employment Prospects: Fair

Advancement Prospects: Fair

Best Geographical Location(s) for Position: Jobs may be located throughout the country; areas hosting many large department stores will offer more opportunities

Prerequisites:

Education and Training—High school diploma or equivalent; on-the-job training; additional training may be required

Experience—Billing or bookkeeping experience preferred, but not always required

Special Skills and Personality Traits—Aptitude for numbers; orderly; detail oriented; office skills; computer skills; communication skills; good judgment; customer relations skills

CAREER LADDER

```
┌─────────────────────────────────┐
│  Billing Supervisor or Manager  │
└─────────────────────────────────┘

┌─────────────────────────────────┐
│         Billing Clerk           │
└─────────────────────────────────┘

┌─────────────────────────────────┐
│   Entry Level or Bookkeeping    │
│     or Accounting Clerk         │
└─────────────────────────────────┘
```

Position Description

Stores make money by selling merchandise to customers. Some customers pay for purchases using cash or checks. Others pay with major credit cards. Many stores also have their own credit cards.

Customers who use these store credit cards may receive special promotions or other considerations. When customers use store credit cards, the store keeps track of purchases. They then send bills to customers. Depending on the store and its structure, bills might be sent monthly or bimonthly.

Billing Clerks work in the billing department. The main function of these individuals is to produce the bills that are used to settle customers' accounts. Billing Clerks take information regarding the customer's purchases and input it into a computer system. They do this by reviewing charge slips to calculate the total amount due from a customer.

Today, most bills are computer generated. Many stores also utilize billing machines or special billing software to help Billing Clerks prepare monthly statements.

Billing Clerks must input information into the computer or billing machine. The individual must be sure the customer's name, address, and account number is correct. In addition to charges for purchases, there may be additional charges. These might include unpaid balances, late charges, and finance charges. Discounts and credits may also be added.

Once bills are prepared, they are printed out. At this point, the Billing Clerk often verifies them for accuracy. The individual is then responsible for sending them to the customer.

Even if bills are computer generated and checked for errors, there may be mistakes. When customers get bills they feel are wrong, they often become angry or irate and call the store to complain. The Billing Clerk is then responsible for checking the bill, trying to find the errors, and preparing a corrected bill. It is essential that the individual practice good customer service skills when speaking to unhappy customers so they feel they are important to the store.

Often the mistake is not a mistake at all. Instead, the customer may be upset about a bill carrying a finance charge he or she does not feel should be included. Perhaps the bill was held up in the mail or the customer forgot to make a payment. Whatever the situation, the Clerk tries to maintain a good relationship with the customer. He or she may, for example, take off the finance charge from a customer's bill or may refer the individual to the billing manager.

In some stores, the Billing Clerk may be expected to monitor customers' payments to make sure they are up to date. If they aren't, the individual may be required to call customers and issue a friendly reminder. In other stores, this may be handled by the collection department.

Many stores have codes for various categories on bills. For example, there may be one code for charges in the men's department, another for charges in the children's department, one for late charges, and yet another for finance charges. The Billing Clerk must be familiar with the codes and have the ability to explain them to customers.

Often customers may call the billing department because they don't understand their bill. Billing Clerks must be able to explain the bills to customers in an easy-to-understand manner.

Other duties of department store Billing Clerks may include:

- Printing out monthly billing and payment reports
- Writing letters and other correspondence regarding customers bills
- Answering customers' questions regarding billings

Salaries

Earnings for Billing Clerks working in retail stores can range from approximately $7.00 to $25 or more per hour. Variables affecting earnings include the geographic location, size, and prestige of the specific store as well as the experience and responsibilities of the individual.

One of the perks for individuals working in stores is that individuals often receive employee discounts.

Employment Prospects

Employment prospects are fair for individuals seeking this position. Jobs may be located in both larger department stores and smaller local stores throughout the country. Depending on the size and structure of the store, there may be one or more Billing Clerks on staff. Individuals may work full or part time.

Advancement Prospects

Billing Clerks working in retail may advance their career in a number of ways. After obtaining experience, individuals may take on additional duties or find similar positions in larger, more prestigious stores. Others may be promoted to billing managers.

Education and Training

Billing Clerks generally must hold a minimum of a high school diploma or the equivalent. Many larger department stores may prefer a college background or some business courses, but don't require it. Classes in bookkeeping, accounting, computers, and accounting software are helpful.

In some situations, the store will provide in-service training in the use of software programs or specific billing procedures used.

Experience, Skills, and Personality Traits

Billing Clerks should have a strong aptitude for numbers. Individuals need to be careful, orderly, and detail oriented. They should be comfortable using computers. There is often a lot of customer contact in this job. The ability to deal well with people is essential. Customer service skills are mandatory.

Unions/Associations

Billing Clerks interested in working in retail environment may get additional career information by contacting the National Retail Federation (NRF). Those working in department stores may belong to house unions.

Tips for Entry

1. Courses and workshops in billing, accounting, and bookkeeping techniques as well as billing software are helpful in making you more marketable.
2. Jobs may be advertised in the classified sections of newspapers. Look under classifications such as "Billing Clerk," "Department Store," "Billing Office," and "Retail Opportunities."
3. Visit the human resources office of larger stores to fill out an application. In smaller stores, ask to see the manager. Ask that your application be kept on file if there are no current openings.
4. Remember to bring with you the names, addresses, and phone numbers of a few people you can use as references when filling out applications. Make sure you ask people if you can use them as references BEFORE you use them.
5. Stores often call local labor offices to post these jobs. Remember to stop by your state employment office.

WINDOW DRESSER

CAREER PROFILE

Duties: Displaying merchandise in retail store windows in a visually pleasing manner

Alternate Titles: Window Designer

Salary Range: $22,000 to $55,000+

Employment Prospects: Fair

Advancement Prospects: Fair

Best Geographical Location(s) for Position: Large metropolitan areas will offer the most opportunities

Prerequisites:

Education and Training—Education and training requirements vary

Experience—Experience designing windows and displays necessary

Special Skills and Personality Traits—Creative; artistic; sense of color and style; good aesthetic judgment

CAREER LADDER

```
┌─────────────────────────────┐
│   Window Dresser in Larger, │
│   More Prestigious Stores   │
└─────────────────────────────┘

┌─────────────────────────────┐
│       Window Dresser        │
└─────────────────────────────┘

┌─────────────────────────────┐
│   Assistant Window Dresser  │
└─────────────────────────────┘
```

Position Description

People often wait with anticipation to see how well-known stores are going to decorate their windows for holiday seasons. Stores such as Saks Fifth Avenue and Bloomingdale's in New York City, for example, may have lines of people waiting to see annual holiday displays. Display windows may showcase products sold in stores as well as attract the attention of potential shoppers.

Every time someone passes by a store's display windows, they are viewing the work of a Window Dresser. In some cases, the person who handles this function may have additional duties, and dress the store's windows as part of his or her job.

Window Dressers are responsible for developing and designing store display windows. Depending on the specific store, they might display clothing and accessories, furniture, CD's, books, computers, software, or food items.

In some cases, the Window Dresser is responsible for creating fantasy windows designed to attract attention instead of just showcasing products sold.

In order to do their job, Window Dressers must know what the store wants to spotlight. The store may want certain products which are currently on sale highlighted in the window. Conversely, they might want to showcase unique products the store sells.

In order to put together aesthetically pleasing windows, the Window Dresser must keep in mind the size, shape, and color of items used in the display. To make the window display exciting, the individual may utilize products or items not sold by the store. The Window Dresser may use prefabricated display items to augment the window or may be responsible for constructing items of various materials. These might include items made of fabric, glass, paper, plastic, or wood, among other things. Sometimes, the Dresser may use items which have movement such as a moving mannequin to create innovative and exciting windows.

Window Dressers may also be responsible for developing interesting displays within the store as well as arranging showcases in a pleasing manner.

No matter what type of project the individual is working on, he or she may be expected to develop sketches ahead of time for approval by store management. These may be done freehand or may be done with the help of a computer.

Additional duties of Window Dressers might include:

- Making changes in window displays as needed
- Dressing mannequins for use in window displays or in displays in other parts of the store
- Adding prices and descriptive signs on backdrops, fixtures, and merchandise

Salaries

Earnings for Window Dressers range from approximately $22,000 to $55,000 or more. Factors affecting earnings include the size, location, and prestige of the specific employer as well as the experience, expertise, and talent of the individual.

Employment Prospects

While employment prospects for Window Dressers can be located throughout the country the greatest number of opportunities will be located in large metropolitan areas where there are more large retail stores. Smaller stores often have other employees handle the functions of the Window Dresser.

Window Dressers are used in a variety of types of stores including department stores, gift shops, furniture stores, and clothing stores. Individuals may be employed on staff or may freelance.

Advancement Prospects

Advancement prospects are difficult to determine. A great deal of advancement for Window Dressers is dependent on the talent, creativity, and aspirations of the individual. The most common method of career advancement for Window Dressers is locating similar positions in larger or more prestigious settings. Some Window Dressers strike out on their own.

Education and Training

Educational requirements for Window Dressers vary. Employers may require individuals to hold a college degree. Good majors include fine art, commercial art, or design. Employers will often hire talented individuals who have proven themselves in this line of work without a college background.

Experience, Skills, and Personality Traits

Some Window Dressers obtained experience putting together store windows and showcases and displays while working in sales. Others worked as assistant Window Dressers prior to their current job.

Successful Window Dressers are creative and artistic. They have a good sense of color, balance, and style. The ability to sketch, draw, and illustrate is helpful in putting together design ideas for windows. Good aesthetic judgment and an eye for detail are essential.

Unions/Associations

Window Designers may get additional information from the National Association of Schools of Art and Design (NASAD).

Tips for Entry

1. Openings may be advertised in the newspaper's classified section under headings including, "Window Dresser," "Window Designer," "Window Design," "Window Display," or "Retail Opportunities."
2. Visit department stores and large retail outlets to see if there are any openings in this area.
3. If you can't find a position right away in a retail outlet, check out design firms and interior design companies.
4. Take pictures of windows and displays you have worked on. Make sure you put together a portfolio of your best work.
5. Check for internships at design firms, interior design firms, department stores, and large retail outlets.

STOCK CLERK

CAREER PROFILE

Duties: Receiving, unpacking, and checking in merchandise; stocking shelves

Alternate Titles: Stock Control Clerk; Inventory Clerk; Shipping Clerk; Receiving Clerk

Salary Range: $5.50 to $7.50+ per hour

Employment Prospects: Good

Advancement Prospects: Good

Best Geographical Location(s) for Position: Jobs may be located throughout the country

Prerequisites:
   Education and Training—On-the-job training
   Experience—No experience required
   Special Skills and Personality Traits—Organized; ability to lift cartons of various weights and sizes

CAREER LADDER

```
┌─────────────────────────────────────┐
│    Stock Clerk in Larger Store,      │
│ Stock Room Manager, or Salesperson   │
└─────────────────────────────────────┘

┌─────────────────────────────────────┐
│            Stock Clerk               │
└─────────────────────────────────────┘

┌─────────────────────────────────────┐
│            Entry Level               │
└─────────────────────────────────────┘
```

Position Description

Stock Clerks have a number of different responsibilities depending on the specific size and structure of the store in which they are working. Their main functions are receiving, unpacking, storing, and tracking merchandise.

Stock Clerks check the merchandise as it comes into the store. This is usually done in the stock room. They might check the number of items and the descriptions of each to be sure that they match packing slips. Individuals might also be responsible for inspecting goods for damage or spoilage.

Stock Clerks may be expected to track merchandise which has been received. They will keep records of merchandise which enters the stock room as well as merchandise that leaves. In many situations, Stock Clerks will be responsible for scanning items into computer systems so that the store knows what is in the inventory. This makes it easier to locate merchandise quickly and easily.

Stock Clerks sort, organize, and mark items with codes which identify the merchandise. This may include prices and stock or inventory control codes. This is often done with hand-held scanners connected to computers. This is necessary to keep inventories in stores up to date.

Stock Clerks bring merchandise to the sales floor and stock shelves and racks as needed. This may be done during store hours or after hours.

Most stores have stock rooms where extra merchandise is stored. Stock Clerks keep it organized until it is ready for display. They may place merchandise in bins, on floors, or on shelves, as well as organize merchandise in an orderly fashion.

In large stores, the Stock Clerk may be expected to handle more specific tasks such as inventory, receiving, or stocking shelves. In smaller stores, the individual will be expected to handle more general stocking duties.

Additional duties of Stock Clerks might include:

• Unpacking cartons of merchandise
• Repacking merchandise
• Checking inventory for specific items
• Handling the duties of a salesperson

Salaries

Stock Clerks earn between $5.50 and $7.50 per hour or more. Variables affecting earnings include the size and geographic location of the store and the experience and responsibilities of the individual.

Employment Prospects

Openings for Stock Clerks can be found throughout the country. The greatest number of openings are located in grocery stores and department stores. Large urban areas hosting a great many shopping centers, groceries, and warehouses will offer the most opportunities.

Advancement Prospects

This is an entry-level position. Advancement prospects are based, to a great extent, on the individual's career aspirations. Individuals may find similar positions at larger stores resulting in increased responsibilities and higher earnings. Others may climb the career ladder by becoming an inventory or stock room manager. Some people move into sales positions.

Education and Training

Generally there is informal on-the-job training provided by the employer. Most employers prefer to hire those who hold a high school diploma or the equivalent or those who are still in school. However, there are many who will hire able people who are eager to work no matter what their educational background.

Experience, Skills, and Personality Traits

As noted previously, this is an entry-level position. As a rule, no prior experience is needed. Stock Clerks should be organized people with stamina. Communications skills are helpful as are computer skills.

Unions/Associations

Depending on the type of store in which the individual works, Stock Clerks might be members of the United Food and Commercial Workers International Union or house unions. Individuals may also get additional career information by contacting the National Retail Federation (NRF).

Tips for Entry

1. There is a great deal of turnover in these positions. Stop in stores and ask the manager if you can fill out an application.

2. Remember to bring the names, addresses, and phone numbers of a few people you can use as references when filling out applications. Make sure you ask people if you can use them as references BEFORE you use them.

3. Look in the classified section of newspapers under heading classifications such as "Retail," "Retail Opportunities," "Stock Clerks," "Inventory Clerks," "Department Stores," or "Grocery Stores."

4. Many stores post job openings in windows. Visit your local mall, department store, or grocery store to check out possibilities.

5. Stores often call local labor offices to post these jobs. Remember to stop by your state employment office.

TRAINER—RETAIL

CAREER PROFILE

Duties: Facilitate classes, seminars, workshops, and other training programs for store employees; prepare training programs

Alternate Titles: Facilitator

Salary Range: $25,000 to $55,000+

Employment Prospects: Fair

Advancement Prospects: Fair

Best Geographical Location(s) for Position: Positions may be located throughout the country

Prerequisites:
Education and Training—College degree preferred
Experience—Experience in training and workshop facilitation
Special Skills and Personality Traits—Leadership skills; communications skills; interpersonal skills; employee relations; writing skills; public-speaking skills; creative; organized

CAREER LADDER

```
┌─────────────────────────────┐
│      Training Manager       │
└─────────────────────────────┘

┌─────────────────────────────┐
│          Trainer            │
└─────────────────────────────┘

┌─────────────────────────────┐
│      College Student        │
│ or Human Resources Associate │
└─────────────────────────────┘
```

Position Description

Trainers working in a retail environment are responsible for preparing and conducting training programs for the company's employees. Depending on the situation and the retail outlet, the individual may train employees to perform specific jobs, customer service skills, selling techniques, or the use of products and merchandise being sold.

Trainers may work under the direction of a human resources director, training manager, or store manager. They confer with management on training needs for the specific retail outlet. Once training needs are identified, the individual must formulate an outline for training sessions. These must include content as well as methods. Some Trainers use comedy in their presentations. Others are more straightforward. The Trainer will use the most effective methods to ensure employees understand the material and can put it to use.

Trainers may present material in a variety of formats. They may facilitate workshops or seminars, or give demonstrations. Some Trainers set up meetings and conferences or give lectures to present material. In some situations, Trainers also may work with employees on a one-on-one basis.

Trainers may prepare handouts, overheads, slides, or PowerPoint presentations to help employees absorb and understand needed skills. They may be expected to develop booklets or other training materials.

Trainers may be responsible for developing and facilitating programs for employees in a variety of subjects depending on the needs of the employer. For example, some stores may have Trainers conduct sessions for all new employees on providing excellent customer service. Other Trainers may be expected to work with employees on handling specialized skills.

Some Trainers may develop and facilitate orientation programs for new employees. During orientation, employees will learn the policies of the retail outlet. The orientation program may also explain to employees the way they are expected to act on the job and responses to difficult situations that are acceptable as well as unacceptable.

No matter the type of retail outlet, good customer service can mean the difference between success and failure. It is therefore essential that each and every employee treat customers in a courteous and gracious manner. An important function of Trainers is teaching employees what good customer service is and how it should be provided.

Trainers may offer classes for management in learning how to communicate with their employees. Other subjects covered in this type of class may include acceptable methods for disciplining employees and how to speak to subordinates without coming across abruptly. The individual may also develop classes for employees dealing with and avoiding sexual harassment in the workplace.

Trainers may also be expected to provide classes specific to certain jobs such as cashiers, salespeople, customer service, or call center representatives.

Other duties of the Trainers may include:

- Training employees in teamwork skills
- Facilitating programs to teach department directors, managers, and supervisors methods of conducting training within their department
- Teaching department directors, managers, and supervisors proper procedures for interview techniques and handling employment reviews

Salaries

Annual earnings for Trainers working in retail environments can range from approximately $25,000 to $50,000 or more. Factors affecting earnings include the geographic location, size, type, and prestige of the specific store. Other factors include the education, experience, and responsibilities of the individual.

Employment Prospects

Employment prospects are fair for Trainers working in retail environments. Individuals may find employment in either the local or corporate office of department stores, chains, or specialty stores. Other opportunities exist for Trainers in call centers or catalog houses.

It should be noted that not every retail outlet employs a Trainer. In many instances, a training manager, human resources director, or even the store manager may handle training functions.

Advancement Prospects

Trainers working in retail environments may advance their careers in a number of ways. Some locate similar positions in larger or more prestigious stores. Others climb the career ladder by becoming training managers. Still others may strike out on their own and become corporate training consultants.

Education and Training

Educational requirements vary from employer to employer. Most require or prefer individuals to hold a minimum of a bachelor's degree. Good majors for those interested in this field might include human resources, communications, retail, business, public relations, marketing, liberal arts, or a related field. There are also stores which may accept individuals with a high school diploma and experience in training, human resources, or the retail industry.

Individuals training employees in a special skill such as selling computers may be hired whatever their educational background as long as they have the ability to train people with easy to understand, effective methods.

Experience, Skills, and Personality Traits

Experience requirements vary. Generally experience in training and development is required or preferred. Additional experience in retailing also may be needed. Some employers will hire individuals out of college who have gone through internship programs.

Good Trainers have the ability to motivate others. They know how to explain things so they are easy to understand and remember.

Individuals should have excellent people and employee-relations skills. They must also have both good verbal and written communications skills. The ability to speak effectively in front of people is essential to this position.

Unions/Associations

Those interested in learning more about careers in this field should contact the American Society of Training Developers (ASTD) and the Society for Human Resources Management (SHRM).

Tips for Entry

1. Become either an active or affiliate member of the American Society of Training Developers (ASTD). This may give you the edge over another applicant with the same qualifications.
2. If you have the opportunity, go to some of the ASTD seminars and workshops. These are valuable for the learning opportunity as well as networking possibilities.
3. Openings are often advertised on the Internet. They may be located via the home pages of department stores, chains, specialty stores, call centers, and catalogs.
4. Positions may be advertised in the classified sections of newspapers. Look under classifications such as "Trainer," "Training and Development," "Retail Opportunities," or "Human Resources."
5. You may be asked to conduct an impromptu training presentation as part of your interview process. Develop a sample program ahead of time and rehearse before the interview.

PROMOTIONS MANAGER—RETAIL STORE

CAREER PROFILE

Duties: Develop, create, and implement promotions for retail store to attract shoppers and create advertising tie-ins

Alternate Titles: Promotions Director

Salary Range: $26,000 to $52,000+

Employment Prospects: Fair

Advancement Prospects: Fair

Best Geographical Location(s) for Position: Jobs may be located throughout the country

Prerequisites:

Education and Training—Bachelor's degree preferred

Experience—Experience in promotions, advertising, marketing special events, publicity, or public relations preferred

Special Skills and Personality Traits—Creativity; detail oriented; imagination; innovation; communications skills; knowledge of retail industry

CAREER LADDER

```
┌─────────────────────────────────┐
│      Director of Marketing,      │
│  Public Relations, or Advertising │
└─────────────────────────────────┘


┌─────────────────────────────────┐
│       Promotions Manager         │
└─────────────────────────────────┘


┌─────────────────────────────────┐
│  Publicity or Promotion Assistant │
└─────────────────────────────────┘
```

Position Description

Many retail stores utilize a variety of promotions throughout the year to attract customers. The programs are designed to keep customers who have already shopped at the store as well as to bring in new ones.

Retail stores generally plan promotions well in advance. Generally, the Promotions Manager must prepare an annual calendar of promotions. In this way the advertising and marketing department will be able to adequately advertise and publicize the promotions.

Depending on the specific situation, Promotions Managers often plan the special sales stores have throughout the year. These may include, for example, seasonal sales such as January white sales, February president's birthday sales, "Spring Into Summer" sales, "July 4th blowouts," back to school sales, and Christmas sales.

Some promotions might utilize contests or sweepstakes. For example, stores might mail out keys to customers on their mailing list. The keys need to be brought in to the store be tried to see if they open a treasure chest full of money or prizes. Another promotion might advertise that every customer who visits the store can pick a key out of a receptacle

and try to see if it starts a car. The customer whose key starts the car wins the automobile.

Promotions Managers might also use sweepstakes in which customers need only put their name, address, and phone number in a drop box to win prizes. Other promotions may encompass special sales, discount coupons, or percentage scratch-off cards. Some promotions are simple; others are more innovative and novel. Whichever type they are, they must have the potential of bringing more customers in to the store.

Promotions are often the result of brainstorming efforts of the Promotions Manager in conjunction with others in the promotions, marketing, public relations, special events, and advertisement departments. The Promotions Manager may develop promotional tie-ins. These may include copromotions with manufacturers of products sold in the store.

The individual handling promotions for a chain of gourmet food products may run chain-wide recipe contests using food items sold in the stores. After the contest has ended, the promotion may include having a tasting of the winning recipes in the store as well as a cookbook giveaway with the top recipe entries included. This type of promotion not only brings people into the store, but makes a lasting impression.

The Promotions Manager works with the community relations department developing promotions that help attract attention to the store as well as helping the community. The individual may, for example, put together programs such as the sponsorship of not-for-profit events or make donations in the store's name to worthwhile causes.

These promotions are used to help keep the store's name in the public eye. They are used for advertising as well as public relations and goodwill purposes.

The Promotions Manager is expected to develop a basic plan for promotions and their implementation. Depending on the structure of the company, this may be given to the director of marketing, advertising, or public relations for approval.

Other duties of the Promotions Manager working for a retail store or chain may include:

- Preparing a budget for promotions
- Working with the advertising department creating promotional ads and direct mail advertising pieces
- Developing marketing materials, including ads and brochures
- Developing promotions for the store's website

Salaries

Earnings for Promotions Managers working in retail stores or chains can range from approximately $26,000 to $52,000 or more. Factors affecting earnings include the specific retail store or chain for which the individual works as well as its size, prestige, and location. Other variables include the education, experience, and responsibilities of the individual.

Employment Prospects

Employment prospects are fair for Promotions Managers. Individuals may find employment in the corporate offices as well as local stores of a variety of chains and other retail outlets. These might include drug stores, department stores, supermarkets, clothing stores, furniture stores, or toy stores.

While jobs may be located throughout the country, individuals may need to relocate for specific positions.

Advancement Prospects

Advancement prospects are fair for Promotions Managers working in retail situations. Individuals may climb the career ladder by landing similar jobs in larger or more prestigious stores or chains. After obtaining experience, they might also be promoted to the director of either marketing, advertising, or public relations.

Education and Training

While there are exceptions, most retail chains and stores require Promotions Managers to hold a minimum of a bachelor's degree. Good majors include communications, public relations, marketing, advertising, business, journalism, retail management, English, liberal arts, or related fields. In some situations, work experience may be accepted in lieu of education.

Seminars and workshops in promotions, public relations, marketing, publicity, and advertising are helpful.

Experience, Skills, and Personality Traits

Promotions Managers are required to have experience in promotions, publicity, marketing, public relations, and advertising. This is often obtained through positions as assistants in publicity, promotion, public relations, marketing, or advertising. Any experience in retail is also useful.

Promotions Managers should be creative, detail-oriented, organized individuals. The ability to work on a variety of projects at one time without becoming flustered is essential.

Communications skills, both written and verbal, are mandatory, as is an understanding of the retail industry.

Unions/Associations

Promotions Managers working in retail may be members of a number of associations and organizations providing professional support and educational guidance. These might include the Public Relations Society of America (PRSA), the International Council of Shopping Centers (ICSC), the National Retail Merchants Association (NRMA) or the National Retail Federation (NRF).

Tips for Entry

1. Contact the International Council of Shopping Centers, the Public Relations Society of America and other organizations to see when and where they hold seminars or workshops in mall promotion and special events.
2. Positions may be located in the newspaper help wanted section. The Sunday classified section is usually the largest of the week. Look under headings such as "Promotions," "Promotion Manager," "Retail," "Retail Opportunities," or "Marketing."
3. Jobs may be advertised on retail store and chain websites.
4. Openings may also be listed or advertised in trade publications.
5. Look for an internship or a position as a promotions assistant in a retail store or chain. These will give you great experience and get your foot in the door.

ART DIRECTOR—RETAIL

CAREER PROFILE

Duties: Develop, design, and create advertisements for retail stores and outlets; design and create advertising sales flyers, posters, show cards, and promotional materials

Alternate Titles: Advertising Art Director; Retail Art Director

Salary Range: $20,000 to $55,000+

Employment Prospects: Fair

Advancement Prospects: Fair

Best Geographical Location(s) for Position: Positions may be located throughout the country

Prerequisites:

Education and Training—Four-year degree in fine arts or commercial art required for some positions; others may not have any specific educational requirements

Experience—Experience working in advertising or art department in any industry helpful, but not always required

Special Skills and Personality Traits—Creativity; artistic ability; understanding of retail advertising industry; knowledge of graphics, layout, paste-ups, photography, and typography

CAREER LADDER

```
┌─────────────────────────────────┐
│   Art Director in Larger,        │
│   More Prestigious Store         │
│ or Art Director in Other Industry │
└─────────────────────────────────┘

┌─────────────────────────────────┐
│        Art Director              │
└─────────────────────────────────┘

┌─────────────────────────────────┐
│        Graphic Artist            │
└─────────────────────────────────┘
```

Position Description

The Art Director working in a retail outlet may work in a number of different job situations. He or she may work for small or large department stores, supermarkets, regional retail chains, or national retail chains. The Art Director might also work for a cataloger. This is a retail business that may or may not have an actual store but sells its products or services through catalogs. Art Directors may also work for on-line catalogs.

The individual's responsibilities vary depending on the size and structure of the retail outlet. The Art Director in the retail world may also be expected to perform the functions of an advertising director. In some stores he or she is also referred to as the Advertising Art Director.

In a small retail store the Art Director may be the only person in the art department. He or she may perform the tasks of a sketch and graphic artist, layout and mechanical person, or letterer. The owners of the store may offer their suggestions. The individual is then responsible for developing, creating, and in some cases actually placing the ads.

The Advertising Art Director may also be in charge of choosing the media in which to advertise.

In larger retail situations, the Art Director may supervise a staff of artists, layout and mechanical preparers, and copywriters, or may work with outside or freelance people. He or she is still usually responsible for developing the advertising concepts and designing the ads.

The Art Director often designs the store posters and flyers used for advertising weekly specials and sales. He or she also designs and creates advertising show cards and counter signs. These are the cards or pieces seen on the countertops or windows or hanging from the ceiling advertising new products, price breaks, and sales specials. As these cards change frequently, the individual usually letters them by hand with markers, paint, or ink or electronically prints them with the use of a computer or other printing mechanism.

The Art Director designs promotional material for the retail store. Depending on the size and structure of the outlet, he or she may just do the designing or may be responsible for the development, writing the promotional copy, or creating the artwork.

Much of the artwork and advertising for large retail chains may be done by an advertising agency. However, the stores often put out local advertisements and catalogs. The Art Director may provide the layout and all graphics for these advertisements, sale flyers, and catalogs.

When creating advertisements, posters, flyers, show cards, and counter signs, the Art Director must make sure that everything used in advertising and promoting the store will retain a unified identity and image. This means that while every ad may be advertising a different weekly special, each must look somewhat like the others. Logos must remain the same and be in a similar position on each ad. The store name must always look the same. In this way, when customers read and see the ads and promotional materials they will automatically think of the store.

Additional duties of the Art Director may include:

- Working with outside printers
- Negotiating prices or getting bids for printing of large quantities of flyers and advertising sales pieces
- Performing functions of copywriter

Salaries

Earnings for the Art Director of the advertising department working in retail stores can vary greatly depending on the job. The range may begin around $20,000 and go up to $55,000 or more.

Generally, individuals with little experience or those working in smaller stores will earn less than their counterparts with more experience in larger, more prestigious stores and retail outlets.

Employment Prospects

Employment prospects are fair for individuals seeking this position. Jobs may be located throughout the country. More and more retail stores are following the current trend toward in-house advertising departments. As noted previously, individuals might find employment in a variety of settings including large department stores, supermarkets, regional retail chains, national retail chains, catalogs, or on-line catalogs and E-tailing websites.

Advancement Prospects

Prospects for career advancement for Art Directors working in the retail industry are fair. Individuals have a number of different options for moving up the career ladder. The most common is to become the Art Director for a larger, more prestigious store. An individual might advance his or her other career by becoming the advertising or art director in a large corporation, depending on his or her qualifications.

The individual might also locate a position as an Art Director in an advertising agency.

Education and Training

Most employers in large retail stores, department stores, or chains will usually require an applicant to have a four-year college degree in fine arts or commercial art. Courses or seminars in advertising are a plus.

Smaller retail stores may or may not require a college degree. Certain stores may accept an applicant with art school training or even a self-taught individual who can demonstrate that he or she possesses the required skills.

Experience, Skills, and Personality Traits

Art Directors working in the advertising department of retail stores need a thorough understanding of the concepts of retail advertising and art. Individuals must be very creative and artistic to come up with concepts for advertisements as well as to design them and bring the ads to fruition. Individuals must be able to sketch, draw, paste up, lay out, put together mechanicals, and choose type. A great deal of this is done by computer today.

A portfolio or "book" made up of the individuals best work is usually necessary in order to show samples and illustrate skills.

Unions/Associations

Art Directors working in the advertising department in a retail setting do not usually belong to any bargaining union. They may, however, belong to a number of trade associations which offer professional guidance, education, and information. These might include the American Advertising Federation (AAF), the Art Director Club, Inc. (ADC), the One Club, the Society of Illustrators (SOI), the Graphic Artists Guild (GAG) and the American Institute of Graphic Arts (AIGA).

Tips for Entry

1. Start working on your portfolio now. A good portfolio can give you an edge over other applicants. In many instances, it can take the place of educational requirements. Make sure your portfolio includes some work relevant to the retail advertising field even if you have to do samples.
2. Join trade associations. Many have student memberships. Others offer critique sessions on improving your portfolio. All of them will help you make important contacts.
3. Many retail chain stores offer internships and training programs. Contact the company headquarters or ask the manager in your local store of the chain about whom to contact to get more information.

4. Obtain experience working in a newspaper advertising department. In addition to gaining experience you will make contact with local advertisers who might have a job opening down the line.

5. Positions are often advertised in the classified sections of the newspaper. Look under the classification headings of "Retail," "Art Director," or "Advertising."

6. Other positions may be located on career websites or specific store sites.

GRAPHIC ARTIST—RETAIL

CAREER PROFILE

Duties: Develop, design, and create graphics for advertisements for retail stores and outlets; design and create graphics for advertising sales flyers, posters, show cards, and promotional materials; design graphics for catalogs

Alternate Titles: Graphic Designer; Artist

Salary Range: $20,000 to $45,000+

Employment Prospects: Good

Advancement Prospects: Good

Best Geographical Location(s) for Position: Positions may be located throughout the country

Prerequisites:

Education and Training—Four-year degree in fine arts or commercial art required for some positions; others may not have any specific educational requirements

Experience—Art and advertising experience helpful but not always required

Special Skills and Personality Traits—Creativity; artistic ability; understanding of retail advertising industry; knowledge of graphics, layout, paste-ups, mechanicals, typography, color, and photography; drawing and illustration skills

CAREER LADDER

```
┌─────────────────────────────────┐
│          Art Director           │
└─────────────────────────────────┘

┌─────────────────────────────────┐
│         Graphic Artist          │
└─────────────────────────────────┘

┌─────────────────────────────────┐
│  Graphic Artist in Other Industry │
│          or Student             │
└─────────────────────────────────┘
```

Position Description

Every retail advertisement in a magazine, store flyer, or catalog has usually been worked on by one or more Graphic Artists. These individuals, who may also be referred to as Graphic Designers or Artists, are the ones who help make advertisements and other promotional pieces look visually attractive.

Graphic Artists working in retail settings may have a number of responsibilities depending on their specific job situation. Their main function is to design the graphics for the retail outlet's promotional material. In larger retail stores, individuals may work under the direction of the store's art director. In smaller stores where there is a one-person art department, the Graphic Artist may also act as the art director. Stores may employ one or more Graphic Artists depending on their size and structure.

Graphic Artists might develop and design the graphics for the retail store's advertisements. It is up to the Graphic Designer to develop graphics that are creative, innovative, appealing, and memorable.

Graphic Artists may design a retail catalog. Others may design weekly sales flyers, counter cards, display signs, or store signs. Depending on the situation, Graphic Artists might come up with store logos, designs for bags and other packaging, and virtually all printed promotional material.

When designing advertising and promotional pieces, logos, and packaging, the Graphic Artist generally tries to keep the image of the company prominently identified. The individual must keep the design of the product names, graphics, and logos closely tied together so that customers will relate the design to the company. In this way, customers who see the logo or name on anything will be able to identify the store, product, or brand easily.

Part of the job of the Graphic Artist may be choosing the kind and size of type to use in advertisements and other promotional material. He or she must choose typefaces as well as background colors.

The Graphic Artist must develop a layout for ads, flyers, or other promotional material. He or she also must design the graphics. Sometimes, Graphic Artists utilize photos. In other situations, the individual may draw, sketch, or use computer-generated graphics.

Graphic Artists often design and create advertising show cards and counter signs. These are the cards or pieces seen on the countertops or windows or hanging from the ceiling advertising new products, price breaks, and sales specials. As these cards change frequently, the individual usually letters them by hand with markers, paint, or ink or electronically prints them with the use of a computer or other printing mechanism.

Additional duties of a Graphic Artist may include:

- Designing the graphics and layout for on-line retailers
- Designing the graphics for other on-line sites
- Performing the functions of a copywriter

Salaries

Earnings for Graphic Artists working in retail can range from approximately $20,000 to $45,000 or more. Factors affecting earnings include the size, type, prestige, and geographic location of the specific retail company for which the individual works. Other variables include the talent, responsibilities, and experience of the individual.

Employment Prospects

Employment prospects are good for Graphic Artists seeking employment in the retail industry. Jobs may be located throughout the country. More and more retail stores are following the current trend toward in-house advertising departments. Individuals might find employment in a variety of settings including large department stores, supermarkets, regional retail chains, national retail chains, traditional paper catalogs, and catalogs on the Internet.

Advancement Prospects

Advancement prospects for Graphic Artists are dependent to a great extent on the talent of the individual as well as his or her career aspirations. Some Graphic Artists climb the career ladder by finding similar positions in larger or more prestigious retail companies resulting in increased responsibilities and earnings. Other individuals land jobs as art directors.

Education and Training

Experience requirements vary for Graphic Artists in the retail industry. Many employers require or prefer an applicant to have a four-year college degree in fine arts or com-

mercial art, or an art school background. However, a good portfolio demonstrating the individual possesses the required skills can often land a job in lieu of education. Courses or seminars in advertising are a plus.

Experience, Skills, and Personality Traits

Graphic Artists should be very artistic individuals with a thorough understanding of the concepts of retail advertising and art. Creativity is essential in order to develop eye-catching ads or promotional material as well as to design them and bring them to fruition. Graphic Artists must be able to sketch, draw, paste up, lay out, put together mechanics, and choose type. A great deal of this is done by computer today. Therefore, computer skills and the ability to use appropriate software programs are mandatory.

A portfolio or "book" made up of the individual's best work is usually necessary in order to show samples and illustrate skills.

Unions/Associations

Graphic Artists working in the advertising department in a retail setting may belong to a number of trade associations which offer professional guidance, education, and information. These might include the American Advertising Federation (AAF), the Art Director Club, Inc. (ADC), the One Club, the Society of Illustrators (SOI), the Graphic Artists Guild (GAG) and the American Institute of Graphic Arts (AIGA).

Tips for Entry

1. Your portfolio can help you get a job. Start working on it now. A good portfolio can give you an edge over other applicants. In many instances, it can take the place of educational requirements. Make sure your portfolio includes some work relevant to the retail advertising field even if you have to do samples.
2. Join trade associations. Many have student memberships. Others offer critique sessions on improving your portfolio. All of them will help you make important contacts.
3. Many retail chain stores offer internships and training programs. Contact the company headquarters or ask the manager in your local chain store about whom to contact to get more information.
4. Positions are often advertised in the classified sections of the newspaper. Look under classification headings such as "Retail," "Graphic Artist," "Artist," "Graphic Designer," or "Advertising."
5. Other positions may be located on career websites or specific store sites.
6. Obtain experience working in a newspaper advertising department. In addition to gaining experience you will make contact with stores who might have a job opening in the future.

PERSONAL SHOPPER

Duties: Working one-on-one with customers; selecting clothing, accessories, and other merchandise for customers

Alternate Titles: None

Salary Range: $25,000 to $70,000+

Employment Prospects: Fair

Advancement Prospects: Fair

Best Geographical Location(s) for Position: Jobs may be located throughout the country

Prerequisites:
   Education and Training—High school diploma or equivalent; training requirements vary
   Experience—Experience working in retail sales
   Special Skills and Personality Traits—A good sense of style; taste; love of shopping; enthusiastic; articulate; good judgment; people skills

```
┌─────────────────────────────────────┐
│  Personal Shopper in More Exclusive  │
│    Store, Personal Shopper with More │
│  Clients, Director of Personal Shoppers, │
│             or Buyer                 │
└─────────────────────────────────────┘

┌─────────────────────────────────────┐
│          Personal Shopper            │
└─────────────────────────────────────┘

┌─────────────────────────────────────┐
│            Salesperson               │
└─────────────────────────────────────┘
```

Position Description

Many stores have found that providing extra services increases customer loyalty, thus increasing sales and profit. These services can encompass a variety of areas such as free gift wrapping, delivery of merchandise, or tailoring. Personal Shoppers are another of those services.

Formerly only the most exclusive stores employed Personal Shoppers. Today, the service is becoming much more prevalent. Generally, the services of Personal Shoppers are free to the customer. The store makes its money by selling the items that the Personal Shopper has selected for the customer.

While some people love shopping, others find it stressful. Additionally, with many people's busy lifestyles today, some just don't have the time to "shop till they drop."

Personal Shoppers have a number of responsibilities depending on the structure of their department. Their main functions are offering customers individualized help and attention, and to make shopping a better and easier experience.

Personal shopping services vary from store to store. In many stores, the customers call the Personal Shopper to make an appointment. In others, customers may see the service advertised and visit the Personal Shopper at his or her office in the store. Some stores send Personal Shoppers and

merchandise to the homes or offices of customers to make it easier for the individual to shop.

Depending on the store, Personal Shoppers may deal exclusively in one area such as clothing and accessories or with all the store's merchandise. The shopper must be not only familiar with the store's merchandise, but must know where it is located so he or she can find it quickly, so he or she can offer better advice to customers.

The Personal Shopper determines what the customer or client wants, and often has consultations with customers to learn their likes, dislikes, needs, and price range, as well as their sizes and lifestyles. Armed with the information, the Personal Shopper goes through the store choosing items to bring back to the customer.

The Shopper brings back a variety of sizes and styles for the customer to try on, and often advises the client on how a garment or outfit looks. If the customer finds something he or she likes, they may buy it. If not, the Personal Shopper will look for something else. It is essential that the individual never make the customer feel obligated to buy something he or she doesn't like or want.

A major function of many Personal Shoppers is helping customers select gifts. Shoppers may, for example, often help select gifts for customers' business associates, family, or friends. One of the perks for customers is they only need give the Personal Shopper a list of people for whom they require gifts, a description of the recipients likes and dislikes or hobbies, and a price range. The individual can then choose a selection of possibilities for customer approval. In many instances the Personal Shopper performs yet another set of services to save the customer time, such as gift wrapping, enclosing cards, and delivering or mailing the gifts.

Most Personal Shoppers keep detailed information on steady customers including sizes, styles, fabrics and color preferences, previously purchased items, birthdays, and anniversaries. They also may keep similar information on the customer's business associates, friends, and family.

Other duties of Personal Shoppers may include:

- Helping customers coordinate outfits and accessories
- Helping customers coordinate home items
- Keeping abreast of new merchandise in the store
- Calling steady customers when new merchandise they might be interested in comes in

Salaries

Earnings for Personal Shoppers range from approximately $25,000 to $70,000 or more. Variables affecting earnings include the size, type, prestige, and geographic location of the store in which the individual works as well as the individual's experience, duties, and reputation in the field.

Personal Shoppers may be compensated in a number of different ways. Some may be paid a straight salary. Others may be paid a salary plus a commission on sales.

Employment Prospects

Employment prospects for Personal Shoppers are getting better every day. While this is a relatively new type of job, it is expanding quickly. Both male and female Personal Shoppers are in demand in a variety of retail establishments including department stores, boutiques, clothing stores, specialty shops, and gift shops.

Advancement Prospects

Personal Shoppers may climb the career ladder in a number of ways. Some individuals advance their careers by locating similar positions in larger or more prestigious stores resulting in increased responsibility and earnings. Others acquire supervisory positions. These might include becoming the director of the personal shopper department, a manager of a different department or in some cases, the store manager.

Some individuals become department buyers. Still others strike out on their own with personal shopping services.

Education and Training

Education and training requirements vary from position to position because of the newness of this job. Generally, most stores require individuals to hold a minimum of a high school diploma or the equivalent. Many prefer a college background or degree.

Good choices for majors for those aspiring to become Personal Shoppers include retailing, merchandising, or fashion. Seminars, workshops, and courses in fashion, color, accessorizing, merchandizing, and retailing are helpful.

Experience, Skills, and Personality Traits

Personal Shoppers usually have worked in retail sales prior to garnering their positions. A background in retailing, merchandising, or fashion is needed.

Successful Personal Shoppers are pleasant people who enjoy working with and helping others. They have panache and a sense of style when selecting clothing, accessories, gifts, or anything else. Customer service skills are essential. Communications skills are mandatory.

Unions/Associations

Individuals may obtain information about a career in this field by contacting the National Retail Merchants Association (NRMA) and the American Collegiate Retailing Association (ACRA).

Tips for Entry

1. Look for an internship with a Personal Shopper in a department store or boutique.
2. Jobs may be advertised in the classified sections of newspapers. Look under headings such as "Personal Shopper," "Retail Opportunities," "Fashion Sales," "Salespeople," "Department Stores," or "Boutiques."
3. Sometimes jobs may not be advertised. You may have to create your own position. If you are currently working in a store that does not yet offer personal shopping services, suggest the idea to store management making sure you ask to be interviewed for the newly created position.
4. If you aren't working for the specific store you think might be open to this type of position, write a letter to the store manager or owner asking for an appointment to discuss the possibility. Make sure to include your resume.
5. Be sure to dress the part. You need to look stylish and well coordinated for this type of job.

SPECIAL EVENTS DIRECTOR—RETAIL STORE

CAREER PROFILE

Duties: Develop and implement special events and promotions for retail store

Alternate Titles: Special Events Manager

Salary Range: $22,000 to $50,000+

Employment Prospects: Fair

Advancement Prospects: Fair

Best Geographical Location(s) for Position: Jobs may be located throughout the country

Prerequisites:

Education and Training—Bachelor's degree

Experience—Experience in special events, publicity, or public relations preferred

Special Skills and Personality Traits—Creativity; detail oriented; imagination; innovation; communications skills

CAREER LADDER

```
┌─────────────────────────────┐
│   Public Relations Director  │
│     or Marketing Director    │
└─────────────────────────────┘

┌─────────────────────────────┐
│    Special Events Director   │
└─────────────────────────────┘

┌─────────────────────────────┐
│   Special Events Assistant   │
│  or Public Relations Assistant│
└─────────────────────────────┘
```

Position Description

Retail stores often have special events and promotions. One of the most well-known special events sponsored by a retail store is the Macy's Thanksgiving Day Parade.

Whether small or large, special events and promotions in retail have a purpose. Some may be designed to attract new customers. Others may enhance the image of the store as well as make it more visible. The Special Events Director formulates the special events in a retail store. He or she generally works in the store's marketing or public relations department. In some stores, the public relations director or marketing director handles the special events functions.

The Special Events Director must devise innovative ideas and then take them from inception through fruition. This must be done within a budget and a time frame.

The Special Events Director often works with store owners, management, public relations, and marketing staff to develop ideas. Special events will, of course, depend on the store. Depending on the situation and budget, events may be small or large and simple or complex. Some events may be industry specific and some may not.

For example, groceries and specialty food stores might hold events such as "Sampling Saturdays," where various food samples are put out for tasting; "Cooking with the Chefs," where chefs illustrate how to prepare dishes using products from the store; or a "Singles Meet and Greet," in the grocery aisles.

Clothing stores may put together fashion shows on or off site, spotlighting the store's clothing or a "Makeover Day" for customers. A furniture store might hold an indoor picnic to bring people into the store or might bring in an interior designer for the day to help customers learn how to decorate their home. Bookstores frequently bring in authors for book signings, workshops, and discussion groups. Department stores might do anything from having art exhibits to holding a concert in their parking lot or hosting a wedding in the public area of the store.

Some stores, like Macy's, sponsor events offsite. This helps the store in a number of ways. It helps build better public relations and good community relations. Off-site events may also obtain publicity and promotion for the store and bring their name to the public in a different manner than advertising can.

The Special Events Director may be responsible for implementing a certain number of events annually. For example, he or she may be expected to develop an event every week or every month. In other situations, the Special Events Director may be notified by the store's upper management when they want events developed. The individual must determine general information about the program. This may include things such as the time frame, proposed budget, and general purpose.

The goal of the Special Events Director is to develop an appropriate event with a novel, workable idea. The individual will brainstorm with other members of the store's management team or members of the public relations, marketing, advertising, or promotions department. The Special Events Director is then responsible for working out the details and writing a basic plan for the event. This includes devising a budget for the project.

After receiving approval, the Special Events Director moves forward and puts the idea into action. He or she often works with one or more assistants to help with the project.

Depending on the specific event the individual may be expected to locate people and items necessary to make the event a success. The Director may need to hire entertainers, talent, caterers, or customers. He or she may need to locate chairs, stages, promotional items, or other important items. Every detail of the entire event becomes the responsibility of the Special Events Director.

Depending on the specific store and its structure, the Special Events Director may be responsible for preparing press releases and other publicity on the upcoming event as well as post-publicity on portions of the programs that have already occurred. The Director may also be expected to call the media and arrange interviews, articles, feature stories, or photo opportunities. In other situations, the public relations department will handle these functions.

Some Special Events Directors are responsible for developing events for an entire chain of stores. This might occur when individuals work in the corporate department of chain stores. The Special Events Director in this circumstance must develop events that will work in multiple stores. An Easter egg hunt or the arrival of Santa Claus, for example, are universal events. In this case, the Special Events Director is often expected to oversee staff in other locations.

Other duties of the Special Events Director working in a retail environment may include:

• Developing special events for employees
• Devising budgets for special events
• Functioning as a public relations person
• Developing and placing advertisements for events
• Supervising staff
• Being present at events

Salaries

Annual earnings for Special Events Directors working in a retail environment can range from approximately $22,000 to $50,000 or more. Factors affecting earnings include the specific retail store as well as its size, prestige, and location. Other variables include the education, experience, and responsibilities of the individual.

Employment Prospects

Employment prospects are fair for individuals seeking this position. Jobs can be located in many retail stores throughout the country. As noted, every store does not have a Special Events Director. In some, the public relations or marketing director or even the store manager may be responsible for these functions.

Advancement Prospects

Advancement prospects are, to a great extent, dependent on the career aspirations of the individual. Some find similar positions in larger or more prestigious retail stores. Others move into handling special events for other industries.

Many Special Event Directors also climb the career ladder by acquiring positions as directors of marketing or public relations.

Education and Training

Individuals seeking positions in special events coordination should generally have a college degree. Good majors include communications, public relations, English, liberal arts, advertising, business, journalism, or retail management.

Seminars and workshops in special events, promotions, public relations, publicity, and advertising are helpful.

Experience, Skills, and Personality Traits

Experience working in special events, publicity, promotion, or retail management is usually required for a position like this. Many Special Events Directors were special events assistants or coordinators prior to their appointment.

Individuals should be creative and innovative with a good imagination. Excellent communications skills are necessary. An understanding of the retail industry is needed.

Special Events Directors should be detail oriented. The ability to deal well under stress is essential.

Unions/Associations

Special Events Directors working in retail might be associated with number of associations and organizations providing professional support and educational guidance. These might include the Public Relations Society of America (PRSA), Business/Professional Advertising Association (B/PAA), the International Communications Association (ICA), and the National Retail Merchants Association (NRMA) or the National Retail Federation (NRF).

Tips for Entry

1. Send a short cover letter and your resume to the corporate office of department or chain stores as well as specialty stores.

2. Positions may be located in the newspaper help wanted section. The Sunday classified section is usually the largest of the week. Look under headings such as "Special Events," "Special Event Director," "Retail Opportunities," "Public Relations," "Marketing," or "Promotion."

3. Job openings may also be listed in trade publications.

4. Contact large stores to see if they offer internships in this area.

5. Jobs may also be located on-line. Start by checking out some of the more popular sites such as www.hotjobs.com.

MYSTERY SHOPPER

CAREER PROFILE

Duties: Shop in stores; determine if stores and employees are up to company standards; write reports on findings

Alternate Titles: Secret Shopper

Salary Range: $7.00 to $20.000+per hour

Employment Prospects: Good

Advancement Prospects: Poor

Best Geographical Location(s) for Position: Jobs may be located throughout the country; large cities will offer more opportunities

Prerequisites:
Education and Training—Educational requirements vary
Experience—Experience usually not required
Special Skills and Personality Traits—Self-confidence; discretion communication skills; organization

CAREER LADDER

```
┌─────────────────────────────┐
│   Mystery Shopper for Larger│
│   or More Prestigious Store │
└─────────────────────────────┘

┌─────────────────────────────┐
│       Mystery Shopper       │
└─────────────────────────────┘

┌─────────────────────────────┐
│        Entry Level          │
└─────────────────────────────┘
```

Position Description

The hope of retail establishments is that customers visiting their stores will have a pleasant shopping experience. It's difficult, however, to know how customers are really treated when the top managers aren't around. In order to find out how customers are treated by employees when they don't think anyone is watching, stores often hire Mystery Shoppers.

These individuals, also known as Secret Shoppers, provide store owners and upper management with a typical consumer's view of shopping in their establishment. In this manner, management can improve customer service and alleviate problems which may exist.

Mystery shopping is a great opportunity for individuals who love to shop. As an added bonus, they get paid for it. Mystery Shoppers can be male or female in virtually every age category from older high school students to senior citizens. Generally, jobs in this field are part time. However, there are some full-time positions available.

What does a Mystery Shopper do? He or she may have varied duties depending on the specific job. Mystery Shoppers are given assignments by their employer. For example, individuals may be asked to go to specific stores and be given a list of merchandise to purchase. The employer either gives the individual money for the purchases or reimburses him or her afterward.

While "shopping," the Mystery Shopper may be asked to check various situations within the store. These might include checking to see if and how employees greet customers, how they react and treat customers and if they are courteous. The Mystery Shopper may be responsible for checking to see if store policies and customer service standards are met, or how different problems are handled.

The Mystery Shopper might additionally be asked to check whether the store is clean and well stocked, rest rooms are clean, and aisles are wide enough. Most of this information is important to make sure store customer service standards are met. Other information may be needed to assure safety requirements are met.

After shopping and observing, the Mystery Shopper is expected to file a report of findings. Depending on the situation, the individual may write a general report or just be expected to fill out forms supplied by the employer.

Additional duties of Mystery Shoppers might include:

• Offering suggestions to employers regarding employees
• Tabulating information collected while shopping
• Visiting the selling floor to assure products are displayed properly
• Visiting the store with specific issues (such as returns) to see how they are handled by employees

Salaries

Salaries of Mystery Shoppers vary depending on the specific type of employment. Individuals working full time for a company specializing in mystery shopping might have annual salaries ranging from $21,000 to $34,000 or more. Mystery Shoppers working on a part-time basis might earn between $7.00 and $20.00 or more per hour. Additionally, some Mystery Shoppers get to keep their purchases.

Employment Prospects

Employment prospects for Mystery Shoppers interested in working on a part-time basis are good. Prospects for full-time employment are much more limited.

Individuals might find employment shopping in a variety of retail establishments including large department stores, chain stores, groceries, auto parts stores, cosmetic stores, drug stores, pharmacies, boutiques, or gift shops. Some Mystery Shoppers might even shop for cars. As noted previously, Mystery Shoppers might work in other industries in addition to retail. Individuals might be Mystery Shoppers in the hospitality industry, restaurants, hotels, travel, banking, insurance, or healthcare.

Some Mystery Shoppers work for mystery shopping companies. Others work for stores, chains, or retail establishments themselves.

Advancement Prospects

Advancement prospects for Mystery Shoppers are poor. The most common method of advancement in this type of job is by obtaining better assignments resulting in increased earnings. Some individuals may strike out on their own and open mystery shopping companies. This, however, is not common.

Education and Training

There are no specific educational requirements for Mystery Shoppers. Those working for companies specializing in mystery shopping may be provided with in-service training programs.

Experience, Skills, and Personality Traits

An important trait for the Mystery Shopper is the ability to "look the part." Individuals for the most part must look like "normal" shoppers in the specific store they're visiting. In some cases, however, Mystery Shoppers may be sent out to see how different groups are treated. For example, a store may want to see how employees treat senior citizen or minority shoppers.

Mystery Shoppers need good communications skills. The ability to be discreet is essential. A Mystery Shopper has no value to a company when everyone knows what he or she is doing in the store.

Unions/Associations

Individuals interested in pursuing a career in this field might also obtain additional information from the National Retail Federation (NRF) and the American Collegiate Retailing Association (ACRA).

Tips for Entry

1. Jobs may be advertised in the newspaper classified section under headings including "Mystery Shopper," or "Secret Shopper."
2. Contact large chains and department stores to see who in the organization you might contact regarding a position in this area. Sometimes it's human resources. Other times it might be another department.
3. Jobs can often be located on-line. Look at some of the major sites such as www.hotjobs.com.
4. Look for companies that specialize in mystery shopping. You might find them advertised in trade journals or via their own websites.

PRODUCT DEMONSTRATOR

CAREER PROFILE

Duties: Demonstrate merchandise and products to customers; answer customers' questions regarding products

Alternate Titles: Product Demonstrator; Sales Demonstrator

Salary Range: $5.50 to $15.00+ or more per hour

Employment Prospects: Good

Advancement Prospects: Fair

Best Geographical Location(s) for Position: Jobs may be located throughout the country; large cities will offer more possibilities

Prerequisites:

Education and Training—Educational requirements vary

Experience—Experience requirements vary

Special Skills and Personality Traits—Communications skills; pleasant personality; enthusiastic; people skills

CAREER LADDER

```
┌─────────────────────────────────┐
│   Product Demonstrator for More │
│  Prestigious Products or in More│
│       Prestigious Stores        │
└─────────────────────────────────┘

┌─────────────────────────────────┐
│      Product Demonstrator       │
└─────────────────────────────────┘

┌─────────────────────────────────┐
│    Entry Level or Sales Position│
└─────────────────────────────────┘
```

Position Description

Many stores have found that when products and merchandise are demonstrated they sell better. They therefore utilize the services of individuals called Demonstrators.

Demonstrators may work directly for stores or for manufacturers or other companies. Responsibilities differ depending on the specific employer and products, but their main function is to promote sales.

Individuals might demonstrate virtually any product, including but not limited to, food, cosmetics, appliances, or housewares.

An individual demonstrating a new ice cream product in a supermarket might scoop out various flavors and give samples and coupons to customers. If he or she is promoting a new kind of frozen pizza, he or she might bake it in a portable toaster, cut it into bite-size pieces, arrange them on plates and give out samples.

Individuals demonstrating cookware might prepare various foods in the cookware in front of customers. During this process, the individual may answer questions and illustrate the benefits of the new product.

Demonstrators working in the cosmetics department of a store might show individuals how to use the cosmetics the store sells. Often, the Demonstrator utilizes the store's makeup to do a makeover on customers.

Individuals may be responsible for developing a mini sales pitch or may be given one.

Some Demonstrators, such as those working in the cosmetics area of department stores, may also double as salespeople. Their function is to demonstrate merchandise and products to customers in stores and other outlets and to create an atmosphere conducive to sales.

In some situations, Demonstrators may not only show new products to customers but record customer reactions as well. For example, did the customers like the new flavor of soda or did they dump half-filled cups into the trash? The Demonstrator often is expected to write reports on consumer reactions to the products being demonstrated.

Additional duties of Demonstrators might include:

• Giving out coupons for products being demonstrated
• Performing functions of sales associate
• Taking payments from customers for purchases
• Writing orders

Salaries

Earnings for Demonstrators are dependent on a number of factors. These include the specific work situation and the type of product being demonstrated as well as the actual responsibilities, education, and experience of the individual.

Some Demonstrators earn $5.50 an hour. Others earn $15 or more per hour. Some Demonstrators may also receive a commission on products sold.

Employment Prospects

Employment prospects for Demonstrators are good. Individuals may find openings at a variety of retail outlets, department stores, specialty shops, and supermarkets throughout the country.

Some Demonstrators work directly for specific companies and manufacturers demonstrating their products in various retail outlets.

Advancement Prospects

Advancement prospects for Demonstrators are dependent to a great extent on an individuals specific career aspiration. Some individuals find more prestigious stores to work in or better products to demonstrate. Others strike out on their own selling products via home parties.

Education and Training

Educational requirements vary for Demonstrators. Some employers prefer individuals have at least some college background if not a college degree. Others will hire individuals who have a high school diploma.

Once hired, employers often provide either formal or informal training programs. Individuals who are demonstrating specialized products may need more specialized training.

Experience, Skills, and Personality Traits

Experience requirements, like education, vary from employer to employer. In many situations this is an entry-level position. Some employers, however, prefer or require experienced employees.

Demonstrators should be well-groomed individuals. An enthusiastic, pleasant personality is helpful in this type of position. Good verbal communications skills are also necessary, as is the ability to repeat the same sales pitch over and over.

Unions/Associations

Individuals interested in pursuing a career in this field might also obtain additional information from the National Retail Federation (NRF), the American Collegiate Retailing Association (ACRA), the American Marketing Association (AMA) and the Direct Selling Association (DSA).

Tips for Entry

1. Jobs may be advertised in the newspaper classified section under headings including "Retail," "Retail Opportunities," "Demonstrator," "Product Demonstrator," "Cosmetics Demonstrator," "Food Demonstrator," or "Housewares Demonstrator."
2. Send your resume and a short cover letter to department stores, supermarkets, and other retail outlets.
3. You might also send your resume to the human resources directors of companies whose products you might be interested in demonstrating.
4. Contact the corporate offices of large chains and department stores to see whom you might contact in their local stores.
5. Get your foot in the door with a sales position. It might give you an edge over another applicant.

COMPARISON SHOPPER

CAREER PROFILE

Duties: Visit competitors' stores; compare prices; compare merchandise; gather other information valuable to employer; write reports on findings

Alternate Titles: None

Salary Range: $15,000 to 24,000+

Employment Prospects: Fair

Advancement Prospects: Fair

Best Geographical Location(s) for Position: Jobs may be located throughout the country; large cities will offer more possibilities

Prerequisites:

Education and Training—Educational requirements vary

Experience—Experience usually not required

Special Skills and Personality Traits—Communication skills; discretion; organization

CAREER LADDER

```
┌─────────────────────────────┐
│      Assistant Buyer         │
│ or Merchandising Assistant   │
└─────────────────────────────┘

┌─────────────────────────────┐
│     Comparison Shopper       │
└─────────────────────────────┘

┌─────────────────────────────┐
│      Entry Level, Sales      │
└─────────────────────────────┘
```

Position Description

It is to the advantage of store owners and management to know as much as possible about what other similar stores are doing in their business. To accomplish this, many stores employ Comparison Shoppers who help stores get the edge over their competitors by gathering important information. This information will vary depending on the specific store.

Comparison Shoppers visit competing types of stores. They must do this in a discreet manner, fitting in with other customers. Individuals may have varied responsibilities depending on the job.

The Comparison Shopper may be given a list of items to view in competing stores. He or she may be asked to check the prices of the merchandise. This information is useful in helping the store become competitive in setting its prices. The individual may also be asked to compare the packaging of items to help the store set prices and package design.

The Comparison Shopper may be expected to check into policies of other stores. For example, he or she may purchase merchandise to see how the competitive store deals with returns. The individual might be asked to observe the number of cashiers or salespeople a store utilizes, the type of customer service they provide, or specific store policies they enforce.

Comparison Shoppers are often responsible for checking the types of merchandise sold in competing stores. If a competing store has the new toy, a new fashion, or fad and the other store does not, it can represent a large loss of sales. Knowing what other stores have can give a store a tremendous edge. This information is also useful to help stores determine buying policies.

In many situations the Comparison Shopper actually buys the merchandise. It is then used to check not only price, but to compare quality. Individuals may visit more than one competitive store to gather information.

Once back at the office, the Comparison Shopper prepares reports of his or her findings. Depending on the situation, the individual may write a general report or just be expected to fill out forms supplied by the employer. This is an extremely important part of the job. This information is used by the employer to make better, more informed decisions on buying, pricing, and merchandising.

Additional duties of Comparison Shoppers might include:

- Checking that merchandise, price, and sales dates are accurately described in advertisement copy
- Checking to be sure merchandise advertised at a specific price by a competitor is available for customer purchase
- Comparing packaging of similar items in competitive stores

Salaries

Salaries of Comparison Shoppers working full time can range from approximately $15,000 to $24,000 or more depending on a number of variables. These include the size, type, prestige, and geographic location of the specific store. Other factors include the responsibilities, education, and experience of the individual.

Comparison Shoppers working on a part-time basis can earn between $6.00 and $10.00 or more per hour.

Employment Prospects

Employment prospects for Comparison Shoppers are fair and getting better every day. As more stores want the edge over their competitors, they will begin employing people in these positions.

Individuals might find employment in a variety of retail establishments including large department stores, chain stores, groceries, cosmetics stores, drug stores, pharmacies, or gift shops.

Advancement Prospects

Advancement prospects for Comparison Shoppers are dependent on the individual's career aspirations. With additional experience, training, or education individuals might move into positions as assistant buyers, merchandising assistants, or sales representatives.

Education and Training

Educational requirements vary for Comparison Shoppers. Some employers prefer individuals have at least some college background if not a college degree. Others will hire individuals who have a high school diploma. Good majors for those in college are marketing, merchandising, retailing, and liberal arts. Once hired, stores often provide either formal or informal training programs.

Experience, Skills, and Personality Traits

Experience requirements vary from employer to employer. Many stores have no experience requirements for this posi-

tion. Others may prefer or require individuals have some type of prior retail experience, such as sales.

The ability to be discreet is essential. Comparison Shoppers should be well groomed with the ability to "look the part." They should be able to walk into a store without attracting undue attention. They don't want to look like they're comparison shopping. Instead, they want to appear that they are "normal" shoppers in the specific store they're visiting.

Comparison Shoppers should be pleasant people with good verbal and written communication skills.

Unions/Associations

Individuals interested in pursuing a career in this field might also obtain additional information from the National Retail Federation (NRF), the American Collegiate Retailing Association (ACRA) and the American Marketing Association (AMA).

Tips for Entry

1. Jobs may be advertised in the newspaper classified section under headings including "Retail," "Retail Opportunities," and "Comparison Shopper."
2. Consider sending your resume and a short cover letter to department stores, supermarkets, and other retail outlets which might hire Comparison Shoppers.
3. You might also visit the human resources department of retail stores and groceries. Remember to dress appropriately when stopping by the human resources department as well as during any interviews.
4. Contact the corporate offices of large chains and department stores to see whom you might contact in their local stores.
5. Get your foot in the door with a sales position. It might give you an edge over another applicant.

STORE MANAGER— GROCERY/SUPERMARKET

Duties: Handle day-to-day management of supermarket; oversee staffing needs of supermarket; deal with customer service issues; make sure store is in compliance with health and safety regulations

Alternate Titles: Supermarket Manager; Grocery Store Manager

Salary Range: $25,000 to $53,000+

Employment Prospects: Good

Advancement Prospects: Fair

Best Geographical Location(s) for Position: Jobs may be located throughout the country

Prerequisites:

Education and Training—Training requirements vary

Experience—Experience in supermarket management

Special Skills and Personality Traits—Problem solving skills; negotiation skills; communications skills; ability to deal well with people, management skills; administrative skills

```
┌─────────────────────────────────────┐
│  Store Manager for Larger Store or   │
│   Super Store, or Area Manager       │
└─────────────────────────────────────┘

┌─────────────────────────────────────┐
│           Store Manager              │
└─────────────────────────────────────┘

┌─────────────────────────────────────┐
│      Assistant Store Manager         │
└─────────────────────────────────────┘
```

Position Description

Grocery stores have changed over the years. Today, while there are still small corner groceries, most of us are more familiar with the large supermarkets, chains, and supercenters. These might encompass not only traditional groceries, but ready-made convenience food, pharmacies, bakeries, and more. The person in charge of overseeing the entire facility is known as the Store Manager.

The Manager handles the day-to-day management of the entire store. Since he or she has many varied duties, the Store Manager generally has one or more assistant managers who help fulfill them.

The Store Manager must be familiar with all the departments in the store. He or she is ultimately responsible for all their activities, and must be sure the facility is kept clean, safe, and well-stocked.

As food spoilage can lead to illness and lawsuits, it is essential the Store Manager be sure that all food sold in the store is fresh. He or she may work with the various department managers to accomplish this task. Dates on merchandise such as dairy products, meats, or baked goods must be checked and expired food must be pulled off the shelves on a regular basis.

There are an array of laws, rules, and regulations which must be followed for health, legal, and safety reasons. It is the responsibility of the Store Manager to make sure all of these are adhered to.

The Store Manager is responsible for staffing the store. If the store is new and just opening or if there are many job openings, the Store Manager may schedule a job fair to attract large numbers of potential employees. He or she may also write and place help wanted advertisements in the newspaper or other media. The Manager will work with assistant managers in interviewing staff including department managers, customer service people, cashiers, baggers, and office staff. In some instances, the department managers will be responsible for interviewing employees for their department and making recommendations to the Store Manager.

The Manager is also responsible for making sure employees are trained. He or she may accomplish this with the help of the assistant and department managers.

Supermarkets which are part of large chains usually have promotions such as loyalty programs, discount coupons, weekly flyers, and ads to attract and retain customers. These are handled by the corporate office. The Manager must only make sure the specials and items advertised in fliers are on the shelves. In non-chain supermarkets, the Manager may be responsible for developing these promotions or handling the store's advertising. The Manager also may be expected to analyze other data as well to help determine what direction the store might take to increase profits.

Customer service is an important function of the Store Manager. A good Store Manager can make a big problem with a customer seem small. A Manager who is not customer service oriented can do just the opposite. Whether it's offering a customer a more expensive product when the one on sale isn't available, calling a company to find out about a recalled product, or opening up another checkout line so people don't have to wait, customer service is essential.

The Manager will usually be the one called when a customer has a problem no one else can or wants to handle. He or she is responsible for dealing with emergencies, crises, and any problems which crop up during the day in the store. He or she is expected to write reports for accidents or other incidents such as when employees or customers are hurt within the store or in the parking lot.

The Manager is responsible for overseeing all monies in the store. He or she may go over reports of the day's receipts as well as weekly and monthly reports. The individual may also be responsible for depositing the days receipts in the bank or may accompany an assistant manager or other employee in this task.

Additional duties of Store Managers in supermarkets and groceries might include:

- Terminating employees
- Recommending raises and promotions for employees
- Handling loss prevention
- Representing the store at community events
- Handling crises

Salaries

Earnings for Store Managers working in supermarkets range from $25,000 to $53,000 or more. Variables affecting earnings include the size, prestige, and geographic location of the supermarket. Other variables include the experience, responsibilities, and education of the individual.

Employment Prospects

Employment prospects are good for supermarket Store Managers. Positions are located throughout the country. Individuals may, however, have to relocate for a specific job.

Advancement Prospects

The most common method of career advancement for Store Managers working in supermarkets or groceries is for individuals to locate similar jobs in larger stores or the new superstores. Another way Store Managers climb the career ladder is by being promoted to positions such as area managers.

Education and Training

Educational and training requirements vary from store to store. Generally larger stores and chains require their Managers to go through formal training programs which include both classroom and in-store training. Some supermarkets will hire individuals who have no formal training, but have worked their way up obtaining on-the-job training along the way.

Educational backgrounds of supermarket Store Managers vary too. While stores may not require individuals to hold anything above a high school diploma, they may prefer Managers with college backgrounds or degrees. Good majors include business, management, marketing, retailing, communications, advertising, liberal arts, or related fields.

Experience, Skills, and Personality Traits

Store Managers working in groceries and supermarkets need a great deal of experience. Most have gone through the ranks either starting out at the bottom and moving up or going through a management program. Store Managers may have been department managers and then assistant store managers prior to their appointment. The Manager must have a knowledge of management principles as well as a total understanding of the retail grocery industry.

Leadership skills, self-confidence, and decisiveness are essential. The ability to deal with and work well with people is mandatory. Individuals need to be good problem solvers who are energetic, detail oriented, and highly motivated. Communication skills, both written and verbal, are necessary as well.

Unions/Associations

Supermarket Store Managers may get additional career information by contacting the Food Marketing Institute (FMI), the National Retail Merchants Association (NRMA), and the American Collegiate Retailing Association (ACRA).

Tips for Entry

1. Many larger supermarkets and chain stores offer management training programs. Contact the headquarters of these stores to find out about requirements.
2. Positions may be advertised in the classified sections of newspapers. Look under classifications including "Store Manager," "Supermarket Opportunities," "Grocery Stores," "Super Centers," "Store Management," "Store Manager-Food," or "Management Opportunities."
3. Openings are also advertised in trade journals.

4. Jobs in this field may be located on-line. Begin your search on some of the more popular job search sites such as Monster board (www.monster.com) and Hot Jobs (www.hotjobs.com).

5. Contact recruiters and executive search firms specializing in management positions in supermarkets.

6. Send your resume and a short cover letter to the corporate offices of supermarkets as well as to the local store.

7. As noted, you need experience in this position to move up. Get your foot in the door, get experience, and learn everything you can.

WRAPPER/BAGGER—GROCERY STORE/SUPERMARKET

CAREER PROFILE

Duties: Wrap merchandise for customers; put merchandise in bags or other packaging for customers; transport customers' purchases to their car

Alternate Titles: Bagger

Salary Range: $5.50 to $7.50+ per hour

Employment Prospects: Excellent

Advancement Prospects: Excellent

Best Geographical Location(s) for Position: Jobs may be located throughout the country

Prerequisites:

Education and Training—On-the-job training

Experience—No experience required

Special Skills and Personality Traits—Ability to stand for extended periods of time; pleasant disposition; customer service skills

CAREER LADDER

```
┌─────────────────────────────┐
│          Cashier            │
└─────────────────────────────┘

┌─────────────────────────────┐
│       Wrapper/Bagger        │
└─────────────────────────────┘

┌─────────────────────────────┐
│        Entry Level          │
└─────────────────────────────┘
```

Position Description

Everyone needs groceries. Whether people do huge weekly shopping trips or just run into the store for a few items for dinner, Wrappers and Baggers make the whole process go quicker.

Wrappers, who are also referred to as Baggers, are the individuals responsible for packaging the merchandise customers purchase. As cashiers operate the cash register, scanning prices or ringing up purchases, they pass the merchandise to a Wrapper or Bagger. In many stores the cashier puts the merchandise on a moving belt as it is rung up. The Bagger then takes the merchandise and packs it for the customer. The individual may ask the customer if he or she prefers paper bags, plastic bags, or even boxes. The Bagger/Wrapper may use double bags if items are heavy.

The Bagger/Wrapper must be sure to package items carefully. He or she is expected to put heavier items on the bottom of bags and lighter or more fragile items on top. The individual must make sure that bags are not too heavy for customers to carry. He or she must also be sure bags are not so heavy they break when customers lift them out of their cart.

The Wrapper/Bagger may put items such as eggs and lightbulbs in separate bags so they don't break when boxes of laundry detergent or six-packs of soda roll on them. He or she may also put small items such as gum, candy, or batteries in separate bags. The individual might package frozen goods and other cold items together. This may help to keep them either frozen or cold until customers get their groceries home as well as making it easier to put them away.

Today, many grocery stores are superstores or supercenters. These stores sell groceries as well as a variety of other merchandise. In these cases, the Wrapper/Bagger may be responsible for packaging items other than those sold in traditional groceries.

After bagging the groceries and other merchandise, individuals are expected to put the bags into the customers' shopping carts.

Additional duties of Wrappers and Baggers may include:

- Carrying customers' packages to their car
- Checking prices for cashiers
- Putting merchandise which customers do not want to purchase back on shelves
- Collecting shopping carts from parking lot

Salaries

Earnings for Baggers and Wrappers working in grocery stores, supermarkets, or other retail establishments can range from approximately $5.50 to $7.50 or more per hour. Variables affecting earnings include the geographic location and size of the store as well as the demand for workers in the specific area.

Employment Prospects

Employment prospects are excellent for Baggers and Wrappers. Individuals may find work throughout the country.

One of the selling points for many people seeking this job is the flexibility of working hours. Individuals may work full time, part time, mornings, afternoons, evenings, weekdays, weekends, or holidays.

Advancement Prospects

Advancement prospects for Wrappers and Baggers are dependent to a great extent on the individual's aspirations. Some people take jobs as Baggers and Wrappers while in school, as a first job, or on a part-time basis to augment other incomes. These individuals can move on to other types of jobs depending on their training. Others may start out as Wrappers and Baggers and move into jobs as cashiers.

Education and Training

Baggers and Wrappers are trained on the job. Individuals will learn how to put items into bags so groceries don't get crushed and bags are not too heavy for customers to carry.

Experience, Skills, and Personality Traits

Jobs for Wrappers and Baggers are usually entry level and don't require any previous experience. Individuals should be able to stand on their feet for long periods of time. Good interpersonal and customer relations skills are essential as is a pleasant personality.

Unions/Associations

Wrappers and Baggers may be members of the United Food and Commercial Workers International Union or house unions. Individuals may get additional career information by contacting the National Retail Federation (NRF).

Tips for Entry

1. There is a great deal of turnover in these positions. Stop in stores where you are interested in working and ask to fill out applications. Ask that your application be kept on file if there are no current openings.
2. Remember to bring with you the names, addresses, and phone numbers of a few people you can use as references when filling in applications. Make sure you ask people if you can use them as references BEFORE you use them.
3. Jobs may be posted in store windows. Look for announcements stating "Baggers/Wrappers Wanted."
4. Jobs may be advertised in the classified sections of newspapers. Look under classifications such as "Baggers," "Wrappers," "Supermarket Opportunities," "Retail Opportunities," or "Grocery Stores."
5. Stores often call local labor offices to post these jobs. Remember to stop by your state employment office.

SALES MANAGER—AUTO SALES

CAREER PROFILE

Duties: Manage sales activities for automotive dealership; assist salespeople; recruit and hire sales staff, train salespeople; motivate salespeople; close deals

Alternate Titles: Auto Sales Manager

Salary Range: $50,000 to $200,000+

Employment Prospects: Good

Advancement Prospects: Fair

Best Geographical Location(s) for Position: Jobs may be located throughout the country

Prerequisites:

Education and Training—Educational requirements vary

Experience—Experience in auto sales

Special Skills and Personality Traits—Management skills; administrative skills; motivation; selling skills; negotiating skills; interpersonal skills; communications skills; ability to work well with numbers

CAREER LADDER

```
┌─────────────────────────────────┐
│      Sales Manager in Larger,    │
│     More Prestigious Dealership  │
│    or Dealership General Manager │
└─────────────────────────────────┘

┌─────────────────────────────────┐
│          Sales Manager           │
└─────────────────────────────────┘

┌─────────────────────────────────┐
│          Salesperson             │
└─────────────────────────────────┘
```

Position Description

Auto dealerships generally have a number of salespeople to help customers when buying cars. The Sales Manager holds an important job. He or she is responsible for leading the dealership's team of salespeople.

A good Sales Manager can mean the difference between success and mediocrity for both the dealership and its salespeople. The individual oversees the sales floor, and develops policies for managing it.

For example, the Sales Manager must determine how walk-ins are assigned to salespeople. (Walk-ins are customers who visit the dealership without being referred to a specific salesperson.) The Sales Manager also must determine how customers calling the dealership not asking for a specific person are assigned to salespeople.

Part of the job of the Sales Manager is recruiting and hiring the sales staff. The individual may develop and place help wanted ads in print or broadcast media. He or she may interview potential sales people. The Sales Manager may also set the work schedules for the sales staff.

One of the most important functions of a good Sales Manager is training the sales staff. The Sales Manager must make sure each salesperson knows as much as possible about each vehicle in order to sell it effectively. He or she may hold regular meetings to inform the sales staff about new cars, new options, and how vehicle features work.

The individual will also train salespeople on selling techniques utilizing policies of the dealership. The Sales Manager may provide training for the sales staff on a one-to-one basis or may be expected to develop formal group training programs.

Another important function of the Sales Manager is motivating the sales staff. Selling cars is not always easy. Every customer who walks in does not make a purchase. Most customers like to comparison shop. It is essential for all salespersons to remain upbeat and motivated. The Sales Manager needs to be effective in this task or he or she may lose salespeople.

When a customer comes in to purchase a car he or she may be indecisive. The Sales Manager often assists salespeople in closing deals or clinching the sale. He or she may explain the various options for obtaining a vehicle such as leasing, purchasing, and financing.

The Sales Manager must be a good negotiator. There is a great deal of negotiation in this type of job and it must be done in a polite and friendly manner to keep the customer.

While salespeople have some leeway in pricing vehicles, the Sales Manager has a great deal more. He or she usually has a great deal more experience in closing deals and may be more successful.

Other duties of car Sales Managers may include:

- Answering customers' questions regarding the dealership
- Handling paperwork
- Tracking weekly, monthly, and annual sales reports
- Ordering needed vehicles
- Arranging for financing
- Developing and setting up sales training programs
- Performing the duties of a salesperson

Salaries

Earnings for Sales Managers working in auto sales can range from approximately $50,000 to $200,000 or more. Factors affecting earnings include the specific dealership, size, location, and type of vehicles being sold.

Sales Managers may be compensated in a number of ways. These include either a straight salary, a low salary plus a high commission, or a higher salary and a lower commission. Commissions may be paid on vehicles sold by the dealership.

Earnings are dependent to a great extent on the aggressiveness, motivation, and sales ability of the individual. Earnings are also dependent on the type of vehicles sold. The more expensive the cars, the higher the commission paid.

Depending on the specific job, one of the perks that Automobile Sales Managers may receive in this line of work are demo cars to drive. Individuals also may receive liberal fringe benefit packages.

Employment Prospects

Employment prospects are good for individuals pursuing a career in this field. Every dealership is on the lookout for good Sales Managers who can motivate their sales staff. Jobs may be located throughout the country.

Advancement Prospects

Sales Managers working in auto sales may advance their career in a number of ways. Individuals may climb the career ladder by locating similar positions in larger or more prestigious dealerships. This would result in increased responsibilities and earnings. Others may be promoted to the position of dealership general manager.

Education and Training

While some dealerships may prefer applicants who have college backgrounds or degrees, most don't require it. Depending on the specific agency, individuals may be required to go through formal training programs or may go through less formal training or on-the-job training.

Any seminars, courses, or workshops in sales or motivation can be useful.

Experience, Skills, and Personality Traits

Prior to becoming Sales Managers, individuals usually have had a great deal of experience as auto salespeople. There are a lot of traits which make a good Automobile Sales Manager. Successful Sales Managers are reliable and loyal to their company, their salespeople, and their customers. Like salespeople, they must be good listeners, and have great selling and negotiating skills. The ability to motivate a sales staff is essential. Interpersonal and organizational skills are also necessary.

Unions/Associations

Those interested in learning more about careers in this field should contact the National Automobile Dealers Association (NADA).

Tips for Entry

1. Jobs may be advertised in the newspaper classified section under headings including "Auto," "Auto Sales," "Car Sales," "Truck Sales," or "Sales Manager—Auto."
2. Stop in to see auto dealers for which you might be interested in working. Ask to speak to the general manager.
3. Many auto dealerships have websites listing job openings.
4. Look for and take training programs, seminars, and workshops in selling and motivation.
5. You might also look for books and listen to tapes in these areas.

CAR SALESPERSON

CAREER PROFILE

Duties: Help customer determine which vehicle best suits individual's needs; accompany customer for test drives; provide customer with price of car

Alternate Titles: Automobile Salesperson; Car Salesman; Car Saleswoman; Auto Sales Consultant; Salesman; Saleswoman

Salary Range: $28,000 to $100,000+

Employment Prospects: Excellent

Advancement Prospects: Fair

Best Geographical Location(s) for Position: Jobs may be located throughout the country

Prerequisites:

    Education and Training—Educational requirements vary

    Experience—Experience requirements vary

    Special Skills and Personality Traits—Sales skills; negotiation skills; interpersonal skills; communications skills; ability to work well with numbers; persuasive; driver's license

CAREER LADDER

```
┌─────────────────────────────────┐
│    Car Salesperson in Larger    │
│  or More Prestigious Dealership  │
│       or Sales Manager          │
└─────────────────────────────────┘

┌─────────────────────────────────┐
│       Car Salesperson           │
└─────────────────────────────────┘

┌─────────────────────────────────┐
│   Salesperson in Other Industry  │
│        or Entry Level            │
└─────────────────────────────────┘
```

Position Description

Other than a home, the largest retail purchase many people make is their vehicle. The individual who sells these is called a Car Salesperson. He or she may also be referred to as a Car Salesman, Car Saleswoman, Auto Salesperson, or Sales Consultant, among other titles.

A Car Salesperson works for a car dealership. (In the context of this job, the word car will encompass all vehicles including automobiles, trucks, SUVs, etc.) He or she may work for a dealership selling new vehicles, used vehicles, or a combination of both.

The Car Salesperson is expected to greet potential customers when they walk into the dealership, and ascertain the type of vehicle in which the customer is interested. The Salesperson determines the options that are important to the customer. Does the customer want an automatic transmission or standard? A sedan or two door? A luxury or an economy model? Does the customer plan on buying the car outright? How about financing? What about leasing? The Salesperson sprinkles small talk into the conversation to put the customer at ease while gathering information.

The more information the Salesperson obtains, the better the opportunity to sell a car to a customer.

Salespeople encourage the customer to look at the car, and may bring the customer out to the car lot to show the various cars available. Salespeople also persuade customers to take a test drive, since customers who begin to take possession of a vehicle in their mind by driving it are more likely to make a purchase.

The Salesperson explains why his or her dealership is better than others and outlines the perks of buying from that particular dealer. These may include free loaner cars when the customer's car is being serviced, discounted service rates for customers, and convenient service hours.

Throughout this process, the customer can be expected to come back to the same question. How much will the car cost? The Salesperson must make the customer feel as if he or she is getting the best possible price. Depending on the structure of the dealership, the Salesperson gives the customer a price or obtains a price from the sales manager. The price, of course, depends on the specific car and whether the customer is buying outright, leasing, financing, or trading in another vehicle. At times, the Salesperson may have the customer talk to the sales manager to clinch the deal. He or she might additionally bring the customer to see the finance manager who can explain payment or lease terms.

The Salesperson must be a good negotiator, and must be able to negotiate in a polite and friendly manner.

There are many dealers and options for people to select from when buying or leasing a vehicle. Some dealerships now offer "no haggle" pricing. Others may have prices set by Internet buying services. In these situations, it is even more important than ever for the Salesperson to be friendly and attentive to his or her customers.

Once a Salesperson has closed a deal, he or she must complete a great amount of paperwork. The Salesperson makes sure contracts or sales agreements are signed and monies are correctly figured. In some dealerships, the Salesperson also may arrange for auto registrations, licensing, etc.

The Salesperson is responsible for making sure the vehicle is prepared for sale. When the customer comes in to take ownership, the Salesperson is expected to take payment. He or she makes sure all transfers for the new vehicle and any trade-ins are signed. At this time, the Salesperson shows the customer how all the features of the car work and covers any last-minute questions.

Other duties of a Car Salesperson may include:

- Answering customers questions regarding vehicles
- Selling extended warranties
- Selling additional options
- Following up after the car has been delivered to the customer to make sure they are happy and have no problems
- Arranging for financing

Salaries

Earnings for Car Salespeople vary tremendously. One of the greatest things about being a Car Salesperson is that the sky is the limit on earnings. Some individuals in this line of work make $28,000 and others earn $100,000 or more annually.

Salespeople may be compensated in a number of different ways. These include a straight salary, a commission on sales, or a combination of both. Earnings depend, to a great extent, on the aggressiveness, motivation, and sales ability of the individual. Earnings also depend on the type of vehicles sold. The more expensive cars are, the higher the commission for the Salesperson.

The success of a Car Salesperson is in repeat business. Customers who feel they got the right vehicle at a fair price will not only come back for their next vehicle, but refer their friends, family, and business associates. Word-of-mouth referrals can increase a Salesperson's income dramatically.

One of the perks that Car Salespeople may receive are demo cars to drive on their personal time. Individuals also may receive liberal fringe benefit packages.

Employment Prospects

Employment prospects for Car Salespeople are excellent. Dealerships are always on the lookout for aggressive, motivated Salespeople. Individuals may find jobs throughout the country.

Depending on the situation, Car Salespeople may sell either new or used vehicles. Some sell both. Individuals may choose between jobs selling foreign or domestic vehicles.

Advancement Prospects

Advancement prospects for a Car Salesperson depend on the career aspirations of the individual. Some Salespeople move up the career ladder by acquiring jobs as sales managers. Others enjoy the selling aspect of their job and want to stay in this type of position. These individuals may advance their careers by locating jobs in larger or more prestigious dealerships. The most common method of career advancement is selling more vehicles resulting in increased earnings.

Education and Training

There is usually no educational requirement for Automobile Salespeople. Some dealerships may prefer a college background, but they do not generally require it. Any seminars, courses, or workshops in sales will be useful. Once on the job, individuals will receive formal or informal training.

Experience, Skills, and Personality Traits

Experience requirements vary from dealership to dealership. While some employers require or prefer experience in auto sales, there are many who will hire motivated eager Salespeople with no experience.

Good car Salespeople are good listeners. They also know the right questions to ask potential buyers. The most successful Salespeople have great selling skills, negotiating skills, and interpersonal skills.

The ability to work well with numbers is essential. A clean driver's license is also needed.

Unions/Associations

Those interested in learning more about careers in this field should contact the National Automobile Dealers Association (NADA), the American Automobile Leasing Association (AALA), and the National Independent Automobile Dealers Association (NIADA).

Tips for Entry

1. Jobs may be advertised in the newspaper classified section under headings including "Auto," "Auto Sales," "Car Sales," "Truck Sales," "Salespeople," or "Auto Salesperson."

2. Stop in to see dealers you might be interested in working with. Ask to speak to the sales manager.
3. Many auto dealerships have websites listing job openings.
4. All sales experience is valuable in learning how to deal with the public.

5. Take advantage of any sales training programs you can find. These are motivational and help you hone your selling skills.

E-COMMERCE, MAIL ORDER, AND DIRECT RESPONSE SHOPPING

MARKETING DIRECTOR—WEB STORE

CAREER PROFILE

Duties: Develop and implement marketing plans and campaigns for company's website store or catalog; handle day-to-day marketing functions; plan and implement special events; oversee advertising and public relations program

Alternate Titles: Internet Catalog Director of Marketing; Marketing Manager

Salary Range: $26,000 to $85,000+

Employment Prospects: Fair

Advancement Prospects: Good

Best Geographical Location(s) for Position: Jobs may be located throughout the country

Prerequisites:

Education and Training—College degree preferred, but not always required

Experience—Marketing, merchandising, publicity, public relations, advertising, and Internet experience necessary

Special Skills and Personality Traits—Creativity; good verbal and written communications skills; knowledge of retail industry; knowledge of consumer products; Internet savvy

CAREER LADDER

```
┌─────────────────────────────────┐
│   Marketing Director at Larger,  │
│   More Prestigious Internet Site │
│            or Store              │
└─────────────────────────────────┘

┌─────────────────────────────────┐
│   Web Store Marketing Director   │
└─────────────────────────────────┘

┌─────────────────────────────────┐
│   Assistant Marketing Director   │
│      or Marketing Director       │
│        in Other Industry         │
└─────────────────────────────────┘
```

Position Description

Today, many traditional retail outlets also have websites to showcase and sell their merchandise. These include department stores, specialty stores, chains and boutiques, catalogs, and even television shopping channels. There are also many companies selling merchandise on the Web that don't have traditional stores or catalogs and sell solely through the Web. Amazon.com is one of the better known of such sites.

There are thousands of websites on the Internet selling merchandise. It is increasingly becoming more important for retail as well as wholesale companies to have a presence on the Web. While some of these "stores" have names well known before their Internet presence, many do not. The Internet has made it possible for people in almost any part of the world to set up a store as small or large as they like on-line. No matter what the size, the site is available to the public. With so many sites available, how does an on-line store attract customers to their site? As in traditional retailing, an on-line store must market their site.

The Marketing Director of a retail website has a very important job. He or she finds ways to market the site to potential customers. The manner in which this is done can mean the success or failure of an on-line retail store.

The Marketing Director develops the concepts and campaigns which will determine how the site will be marketed to potential shoppers. The individual determines the most effective techniques and programs to market the site and its products.

As part of this job, the Marketing Director plans and coordinates all of the site's marketing goals and objectives. How will people know the store is on-line? To whom will they market the site? What types of customers will they try to attract?

Marketing an on-line store is slightly different from marketing a traditional store. Customers for on-line stores can come from virtually anywhere in the world.

It is essential that the Marketing Director find ways to include the store's Web address in as many places as possible. In some situations, the store may have one or more traditional retail outlets. This often makes it easier to let people know of an on-line store.

The Marketing Director must be sure that the on-line store's website address is added to all television commercials, print advertisements, and packaging. This helps get the name and address of the web store in front of the public.

The Marketing Director's job becomes more challenging if the store's name isn't recognizable. In this case, he or she must find ways to bring the store to the public's attention. Marketing Directors may utilize a variety of programs to help attract shoppers and bring people to the store's site.

The Marketing Director must decide which of these programs and services are most viable for his or her specific audience. Often, Marketing Directors advertise the site. They may do this in print, television, or banner ads on other sites. Banner ads are the advertisements commonly seen on a website where an individual need only click on the banner to go to the site of the advertiser.

The Marketing Director often does research to obtain information about current and potential customers. He or she may prepare questionnaires or surveys to be placed on the site. In order to entice people to answer questionnaires, the Marketing Director may offer a gift, free shipping, or a percentage off on future orders.

Marketing Directors must devise innovate ideas to attract new visitors to the site. In many situations, on-line store Marketing Directors utilize sweepstakes and contests for this purpose. Once people log on to the on-line store site to enter the contest, the hope is they will return to the site to browse and buy. To accomplish this, many Marketing Directors run contests that customers can enter daily. This means customers may visit the site daily and see merchandise they want to purchase.

Another reason Marketing Directors of on-line stores use sweepstakes is to help build mailing lists. When people enter contests they must usually give their names, addresses, phone numbers, and email address. Additional information may be gathered as well which may be helpful in targeting shoppers to the site.

Marketing Directors also use contests to build lists for email newsletters. These newsletters are useful for informing customers about store specials, new merchandise, and promotions.

Promotions in traditional stores are designed to bring people in to browse and buy. Marketing Directors for on-line stores often utilize marketing efforts such as on-line coupons, offers of "buy one, get one for half price," or free shipping.

The Marketing Director who can come up with innovative and creative ideas might get the attention of journalists or others doing articles or stories on interesting websites. The individual may, for example, contact a television talk or news show to do a segment on an interesting product being sold on the site. Depending on which show a story ends up on, it can lead to thousands of website hits.

Depending on the size and structure of the site, the Marketing Director may work with an advertising and public relations director. In some situations, the Marketing Director may also be responsible for handling the public relations and advertising functions.

Additional duties of a web store Marketing Director might include:

- Supervising marketing, public relations, and advertising staff
- Developing marketing budgets
- Designing and developing marketing materials
- Conducting marketing research
- Developing and providing advertising content for site

Salaries

Annual earnings for Marketing Directors for on-line stores can range from approximately $26,000 to $85,000 or more. Variables affecting earnings include the size and prestige of the specific on-line store as well as the experience and responsibilities of the individual. Many on-line companies also offer stock options to their employees as part of their employment package.

Employment Prospects

Employment prospects are fair for this position. As more companies open on-line stores, prospects will improve. As Web stores can be located anyplace, jobs may be found throughout the country. Individuals who have a proven track record are most employable.

Advancement Prospects

Marketing Directors working in this industry have a number of options for career advancement. Some individuals get experience, prove themselves, and move on to positions at larger or more prestigious on-line stores. This results in increased responsibilities and earnings. Often, other on-line stores try to recruit the Marketing Director from a successful on-line store.

Other individuals move into positions as Marketing Directors for other types of websites or in other industries. Still others strike out on their own and start their own marketing firms.

Education and Training

Educational requirements vary for Marketing Directors working for on-line stores. Smaller or lesser known on-line stores may prefer a college degree, but not always require it. Generally larger, more prestigious, or better-known on-line stores will require their Marketing Directors to hold a minimum of a four-year college degree. Good choices for majors include public relations, advertising, business, journalism, marketing, liberal arts, English, communications, and business.

Courses and seminars in marketing, public relations, publicity, promotion, the retail industry, and Web marketing are also helpful.

Experience, Skills, and Personality Traits

Marketing Managers in this industry must be Web savvy. Communications skills, both written and verbal, are essential. Individuals should be creative, innovative, ambitious, articulate, and highly motivated. Marketing Directors also need to be energetic with the ability to handle many details and projects at one time without getting flustered and stressed.

A knowledge of publicity, promotion, public relations, and advertising as well as research techniques is also necessary.

Unions/Associations

Marketing Directors may belong to a number of trade associations providing support and guidance. These might include the American Marketing Association (AMA), the Marketing Research Association (MRA), the Public Rela-

tions Society of America (PRSA), and Electronic Retailing Association (ERA).

Tips for Entry

1. Positions may be advertised in the classified ad section of newspapers. Look under headings including "Marketing," "Marketing Director," "Web Store," "On-Line Store," or "E-Tailing."
2. Send your resume and a cover letter to stores or sites in which you are interested in working. Ask that your resume be kept on file.
3. Join trade associations. These will help you in searching for internships, scholarships, and training programs in marketing.
4. Jobs may also be advertised in trade journals.
5. Look for jobs on-line. Check out sites such as www.hotjobs.com and www.monster.com to get started.
6. Take seminars and courses in marketing, promotion, public relations, publicity, and Web marketing. These will give you an edge over other applicants as well as helping you hone your skills and make valuable contacts.

WEBMASTER—
ON-LINE STORE OR CATALOG

CAREER PROFILE

Duties: Design on-line retail store or catalog; create content for site; manage and maintain site

Alternative Titles(s): Website Administrator

Salary Range: $28,000 to $150,000+

Employment Prospects: Good

Advancement Prospects: Good

Best Geographical Location(s) for Position: Positions located throughout the country

Prerequisites:

Education and Training—Education and training requirements vary

Experience and Qualifications—Experience designing websites necessary

Special Skills and Personality Traits—Creative; knowledge of retail industry; computer skills; Internet savvy; knowledge of HTML and other programming languages; graphic and layout skills.

CAREER LADDER

```
┌─────────────────────────────────┐
│      Webmaster for Larger,       │
│   More Prestigious On-Line Store │
│     or Webmaster Consultant      │
└─────────────────────────────────┘

┌─────────────────────────────────┐
│           Webmaster             │
└─────────────────────────────────┘

┌─────────────────────────────────┐
│    Webmaster in Other Industry   │
└─────────────────────────────────┘
```

Position Description

Every day more companies are getting a presence on the World Wide Web. Retail businesses are no exception. Whether they are small retail companies aspiring to make it big or large companies who don't want to miss the boat with on-line sales, retail stores on the Internet are here to stay. An on-line store means a retailer can have customers around the corner or around the world.

In order to open an on-line store, a company must rent a space or location on the Web. This may be done by obtaining a host. The store pays the host for the right to place their store on-line on the host's space. In some instances, the store and the host are one.

In order for potential customers to find the store, it must have a web address. This is the domain name. For example, the web address of amazon.com is www.amazon.com. The web address of the television shopping channel QVC is www.iqvc.com.

The individual responsible for putting together the website for the on-line store is called the Webmaster. The Web-

master's job is very important to the on-line retailer. His or her skill and talent can mean the difference between a web store's success and failure.

Web stores are very much like traditional stores. If people don't go and visit, no one will buy anything. Traditional stores need foot traffic. Web stores need visitors. Every time an individual visits a web page it is called a hit. Just as the more people who visit a store, the better the chance of sales, similarly, the more hits a web store gets the better the chance of people buying. It is also essential that people not only visit a web store, but revisit it on a consistent basis.

The Webmaster develops and creates the web store site on the World Wide Web. He or she must design and program the on-line store site so it is exciting and easy to use. The Webmaster must be sure that the each web page on the store site opens easy and quickly. If they don't, people often leave the site and surf to another location. This results in a loss of sales.

The Webmaster develops the site and adds pictures of products, animations, and other graphics. These are useful to help potential customers get a better idea of what the merchandise looks like as well as adding excitement to the various pages.

The individual may manipulate images to the proper size and format. This is necessary because if an image is too large it will slow down the loading of a web page on an individual's computer. If an image is too small, a customer may not be able to see it clearly. The Webmaster must therefore know how many graphics to add and how to size them properly to make each page graphically pleasing, yet quick to open.

The Webmaster often develops a system for people to search for products on the store site. The easier it is for people to find what they are looking for, the better the chance of a sale. He or she may program pop-up windows, product compare features, shopping carts, secure payment systems, or other functions to make on-line shopping easier for the customer.

Developing and designing the web store site is just one part of the job of the Webmaster. He or she is additionally responsible for the continued management and maintenance of the site.

In order to keep an on-line store site fresh and timely retailers often change the merchandise they are offering, update sale items, or have promotions to attract customers to their store site. Sometimes the on-line stores change content daily. The Webmaster must make ad changes and remove stale content.

Websites are created in special languages so they can be displayed on the Internet. Text, for example, is converted into a language called HTML, or Hypertext Markup Language. Other languages may used as well. The Webmaster must know how to format the special languages.

Webmasters are expected to monitor the site continuously. Every time new content or a link is added, the individual must be sure everything on the site is working and all links are accurate.

Depending on the situation and the size of the on-line store, the Webmaster may work alone or may have one or more people working under his or her direction. He or she may also work with graphic designers and artists, photographers, copywriters, or editors.

Other duties of Webmasters for on-line stores include:

- Developing web content
- Making sure the store site is user friendly
- Responding to inquiries from customers and other browsers having problems with the site
- Handling problems with the site
- Finding the best way to present information and graphics on the store site

Salaries

Annual earnings for Webmasters working for on-line retailers may vary from approximately $28,000 to $150,000 or more annually. Variables include the size and prestige of the specific retailer as well as the responsibilities, experience, and reputation of the individual.

Webmasters who have a proven track record for developing creative sites which attract attention will earn the highest salaries.

It should be noted that some retailers hire consultants to handle their website stores. These individuals may earn between $50 and $200 or more per hour.

Employment Prospects

Employment prospects are good for Webmasters seeking to work for on-line retailers and getting better every day. Depending on the experience of the individual, he or she might work for small start-up retailers or those that are well established.

Individuals may find positions with retailers who are currently on line, retailers who are planning an on-line presence and on-line catalogers. Jobs may be located throughout the country.

As a result of the nature of the job, some retailers may allow their Webmasters to telecommute all or part of the time. Individuals may also find part-time or consulting positions.

Advancement Prospects

Webmasters working for retailers with on-line stores can advance their careers in a number of ways. Those who build websites which consistently attract visitors will have no trouble climbing the career ladder. The most common method of career advancement for Webmasters is locating similar positions with larger or more prestigious retailers. This will result in increased responsibilities and earnings. Other Webmasters decide to strike out on their own and begin consulting firms.

Education and Training

Education and training requirements vary for Webmasters working for on-line retailers. Many Webmasters are self-taught. Some have taken classes. Others have college backgrounds or degrees in computers, programming, languages, graphics, web authoring, and the Internet. However it is learned, Webmasters must know HTML. It is also necessary to know other programming languages such as Cold Fusion, PERL, and Active Server Pages. It is helpful for those working on retail store sites to also know how to integrate databases.

Technology is constantly changing in this field. It is essential that Webmasters update their skills by self-study and/or classes, seminars, and workshops to keep up. Additional classes in understanding retail will also be helpful.

Experience, Skills, and Personality Traits

Experience requirements depend, to a great extent, on the size and prestige of the on-line store. Smaller on-line stores or those just starting up, may not require Webmasters with a great deal of experience as long as they illustrate that they can do an effective job. Larger, more prestigious on-line stores will generally want their Webmasters to have a proven track record and experience with retail sites.

Individuals must have a total competence with web dynamics, HTML authorship, and other programming languages. While some graphics work is outsourced or done by graphic designers within the company, graphic talent is necessary.

Webmasters additionally need excellent communications skills, both verbal and written. Creativity is essential.

Unions/Associations

Individuals interested in learning more about careers in the field may obtain additional information by contacting the Internet Professionals Association (IPA), the National Association of Webmasters (NAW), and National Retail Federation (NRF).

Tips for Entry

1. Positions may be located in the classified section of newspapers. Look under heading such as "Webmaster," "Retail Opportunities," or "On-Line Store." Also look for ads under specific store and on-line store names.
2. Trade journals may also list openings.
3. Look for a job on-line. Start with the more popular job sites such as www.hotjobs.com and www.monster.com.
4. Check out the websites of stores and catalogs on-line. Many post job openings.
5. Get experience putting together websites for not-for-profit organizations or civic groups. Don't forget to add your name as the creator and Webmaster.

CUSTOMER SERVICE MANAGER— ON-LINE STORE OR CATALOG

CAREER PROFILE

Duties: Supervise customer service representatives; oversee customer service department; handle problems and difficulties for customers; provide information regarding the web store to customers.

Alternate Titles(s): None

Salary Range: $23,000 to $48,000+

Employment Prospects: Good

Advancement Prospects: Fair

Best Geographical Location(s) for Position: Positions located throughout the country

Prerequisites:

Education and Training—Education and training requirements vary

Experience and Qualifications—Experience working in retailing, customer service, or with on-line stores

Special Skills and Personality Traits—Excellent writing skills; knowledge of retail industry; Internet savvy; communications skills; customer service skills

CAREER LADDER

```
┌─────────────────────────────────────┐
│  Customer Service Manager for Larger │
│   or More Prestigious On-Line Store  │
│            or Catalog                │
└─────────────────────────────────────┘

┌─────────────────────────────────────┐
│      Customer Service Manager        │
└─────────────────────────────────────┘

┌─────────────────────────────────────┐
│   Customer Service Representative    │
└─────────────────────────────────────┘
```

Position Description

Web stores and catalogs, like other retail outlets must provide exemplary customer service in order to survive. While e-commerce is thriving, in order to be successful, web stores and catalogs must still remember the golden rules of retailing. "The customer is always right," and "The customer needs to feel valued and important."

Most web stores and on-line catalogs employ a Customer Service Manager or customer service representatives to handle any problems or difficulties customers may have shopping on the site. In smaller retail sites, the webmaster or store owner may handle these functions. However, larger sites and stores usually have at least one Manager and may have a number of customer service representatives.

While shopping on-line is convenient and, to many, the best way to make purchases today, to some the process is new and unfamiliar. People may be uncomfortable with putting their credit card on-line, worried about shipping dates, extra charges, returns, or an array of other problems.

In a traditional store, a customer can pose a question and someone will answer face to face. In an on-line store, the question is often emailed to the customer service department. The Customer Service Manager receives the email with the question and is expected to respond. Most of the time, this is done by email. In some cases, the Customer Service Manager will assign these duties to customer service representatives.

The Customer Service Manager handles a variety of situations ranging from technical difficulties to problems with returns. For example, a customer might email customer service when a web store link isn't working correctly. Another customer might email that he or she is having problems adding items to their shopping cart on the site. In these cases, the Customer Service Manager must contact the webmaster to check out the situations and see how quickly the situations can be resolved. The Customer Service Manager must also email customers to thank them for bringing problems to their attention and advise them of a solution.

Sometimes the problems the Customer Service Manager faces are not technical in nature or web specific. For example, a customer may have placed an order for merchandise and it didn't arrive in a timely manner. Understandably, the customer is irate and wants an answer. The Customer Service Manager may respond with an email apologizing and offer the customer something to make up for the trouble he or she experienced. Depending on the situation, this might be a discount on the order, free-shipping, or a gift certificate toward a future purchase. The Customer Service Manager may also send a letter through the mail to apologize.

Depending on the specific on-line store, customers may want more information on a product than is offered on the website. They may contact customer service to find out if additional colors are offered, when stock will be in, or warranty information. The Customer Service Manager or a subordinate will contact the buyers to get the information and e-mail back an answer.

Web-store customers generally want their queries answered in as immediate a fashion as possible. The Customer Service Manager must see that queries, questions, and problems are handled quickly. At the very least, the individual must email a note informing customers they are working on a solution. In many companies, this is automated.

Other duties of Customer Service Managers for on-line stores include:

- Overseeing customer service representatives
- Training customer service representatives
- Developing policies to handle customer service issues
- Working with other members of the on-line store development team to make sure the site is customer friendly
- Preparing reports on customer service inquires for the on-line store owners or management
- Handling difficult returns for customers
- Issuing credits or gift certificates to make up for unsatisfactory service

Salaries

Earnings for Customer Service Managers working for on-line stores can range from $23,000 to $48,000 or more annually. Variables include the size and prestige of the specific on-line retailer as well as the responsibilities and experience of the individual.

Employment Prospects

Employment prospects are good for Customer Service Managers interested in working for on-line stores. While jobs may be located throughout the country, individuals may need to relocate for the position.

Individuals may work for large established on-line stores and on-line catalogs as well as smaller retail sites which are just starting up.

Advancement Prospects

Customer Service Managers working with on-line stores may advance their careers by locating similar jobs at larger or more prestigious on-line retailers. This results in increased responsibilities and earnings. Some individuals may also become customer service directors with large on-line retailers.

Education and Training

Educational requirements vary. Generally, the more well known on-line retailers will require or prefer a college degree. Smaller or lesser known on-line stores may not have an educational requirement as long as individuals illustrate that they can handle the job.

College gives individuals the opportunity to gain experience and may be useful in career advancement. It may also give one applicant an edge over another who doesn't have a college degree.

Experience, Skills, and Personality Traits

Customer Service Managers need the ability to make decisions quickly and effectively. This is mandatory with on-line stores. As noted previously, because of the nature of electronic retailing, people expect an answer shortly after posing a question.

As so much of this job entails writing, it is essential for Customer Service Managers to have excellent written communications skills. An understanding of the retail industry, customer service, and the workings of the Internet are also necessary.

Unions/Associations

Individuals may be members of a number of organizations which provide career guidance and support. These include the Internet Professionals Association (IPA) and the Electronic Retailing Association. Additional career information may also be obtained by contacting the National Retail Federation (NRF).

Tips for Entry

1. Jobs may be advertised in the classified sections of newspapers. Look under classifications such as "Internet Opportunities," "On-line Opportunities," "On-line Retailing," "Customer Service Manager," or "E-Commerce Opportunities." Specific on-line stores may also list multiple jobs in an advertisement.
2. Visit the websites of on-line retailers. Many post job openings.
3. Look for a job on-line. Start with some of the better known sites such as www.hotjobs.com and www.monster.com.

4. Make sure you are Internet savvy. If necessary, take a class at a local vocational-technical school or community college.

5. Seminars on Internet customer service will also be helpful. Many are offered throughout the country.

6. You might also stop at the library to get some books on customer service on the Internet and on-line retailing. The more you know, the better the job you can perform.

DIRECT RESPONSE COPYWRITER

CAREER PROFILE

Duties: Develop and write copy for direct response advertising; prepare copy for brochures, marketing pieces, etc.

Alternate Titles: Copywriter

Salary Range: $24,000 to $75,000+

Employment Prospects: Good

Advancement Prospects: Good

Best Geographical Location(s) for Position: Positions located throughout the country

Prerequisites:

Education and Training—Bachelor's degree in advertising, business, journalism, public relations, marketing, liberal arts, English, communications, business, etc.

Experience—Experience as junior copywriter, trainee, or intern helpful

Special Skills and Personality Traits—Creativity; excellent writing skills; good command of the English language; knowledge and understanding of direct response copywriting

CAREER LADDER

```
┌─────────────────────────────────────┐
│          Copy Supervisor            │
│  or Copywriter at Large, Prestigious│
│       Direct Response Agency        │
└─────────────────────────────────────┘

┌─────────────────────────────────────┐
│      Direct Response Copywriter     │
└─────────────────────────────────────┘

┌─────────────────────────────────────┐
│     Junior Copywriter or Trainee    │
└─────────────────────────────────────┘
```

Position Description

In addition to traditional retail stores, many products today are sold through direct response. One of the oldest forms of direct-response selling is the catalog. The newest are home shopping channels and infomercials, and other forms include direct mail as well as certain television or radio shows that are actually paid programming.

The individual responsible for writing and developing the copy for direct response advertising is called the Direct Response Copywriter. His or her main duty is writing copy for products generally sold through nontraditional retail outlets, and the exact duties of the job may vary among employers. The individual may write copy for print advertisements, sales letters, brochures, marketing pieces, copy for television or radio commercials, catalogs, or scripts for those selling products on home shopping channels or infomercials.

The Direct Response Copywriter may write simple copy such as headlines or may develop copy for entire mailings, advertisements or promotional packages. Direct Response Copywriters generally focus in on a specific group of people or market that may be interested in a product, and direct response pieces may be sent in the mail, advertised in a specialized publication, or seen during a televised program that targets these groups. Generally, the products being advertised can be ordered either by phone or mail.

Some Direct Response Copywriters, for example, may develop copy for literature sent in monthly credit card statements selling merchandise. This concept, often called piggybacking, may offer merchandise at a discounted price for credit card holders. It is essential to the success of this type of selling that the Direct Response Copywriter develop ads and brochures that grab people's attention. The ad, letter, or sales piece must make people want to read it, pick up a phone or write out a check, and order the merchandise at that very moment. Successful Direct Response Copywriters develop ads that make a consumer want to take action immediately. In many situations, the Direct Response Copywriter inserts a coupon into the advertising or promotional piece in order to stimulate quick and immediate response. Direct response earned its name from this type of direct action.

One of the interesting things about the job of a Direct Response Copywriter is that the results of his or her work can be seen almost immediately. People may either order a product, call an "800" number and charge it for a purchase, throw a brochure away or ignore it completely. If a sales letter, commercial, or advertisement does not draw orders almost immediately, the Direct Response Copywriter may be asked to change it rapidly.

Depending on the specific employment situation, The Direct Response Copywriter may also be responsible for developing advertising and sales concepts. He or she may come up with an idea to use as the selling point such as the low price, a money back guarantee, the trial period, or the extra added value if the customer acts immediately.

Additional duties of Direct Response Copywriters may include:

- Preparing copy for web retail stores
- Doing research to gather information for copy
- Revising or rewriting copy that the copy supervisor may find unsatisfactory

Salaries

Earnings for Direct Response Copywriters can range from approximately $24,000 to $75,000 or more annually. Factors affecting earnings include the size and prestige of the specific employer, as well as the responsibilities, experience, education, and reputation of the individual. Those who have proved themselves will earn salaries towards the upper end of the scale.

Employment Prospects

Talented Direct Response Copywriters are always in demand. Individuals may find employment throughout the country in a variety of settings. These include small, mid-sized and large catalog companies, direct response agencies, retail web sites, direct television agencies, and manufacturers of products sold through direct response methods.

Advancement Prospects

Direct Response Copywriters who develop persuasive copy which shows results will have no trouble advancing their careers. Individuals may climb the career ladder by becoming copy supervisors or locate jobs at large direct response agencies.

Education and Training

Generally, employers prefer individuals hold a minimum of a four-year college degree. Good choices for majors include advertising, marketing, public relations, English, liberal arts, or communications.

Courses and seminars in advertising or copywriting are useful to hone skills.

Experience, Skills, and Personality Traits

Direct Response Copywriters should be very creative, with a flair for writing exciting, persuasive headlines and body copy. They need a way with words that can make people want to take action right away.

Excellent writing skills are mandatory. A complete working knowledge of word usage, grammar, and spelling is necessary. The ability to work on multiple projects at one time and meet deadline is essential.

Individuals are often asked to show their portfolio or "book" of their work prior to being hired. This book is used to illustrate talent to potential employers.

Unions/Associations

Direct Response Copywriters may belong to a number of trade associations providing support and guidance. These may include the American Advertising Federation (AAF), the Business/Professional Advertising Association (B/PAA), the American Marketing Association (AMA), the Direct Marketing Association (DMA), and the Mail Advertising Service Association (MASA).

Tips for Entry

1. Join trade associations and attend their meetings and conventions. These are invaluable sources of information and networking opportunities.
2. Many associations have student memberships. Some of these also offer scholarships or internship opportunities.
3. Get experience in all facets of writing. This will help prepare you for your writing career.
4. Collect samples of direct response copy to see what might make you take action now. Practice writing your own copy for products.
5. Put together a portfolio of your writing samples. Include a variety of samples to illustrate your writing talents.
6. Positions are often advertised in the classified sections of newspapers. Keep in mind the Sunday paper usually has the largest classified section. Look under headings including "Direct Response," "Direct Mail," "Copywriter," or "Direct Response Copywriter." Companies may also advertise a number of opportunities in a boxed classified ad.

CATALOG COPYWRITER

CAREER PROFILE

Duties: Develop and write copy for catalogs

Alternate Titles: None

Salary Range: $24,000 to $55,000+

Employment Prospects: Fair

Advancement Prospects: Fair

Best Geographical Location(s) for Position: The greatest number of positions will be in areas hosting catalogs

Prerequisites:

Education and Training—Bachelor's degree in advertising, business, journalism, public relations, marketing, liberal arts, English, communications, business

Experience—Experience as junior copywriter, trainee, or intern helpful

Special Skills and Personality Traits—Creativity; excellent writing skills; good command of the English language; knowledge and understanding of catalog copywriting

CAREER LADDER

```
┌─────────────────────────────────┐
│  Copy Supervisor or Copywriter  │
│   at Direct Response Agency     │
└─────────────────────────────────┘

┌─────────────────────────────────┐
│       Catalog Copywriter        │
└─────────────────────────────────┘

┌─────────────────────────────────┐
│   Junior Copywriter or Trainee  │
└─────────────────────────────────┘
```

Position Description

With today's busy lifestyles, more people than ever are catalog shopping. There are literally thousands of different catalogs selling everything from soup to nuts and masses of items in between. Some catalogs sell a variety of merchandise, much like a department store. Others sell specialty items such as crafts, clothing, toys, shoes, electronics, plants, gourmet food, jewelry, tools, vitamins, music, videos, and books.

Copywriters working for catalog companies have challenging jobs. Individuals must describe a product in few words in such a way that people are enticed to purchase it. A common saying in the advertising industry is "Sell the sizzle, not the steak." Catalog Copywriters must do the same. They must make products in the catalog seem exciting no matter what they are.

Successful Catalog Copywriters use descriptive terms so that those who read the copy can imagine seeing and feeling the product being described. They can often even make people imagine the smell and taste of a product. For example, a talented Copywriter might write the following blurb in a gourmet food catalog under a can of chocolate chip cookies. *"Double Decadent Chocolate-Chocolate Chip Cookies. Four dozen chewy, chocolaty, fresh baked, bite sized chocolate chip cookies. Each mouth-watering chocolate morsel is chock full of chips and covered in a crunchy chocolate coating. Tucked into a decorative collector's tin and wrapped separately for you to savor alone or share with a friend."*

One of the problems catalog shoppers often face is that they do not have the actual product in front of them to pick up and see. The more descriptive the words a Copywriter uses, the easier it is for a potential customer to imagine what a product will be like.

Catalog Copywriters are expected to write headline copy, as well as the body of the description for each product. The individual must be able to describe each product in just a few words. Although there are exceptions, this usually ranges from approximately thirty words to one hundred words per product.

In order to perform their job, Catalog Copywriters may read the product literature and look at photos as well as touch and feel the actual product. In this manner, the individual will better be able to describe the product. In some instances, the manufacturer of the product also provides some descriptive copy. The writer may use this as the basis of his or her copy. Generally, a picture will accompany the product in the catalog.

The Copywriter must make sure the copy makes sense and relates to the accompanying photograph.

Some catalogs have hundreds of products. Each product sold in the catalog needs copy to describe it. Depending on the size and structure of the catalog, the individual may handle all the product copywriting duties or may work with one or more Copywriters. As a rule, copy must be approved by the catalog's copy supervisor. In some instances, the manufacturer of specific products may also need to approve copy.

It should be noted that many companies today also put their catalog on-line. Additionally, there are companies which solely have on-line catalogs. Catalog Copywriters may be responsible for handling the product copy for either variety.

Additional duties of Catalog Copywriter may include:

- Preparing copy for the catalog cover and back pages
- Doing research to gather information for copy
- Revising or rewriting copy that the copy supervisor may find unsatisfactory

Salaries

Earnings for Catalog Copywriters can range from approximately $24,000 to $55,000 or more annually. Factors affecting earnings include the size and prestige of the specific catalog as well as the responsibilities, experience, education, and reputation of the individual.

Employment Prospects

Employment prospects are fair for Catalog Copywriters. Individuals may find employment throughout the country. These include small, mid-sized, and large catalog companies. Additionally, there are increasing numbers of positions for Catalog Copywriters for on-line catalogs.

Advancement Prospects

Catalog Copywriters who consistently write persuasive copy will have no trouble advancing their careers. A common method of climbing the career ladder is landing a job with a larger or more prestigious catalog company. Some individuals advance their career by being promoted to copy supervisors. Still others locate jobs at advertising or direct-response agencies.

Education and Training

Most catalog companies prefer individuals hold a minimum of a four-year college degree. Relevant majors include advertising, marketing, public relations, English, liberal arts, and communications. Courses and seminars in advertising and copywriting are useful to hone skills.

Experience, Skills, and Personality Traits

Catalog Copywriters need to be very creative, with a flair for writing attention-grabbing, persuasive headlines and body copy. They need a way with words that can explain an item in an interesting manner with just a few words.

Excellent writing skills are mandatory. A complete working knowledge of word usage, grammar, and spelling is necessary. The ability to work on multiple projects at one time and meet deadlines is essential. Individuals are often asked to show their portfolio or "book" of their work prior to being hired. This book is used to illustrate talent to potential employers.

Unions/Associations

Catalog Copywriters may belong to a number of trade associations providing support and guidance. These may include the American Advertising Federation (AAF), the Business/Professional Advertising Association (B/PAA), the American Marketing Association (AMA), the Direct Marketing Association (DMA), and the Mail Advertising Service Association (MASA).

Tips for Entry

1. Join trade associations and attend their meetings and conventions. These are invaluable sources of information and networking opportunities.
2. Get experience in all facets of writing. This will help prepare you for your writing career.
3. Collect samples of catalog copy to see what you might buy. Practice writing your own copy for products.
4. Put together a portfolio of your writing samples. Include a variety of samples to illustrate your writing talents.
5. Positions are often advertised in the classified sections of newspapers. Keep in mind the Sunday paper usually has the largest classified section. Look under headings including "Catalogs," "Catalog Copywriter," or "Copywriter." Catalogs may also advertise a number of opportunities in a boxed classified ad.
6. Send your resume and a cover letter to the corporate offices of companies at which you are interested in working. Ask that your resume be kept on file.

CALL CENTER REPRESENTATIVE

Duties: Answer telephone calls from potential customers; answer questions about products being sold; take orders for products

Alternate Titles: Call Center Associate; Customer Representative; Order Entry Operator

Salary Range: $5.50 to $19.00+ per hour

Employment Prospects: Excellent

Advancement Prospects: Fair

Best Geographical Location(s) for Position: Greatest number of opportunities will be located in areas hosting large numbers of call centers

Prerequisites:

Education and Training—On-the-job training

Experience—Experience may be preferred, but not always required

Special Skills and Personality Traits—Pleasant telephone manner; interpersonal skills; people skills; communications skills; computer skills

```
┌─────────────────────────────────┐
│   Call Center Shift Supervisor  │
└─────────────────────────────────┘

┌─────────────────────────────────┐
│   Call Center Representative     │
└─────────────────────────────────┘

┌─────────────────────────────────┐
│          Entry Level            │
└─────────────────────────────────┘
```

Position Description

A great deal of retailing is done through methods other than traditional store shopping. With today's busy lifestyles many individuals also shop on the Internet, buy from catalogs, or make purchases from infomercials or television shopping channels. Those who shop on the Web may just need to point and click to make a purchase. Those buying from catalogs or television often pick up a telephone and place their order.

Call Center Representatives are the individuals who answer the telephone calls from potential customers and take the orders. Depending on where they work, they may also be referred to as Order Entry Operators, Call Center Associates, or Customer Representatives. Some retailers farm out their order taking to huge call centers. Others have their own employees handling orders.

The Call Center Representative may answer questions and provide information regarding the company and it's products. The individual is expected to answer the phone in a pleasant and friendly manner.

The first contact many people have with the company they are calling is with the Call Center Representative. If he or she sounds unfriendly, the customer may be taken aback and not place an order.

The individual may greet customers and thank them for calling. The Representative will then ask the customer how he or she can be of assistance. The Call Center Representative answers customer's inquiries to the best of his or her knowledge.

In some situations, the customer may want some information on a product or a price or may want to check availability. The Call Center Representative must be as helpful as possible. He or she often will punch information such as an item number or key word into a computer. In this manner the Representative may be able to check availability, descriptions, and prices.

Once customers have decided what they want to purchase, the Call Center Representative will take the order. In some situations, the Call Center Representative will ask the individual for some information. This might, for example, include a customer's name, address, phone number, the code on the back of a catalog, a customer number, item numbers, colors, or sizes. This information is generally input into a computer.

The Representative must obtain information on the customer's method of payment. Will he or she be sending a check? Is the item being shipped C.O.D.? Is a credit card being used? The Representative will total the order including merchandise and any shipping, handling, and taxes and inform the customer of the final price. At this time the Call Center Representative will process the order and also let the customer know when the order should arrive.

The more familiar a Call Center Representative is with the products the company sells the better. In some situations, the Representative may suggest products for customers or give explanations of merchandise.

A great deal of the success of companies selling products ordered by customers via the telephone is based on good customer service skills. Call Center Representatives who are good at their job are usually pleasant and helpful in making customers feel good about calling.

Additional duties of the Call Center Associates may include:

- Promoting the company's products
- Informing customers about current specials and promotions
- Giving customers phone number or addresses for additional customer service or contact information
- Handling customer service issues
- Searching the database for merchandise for which customers don't have item numbers

Salaries

Call Center Representatives earn hourly wages ranging from approximately $5.50 to $19.00 or more. Variables affecting earnings include the geographic location and size of the specific company for which the individual works as well as his or her experience and responsibilities. In some companies, individuals working overnight shifts or weekends will earn higher wages than those working more traditional hours and workdays.

Employment Prospects

Employment prospects are good for Call Center Representatives. While jobs may be located throughout the country, the most opportunities will be found in areas hosting large call centers. Individuals may work full time or part time.

Advancement Prospects

Advancement prospects are fair for Call Center Representatives. After obtaining experience, motivated individuals may advance their careers by acquiring positions as shift supervisors or call center managers.

Education and Training

Most employers require individuals to hold a minimum of a high school diploma or the equivalent. However, there are many Call Center Representatives who are still in school.

Generally, training is provided on the job. In some companies, formal training programs are provided to Call Center Representatives.

Experience, Skills, and Personality Traits

This is usually an entry-level job. While experience may give one applicant an edge over another, it is not generally required.

Call Center Representatives need a pleasant speaking voice and a good phone manner. Excellent customer service skills are mandatory. Computer skills are essential.

Unions/Associations

Individuals interested in learning more about careers in this field may obtain information by contacting the National Retail Federation (NRF) and the American Wholesale Marketers Association (AWMA).

Tips for Entry

1. Openings may be advertised in the classified sections of newspapers. Look under heading classifications such as "Call Centers," "Call Center Opportunities," "Catalog Opportunities," "Television Shopping Opportunities," "Call Center Representative," "Order Entry Operator," "Call Center Associate," or "Customer Representative." You might also look under ads for specific catalog companies, television shopping channels, or the mail order division of retail stores.
2. Check out openings on the Internet. Many call centers, catalogs, and television shopping channels have their own websites listing employment opportunities.
3. You might also find openings on the World Wide Web's job sites. Start with the more popular ones such as www.hotjobs.com and www.monster.com. A new site, www.abracat.com, is easy to use and has many job openings in all industries by geographical area.
4. Contact call centers, retail stores with mail order outlets, catalog companies, and television shopping channels. Ask to fill out an application.

WHOLESALE

SALES MANAGER—WHOLESALE

CAREER PROFILE

Duties: Supervise and coordinate the activities of sales representatives; establish territories; determine goals for sales representatives; motivate sales staff

Alternate Titles: Sales and Marketing Manager

Salary Range: $35,000 to $250,000+

Employment Prospects: Good

Best Geographical Location(s) for Position: Jobs may be located throughout the country; large cities will offer more possibilities

Prerequisites:

Education and Training—Educational requirements vary
Experience—Experience in wholesale or retail sales
Special Skills and Personality Traits—Sales ability; aggressiveness; organization; communication skills; ability to motivate others

CAREER LADDER

```
┌─────────────────────────────────────┐
│      Sales Manager for Larger        │
│  or More Prestigious Manufacturer    │
│     or Vice President of Sales       │
└─────────────────────────────────────┘

┌─────────────────────────────────────┐
│           Sales Manager              │
└─────────────────────────────────────┘

┌─────────────────────────────────────┐
│   District or Regional Sales Manager │
└─────────────────────────────────────┘
```

Position Description

Wholesalers sell a large amount of products to other companies who in turn sell them to consumers. Merchandise includes, but is not limited to, food, clothing, pharmaceuticals, office equipment, computers, cosmetics, machinery parts, hardware, electronics, automobile parts, exercise and sports equipment, and furniture. Wholesale companies often hire salespeople or manufacturer's representatives to sell their products to retailers or other consumers.

Sales Managers working in the wholesale industry are the individuals responsible for managing the activities of a company's sales staff. Within the scope of their job, they have many responsibilities. The Sales Manager recruits and hires the sales staff and other key employees. In others, the human resources department will handle the recruiting function. However, the Sales Manager may still do final interviews of sales staff.

Depending on the specific product, there may be many areas and avenues in which a company can sell their products. A clothing company may, for example, sell their merchandise to department stores, chain stores, boutiques, specialty stores, and catalogs from coast to coast as well as other countries. Without the direction of the Sales Manager, the sales staff might go on their own, haphazardly

selling wherever they chose and without any clear sales plan.

The Sales Manager separates geographic areas into territories. Sizes of territories depend on the specific company and the products they sell. A territory for one manufacturer might include the entire Northeast. For another, a territory might be southern New Jersey. Whatever the size of the territory, the Sales Manager is responsible for assigning territories to each sales representative. In many instances, the Sales Manager may work with district managers who also handle some of these functions.

Sometimes, the Sales Manager may also assign specific types of accounts to sales representatives. For example, the Sales Manager working for a photocopy machine manufacturer may assign one representative all the corporate business accounts in an area and another all the office supply stores and other retail outlets in the same area.

The Sales Manager will assign leads to the sales representatives or to the district manager who will handle the task. Leads are calls or other correspondence which come in to the company from potential buyers. For example, a company may manufacture a product which was shown on television. A spurt of business occurs. Stores may start calling the manufacturer because they want to carry the product.

The sales staff must respond to these requests. The Sales Manager must see to it that it happens quickly.

The Sales Manager is expected to assist the manufacturers' sales representatives and the district managers in their job. He or she is in place to help them succeed. No matter what type of products are being sold, the main function of the representative is to interest buyers and purchasing agents in their merchandise. Some representatives pick right up on this task. Others need help. The Sales Manager may accompany new representatives on sales calls to current company client as well as prospective buyers to show them the ropes. The Manager may also go with the representative to visit clients in their places of work or set up sales meeting in other locations when the representative needs some assistance clinching a big sale.

One of the most important functions of a good Sales Manager is training the sales staff. In order to be able to sell effectively, the Sales Manager must make sure each representative knows as much about the manufacturer's products as possible. He or she may hold regular meetings to inform the representatives about new merchandise or the use of products.

The individual will also train representatives and salespeople on selling techniques utilizing policies of the manufacturer. The Sales Manager may provide training for the sales staff on a one-on-one basis or may be expected to develop formal group training programs. This may be the case, even if there is a formal training program provided by the manufacturer.

Sales Managers may help their sales staff develop a strong sales pitch, give representatives information on the company's products or even information on the competitors products. This is essential so that the sales representatives are knowledgeable about the strengths and weakness of their merchandise and competing products in the marketplace.

The Sales Manager works closely with the marketing manager. He or she must be aware of any promotions or specials the company is running. The individual must then communicate the pricing of products and any specials to the sales staff. This may occur in regular sales meetings.

The Sales Manager is responsible for handling a great deal of paperwork. He or she must keep records of what is selling and what is not as well as tracking orders, invoices, and bills. Individuals might also be responsible for developing sales letters or brochures to new or established accounts.

The Sales Manager is expected to set goals for the sales staff. He or she must be aware of how representatives are performing and meeting quotas. An important function of the Sales Manager is motivating the sales staff. Selling any product is not always easy. Every meeting does not always culminate in a sale. It is essential for representatives to remain upbeat and motivated. The Sales Manager needs to be effective in this task or he or she may lose his or her sales staff.

The Sales Manager may run sales meetings for representatives and other employees to review sales performance, product development, sales goals, and profitability.

Sales Managers are also expected to attend conferences and conventions on behalf of the manufacturer to meet new clients and discuss product developments.

Additional duties of Sales Managers in wholesale industry might include:

- Answering questions about new products and merchandise
- Addressing concerns of clients
- Providing advice to clients on increasing sales
- Developing sales letters, product literature, and pricing sheets
- Recommending raises and promotions or terminating sales staff

Salaries

Annual earnings for Sales Managers working in the wholesale industry can vary greatly ranging from approximately $35,000 to $250,000 or more. Variables include the specific manufacturer for which the individual works, its size, location, and prestige as well as the types of products being sold. Other factors affecting earnings include the experience, reputation, and responsibilities of the individual. In some instances, the Sales Manager will receive a commission on sales as well as his or her salary. He or she might also receive bonuses for outstanding sales.

Employment Prospects

Employment prospects for Sales Managers in the wholesale industry are good. Prospects are best for individuals who have a proven track record. Positions can be located throughout the country, although the most opportunities will be in areas hosting large numbers of manufactures.

Advancement Prospects

Advancement prospects are fair for individuals in this line of work. The most common method of climbing the career ladder for Sales Managers is landing similar jobs at larger or more prestigious manufacturers. This leads to increased responsibilities and earnings. Some Sales Managers advance to positions as vice presidents of sales.

Education and Training

Educational requirements vary from company to company. A college degree or background may be preferred, but is not always required. A degree may give one applicant an edge over another who doesn't possess one.

Many companies send their Sales Managers to formal training programs. These programs help individuals learn new methods of motivating employees, selling new techniques, and may offer a different spin on sales strategies. Programs may also help Sales Managers learn more about the company's products.

Experience, Skills, and Personality Traits

Sales Managers are usually required to have a great deal of selling experience. Individuals must have a complete knowledge of the products being sold by the manufacturer.

Leadership skills are mandatory. The ability to motivate others is essential in this type of job. Successful Sales Managers are confident, assertive individuals. Communication skills, both written and verbal, are necessary. The ability to train others is helpful.

Unions/Associations

Sales Managers working in the wholesale industry may belong to a number of organizations providing professional support and guidance. These include Sales and Marketing Executives International (SMEI), the Manufacturers' Agents National Association (MANA), the American Management Association, the American Wholesale Marketers Association (AWMA), or associations specific to the products being sold.

Tips for Entry

1. Jobs as Sales Managers can often be located on-line. Start with some of the more well-known sites such as www.monster.com and www.hotjobs.com.

2. Positions are often advertised in the classified sections of newspapers under heading including "Sales Manager," "Wholesale-Retail Opportunities," "Wholesale Opportunities," "Wholesale Sales," or "Retail Opportunities." You might also look under industries specific to the products you are interested in representing.

3. Sunday's papers usually have the largest classified section. Most companies try to have their help wanted ads run on a Sunday.

4. If you are interested in working with a specific manufacturer or wholesaler, check to see if they have a website. Many companies today have websites featuring job opportunities.

5. Visit www.hoovers.com to get websites for specific companies as well as basic information on what various companies sell. Hoovers also often has information regarding specific names of people to send resumes in a company.

6. The yellow pages are a wealth of information in your job search. Check them to find the names, addresses, and phone numbers of manufacturers in your area.

7. Take classes, seminars, and workshops in selling techniques and motivation to give you an edge over other applicants. These classes are also useful in giving you ideas to motivate your sales force.

DISTRICT MANAGER—WHOLESALE

CAREER PROFILE

Duties: Supervise and coordinate the activities of sales representatives in the district; train sales staff; assist sales staff in meeting district's sales goals; motivate sales staff; handle paperwork

Alternate Titles: Territory Manager

Salary Range: $31,000 to $85,000+

Employment Prospects: Good

Advancement Prospects: Fair

Best Geographical Location(s) for Position: Jobs may be located throughout the country; large cities will offer more possibilities

Prerequisites:

Education and Training—Educational requirements vary

Experience—Experience in wholesale sales

Special Skills and Personality Traits—Sales ability; aggressiveness; ability to handle multiple projects; administrative skills; organization; communication skills; ability to motivate others

CAREER LADDER

```
┌─────────────────────────────────────┐
│  Regional Manager or Sales Manager   │
└─────────────────────────────────────┘

┌─────────────────────────────────────┐
│          District Manager            │
└─────────────────────────────────────┘

┌─────────────────────────────────────┐
│        Sales Representative           │
└─────────────────────────────────────┘
```

Position Description

Wholesale companies may manufacture merchandise or purchase it from manufacturers. They then sell the products to other companies who in turn sell them to consumers. Merchandise can include, but is not limited to, food, clothing, pharmaceuticals, office equipment, computers, cosmetics, machinery parts, hardware, electronics, automobile parts, exercise and sports equipment, or furniture.

Wholesale companies often have a sales staff responsible for selling the company's products to retailers or other consumers. This staff may be headed by a sales manager. Depending on the size and structure of the company, the sales staff may include salespeople, manufacturers representatives, regional managers, and District Managers.

It is not uncommon for wholesale companies to sell their merchandise throughout the country. This means that sales forces will be required in a number of different areas or districts. In order to assure all sales districts are run properly, areas of the country are often divided into regions, which are overseen by regional managers. These regions are then divided into districts or territories. Each district is then overseen by an individual called a District Manager.

District Managers manage all of the accounts in a specific area or district. They are expected to make sure each account or business in the district is serviced by salespeople.

Whether retail or wholesale, all customers want to feel important. They need to know they are being taken care of by the companies with which they are doing business. Not doing so can lead to a loss of sales. The District Manager makes sure clients are satisfied.

He or she may assign salespeople to call or visit established accounts. It is important to wholesale companies to constantly look for new business. The District Manager often works with salespeople and representatives to develop new clients.

District Managers often recruit and hire representatives and other sales staff for their districts. In some situations, the human resources department of the company or the sales manager may handle the recruiting function. However, the district manager may still take part in final interviews of his or her sales staff.

District Managers assign specific territories to each sales person and representative. In this manner, salespeople are not repeating their efforts calling on clients or ignoring the needs of others.

The District Manager may assign leads to the sales representatives in his or her district. Leads are calls which come in to the company from potential buyers. For example, a retail store may call the manufacturer of a line of dresses in which they have an interest.

The District Manager is expected to assist the sales staff in his or her district with their jobs. He or she is there to help them succeed. The individual may accompany new representatives on sales calls to current company client as well as prospective buyers to show them the ropes. The individual may also go with the representative to visit clients in their places of work or set up sales meetings in other locations when the representative needs some help clinching a big sale.

The District Manager works with the sales manager in training the sales staff. Some companies also have a trainer who develops and runs programs. The Manager works with each member of the sales staff either one on one or as a group making sure each knows as much about the manufacturer's products as possible. He or she may hold regular meetings to inform the representatives about new merchandise or the use of products.

The individual communicates with each salesperson on a regular basis. During these conversations, the Manager will check to see if there are any problems with any accounts and make sure each is being taken care of. He or she will usually need to know how sales are going.

The District Manager must keep accurate records of sales figures on a daily, weekly, monthly, and annual basis. This information is used to help the company project profits. Based on these figures, along with various other information, the corporate office sets sales goals. In many situations, the sales representatives are expected to call in or fax sales figures to the District Manager on a daily or weekly basis.

The District Manager works with the sales staff in his or her district to make sure they meet corporate sales and profit goals. He or she may hold meetings with staff to motivate them as well as giving them product information helpful in making sales.

The District Manager is the liaison between the corporate office and his or her sales staff. He or she is responsible for communicating routine corporate policies as any policy changes. For example, the corporate office may want new customers to fill in a credit report before credit is issued. The District Manager must make sure all sales representatives know the policies and be sure they are being followed.

The District Manager often handles a customer service problem when it can't be handled by the sales representative. A customer, for example, may need additional credit and want to deal with it on a higher level.

The District Manager handles a great deal of paperwork. He or she must keep records of what is selling and what is not, as well as tracking orders, invoices, and bills.

The District Manager must be aware of how representatives are performing and meeting quotas. The individual will constantly work to motivate the sales staff. Selling a product is not always easy. Every meeting does not culminate in a sale. It is essential for a sales staff to remain upbeat and motivated. The District Manager needs to be effective in this task or he or she may lose his or her staff.

District Managers are also expected to attend conferences and conventions on behalf of the manufacturer to meet new clients and discuss product developments.

Additional duties of District Managers might include:

- Answering questions about new products and merchandise
- Addressing concerns of clients
- Providing advice to clients on increasing sales
- Assisting sales manager in running sales meetings
- Recommending raises and promotions or terminating sales staff

Salaries

Annual earnings for District Managers working in the wholesale industry can vary greatly, ranging from approximately $31,000 to $85,000 or more. Variables include the specific manufacturer for which the individual works, its size, location, and prestige as well as the types of products being sold. Other factors affecting earnings include the experience, reputation, and responsibilities of the individual. In some instances, the District Manager will receive a commission on sales as well as his or her salary. He or she might also receive bonuses for outstanding sales.

Employment Prospects

Employment prospects are good District Managers interested in working in the wholesale industry. Prospects are best for individuals who have a proven track record. Positions can be located throughout the country although the most opportunities will be in areas hosting large numbers of manufacturers and wholesalers.

Advancement Prospects

Advancement prospects are fair for individuals in this line of work. The most common method of climbing the career ladder for District Managers is by landing similar jobs at larger or more prestigious manufacturers. This leads to increased responsibilities and earnings. District Managers may also advance to positions as regional managers or even sales managers.

Education and Training

Educational requirements vary. In many companies, experience is accepted in lieu of education. A college degree or background may be preferred, but is not always required. However, a college degree may give one applicant an edge over another who doesn't have one. Good majors include marketing, retailing, merchandising, business, management, communications, advertising, liberal arts, or related fields.

Once hired, many companies send their District Managers through formal training programs. These programs help individuals learn new methods of motivating employees, new selling techniques, and may offer a different spin on sales strategies. Programs may also help District Managers learn more about the company's products.

Experience, Skills, and Personality Traits

District Managers are usually required to have a great deal of selling experience. Individuals must have a complete knowledge of the products being sold by the manufacturer.

Leadership and management skills are mandatory. The ability to motivate others is essential. The ability to deal well with others is necessary. Communications skills, both written and verbal, are also necessary. The ability to train others is helpful.

Unions/Associations

District Managers working in the wholesale industry may belong to a number of organizations providing professional support and guidance. These include Sales and Marketing Executives International (SMEI), the Manufacturers' Agents National Association (MANA), the American Management Association, the American Wholesale Marketers Association (AWMA), or associations specific to the products being sold.

Tips for Entry

1. Positions as District Managers can often be located on-line. Start with some of the more popular sites such as www.monster.com and www.hotjobs.com.

2. Positions are often advertised in the classified sections of newspapers under headings including "District Manager," "Wholesale-Retail Opportunities," "Wholesale Opportunities," or "Wholesale Sales." You might also look under industries specific to the products you are interested in representing.

3. Sunday's paper usually has the largest classified section. Most companies try to have their help wanted ads run on a Sunday.

4. If you are interested in working with a specific company, check to see if they have a website. Many companies have websites featuring job opportunities.

5. Visit www.hoovers.com to get websites for specific companies as well as basic information on what various companies sell, and information regarding specific names of people to send resumes to a company.

6. The yellow pages are a wealth of information in your job search. Check them to find the names, addresses, and phone numbers of manufacturers in your area.

7. Take classes, seminars, and workshops in selling techniques and motivation to give you an edge over other applicants. These classes are also useful in giving you ideas to motivate your sales force.

8. Contact larger companies to see if they have internship programs.

MARKET RESEARCHER—MANUFACTURER

CAREER PROFILE

Duties: Perform market research to determine potential sales of new products; research demographics, pricing, packaging, and promotion of products produced by manufacturers; retailers; tabulate results; write reports

Alternate Titles: Market Analyst, Product Analyst; Market Research Specialist

Salary Range: $28,000 to $68,000+

Employment Prospects: Good

Advancement Prospects: Fair

Best Geographical Location(s) for Position: Jobs may be located throughout the country; the greatest number of opportunities will exist in areas with large numbers of manufacturers

Prerequisites:

Education and Training—Bachelor's degree

Experience—Experience performing surveys and tabulating results

Special Skills and Personality Traits—Excellent written and verbal communication skills; analytical mind; ability to solve problems; math skills; familiarity with statistics; computer skills

CAREER LADDER

```
┌─────────────────────────────────────┐
│  Research Supervisor or Director     │
└─────────────────────────────────────┘


┌─────────────────────────────────────┐
│         Market Researcher            │
└─────────────────────────────────────┘


┌─────────────────────────────────────┐
│         Research Assistant           │
└─────────────────────────────────────┘
```

Position Description

Manufacturers do a great deal of research prior to developing products. Without performing this research they might produce something that does not meet the needs of the market or the population. Manufacturers also perform market research to assure proper pricing, competitive stature of their product, and that specific product targets are included.

Manufacturers employ individuals called Market Researchers to handle this job. The Market Researcher determines the need, interest, and willingness of a given market to pay for specific products. For example, a Market Researcher at a pharmaceutical manufacturer might research the needs of an arthritis drug which could be taken every other day instead of daily. The Market Researcher at a record company might research the willingness of the marketplace to purchase compilation CDs of their artist's greatest hits. The Market Researcher working for a food manufacturer might research the amount the general population might pay for specialty or convenience food items. Depending on the manufacturer and the specific project, the Market Researcher may also do research on types of packaging, product names, or advertising.

This is an interesting job. Market Researchers have the opportunity to talk to people, get their ideas, and help a manufacturer determine if a product can succeed in the marketplace.

Market Researchers research the market conditions in various areas to determine the potential sales of the manufacturer's product. The Researcher may also determine the type of words that potential customers might look for in the company's advertisements. Would the word "convenience" sell a product better than the words "cooks quickly?" How about the words "may reduce the risk of cancer" on a food product?

As part of the job, the Market Researcher uses a number of research techniques. The individual might develop a survey or questionnaire to find the answers to questions. Depending on the specific company and what is being manufactured, the questionnaires might ask about a person's age, gender, and income level. It may ask about potential buyers' shopping habits and preferences.

The Market Researcher may execute questionnaires and surveys on the phone or visit various areas to personally interview various groups of individuals. He or she may personally handle this function or have it done by research assistants.

The Market Researcher may send questionnaires and surveys in the mail offering free samples or other incentives for people to respond. Today, a great deal of market research by manufacturers is also done on the Internet. Many companies find it easier to get people to answer questions by holding on-line sweepstakes offering prizes. With this method the survey or questionnaire is put on-line as part of the entry form. At the end of the sweepstakes period, the manufacturer has the results of the questionnaire.

The Market Researcher may also use data from many sources including information compiled by federal, state, and local agencies as well as private sources. The individual may put together focus groups and panels of consumers to test products. He or she may also conduct consumer buyer surveys, audits, and new product sales surveys.

Once the Market Researcher performs surveys and questionnaires and other research, he or she must analyze the results. The individual is then expected to write a report on his or her findings. The manufacturer will then decide if there is a market for the product, pricing strategies, name possibilities, target markets, and potential advertising mediums.

Additional duties of Market Researchers working for manufacturers might include:

- Putting together focus groups to determine the need for a product
- Supervising research assistants
- Working with a manufacturer's advertising agency
- Working with the manufacturer's development team on new products

Salaries

Annual earnings of Market Researchers working for manufacturers can range from approximately $28,000 to $68,000 or more. Factors affecting earnings include the size, structure, and prestige of the manufacturer as well as the education, experience, and responsibilities of the individual.

Employment Prospects

Employment prospects for Market Researchers are good. Positions may be located throughout the country. However, the greatest number of openings are located in areas hosting large numbers of manufacturers.

Advancement Prospects

Advancement prospects for Market Researchers working for manufacturers are fair. The most common method of career advancement is landing a similar job with a larger or more prestigious manufacturer. Individuals may also climb the career ladder by being promoted to positions of research supervisor or director.

Education and Training

Generally, the minimum educational requirement for a position in this field is a bachelor's degree. Some employers may require a graduate degree. Classes in business, statistics, marketing, advertising, or behavioral sciences will be useful for a career in this field. A doctorate is helpful for career advancement.

Experience, Skills, and Personality Traits

Market Researchers should be excellent problem solvers with good analytical minds. The ability to perform math skills and familiarity with statistics are essential.

Communications skills, both oral and written are necessary. An understanding of people and their behavior is mandatory. Computer skills are also needed.

Unions/Associations

Market Researchers may learn more about this career by contacting the Council of American Survey Research Organizations (CASRO).

Tips for Entry

1. The better your education, the better the job you can get in this field. If you can, earn a master's degree. Some companies will pay for your continuing education.
2. Jobs are often advertised in the classified section of the newspaper. Look under headings such as "Research Analyst," "Market Researcher," "Manufacturing Opportunities," or "Market Research." Specific companies may also advertise a number of job opportunities in one advertisement.
3. Sunday's paper usually has the largest classified section. Most companies try to have their help wanted ads run on a Sunday.
4. Contact manufacturers to see if they have any internships in this area. Once in, learn everything you can.
5. Send your resume and a short cover letter to manufacturers you are interested in working with and inquiring about openings.

6. If you are interested in working for a specific manufacturer, check to see if they have a website. Many companies now have websites featuring job opportunities. Check the appendix for some of the larger manufacturers.

7. Visit www.hoovers.com to get websites for specific companies as well as basic information on what various companies sell.

8. The yellow pages are a wealth of information in your job search. Check them to find the names, addresses, and phone numbers of manufacturers in your area.

CONSUMER AFFAIRS MANAGER— MANUFACTURER/WHOLESALER

CAREER PROFILE

Duties: Supervise the consumer affairs department; oversee the activities of customer services and consumer affairs staff; assist consumers in solving problems with company's products.

Alternate Titles: Consumer Affairs Coordinator

Salary Range: $25,000 to $55,000+

Employment Prospects: Fair

Advancement Prospects: Fair

Best Geographical Location(s) for Position: Positions located throughout the country

Prerequisites:

Education and Training—Bachelor's degree

Experience—Experience working in consumer affairs, customer relations, customer service, or public relations necessary

Special Skills and Personality Traits—Ability to remain calm; good interpersonal skills; communications skills; writing skills; empathy; supervisory skills

CAREER LADDER

```
┌─────────────────────────────────┐
│     Consumer Affairs Director    │
│  or Director of P.R. or Marketing│
└─────────────────────────────────┘

┌─────────────────────────────────┐
│     Consumer Affairs Manager     │
└─────────────────────────────────┘

┌─────────────────────────────────┐
│ Consumer Affairs Assistant Manager│
│ or Customer Relations Representative│
└─────────────────────────────────┘
```

Position Description

Manufacturers and wholesalers, as other businesses, like to keep their customers happy and satisfied. Many employ Consumer Affairs Managers to handle these customer service and consumer affairs issues. The Consumer Affairs Manager supervises and coordinates the consumer affairs, customer services and customer-relations services of the manufacturer or wholesaler's company. The individual may have varied duties, depending on the specific company for which he or she works.

First and foremost, the Consumer Affairs Manager makes sure customers are satisfied with the company's products. The manufacturer or wholesaler may, for example, have an "800" number set up for customers to call. The Consumer Affairs Manager and his or her staff resolves any complaints or problems customers may have. The Consumer Affairs Manager often supplies customers with useful information about the company's products. In some cases, the Consumer Affairs Manager develops pamphlets, leaflets,

or other literature for this purpose. In other cases, he or she may train customer service representatives on methods to answer questions and provide information.

The Consumer Affairs Manager may have additional duties when a manufacturer has a product recall or other similar problem. He or she may, for example, develop literature to explain the recall procedures to customers. The individual might also train customer service representatives in dealing with frightened or angry consumers. It is always important to find ways to maintain customer confidence in the company as well as to alleviate any additional problems which may occur.

The Consumer Affairs Manager often works with the company's public relations department and others in upper management. Together they create corporate policies as they relate to consumers. It is essential that the Consumer Affairs Manager understand and have the ability to explain these policies to consumers and customer service representatives.

The Consumer Affairs Manager trains customer service representatives or develops the training program with the company's training manager. He or she may be expected to develop training manuals for the customer service representatives as well as others in the company dealing with the public.

The individual sets the policies on how consumer letters and calls should be handled, answered, and taken care of. The Consumer Affairs Manager must explain to each representative what information should be taken from each consumer when they call and how to maintain files.

Generally, the Consumer Affairs Manager will not handle routine calls from customers. However, he or she will often deal with phone calls, letters, or emails from extremely upset, "difficult" consumers. The individual also handles calls regarding major consumer problems, such as a customer suggesting that a lawsuit will ensue unless he or she is satisfied.

Sometimes the situation is easily resolved. The consumer may only want need to vent his or her frustration with an employee of the company they have a complaint with. One of the important functions of the Consumer Affairs Manager is being able to calm people down so that problems can be resolved.

Additional duties of Consumer Affairs Managers may include:

- Preparing copy for the company's website regarding consumer affairs
- Developing and writing consumer oriented materials such as leaflets, booklets, flyers
- Preparing consumer newsletters.

Salaries

Annual earnings for Consumer Affairs Managers working for manufacturers or wholesalers can range from approximately $25,000 to $55,000 or more annually. Factors affecting earnings include the size and prestige of the company as well as the responsibilities and experience of the individual.

Employment Prospects

Employment prospects are fair for Consumer Affairs Managers seeking employment with manufacturers or wholesalers. Most mid-sized and larger companies have someone in this position on staff. Positions may be located throughout the country. More opportunities will be available in areas hosting greater numbers of manufacturers and wholesalers.

Advancement Prospects

Advancement prospects are fair for Consumer Affairs Managers. Some individuals advance their careers by locating similar positions with larger, more prestigious manufacturers or wholesalers. Others may climb the career ladder by becoming the director of consumer affairs or the director of public relations or marketing.

Education and Training

Generally, employers prefer individuals hold a minimum of a four year college degree. Good choices for majors include public relations, marketing, advertising, English, communications, liberal arts, business administration or a related field.

Experience, Skills, and Personality Traits

Experience working in consumer affairs, customer service or public relations is usually necessary. Often individuals have gone through internships as well.

Supervisory skills are essential in this position. Good interpersonal skills are also necessary. The ability to deal well with subordinates, superiors and customers is needed.

Individuals must have a great deal of empathy for others and be able to keep people calm when they are upset and irate. Communication skills, both verbal and written are mandatory.

Unions/Associations

Consumer Affairs Managers may be members of the Society of Consumer Affairs Professionals (SOCAP). This organization provides professional guidance and support to its members. Individuals may also be members of the Public Relations Society of America (PRSA), Women in Communications (WIC), or private and voluntary consumer organizations.

Tips for Entry

1. Join SOCAP and take advantage of their membership opportunities. Go to meetings, get their literature and make important contacts.
2. Jobs may be located on-line at company websites. Many manufacturers and wholesalers list job openings on their website. Use the listing in the appendix to get you started.
3. Job openings may also be located in the classified section of newspapers. Look under headings such as "Consumer Affairs Manager," "Consumer Affairs," "Manufacturing Opportunities," "Wholesaling Opportunities," "Customer Service," "Customer Relations," or "Public Relations."
4. Get experience working in consumer affairs by volunteering your time to work with consumer organizations. This gives you valuable hands-on experience and looks good on your resume.
5. Get more experience by working as a customer service or customer relations representative. Learn what you can and climb the career ladder.

WHOLESALE SALES REPRESENTATIVE

Duties: Represent wholesaler by marketing and selling their product to distributors and retail establishments in specific territories

Alternate Titles: Sales Representative

Salary Range: $18,000 to $100,000+

Employment Prospects: Excellent

Best Geographical Location(s) for Position: Jobs may be located throughout the country; large cities will offer more possibilities

Prerequisites:

Education and Training—Educational requirements vary

Experience—Experience in wholesale or retail sales

Special Skills and Personality Traits—Sales ability; motivation; persuasive; organized; communication skills; people skills

```
┌─────────────────────────────────────┐
│  Wholesale Sales Representative with │
│  Better Territory, Representative for │
│  Larger, More Prestigious Wholesaler │
└─────────────────────────────────────┘


┌─────────────────────────────────────┐
│   Wholesale Sales Representative     │
└─────────────────────────────────────┘


┌─────────────────────────────────────┐
│     Salesperson or Entry Level       │
└─────────────────────────────────────┘
```

Position Description

Wholesale Sales Representatives are the individuals responsible for selling a company's products to manufacturers, distributors, retail establishments, government agencies, and other institutions. Individuals might also be called Sales Representatives. The difference between Wholesale Sales Representatives and Manufacturer's Representatives is that Wholesale Representatives usually work solely for a wholesaler.

Wholesale Sales Representatives may work in any industry selling a variety of products. These might include raw materials, wholesale food, clothing, pharmaceuticals, office equipment, computers, cosmetics, machinery parts, electronics, automobile parts, exercise and sports equipment, or furniture.

No matter what type of products the Wholesale Sales Representative sells, the main function of the individual is to interest manufacturers and purchasing agents in their merchandise. Wholesale Sales Representatives are expected to make sales calls to current clients as well as prospective buyers. They may visit clients at their place of work or set up sales meetings in other locations.

The Wholesale Sales Representatives must learn the needs of the customer and then show him or her how the wholesaler's specific product can help meet those needs. There is often a great deal of competition in this field. As a result, the Wholesale Sales Representative must be aware of the unique qualities of the merchandise his or her company sells. In this manner, the Wholesale Sales Representatives can be more effective in the selling process. For example, the individual may work for a company that wholesales a variety of exercise equipment. The Representative must know everything about not only his company's exercise equipment, but that of the competitors. Individuals must have the ability to speak knowledgeably discussing the strengths and weakness of their products and others in the marketplace.

Depending on the specific company and the products the individual is selling, he or she may show the client samples or pictures in a catalog of merchandise offered. It is essential for Wholesale Sales Representatives to develop a strong sales pitch to sell their merchandise.

It is the responsibility of the Wholesale Sales Representative to supply each client with a pricing formula for merchandise. He or she will explain the different price breaks depending on the amount purchased by the customer. The Wholesale Sales Representative is expected to answer any of the customer's questions.

If all goes well, the Wholesale Sales Representative will then close the sale. The individual is expected to take and write up the customers order. At this point, he or she may explain payment options or provide shipping dates.

The Wholesale Sales Representative must keep in contact with clients to make sure merchandise has arrived, is satisfactory, and there are no problems with the order. He or she will also try to get reorders by determining the quantity of products which have been sold since the last sales call. Many Wholesale Sales Representative make regular scheduled calls to make sure they don't lose reorders.

Wholesale Sales Representatives might work from their office, making appointments and sales calls by telephone. Today, many make calls on their cell phones while enroute to other appointments.

Wholesale Sales Representatives also make sales calls in person visiting established accounts or making cold calls to potential new customers.

It is important for the individual to look constantly for new business and new accounts. He or she often does this by making cold calls to new prospects. The Wholesale Sales Representative may also get referrals from satisfied customers.

Wholesale Sales Representatives often are expected to attend trade shows, conferences, and conventions to meet other people from their industry as well as clients. They may also attend company sponsored sales meetings to review sales performance, product development, sales goals, and profitability.

Additional duties of Wholesale Sales Representatives might include:

- Keeping accurate records of orders, invoices, and bills
- Developing and sending sales letters or brochures to new or established accounts
- Addressing concerns of clients
- Visiting established accounts

Salaries

Earnings for Wholesale Sales Representatives can vary greatly ranging from approximately $18,000 to $100,000 or more annually. Variables include the specific wholesaler for which the individual works, the product being sold and the sales territory which is assigned. Other factors affecting earnings include the experience of the Representative as well as his or her sales ability, motivation, and aggressiveness.

There are a number of different methods by which Wholesale Sales Representatives may be compensated. Individuals might receive a straight salary, a commission, or a combination of the two. Individuals also may receive bonuses for outstanding sales. In many cases the Wholesale Sales Representative additionally receives a company car or a car allowance.

Employment Prospects

Employment prospects for Wholesale Sales Representatives are excellent. Those who are aggressive and motivated should have no problem finding a job. Positions are plentiful and can be located throughout the country although the most opportunities will be in areas hosting large numbers of wholesale companies.

Advancement Prospects

Advancement prospects are excellent for aggressive and motivated Wholesale Sales Representatives. There are a number of options for climbing the career ladder in this field. The most common is locating similar positions with a larger or more prestigious wholesaler. Individuals might also stay in the same company and get better territories. Some Wholesale Sales Representatives move into supervisory and management positions.

Education and Training

Educational and training requirements vary depending on the specific company and the product line. Some companies just require their Representatives to hold a high school diploma while others prefer or require a college background or degree. If the wholesaler is selling a product which is technical in nature such as computers or software, any technical knowledge the individual has will be useful.

Companies often have formal training programs for new employees as well as continuing programs for those with more experience. These programs help motivate employees and offer new ideas and selling techniques.

Other companies offer informal training with managers or supervisors helping employees learn sales techniques and policies. Some Representatives learn the trade by accompanying more experienced individuals on calls in the field.

Experience, Skills, and Personality Traits

Background and experience requirements Wholesale Sales Representatives vary. Experience selling in either the retail or wholesale industry may be preferred. However, there are often entry-level jobs available.

Successful Wholesale Sales Representatives like to sell. They are confident, assertive, motivated individuals with sales ability. Communications skills are essential. Wholesale Sales Representatives should have the ability to work well both independently and as part of a team. People skills are mandatory.

Depending on the specific job, the individual may be required to hold a valid driver's license.

Unions/Associations

Wholesale Sales Representatives may belong to a number of organizations providing professional support and guidance. These include the Sales and Marketing Executives International (SMEI), the American Management Association (AMA), the American Wholesale Marketers Association (AWMA), or associations specific to the products being sold.

Tips for Entry

1. Contact wholesalers with your resume and a short cover letter. Ask about openings for Wholesale Sales Representatives.

2. Jobs can often be located on-line. Start with some of the more popular sites such as www.monster.com and www.hotjobs.com.

3. Positions are often advertised in the classified sections of newspapers under heading including "Wholesale Sales Representative," "Wholesale Opportunities," "Wholesale Sales," "Sales Representative," or "Sales Representatives." Also check out manufacturers' ads, where they might advertise more than one job opening.

4. If you are interested in working with a specific wholesaler, check to see if they have a website. Many company websites now list job opportunities.

5. Visit www.hoovers.com to get websites for specific wholesalers as well as basic information on what various companies sell.

6. Take classes, seminars, and workshops in selling techniques and motivation to give you an edge over other applicants.

SALES TRAINER—WHOLESALE

CAREER PROFILE

Duties: Facilitate classes, seminars, workshops, and other training programs for company representatives, salespeople, and account managers; prepare training programs.

Alternate Titles: Facilitator; Trainer; Corporate Trainer

Salary Range: $25,000 to $55,000+

Employment Prospects: Good

Advancement Prospects: Fair

Best Geographical Location(s) for Position: Positions may be located throughout the country; larger cities hosting many manufacturers will offer more opportunities

Prerequisites:
Education and Training—College degree preferred
Experience—Experience in training and workshop facilitation
Special Skills and Personality Traits—Leadership skills; sales skills; communications skills; interpersonal skills; employee relations; writing skills; ability to speak in public; creative; organized

CAREER LADDER

```
┌─────────────────────────────────┐
│        Training Manager         │
└─────────────────────────────────┘

┌─────────────────────────────────┐
│            Trainer              │
└─────────────────────────────────┘

┌─────────────────────────────────┐
│     Sales Representative,        │
│   Account Representative,        │
│      District Manager,           │
│  or Human Resources Associate    │
└─────────────────────────────────┘
```

Position Description

Wholesalers, distributors, and manufacturers may employ an array of salespeople to move their products to the retail market. These may include sales representatives, manufacturers' representatives, account representatives, account managers, sales managers, district managers, or regional and territory managers.

In order to assure the staff be as effective as possible, many companies hire Sales Trainers. These individuals are responsible for preparing and conducting training programs for the company's sales staff. Depending on the situation and the specific company the individual may train employees to perform specific jobs, customer service skills, selling techniques, or the use of products and merchandise being sold.

Sales Trainers in this setting may work under the direction of a human resources director, training manager, or sales manager. They confer with management on training needs for the specific company. Once training needs are identified, the individual must formulate an outline for training sessions. These must include content as well as methods. Some Trainers use comedy in their presentations.

Others are more straightforward. Many Sales Trainers develop programs with role playing and games which help employees absorb material as well as retain it. The Trainer will use the most effective methods to ensure employees understand and can put the material presented into use.

In many situations, companies hire sales representatives or account representatives who may have limited experience either selling or selling the specific product. The Sales Trainer must be sure the representatives know how to sell and use the specific product, how to deal with the clients for those products, and what the products can and cannot do. A pharmaceutical company, for example, may hire representatives to sell their products to hospitals and other health care facilities. A lack of knowledge on the part of any of the sales force could lead to possible injury, death, or malpractice suits.

The Trainer also develops methods of teaching sales strategies. Selling can be a difficult job in the best of circumstances. Trainers must find ways to help motivate a sales staff even when sales are not going well.

Trainers may present material in a variety of ways. They may facilitate workshops or seminars, or give lectures or demonstrations. In many cases, manufacturers who hire Trainers have them give general training sessions to new employees as well as on-going sessions to seasoned employees.

Depending on the company, Trainers may have the capability to set up training sessions as part of sales conferences or trade shows. In some situations, Trainers may also work with employees on a one-on-one basis.

Trainers may be responsible for preparing handouts, overheads, slides, or PowerPoint presentations to help employees absorb and understand needed skills. They additionally may be expected to develop booklets or other training materials.

In many cases, Trainers working for manufacturers or other wholesalers may be responsible for developing materials to help the sales staff understand how to use and sell new products when they are launched.

Trainers may be responsible for developing and facilitating programs for employees in a multitude of areas and a variety of subjects depending on the needs of the specific manufacturer or wholesaler. For example, companies may have Trainers conduct sessions for all employees on dealing with providing customer service for established accounts. Other Trainers may be expected to work with employees on handling specialized skills. For example, a Trainer working with a software manufacturer will need to prepare training programs on working with the software in order for salespeople to have the ability to sell it effectively.

Many companies have routine orientation for new employees. In these cases, Trainers may be expected to develop and facilitate orientation programs. During orientation, the Trainer must explain company policies as well as acceptable and unacceptable behavior on the job.

Some Trainers working for manufacturers, distributors, and other wholesalers may offer management classes to teach methods for communicating with their employees. This is essential in retaining employees. Other subjects covered in this type of class may include acceptable methods for disciplining staff and how to speak to subordinates without coming across abruptly. The individual may also develop classes for employees dealing with and avoiding sexual harassment in the workplace. This is especially important to a sales staff who must go out and sell in various locations and businesses.

Trainers may also be expected to provide classes specific to certain jobs. Other duties of Trainers working for wholesalers, manufacturers, and distributors may include:

- Training employees in team building
- Preparing development programs for sales staff
- Facilitating programs to teach department directors, managers, and supervisors methods of conducting training within their department
- Teaching department directors, managers, and supervisors proper procedures for interview techniques and handling employment reviews

Salaries

Annual earnings for Trainers working for wholesalers, manufacturers, and distributors can range from approximately $25,000 to $55,000 or more. Factors affecting earnings include the geographic location, size, and type of the specific company as well as the education, experience, and responsibilities of the individual.

Employment Prospects

Employment prospects are good for Trainers working for wholesalers, distributors, and manufacturers. The greatest number of positions will be located in areas hosting a lot of industry and many manufacturers.

Advancement Prospects

Trainers may advance their careers in a number of ways. The most common is to locate similar positions in larger or more prestigious companies. Another method of climbing the career ladder for a Sales Trainer is being promoted to the position of training manager. Some Trainers strike out on their own and become corporate training consultants.

Education and Training

Educational requirements vary. Most require or prefer individuals to hold a minimum of a bachelor's degree. Good majors for those interested in this field might include human resources, communications, retail, business, public relations, marketing, liberal arts, or a related field. There are some companies who may accept individuals with a high school diploma and a background and experience in training and human resources. Other companies may hire an individual without an educational background who has worked in sales management and has the ability to train others.

Experience, Skills, and Personality Traits

Experience requirements vary. Generally experience in training and development is required or preferred. Sales experience may also be needed. Some employers will hire individuals out of college who have gone through internship programs.

Good Trainers have the ability to motivate others. They know how to explain things in an easy-to-understand and easy-to-remember manner.

Sales Trainers need exemplary people and employee relations skills. Good verbal and written communication skills are also necessary. The ability to speak effectively in front of people is essential to this position. An understanding of the products being sold is mandatory to prepare programs.

Unions/Associations

Those interested in learning more about careers in this field should contact the American Society of Training Developers

(ASTD), the Society for Human Resources Management (SHRM), Sales and Marketing Executives International (SMEI), the Manufacturers' Agents National Association (MANA), the American Management Association, the American Wholesale Marketers Association (AWMA) or associations specific to the products being sold.

Tips for Entry

1. Experience as a sales representative for a manufacturer or distributor is helpful in understanding the sales process.
2. Become either an active or affiliate member of the American Society of Training Developers (ASTD). This may give you the edge over another applicant with the same qualifications.
3. If you have the opportunity, go to some of the ASTD seminars and workshops. These are valuable for the learning opportunity as well as networking possibilities.
4. Openings are often advertised on the Internet. They may be located via the home pages wholesalers, distributors, or manufacturers.
5. Positions may be advertised in the classified sections of newspapers. Look under classifications such as "Trainer," "Training and Development," "Wholesale Opportunities," or "Human Resources." Also look at specific company advertisements.
6. You may be asked to conduct an impromptu training presentation as part of your interview process. Develop a sample program ahead of time and rehearse before the interview.
7. Send your resume and a short cover letter to wholesalers, distributors, and manufacturers. Inquire about openings and an interview. Get started by contacting some of the companies listed in the appendix.

MANUFACTURER'S REPRESENTATIVE

CAREER PROFILE

Duties: Represent manufacturer by marketing and selling their product to wholesale and retail establishments in specific territories

Alternate Titles: Sales Representatives

Salary Range: $18,000 to $100,000+

Employment Prospects: Excellent

Advancement Prospects: Excellent

Best Geographical Location(s) for Position: Jobs may be located throughout the country; large cities will offer more possibilities

Prerequisites:

Education and Training—Educational requirements vary

Experience—Experience in wholesale or retail sales

Special Skills and Personality Traits—Sales ability; aggressiveness; persuasiveness; organization; communication skills; people skills

CAREER LADDER

```
┌─────────────────────────────────────┐
│     Manufacturer's Representative    │
│        with Better Territory,        │
│     or Representative for Larger,    │
│       More Prestigious Company       │
│          or Sales Manager            │
└─────────────────────────────────────┘

┌─────────────────────────────────────┐
│     Manufacturer's Representative    │
└─────────────────────────────────────┘

┌─────────────────────────────────────┐
│       Salesperson or Entry Level     │
└─────────────────────────────────────┘
```

Position Description

Manufacturer's Representatives market a company's products to wholesale and retail establishments, government agencies, and other institutions. Individuals might also be called Manufacturers' Representatives or Sales Representatives.

Manufacturer's Representatives work in any industry selling a variety of products, including both retail and wholesale food, clothing, pharmaceuticals, office equipment, computers, cosmetics, machinery parts, electronics, automobile parts, exercise and sports equipment, furniture, and so on. No matter what type of products the Manufacturer's Representative sells, their main function is to interest wholesale and retail buyers and purchasing agents in their merchandise. Manufacturer's Representatives make sales calls to current clients as well as prospective buyers. They may visit clients at their place of work or set up sales meetings in other locations.

The Manufacturer's Representative must learn the needs of the customer and then show him or her how their specific product meets those needs. The individual may show the client samples or pictures in a catalog of merchandise he or she has to offer.

Successful Manufacturer's Representatives develop a strong sales pitch to sell their merchandise. Individuals must have the ability to discuss the strengths and weaknesses of their products and others in the marketplace. It is essential that the Manufacturer's Representative know everything there is about not only his or her company's products but those of competitors. In this way, the individual can explain and emphasize the unique qualities of his or her specific merchandise in comparison to similar products sold by others.

The Manufacturer's Representative is expected to give pricing schedules for merchandise, answer questions, and then hopefully close a sale. At this point, the Manufacturer's Representative will take and write up orders.

The Representative must keep in contact with clients to make sure merchandise has arrived, is satisfactory, and that there are no problems with the order. He or she will also try to get reorders by determining the quantity of products which have been sold since the last sales call.

At times, the Manufacturer's Representative might work from his or her office, making appointments and sales calls by telephone. At other times, the individual might make sales calls in person visiting established accounts or making cold calls to potential new customers.

It is essential that the Manufacturer's Representative keep abreast of new merchandise and the changing needs of their customers. Individuals often are expected to attend trade shows where new products are showcased. They might also attend conferences and conventions to meet other Sales Representatives and clients and discuss new product developments. Companies often sponsor sales meetings to review sales performance, product development, sales goals, and profitability.

There is a fair amount of office work in this type of position. Individuals might be responsible for developing and sending sales letters or brochures to new or established accounts. It is also necessary for the Manufacturer's Representative to keep accurate records of orders, invoices and bills.

Additional duties of Manufacturer's Representatives might include:

- Answering questions about new products and merchandise
- Addressing concerns of clients
- Providing advice to clients on increasing sales
- Visiting established accounts
- Writing sales letters and sending product literature and pricing sheets to customers

Salaries

Earnings for Manufacturer's Representatives vary greatly ranging from approximately $18,000 to $100,000 or more annually. Variables include the specific company for which the individual works, the product being sold, and the sales territory which is assigned. Other factors affecting earnings include the experience of the Representative as well as his or her sales ability, motivation, and aggressiveness.

There are a number of different ways Manufacturer's Representatives are compensated. Individuals might receive a straight salary, a commission, or a combination of the two. Manufacturer's Representatives might also receive bonuses for outstanding sales. In many cases the Manufacturer's Representative additionally receives a company car or a car allowance.

Employment Prospects

Employment prospects for Manufacturer's Representatives are excellent. Those who are aggressive and motivated should have no problem finding a job. Positions are plentiful and can be located throughout the country although the most opportunities will be in areas hosting large numbers of manufacturers.

Advancement Prospects

Advancement prospects are excellent for aggressive and motivated Manufacturer's Representatives. There are a number of options for climbing the career ladder in this field. The most common is locating similar positions with larger or more prestigious companies. Individuals might also stay in the same company and get better territories. Some Manufacturer's Representatives move into supervisory and management positions.

Education and Training

Educational and training requirements vary depending on the specific company and the product line. Some companies just require their Representatives to hold a high school diploma while others prefer or require a college background or degree.

Companies often have formal training programs for new employees as well as continuing programs for those with more experience. These programs help motivate employees and offer new ideas and selling techniques.

Other companies offer informal training with managers or supervisors helping employees learn sale techniques and policies. Some Representatives learn the trade by accompanying more experienced individuals on calls in the field.

Experience, Skills, and Personality Traits

Background and experience requirements for Manufacturer's Representatives vary. Experience selling in either the retail or wholesale industry may be preferred. However, there are often entry-level jobs available.

Successful Manufacturers' Representatives are confident, assertive, motivated individuals with sales ability. Communications skills are essential. Manufacturer's Representatives need the ability to work well both independently and as part of a team. Depending on the specific job, the individual may be required to hold a valid driver's license.

Individuals must have a great deal of patience and perseverance. Sales don't always happen overnight.

Unions/Associations

Manufacturer's Representatives may belong to Sales and Marketing Executives International (SMEI), the Manufacturers' Agents National Association (MANA), or associations specific to the products they are selling. Individuals may also obtain additional career information from the Manufacturer's Representatives Educational Research Foundation.

Tips for Entry

1. Jobs can often be located on-line. Start with some of the more popular sites such as www.monster.com or www.hotjobs.com.
2. Send your resume and a short cover letter to manufacturers in your area.
3. Positions are often advertised in the classified sections of newspapers under heading including "Manufacturer's Representative," "Manufacturer's Rep,"

"Wholesale Opportunities," "Wholesale Sales," "Retail Opportunities," or "Sales Representatives." You might also look under industries specific to the products you are interested in representing.

4. If you are interested in working with a specific company, check to see if they have a website. Many companies have websites featuring job opportunities.

5. Visit www.hoovers.com to get websites for specific companies as well as basic information on what various companies sell.

6. You might also check product packaging to obtain the address of a specific product you are interested in selling.

7. The yellow pages can be a wealth of information in your job search. Check them to find the names, addresses, and phone numbers of manufacturers in your area.

8. Take classes, seminars, and workshops in selling techniques and motivation to give you an edge over other applicants.

TRADE SHOW REPRESENTATIVE— WHOLESALE

CAREER PROFILE

Duties: Represent manufacturer or wholesaler at trade shows and conventions; demonstrate products; staff the booth; take orders for products.

Alternate Titles: Trade Show Representative; Trade Show Sales Representative

Salary Range: $23,000 to $75,000+

Employment Prospects: Good

Advancement Prospects: Fair

Best Geographical Location(s) for Position: Jobs may be located throughout the country; areas hosting large numbers of manufacturers and wholesalers will offer more possibilities

Prerequisites:

Education and Training—Educational requirements vary
Experience—Experience dealing with the public is helpful
Special Skills and Personality Traits—Sales ability; articulate; people skills; organization; detail oriented; communication skills; ability to travel

CAREER LADDER

```
┌─────────────────────────────────┐
│  Trade Show Representative with  │
│ Larger or More Prestigious Company│
└─────────────────────────────────┘

┌─────────────────────────────────┐
│   Trade Show Representative      │
└─────────────────────────────────┘

┌─────────────────────────────────┐
│ Entry Level, Sales Representative,│
│   Manufacturers Representative,  │
│      or Marketing Assistant      │
└─────────────────────────────────┘
```

Position Description

Manufacturers and wholesalers sell their products to retailers who in turn sell them to consumers. Manufacturers' representatives and other salespeople often make sales calls to current clients as well as prospective buyers. They may visit clients at their place of work or set up sales meetings in other locations. Sometimes clients visit manufacturers' or wholesalers' showrooms to place orders for merchandise. Another common way of selling merchandise is through trade shows.

Trade shows are events where companies have booths and showcase their products. Companies may spotlight new items at these shows as well as current inventory. Customers, or in this case retailers, visit the show to see a variety of products all in one location. Trade shows may run from one day to four or five days depending on the specific event.

Trade Show Representatives work for the wholesaler or manufacturer and act as their representatives in the field. Their main function is to help sell the company's product. Depending on the specific industry, there may be many dif-

ferent trade shows held in cities from coast to coast. Shows may also be held in other countries. As part of the job, the Trade Show Representative is expected to travel to the different locations where events are being held.

Trade shows traditionally are set up with convention style booths in which companies create their own space. In this space they may include things such as product displays, merchandise, literature, signs, giveaways, promotional material, computers, or audiovisual equipment. Before a Trade Show Representative leaves the company's main office, he or she must be sure arrangements have been made to have everything shipped to the venue as well as shipped back or on to the next trade show.

Once at the venue, the Trade Show Representative is expected either to set up the booth or to oversee the set up. He or she may also work with union personnel present in many venues during the setup and break down.

The Trade Show Representative's main function during a show is attracting people to the booth and talking to them about the company's products. In this manner, the Trade Show Representative can interest potential customers.

The Trade Show Representative must know as much as possible about the manufacturer's products. He or she often spends a great deal of time before trade shows with company salespeople, technicians, and marketing people to obtain this information. The Trade Show Representative may read company literature and marketing pieces, or view commercials, ads, and videos to make him- or herself familiar with the merchandise and the company.

Depending on the structure of the company, the individual may work with one or more Representatives or salespeople at the show. Sometimes, if the show is very large and considered important in the industry, the company may also send others from upper management including the marketing manager and sales manager.

The Trade Show Representative arrives at the trade show before it opens to the public. Once retailers begin to come in, the Representative is expected to work the booth, demonstrate the merchandise, and answer questions from prospective customers.

Depending on the specific situation, some Trade Show Representatives may be responsible for taking orders for merchandise. Others might just take names, addresses, and phone numbers and set up meetings for company sales people.

Trade Show Representatives often meet with prospective clients after show hours to explain products in more detail or to help create good business relationships. Often manufacturers and wholesalers host informal get-togethers, cocktail parties, or receptions for potential clients after hours as well. The Trade Show Representative is expected to be on hand at these events, acting as host and setting up sales meetings, appointments, and presentations.

Additional duties of Trade Show Representatives working in the wholesale industry might include:

- Making travel and lodging arrangements for staff attending show
- Making sure trade show promoter has provided all equipment and space for which the company has contracted
- Breaking down booths at conclusion of trade show
- Answering questions about new products and merchandise
- Representing company during media interviews in areas where trade show is being held

Salaries

Annual earnings for Trade Show Representatives working for manufacturers in the wholesale industry can range from approximately $23,000 to $75,000 or more. Variables include the specific company for which the individual works as well as the experience and responsibilities of the individual.

Trade Show Representatives whose main responsibility is staffing a booth or demonstrating a product will earn the lower salaries. Those who have more responsibility or those who sell will have earnings at the higher end of the pay scale. Some Representatives also receive commissions on sales in addition to their base salary.

Employment Prospects

Employment prospects for Trade Show Representatives in the wholesale industry are good. Most companies attend trade shows on a regular basis and need individuals for this position. The greatest opportunities will exist in areas hosting large numbers of manufacturers and wholesalers. It is important to note that some companies utilize freelance Trade Show Representatives.

Advancement Prospects

Advancement prospects are dependent, to a great extent, on an individual's career expectations. Some people love the life of being on the road. They enjoy traveling and they can't think of a better career than working trade shows. These individuals will most likely climb the career ladder by landing jobs with larger or more prestigious companies. Others move into positions in marketing or sales.

Education and Training

Educational requirements vary. A college degree or background may be preferred, but is not always required. A degree may give one applicant an edge over another who doesn't have one.

Good majors to consider for positions in this field include sales, marketing, business, advertising, public relations, and communications.

Experience, Skills, and Personality Traits

Trade Show Representatives spend a great deal of time on the road. People in this field must like to travel and not mind "living out of a suitcase."

Individuals should be neat, articulate, and personable with excellent communication skills. The most successful Trade Show Representatives have pleasant personalities mixed with sales skills.

Unions/Associations

Depending on their duties and the industry in which the individual is working, he or she may be a member of industry specific associations. The Trade Show Representative may also be a member of a number of other organizations providing professional support and guidance including the Public Relations Society of America (PRSA), the Sales and Marketing Executives International (SMEI), the Manufacturers' Agents National Association (MANA), and the American Wholesale Marketers Association (AWMA).

Tips for Entry

1. Jobs as Trade Show Representatives can often be located on-line. Start with some of the more prevalent sites such as www.monster.com and www.hotjobs.com.

2. Positions are often advertised in the classified sections of newspapers under heading including "Wholesale Opportunities," "Wholesale-Retail Opportunities," "Trade Show Representative," "Wholesale Sales," "Marketing Opportunities," or "Sales." You might also look under industries specific to the products you are interested in representing.

3. Sunday's paper usually has the largest classified section. Most companies try to have their help wanted ads run on a Sunday.

4. If you are interested in working with a specific company, check to see if they have a website. Many companies have websites featuring job opportunities.

5. Visit www.hoovers.com to get websites for specific companies as well as basic information on what various companies sell. Hoovers also often has information regarding specific names of people in a company to whom to send resumes.

6. The yellow pages are a wealth of information in your job search. Check them to find the names, addresses, and phone numbers of manufacturers/wholesalers in your area.

7. Many wholesalers and manufacturers have freelance or part-time positions for Trade Show Representatives. Visit the human resources department to find out about possibilities. Often a part-time position leads to a full-time opportunity.

8. Get some experience by working as a freelance Trade Show Representative. Contact trade show companies to find out when and where they are holding events. Ask for a list of exhibitors. Send your resume and a short cover letter asking about possibilities.

9. You might also contact convention bureaus or convention managers of hotels to find out what trade shows are coming in. Contact their trade show manager to find a list of exhibitors.

RACK JOBBER

CAREER PROFILE

Duties: Supply wholesale or manufacturer's merchandise to stores; service accounts; bring in new merchandise

Alternate Titles: Subdistributor

Salary Range: $22,000 to $70,000+

Employment Prospects: Fair

Advancement Prospects: Fair

Best Geographical Location(s) for Position: Jobs may be located throughout the country; large cities will offer more possibilities

Prerequisites:

Education and Training—Educational requirements vary

Experience—Selling experience (retail and/or wholesale) helpful

Special Skills and Personality Traits—Salesmanship; aggressiveness; good business skills; ability to handle multiple projects; administrative skills; organization; communication skills; ability to work well with figures and calculations

CAREER LADDER

```
┌─────────────────────────────┐
│      Owner of Shop          │
│ or Company Representative    │
└─────────────────────────────┘


┌─────────────────────────────┐
│        Rack Jobber          │
└─────────────────────────────┘


┌─────────────────────────────┐
│ Rack Jobber Field Representative │
└─────────────────────────────┘
```

Position Description

Rack Jobbers offer merchandise that is not covered by existing inventory to retail stores. Rack Jobbers may be representatives of manufacturers or wholesalers or may be the manufacturer or wholesaler themselves.

Rack Jobbers are granted shelf space in retail stores for their merchandise. Rack Jobbers may bring in a variety of merchandise depending on the company they represent. Many of the record, book, and cosmetic displays seen in supermarkets, department stores, automotive shops, discount stores, and drug stores are put together by Rack Jobbers.

It is the responsibility of the Rack Jobber to select the products to display and sell in a section of someone else's store or market. He or she receives the space in return for either a rental fee, a leasing fee, a percentage of sales, or a combination of both.

The job of a Rack Jobber is much like that of owning a retail store. However, the merchandise is in a space that hopefully already draws a stream of customer traffic. The Rack Jobber may have a space in more than one store.

The Rack Jobber buys merchandise from a distributor or wholesaler. Since he or she has limited space it is impossi-

ble to stock everything. Instead, the individual will stock the merchandise customers are most likely looking for.

Rack Jobbers offer stores the opportunity to have a specific department without the risk. For example, a convenience store may not want to pay the expense for a compact disc, cassette, and videotape department. The Rack Jobber gives the store a department and merchandise. If something doesn't sell, the Rack Jobber takes it back. This is a no-risk situation for the store's management.

After selecting merchandise, the Rack Jobber makes sure it gets to the store. He or she must also make sure that merchandise is displayed properly. The display must be eye catching and draw potential customers. In this way they will see merchandise and hopefully make a purchase.

It is the responsibility of the Rack Jobber to periodically come into the store and take inventory. At this time, he or she will take back merchandise which isn't moving, and bring in "hot" sellers. Those selling CDs and tapes, for example, might bring in those by artists who have top twenty hits. As the "Top 20" changes, so will the merchandise. In some cases, such as where the Rack Jobber is selling perishable merchandise, he or she may have to return to the store more often to bring in fresh merchandise. This might be the case, for example, when a Rack Jobber is representing the manufacturer of baked goods.

Depending on the situation, the Rack Jobber must either hire a staff of salespeople (if it is a lease situation) or train and supervise members of the store's existing staff who will be working in the specific department. In this instance, the Rack Jobber may pay a rental fee or percentage to the store. In other instances, the Rack Jobber will just provide the merchandise and it will be run through the store's register when sold.

The Rack Jobber often will visit the store managers of established accounts. He or she will also look for new businesses in which to put merchandise. The individual must constantly keep the stores happy and satisfied or they will not renew their contracts.

Additional duties of Rack Jobbers might include:

- Answering questions about new products and merchandise
- Addressing concerns of clients
- Providing advice to salespeople on increasing sales
- Keeping accurate records of merchandise inventory and sales from his or her space
- Supplying the store with advertising and promotional material to help sell the merchandise

Salaries

Annual earnings for Rack Jobbers can range from approximately $22,000 to $70,000 or more depending on a number of factors. These include the size and prestige of the wholesaler or distributor with whom the individual is working, the specific product, how much is sold, and the type of salary received.

Rack Jobbers may be paid in the form of a straight commission or may be guaranteed a salary against a commission.

Employment Prospects

Employment prospects are fair for Rack Jobbers. Rack Jobbers may work for themselves or for wholesalers or distributors. There are many stores and shops that want departments serviced by Rack Jobbers. An individual may take over an entire rack jobbing operation or be a field representative.

Advancement Prospects

Advancement prospects are fair for individuals in this line of work. The most common method of climbing the career ladder is by increasing the size of an individual's business by broadening the base of the operation.

As Rack Jobbers meet and work closely with distributors of companies, they often make a large number of contacts. These individuals often offer the Rack Jobber a position in the distribution department of their company. Some Rack Jobbers strike out and open their own stores.

Education and Training

Generally, there is no specific educational background required to be a Rack Jobber or to work for one other than having a high school diploma. However, a college background or courses in business, merchandising, marketing, and related fields will be useful in honing skills and making contacts.

Experience, Skills, and Personality Traits

Rack Jobbers usually experience selling in both the retail and wholesale industries. Individuals must have a complete knowledge of the products being sold.

Management, organization, and communications skills are essential to the success of Rack Jobbers. Salesmanship and assertiveness are also useful.

Unions/Associations

Rack Jobbers may belong to a number of organizations providing professional support and guidance. These include Sales and Marketing Executives International (SMEI), the Manufacturers' Agents National Association (MANA), the American Management Association, the American Wholesale Marketers Association (AWMA), or associations specific to the products being sold.

Tips for Entry

1. Positions as Rack Jobbers can often be located online. Start with some of the more popular sites such as www.monster.com and www.hotjobs.com.
2. Positions are often advertised in the classified sections of newspapers under headings including "Rack-Jobber," "Wholesale-Retail Opportunities," "Wholesale Opportunities," "Wholesale Sales," or "Rack Jobber Field Representative."
3. Sunday's paper usually has the largest classified section. Most companies try to have their help wanted ads run on a Sunday.
4. If you are interested in working with a specific company, check to see if they have a website. Many companies have websites featuring job opportunities.
5. Visit www.hoovers.com to get websites for specific companies as well as basic information on what various companies sell.
6. The yellow pages are a wealth of information in your job search. Check them to find the names, addresses, and phone numbers of manufacturers in your area.
7. Many major department stores around the country have departments serviced by Rack Jobbers. Contact the store and ask. Then contact the Rack Jobber and ask for a job as a clerk or sales associate in that department.
8. You might also visit drug stores, supermarkets, or convenience stores to determine their Rack Jobbers. Get addresses and phone numbers so you can send a resume and set up an interview.

PURCHASING MANAGER—WHOLESALE

Duties: Acquire products, material, intermediate goods, machines, supplies, and other items used in the production of a final product; find suppliers and vendors; negotiate lowest prices; solicit bids; award contracts.

Alternate Titles: Industrial Purchasing Manager

Salary Range: $28,000 to $75,000+

Employment Prospects: Fair

Advancement Prospects: Fair

Best Geographical Location(s) for Position: Jobs may be located throughout the country; large cities and areas with a great many manufacturers and industry will offer more possibilities

Prerequisites:

Education and Training—College degree preferred
Experience—Experience in buying and purchasing
Special Skills and Personality Traits—Negotiation skills; leadership; communication skills; organization; planning skills; decision making skills

Purchasing Director

Purchasing Manager

Purchasing Agent

Position Description

There is a chain of supply in the production of merchandise. First it must be manufactured and then sold to wholesalers or distributors. These companies then sell the merchandise to retail outlets for the public to buy. In some cases, the manufacturer is also the wholesaler and/or the distributor.

In order to manufacture merchandise and products, raw materials and machinery are often needed by the manufacturer. The individual responsible for overseeing the acquisition of these products is called the Purchasing Manager.

Responsibilities of Purchasing Managers can vary depending on the specific employment situation. Purchasing Managers may buy product materials, intermediate goods, machines, supplies, and other materials used in the production of a final product. In some cases, individuals may specialize in a certain type of purchasing. For example, they may specialize in machinery or supplies. Others may specialize in wood, lumber, steel, plastic, or fabric materials.

Depending on the type of products the manufacturer sells, the Purchasing Manager may be expected to obtain goods

ranging from the actual raw materials (such as wood), to fabricated parts or the machinery needed to complete the process.

Purchasing Managers usually have a number of different vendors to choose from when selecting materials. As part of their job, they must evaluate and select vendors or suppliers based on a number of criteria. While price is important, it can not be used solely in choosing suppliers of merchandise. Other factors to be considered when choosing suppliers include the quality of the merchandise, availability, selection, and reliability of the vendor.

It is essential to the success of a manufacturer to have the correct materials on hand when needed for a project. Not doing so can hold up manufacturing, which can have a serious impact on sales.

Depending on the size and structure of the manufacturer, Purchasing Managers may supervise and oversee the work of one or more purchasing agents. In others, he or she may work alone.

In some companies, the Purchasing Manager is expected to work on product development. This is because the Purchasing Manager is the one in the organization who often is best able to forecast which materials will be most available, cost effective, and acceptable in relation to production standards.

The Purchasing Manager may seek suppliers and vendors both domestically and internationally. Individuals find supplies in a variety of ways. They may meet with vendors to look at merchandise in their own offices or may visit warehouses, showrooms, or factories. Individuals might review listings in catalogs, industry periodicals, directories, and trade journals. Purchasing Managers often research the reputation and history of suppliers to assure that they are reliable in their business dealings.

Some Purchasing Managers must travel a great deal. Individuals may go on trips to purchase supplies as well as attending meetings, trade shows, and conferences. Many Purchasing Managers may also visit vendors' plants and distribution centers. In this manner they can examine products as well as assess the vendor's production and distribution capabilities.

The Purchasing Manager solicits bids from vendors to obtain the best prices for the best merchandise. A difference of even one cent per item can make a huge difference in the final cost of a product to a manufacturer. Once the Purchasing Manager obtains bids and analyzes them, he or she will award contracts.

In some instances, the Purchasing Manager may seek bids for contractors to handle certain parts of a manufacturing job. Because these might be long-term contracts, the Purchasing Manager must choose a suitable supplier.

It is mandatory to the success of the Purchasing Manager to have a good business relationship with suppliers. He or she may be expected to work out any problems and handle customer service issues.

Additional duties of Purchasing Managers might include:

- Supervising supply contracts
- Developing bid forms
- Handling quality control of materials
- Developing good working relationships with vendors

Salaries

Annual earnings for Purchasing Managers can range from approximately $28,000 to $75,000 or more depending on a number of variables. These include the size, geographic location, and specific employer as well as the experience, responsibilities, and education of the individual.

Employment Prospects

Employment prospects for Purchasing Managers are good. Individuals may find employment with a variety of manufacturers. The greatest opportunities will exist in areas hosting large numbers of manufacturers.

Advancement Prospects

Advancement prospects for Purchasing Managers are fair. Some individuals find similar positions with larger manufacturers. This results in increased responsibilities and earnings. After obtaining experience, other individuals may climb the career ladder by becoming Purchasing Directors.

Education and Training

Educational requirements vary depending on the specific employer. While there are exceptions, most employers prefer their Purchasing Managers hold a minimum of a four-year college degree.

Once on the job, individuals often go through either formal or informal training programs. Voluntary certification is available through the National Association of Purchasing Management and the American Purchasing Society.

Experience, Skills, and Personality Traits

Purchasing Managers need a great deal of experience in purchasing and often have started out as purchasing agents.

Individuals should be self-confident with the ability to make decisions. They should have a complete knowledge of the products they are purchasing and the industries they are working with. Good communications skills and the ability to deal with stress and pressure are necessary.

Unions/Associations

Purchasing Managers might belong to a number of associations including the American Purchasing Society, Inc. (APS) or the National Association of Purchasing Management, Inc. (NAPM). Both these organizations provide certification programs, professional support, and career guidance.

Tips for Entry

1. Contact the American Purchasing Society, Inc. (APS) and the National Association of Purchasing Management, Inc. (NAPM). Ask about certification requirements.
2. Jobs often can be located on-line too. Look at some of the major sites such as www.hotjobs.com and www.monster.com.
3. Positions are often advertised in the classified sections of newspapers under heading including "Wholesale Opportunities," "Manufacturing Opportunities," "Industry," "Purchasing Professional," "Purchasing Manager," or "Purchasing."
4. Send your resume and a short cover letter to manufacturers and inquire about internships or training programs. Contact manufacturers in your local area or some of those listed in the appendix of this book.

WAREHOUSE MANAGER—WHOLESALE MANUFACTURER OR DISTRIBUTOR

CAREER PROFILE

Duties: Oversee management of warehouse or distribution center; supervise and coordinate activities of warehouse workers; organize the receiving, storing, and shipping of merchandise and goods

Alternate Titles: Distribution Warehouse Manager

Salary Range: $26,000 to $75,000

Employment Prospects: Good

Advancement Prospects: Fair

Best Geographical Location(s) for Position: Jobs may be located throughout the country; the greatest number of opportunities will exist in areas with large numbers of manufacturers or distributors

Prerequisites:

Education and Training—Educational requirements vary

Experience—Experience working in warehouse and/or distribution center

Special Skills and Personality Traits—Supervisory skills; organization; time management skills

CAREER LADDER

```
┌─────────────────────────────┐
│  Operations Manager—Warehouse │
│   or Distribution Center      │
└─────────────────────────────┘

┌─────────────────────────────┐
│     Warehouse Manager         │
└─────────────────────────────┘

┌─────────────────────────────┐
│    Warehouse Supervisor       │
│     or Area Manager           │
└─────────────────────────────┘
```

Position Description

Manufacturers must store the merchandise they make so that it can be transported to distributors. Once received, the distributor must store the merchandise until it is sold to retailers or other consumers. Both manufacturers and distributors utilize warehouses to store these goods. The individual responsible for overseeing the warehouse is called the Warehouse Manager. He or she works under the direction of the warehouse operations manager.

The Warehouse Manager holds an important position in the supply chain of goods. He or she helps plan and prepare for the management of the warehouse. If the individual works for a distributor he or she will be in charge of the distribution center warehouse. Depending on the specific facility, he or she will be responsible for receiving, storing, and sending out stock from the warehouse. Within the scope of the job, he or she has additional responsibilities.

The Warehouse Manager supervises and coordinates the activities of the workers in the facility. Depending on the specific situation, this may include traffic workers, loading and unloading workers, clerks, area supervisors, and more. He or she will assign duties to each worker so that the warehouse is run effectively and efficiently.

Depending on the type of goods, merchandise may be stored in a number of ways. It is up to the Warehouse Manager to determine the best method. Sometimes it may be on pallets. Other times it may be stored in areas called cages. If the merchandise or goods are perishable, such as certain food items, they must often be stored in cold areas, refrigerated storage, or huge freezers.

A great deal of machinery and equipment may be used within the warehouse. It is the responsibility of the Warehouse Manager to be sure all machinery is working and available. If there is a problem with machinery, he or she is responsible for reporting it immediately and making sure it is repaired. Failure to do so may result in a backup moving merchandise in, out, or around the facility.

A major function of the Warehouse Manager is assuring that all employees know how to use equipment properly. He or she must also be sure that employees practice safety methods and rules when working in the warehouse. Failure to do this might result in accidents injuring employees and/or damaging merchandise.

The Warehouse Manager assists in the planning of the distribution chain. He or she is responsible for assuring the quality of merchandise that comes in and leaves the warehouse. For example, if a distribution center brings in a truckload of frozen foods and they are not kept frozen at all times, the food will be spoiled.

The Warehouse Manager coordinates the receipt of goods coming into the warehouse as well as those leaving the facility. He or she makes sure all merchandise is accounted for. This is often done with the help of scanners and computer equipment used by receiving and shipping clerks and workers depending on whether merchandise is coming in or leaving the facility.

The Warehouse Manager orders and schedules deliveries of packaging and raw materials as needed. This is necessary in order to ship merchandise out of the facility.

The individual must keep accurate records of stock received and merchandise which is returned. He or she reviews these records and determines any discrepancies. The Warehouse Manager must also be sure that procedures regarding returning defective merchandise are followed.

In some cases, the Warehouse Manager may drive a forklift him- or herself helping to move merchandise. In other situations, the Warehouse Manager will just oversee employees handling these tasks.

Additional duties of a Warehouse Manager might include:

- Communicating with management
- Supervising the loading and unloading of bulk merchandise and goods on pallets
- Overseeing inventory control
- Hiring and terminating employees who do not perform satisfactorily
- Organizing and planning daily activities
- Receiving orders for goods
- Handling complaints regarding the warehouse

Salaries

Annual earnings of Warehouse Managers working for manufacturers or distributors can range from approximately $26,000 to $75,000 or more. Variables affecting earnings include the specific employer, the size, and geographic location of the warehouse and the experience and responsibilities of the individual.

Employment Prospects

Employment prospects for Warehouse Managers are good. Positions may be located throughout the country. The greatest number of openings are located in large areas hosting large numbers of manufacturers and distribution centers.

Advancement Prospects

The most common method of career advancement for Warehouse Managers is locating similar positions for companies with warehouses. This will result in increased responsibilities and earnings. Individuals may also climb the career ladder through promotion to operations manager of a warehouse or distribution center.

Education and Training

Educational requirements vary. Some companies require or prefer individuals to hold a college degree. Other companies will hire individuals without a college degree or background who have moved up the ranks and prove they can handle the job. A college degree will help individuals move up the career ladder. Good possibilities for majors include operations, logistics, materials management, or related fields.

There are also trade schools and colleges which have certificate programs in warehouse work.

Experience, Skills, and Personality Traits

Prior experience working in a warehouse is needed as is supervisory experience. Warehouse Managers need to be detail oriented, organized individuals with excellent time management skills. Good verbal and written communications skills are also necessary. Interpersonal skills are needed. Computer skills are necessary. The ability to remain calm is essential.

Unions/Associations

Warehouse Managers may be members of the American Wholesale Marketers Association (AWMA) or associations or associations specific to the products and merchandise in their warehouse.

Tips for Entry

1. Jobs are often advertised in the classified section of the newspaper. Look under headings such as "Warehouse Manager," "Warehouse," "Distribution Center," "Wholesale Opportunities," or "Distribution Center Manager." Specific companies may also advertise a number of job opportunities in one advertisement.
2. Sunday's paper usually has the largest classified section. Most companies try to have their help wanted ads run on a Sunday.
3. Get your foot in the door and get experience. Learn what you can and move up the career ladder.
4. Contact manufacturers, wholesalers, and distributors. Send your resume and a short cover letter inquiring about openings.

5. If you are interested in working for a specific manufacturer or distributor, check to see if they have a website. Many companies now have websites featuring job opportunities. Check the appendix for some of the larger manufacturers.

6. Visit www.hoovers.com to get websites for specific companies as well as basic information on what various companies sell.

7. The yellow pages are a wealth of information in your job search. Check them to find the names, addresses, and phone numbers of manufacturers in your area.

APPENDIXES

APPENDIX I
DEGREE AND NON-DEGREE PROGRAMS

A. FOUR-YEAR COLLEGES AND UNIVERSITIES OFFERING MAJORS IN RETAIL MANAGEMENT

Although possession of a college degree does not guarantee a job in the field of retail management, many people feel that it is in their best interest to pursue an education after high school to learn additional information, gain new skills and make important contacts. A degree or background in higher education may give one person an edge over another who doesn't continue his or her schooling.

The following is a list of four-year schools that grant degrees in retail management, grouped by state. More colleges are beginning to grant degrees in this area every year. Check the newest copy of *Lovejoy's* (found in the reference section of libraries, in guidance or counseling centers, and in bookstores) for additional schools giving degrees in this field. There are also numerous two-year schools offering study in retail management, as well as four-year schools with courses in the retail industry.

ALABAMA

University of Alabama
Box 870132
Tuscaloosa, AL 35487

University of Montevallo
Station 6030
Montevallo, AL 35115

ARKANSAS

Southern Arkansas University—Magnolia
SAU Box 1382
Magnolia, AR 71753

CALIFORNIA

California State University
5151 State University Drive
Los Angeles, CA 90032

San Francisco State University
1600 Holloway Avenue
San Francisco, CA 94132

Santa Clara University
Santa Clara, CA 95053

COLORADO

University of Colorado at Colorado Springs
P.O. Box 7150
Austin Bluff Parkway
Colorado Springs, CO 80933

CONNECTICUT

University of Bridgeport
126 Park Avenue
Bridgeport, CT 06601

FLORIDA

University of South Florida
4202 East Fowler Avenue
Tampa, FL 33620

University of West Florida
11000 University Parkway
Pensacola, FL 32514

IDAHO

Idaho State University
P.O. Box 8468
Pocatello, ID 83209

Lewis-Clark State College
500 8th Avenue
Lewiston, ID 83501

ILLINOIS

Chicago State University
9501 South King Drive
Chicago, IL 60628

Governors State College
University Parkway
University Park, IL 60466

INDIANA

Indiana University Bloomington
300 North Jordan Avenue
Bloomington, IN 47405

Purdue University
1080 Schleman Hall
West Lafayette, IN 47907

KENTUCKY

Eastern Kentucky University
Lancaster Avenue
Richmond, KY 40745

Sullivan College
P.O. Box 33-308
Louisville, KY 40232

Western Kentucky University
One Big Red Way
Bowling Green, KY 42101

MAINE

Thomas College
180 West River Road
Waterville, ME 04901

MARYLAND

Hood College
401 Rosemont Avenue
Frederick, MD 21701

MASSACHUSETTS

Endicott College
376 Hale Street
Beverly, MA 01915

LaSell College
1844 Commonwealth Avenue
Newton, MA 02466

Salem State College
P.O. Box 10548
Salem, MA 27108

Simmons College
300 The Fenway
Boston, MA 02115

MICHIGAN

Alma College
West Superior Street
Alma, MI 48801

Baker College of Flint
G-1050 West Bristol Road
Flint, MI 48507

Baker College of Muskegon
Muskegon, MI 56716

Baker College of Owosso
10205 Washington
Owosso, MI 48867

Ferris State University
420 Oaks Street, PRK 101
Big Rapids, MI 49307

Northern Michigan University
1401 Presque Isle Avenue
Marquette, MI 49855

Northwood University
3225 Cook Road
Midland, MI 48640

Western Michigan University
West Michigan Avenue
Kalamazoo, MI 49008

MINNESOTA

University of Minnesota—Crookston
170 Owen Hall
2900 University Avenue
Crookston, MN 56716

Winona State University
P.O. Box 5838
Winona, MN 55987

MISSISSIPPI

Mississippi College
P.O. Box 4203
Clinton, MS 39058

University of Mississippi
117 Lyceum
University, MS 38677

MISSOURI

Fontbonne College
6800 Wydown Boulevard
St. Louis, MO 63105

Lindenwood College
St. Charles, MO 63301

Northwest Missouri State University
800 University Drive
Maryville, MO 64468

MONTANA

University of Montana
Lodge 101
Missoula, MT 59812

NEBRASKA

University of Nebraska at Omaha
60th and Dodge Streets
Omaha, NE 68182

NEW HAMPSHIRE

New Hampshire College
2500 North River Road
Manchester, NH 03106

NEW JERSEY

Jersey City State College
2039 Kennedy Memorial Boulevard
Jersey City, NJ 07305

Montclair State University
Upper Montclair, NJ 07043

Rider University
2083 Lawrenceville Road
Lawrenceville, NJ 08548

Rowan College of New Jersey
Glassboro, NJ 09028

Thomas Edison State College
101 West State Street
Trenton, NJ 08625

NEW YORK

Cazenovia College
Cazenovia, NY 13035

Fashion Institute of Technology
Seventh Avenue at 27th Street
New York, NY 10001

New York University
22 Washington Square North
New York, NY 10011

Syracuse University
200 Administration Building
Syracuse, NY 13210

OHIO

Bluffton College
Box 638 Marbeck Center
Bluffton, OH 45817

David N. Meyers College
112 Prospect Avenue
Cleveland, OH 44115

Youngstown State University
1 University Plaza
Youngstown, OH 44555

University of Toledo
2801 West Bancroft Street
Toledo, OH 43606

OKLAHOMA

Southeastern Oklahoma State University
Box 4118 Station A
Durant, OK 74701

University of Central Oklahoma
100 North University Drive
Edmond, OK 73034

OREGON

Bassist College
Portland, OR 97201

PENNSYLVANIA

Cedar Crest College
100 College Drive
Allentown, PA 18104

Drexel University
32nd and Chestnut Streets
Philadelphia, PA 19104

La Salle University
20th Street and Olney Avenue
Philadelphia, PA 19141

Marywood College
2300 Adams Avenue
Scranton, PA 18509

Philadelphia University
School House Lane & Henry Avenue
Philadelphia, PA 19144

Saint Vincent College
300 Fraser Purchase Road
Latrobe, PA 15650

Seton Hill College
Seton Hill Drive
Greensburg, PA 15601

York College of Pennsylvania
York, PA 17405

RHODE ISLAND

Johnson & Wales University
8 Abbott Park Place
Providence, RI 82903

TENNESSEE

Belmont University
1900 Belmont Boulevard
Nashville, TN 37203

University of Tennessee—Knoxville
320 Student Services Building
Knoxville, TN 37996

TEXAS

Weber State University
1001 University Circle
Ogden, UT 84408

West Texas A&M University
WTAMU Box 748
Canyon, TX 79016

UTAH

Brigham Young University
A-153 ASB
Provo, UT 84602

Weber State University
Box 1015-3750 Harrison Boulevard
Ogden, UT 84408

VIRGINIA

Christopher Newport University
Newport News, VA 23606

Marymount University
2807 North Glebe Road
Arlington, VA 22207

WASHINGTON

Central Washington University
Mitchell Hall
Ellensburg, WA 98826

WEST VIRGINIA

Fairmont State College
1201 Locust Avenue Extension
Fairmont, WV 26544

Marshall University
400 Hal Greer Boulevard
Huntington, WV 25701

Shepherd College
Shepherdstown, WV 25443

WISCONSIN

University of Wisconsin-Stout
P.O. Box 790
Menomonee, WI 54751

B. TWO-YEAR COLLEGES OFFERING MAJORS IN RETAIL MANAGEMENT

Although possession of a college degree does not guarantee a job in the field of retail management, many people feel that it is in their best interest to pursue an education after high school to learn additional information, gain new skills, and make important contacts. A degree or background in higher education may give one person an edge over another who doesn't continue his or her schooling.

The following is a list of two-year schools that grant degrees in retail management, grouped by state. More colleges are beginning to grant degrees in this area every year. Check the newest copy of *Lovejoy's* (found in the reference section of libraries, in guidance or counseling centers, and in bookstores) for additional schools giving degrees in this field. There are also numerous four-year schools offering study in retail management, as well as both two- and four-year schools with courses in the retail industry.

ALABAMA

Bessemer State Technical College
Bessemer, AL 35201

Jefferson State Community College
Birmingham, AL 35215

John C. Calhoun State Community College
Decatur, AL 35609

Enterprise State Junior College
Enterprise, AL 36331

ARIZONA

Eastern Arizona College
Thatcher, AZ 85552

Glendale Community College
Glendale, AZ 85302

CALIFORNIA

American River College
4700 College Oaks Drive
Sacramento, CA 95841

Cabrillo College
Aptos, CA 95003

Candad College
Redwood City, CA 94061

Chabot College
Hayward, CA 94545

College of Marin
Kentfield, CA 94904

College of San Mateo
Mateo, CA 94402

**Fashion Institute of Design
and Merchandising—Costa Mesa**
Costa Mesa, CA 92925

**Fashion Institute of Design
and Merchandising—Los Angeles
Campus**
919 South Grand Avenue
Los Angeles, CA 90015

**Fashion Institute of Design
and Merchandising—San Diego
Campus**
1010 Second Avenue
San Diego, CA 92101

**Fashion Institute of Merchandising—
San Francisco Campus**
55 Stockton Street
San Francisco, CA 94108

Golden West College
Huntington Beach, CA 92647

Grossmont College
8800 Grossmont College Drive
El Cajon, CA 92020

Long Beach City College
4901 East Carson Street
Long Beach, CA 90806

Los Angeles City College
855 North Vermont Avenue
Los Angeles, CA 90029

Los Angeles Valley College
Van Nuys, CA 91401

Merced College
Merced, CA 95348

Modesto Junior College
435 College Avenue
Modesto, CA 95359

Rancho Santiago College
1530 West 17th Street
Santa Ana, CA 90601

Saddleback College
Mission Viejo, CA 92692

Shasta College
Redding, CA 96049

West Los Angeles College
4800 Freshman Drive
Culver City, CA 90203

COLORADO

Arapaho Community College
Littleton, CO 80160

**Colorado Mountain College—Alpine
Campus**
P.O. Box 1001
Glenwood Springs, CO 81602

Parks College
Denver, CO 80229

CONNECTICUT

Briarwood College
Southington, CT 06489

Gateway Community-Technical College
80 Sergeant Drive
New Haven, CT 06511

**Three Rivers Community-Technical
College**
Mahan Drive
Norwich, CT 06360

DELAWARE

**Delaware Technical & Community
College-Jack F. Owens Campus**
Box 610
Georgetown, DE 19947

FLORIDA

**Florida Community College at
Jacksonville**
501 West State Street
Jacksonville, FL 32202

Indian River Community College
Fort Pierce, FL 34981

GEORGIA

Dekalb College
555 North Indian Creek Drive
Decatur, GA 30021

HAWAII

Heald Business College
1500 Kapiolani Boulevard
Honolulu, HI 06814

**University of Hawaii—Leeward
Community College**
Pearl City, HI 96782

IDAHO

College of Southern Idaho
Twin Falls, ID 83303

ILLINOIS

Black Hawk College
Moline, IL 61265

**City Colleges of Chicago—Harold
Washington College**
30 East Lake Street
Chicago, IL 60601

College of Lake County
Grayslake, IL 60031

Elgin Community College
Elgin, IL 60123

John A. Logan College
Carterville, IL 62918

Kankakee Community College
Kankakee, IL 60901

Lake Land College
Mattoon, IL 61938

Lincoln Land Community College
Springfield, IL 62794

MacCormac Junior College
506 South Wabash Avenue
Chicago, IL 60605

Moraine Valley Community College
10900 South 88th Avenue
Palos Hills, IL 60465

Parkland College
Champaign, IL 61821

Rock Valley College
3301 North Mulford Road
Rockford, IL 61114

South Suburban College
South Holland, IL 60473

Triton College
River Grove, IL 60171

IOWA

American Institute of Business
2500 Fleur Drive
Des Moines, IA 50321

American Institute of Commerce
Davenport, IA 52807

Ellsworth Community College
Iowa Falls, IA 50126

Des Moines Area Community College
Ankeny, IA 50021

Iowa Lakes Community College
Estherville, IA 51334

Iowa Western Community College
Council Bluffs, IA 51502

North Iowa Area Community College
Mason City, IA 50401

Northwest Iowa Community College
602 West Park Street
Sheldon, IA 51201

Southwestern Community College
Creston, IA 50801

Kirkwood Community College
Cedar Rapids, IA 52406

KANSAS

Allen County Community College
Iola, KS 66749

Butler County Community College
El Dorado, KS 67042

Coffeyville Community College
Coffeyville, KS 67337

**Cowley County Community College
and Vocational—Technical School**
Arkansas City, KS 67005

Fort Scott Community College
Fort Scott, KS 66701

Garden City Community College
Garden City, KS 67846

**Hutchinson Community College and
Area Vocational School**
Hutchinson, KS 67501

KENTUCKY

**University of Kentucky—Madisonville
Community College**
Madisonville, KY 42431

**University of Kentucky—Maysville
Community College**
Maysville, KY 41056

**University of Kentucky—Paducah
Community College**
Paducah, KY 42002

MARYLAND

Anne Arundel Community College
Arnold, MD 21012

Hardford Community College
401 Thomas Run Road
Bel Air, MD 21015

Howard Community College
Columbia, MD 21044

**Montgomery College—Germantown
Campus**
20200 Observation Drive
Germantown, MD 20876

MASSACHUSETTS

Bay State College
122 Commonwealth Avenue
Boston, MA 02116

Bristol Community College
777 Elsbree Street
Fall River, MA 02720

Bunker Hill Community College
Rutherford Avenue
Boston, MA 02129

Cape Cod Community College
West Barnstable, MA 02668

Holyoke Community College
Holyoke, MA 01040

Dean College
Franklin, MA 02038

Newbury College
129 Fisher Avenue
Brookline, MA 02146

Roxbury Community College
1234 Columbus Avenue
Roxbury Crossing, MA 02120

Massachusetts Bay Community College
Wellesley, MA 02181

Middlesex Community College
33 Kearney Square
Bedford, MA 01852

Mount Ida College
Newton Centre, MA 01440

Quincy College
Quincy, MA 02169

Quinsigamond Community College
670 West Boylston Street
Worcester, MA 01606

MICHIGAN

Delta College
University Center, MI 48710

Lansing Community College
P.O. Box 40010
Lansing, MI 48901

Oakland Community College
Bloomfield Hills, MI 48304

West Shore Community College
Scottsville, MI 49454

MINNESOTA

Alexandria Technical College
Alexandria, MN 56308

North Hennepin Community College
Minneapolis, MN 55445

Northland Community and Technical
College
Thief River Falls, MN 56701

Ridgewater College
P.O. Box 1097
Willmar, MN 56201

St. Cloud Technical College
1540 Northway Drive
St. Cloud, MN 56303

MISSOURI

Jefferson College
Hillsboro, MO 63050

State Fair Community College
Sedalia, MO 65301

MONTANA

Miles Community College
Miles City, MT 59301

NEBRASKA

Southeast Community College—
Lincoln Campus
Lincoln, NE 68520

NEVADA

Community College of Southern Nevada
North Las Vegas, NV 89030

NEW HAMPSHIRE

Hesser College
3 Sundial Avenue
Manchester, NH 03103

NEW JERSEY

Atlantic Community College
Mays Landing, NJ 08330

Bergen Community College
Paramus, NJ 07652

Berkeley College
44 Rifle Camp Road
West Paterson, NJ 07424

County College of Morris
Randolph, NJ 07869

Gloucester Community College
Tanyard Road
RR 4, Box 203
Sewell, NJ 08080

Middlesex County College
Edison, NJ 08818

Ocean County College
Toms River, NJ 08754

Passaic County Community College
One College Boulevard
Paterson, NJ 07505

Raritan Valley Community College
P.O. Box 3300
Somerville, NJ 08876

Salem Community College
Caraneys Point, NJ 08069

Sussex County Community College
Newton, NJ 07860

NEW MEXICO

Dona Ana Branch Community College
Box 30001
Las Cruces, NM 88003

NEW YORK

Berkeley College
3 East 43rd Street
New York, NY 10017

Berkeley College
White Plains, NY 10604

Borough of Manhattan Community
College of the City University of
New York
199 Chambers Street
New York, NY 10007

Cayuga County Community College
Auburn, NY 13021

Central City Business Institute
224 Harrison Street
Syracuse, NY 13202

Clinton Community College
Plattsburgh, NY 12901

Dutchess Community College
Poughkeepsie, NY 12601

Erie Community College, City Campus
Main Street and Youngs Road
Williamsville, NY 14221

Finger Lakes Community College
Canandaigua, NY 14424

Genesee Community College
Batavia, NY 14020

Jefferson Community College
Watertown, NY 13601

Kingsborough Community College of
the City University of New York
2001 Oriental Boulevard
Manhattan Beach
Brooklyn, NY 11235

Mohawk Valley Community College
Utica, NY 13501

Monroe Community College
Rochester, NY 14263

Nassau Community College
Garden City, NY 11530

Niagara County Community College
Sanborn, NY 14132

North Country Community College
Saranac Lake, NY 12983

State University of New York College of Technology at Alfred
Alfred, NY 14802

State University of New York College of Technology at Canton
Canton, NY 13617

Suffolk County Community College—Ammerman Campus
Selden, NY 11784

Suffolk County Community College—Eastern Campus
Riverhead, NY 11901

Suffolk County Community College—Western Campus
Brentwood, NY 11717

Sullivan County Community College
Loch Sheldrake, NY 12759

Ulster County Community College
Stone Ridge, NY 12484

Westchester Community College
Valhalla, NY 10595

NORTH CAROLINA

Central Piedmont Community College
P.O. Box 35009
Charlotte, NC 28235

Lenoir Community College
Kingston, NC 28502

Surry Community College
P.O. Box 304
Dobson, NC 27017

NORTH DAKOTA

Bismarck State College
Bismarck, ND 58501

Minot State University-Bottineau
Bottineau, ND 58318

OHIO

Bowling Green State University-Firelands College
Huron, OH 44839

Columbus State Community College
Box 1609
Columbus, OH 43216

Edison State Community College
Piqua, OH 45356

Hocking College
Nelsonville, OH 45764

Jefferson Community College
Steubenville, OH 43952

Lima Technical College
4240 Campus Drive
Lima, OH 45804

Lorain County Community College
Elyria, OH 44035

Sinclair Community College
444 West Third Street
Dayton, OH 45402

Wright State University, Lake Campus
Celina, OH 45822

OKLAHOMA

Tulsa Junior College
6111 Shelly Drive
Tulsa, OK 74135

Western Oklahoma State College
Altus, OK 73531

PENNSYLVANIA

Art Institute of Pittsburgh
526 Penn Avenue
Pittsburgh, PA 15222

Bucks County Community College
Newton, PA 18940

Butler County Community College
Butler, PA 16003

Central Pennsylvania Business School
Summerdale, PA 17093

Community College of Allegheny County–Allegheny Campus
808 Ridge Avenue
Pittsburgh, PA 15233

Community College of Allegheny County–Boyce Campus
Monroeville, PA

Community College of Allegheny County–North Campus
Pittsburgh, PA

Community College of Allegheny County–South Campus
West Mifflin, PA

Community College of Philadelphia
1700 Spring Garden Street
Philadelphia, PA 19130

Delaware County Community College
Media, PA 19063

Harcum College
Bryn Mawr, PA 19010

Harrisburg Area Community College
1 HACC Drive
Harrisburg, PA 17110

Newport Business Institute
Lower Burrell, PA 15068

Pennsylvania College of Technology
Williamsport, PA 17701

Reading Area Community College
Reading, PA 19603

Westmoreland County Community College
Youngwood, PA 15697

RHODE ISLAND

Community College of Rhode Island
Warwick, RI 02886

SOUTH CAROLINA

Spartanburg Methodist College
1200 Textile Road
Spartanburg, SC 29301

TENNESSEE

Chattanooga State Technical Community College
4501 Amnicola Highway
Chattanooga, TN 37406

TEXAS

Austin Community College
5930 Middle Fiskville Road
Austin, TX 78752

Brookhaven College
Farmers Branch, TX 75244

Central Texas College
P.O. Box 1800
Killeen, TX 76542

Cisco Junior College
Cisco, TX 76437

Midland College
Midland, TX 79705

Navarro College
3200 West 7th Avenue
Corsicana, TX 75130

South Plains College
Levelland, TX 79336

Tarrant County Junior College
1500 Houston Street
Fort Worth, TX 76102

Texarkana College
2500 North Robinson Road
Texarkana, TX 75599

Texas Southmost College
83 Fort Brown
Brownsville, TX 78520

Del Mar College
Baldwin and Agres
Corpus Christi, TX 78404

UTAH

LDS Business College
411 East South Temple Street
Salt Lake City, UT 84111

Salt Lake Community College
P.O. Box 30808
Salt Lake City, UT 84130

Utah Valley State College
Orem, UT 84058

VERMONT

Champlain College
163 South Willard Street
Burlington, VT 05401

VIRGINIA

Central Virginia Community College
Lynchburg, VA 24502

WASHINGTON

Centralia College
Centralia, WA 98531

Clark College
Vancouver, WA 98663

Edmonds Community College
Lynnwood, WA 98036

Green River Community College
12401 Southeast 320th Street
Auburn, WA 98092

Shoreline Community College
Seattle, WA 98133

Skagit Valley College
Mount Vernon, WA 98273

Spokane Falls Community College
3140 West Fort George Wright Drive
Spokane, WA 98224

Walla Walla Community College
Walla Walla, WA 99362

WISCONSIN

Fox Valley Technical College
Appleton, WI 54913

Mid-State Technical College
Wisconsin Rapids, WI 54494

Milwaukee Area Technical College
700 West State Street
Milwaukee, WI 53233

Western Wisconsin Technical College
304 North Sixth Street
La Crosse, WI 54602

WYOMING

Casper College
Casper, WY 82601

Central Wyoming College
2600 Peck Avenue
Riverton, WY 82501

Laramie County Community College
Cheyenne, WY 82007

Northwest College
Powell, WY 82435

C. FOUR-YEAR COLLEGES AND UNIVERSITIES OFFERING MAJORS IN PUBLIC RELATIONS

A degree or background in public relations is helpful in many jobs in the retail industry. A college background may give an applicant an edge in marketability and advancement prospects, as well as providing experience not otherwise available.

The following is a list of four-year schools that offer majors in public relations, grouped by state. More colleges are beginning to grant degrees in this area every year. Check the newest copy of *Lovejoy's* (found in the reference section of libraries, in guidance or counseling centers, and in bookstores) for additional schools giving degrees in this field.

ALABAMA

Alabama State University
P.O. Box 271-915 South Jackson Street
Montgomery, AL 36101

Auburn University
Mary E. Martin Hall
Auburn University, AL 36849

University of Alabama
Box 870132
Tuscaloosa, AL 35487

University of North Alabama
Wesleyan Avenue
Florence, AL 35632

ARIZONA

Northern Arizona University
Box 4084
Flagstaff, AZ 86011

ARKANSAS

Arkansas State University
P.O. Box 1630
State University, AR 72467

Harding University
Box 762-Station A
Searcy, AR 72143

John Brown University
Siloam Springs, AR 72761

Southern Arkansas University
SAU Box 1382
Magnolia, AR 71753

CALIFORNIA

California Polytechnic State University
San Luis Obispo, CA 93407

**California State Polytechnic
University—Pomona**
3801 West Temple Avenue
Pomona, CA 91768

California State University—Chico
Chico, CA 95929

California State University—Fullerton
Fullerton, CA 92634

Chapman College
333 North Glassell Street
Orange, CA 92666

La Sierra University
4700 Pierce Street
Riverside, CA 92515

Pacific Union College
Angwin, CA 94508

Pepperdine University
24255 Pacific Coast Highway
Malibu, CA 90263

San Diego State University
5300 Campanile Drive
San Diego, CA 92182

San Jose State University
One Washington Square
San Jose, CA 95192

University of Southern California
University Park
Los Angeles, CA 90089

University of the Pacific
3601 Pacific Avenue
Stockton, CA 95211

COLORADO

Colorado State University
Administration Annex
Fort Collins, CO 80523

Regis University
3333 Regis Boulevard
Denver, CO 80221

University of Northern Colorado
Greeley, CO 80639

University of Southern Colorado
2200 Bonforte Boulevard
Pueblo, CO 81001

CONNECTICUT

University of New Haven
300 Orange Avenue
West Haven, CT 06516

FLORIDA

Barry University
11300 Northeast Second Avenue
Miami Shores, FL 33161

**Florida Agriculture and Mechanical
University**
Tallahassee, FL 32307

Florida International University
University Park
Miami, FL 33199

Florida Southern College
111 Lake Hollingsworth Drive
Lakeland, FL 33801

Florida State University
Tallahassee, FL 32306

University of Florida
135 Tigert Hall
Gainesville, FL 32611

University of Miami
P.O. Box 248025
Coral Gables, FL 33124

University of West Florida
11000 University Parkway
Pensacola, FL 32514

GEORGIA

Clark Atlanta University
240 James P. Brawley Drive
Atlanta, GA 30314

Georgia Southern University
Box 8024
Statesboro, GA 30458

Shorter College
315 Shorter Avenue
Rome, GA 30165

**The Women's College of Brenau
University**
1 Centennial Circle
Gainesville, GA 30501

Toccoa Falls College
Toccoa Falls, GA 30598

University of Georgia
114 Academic Building
Athens, GA 30602

Wesleyan College
4760 Forsyth Road
Macon, GA 31297

ILLINOIS

Bradley University
1501 West Bradley
Peoria, IL 61625

Columbia College
600 South Michigan
Chicago, IL 60605

Illinois State University
201 Hovey Hall
Normal, IL 61761

McKendree College
701 College Road
Lebanon, IL 62258

Quincy University
1800 College Avenue
Quincy, IL 62301

Roosevelt University
430 South Michigan Avenue
Chicago, IL 60605

Southern Illinois University at Carbondale
Woody Hall
Carbondale, IL 62901

INDIANA

Franklin College
Monroe Street
Franklin, IN 46131

Goshen College
1700 South Main Street
Goshen, IN 46526

Indiana State University
217 North Sixth Street
Terre Haute, IN 47809

Purdue University
Hovde Hall
West Lafayette, IN 47907

St. Mary-of-the-Woods College
St. Mary-of-the-Woods, IN 47876

Taylor University-Fort Wayne
1025 West Rudisill Boulevard
Fort Wayne, IN 46807

University of Evansville
1800 Lincoln Avenue
Evansville, IN 47722

University of Southern Indiana
8600 University Boulevard
Evansville, IN 47714

Valparaiso University
Valparaiso, IN 46383

IOWA

Clarke College
1550 Clarke Drive
Dubuque, IA 52001

Drake University
25th and University Streets
Des Moines, IA 50311

Loras College
1450 Alta Vista
Dubuque, IA 52001

Mount Mercy College
1330 Elmhurst Drive Northeast
Cedar Rapids, IA 52402

St. Ambrose College
518 West Locust Street
Davenport, IA 52803

University of Northern Iowa
West 27th Street
Cedar Falls, IA 50614

KANSAS

Fort Hays State University
600 Park Street
Hays, KS 67601

Kansas Newman College
3100 McCormick
Wichita, KS 67213

Pittsburg State University
1701 South Broadway
Pittsburg, KS 66762

Washburn University
1700 College Street
Topeka, KS 66621

Wichita State University
1845 Fairmount Street
Wichita, KS 67208

KENTUCKY

Eastern Kentucky University
Lancaster Avenue
Richmond, KY 40475

Kentucky Wesleyan College
3000 Frederica Street
Owensboro, KY 42301

Murray State University
Murray, KY 42071

Western Kentucky University
Wetherby Administration Building
Room 209
Bowling Green, KY 42101

LOUISIANA

Louisiana State University-Shreveport
One University Place
Shreveport, LA 71115

Northeast Louisiana University
700 University Avenue
Monroe, LA 71209

University of Southwestern Louisiana
P.O. Box 41770
Lafayette, LA 70504

MARYLAND

Bowie State University
Jericho Park Road
Bowie, MD 20715

Columbia Union College
7600 Flower Avenue
Tacoma Park, MD 20912

University of Maryland—College Park
College Park, MD 20742

MASSACHUSETTS

Boston University
121 Bay State Road
Boston, MA 02215

Curry College
1071 Blue Hill Avenue
Milton, MA 02186

Emerson College
100 Beacon Street
Boston, MA 02116

North Adams State College
Church Street
North Adams, MA 01247

Salem State College
352 Lafayette Street
Salem, MA 01970

Simmons College
300 The Fenway
Boston, MA 02115

MICHIGAN

Andrews University
Berrien Springs, MI 49104

Eastern Michigan University
400 Pierce Hall
Silanti, MI 48197

Ferris State College
Big Rapids, MI 49307

Grand Valley State University
1 Seidman House
Allendale, MI 49401

Madonna College
36600 Schoolcraft Road
Livonia, MI 48150

Northern Michigan University
Cohodas Administration Center
Marquette, MI 49855

University of Detroit Mercy
4001 West McNichols Road
Detroit, MI 48221

Wayne State University
Detroit, MI 48202

Western Michigan University
Administration Building
Kalamazoo, MI 49008

MINNESOTA

Concordia College
Moorhead, MN 56560

Mankato State University
Box 55
Mankato, MN 56001

Moorhead State University
1104 7th Avenue South
Moorhead, MN 56560

St. Mary's College of Minnesota
700 Terrace Heights
Winona, MN 55987

University of St. Thomas
2115 Summit Avenue
St. Paul, MN 55105

Winona State University
Winona, MN 55987

MISSISSIPPI

Jackson State University
1325 J.R. Lynch Street
Jackson, MS 39217

MISSOURI

Central Missouri State University
Warrensburg, MO 64093

Culver-Stockton College
Canton, MO 63435

Fontbonne College
6800 Wydown Boulevard
St. Louis, MO 63105

Missouri Western State College
4525 Downs Drive
St. Joseph, MO 64507

Northwest Missouri State University
Maryville, MO 64468

Stephens College
Columbia, MO 65215

Webster University
470 East Lockwood
St. Louis, MO 63119

William Jewell College
Liberty, MO 64068

MONTANA

Carroll College
North Benton Avenue
Helena, MT 59625

NEBRASKA

Creighton University
California at 24th Street
Omaha, NE 68178

Hastings College
7th and Turner Avenues
Hastings, NE 68901

Midland Lutheran College
720 East 9th Street
Fremont, NE 68025

Union College
3800 South 48th Street
Lincoln, NE 68506

University of Nebraska—Omaha
60th and Dodge Streets
Omaha, NE 68182

NEVADA

University of Nevada—Las Vegas
4505 Maryland Parkway
Las Vegas, NY 89154

NEW HAMPSHIRE

New England College
Henniker, NH 03242

NEW JERSEY

Monmouth College
Cedara Avenue
West Long Branch, NJ 07764

Rowan College of New Jersey
201 Mullica Hill Road
Glassboro, NJ 08028

Seton Hall University
400 South Orange Avenue
South Orange, NJ 07079

NEW MEXICO

New Mexico State University
Box 30001
Department 3A
Las Cruces, NM 88003

NEW YORK

City College of New York
Convent Avenue at 138th Street
New York, NY 10031

College of New Rochelle
Castle Place
New Rochelle, NY 10805

Iona College
715 North Avenue
New Rochelle, NY 10801

Long Island University—C.W. Post Campus
College Hall
Northern Boulevard
Greenvale, NY 11548

Long Island University-Southampton Campus
Montauk Highway
Southampton, NY 11968

Medaille College
18 Agassiz Circle
Buffalo, NY 14214

Mount Saint Mary College
330 Powell Avenue
Newburgh, NY 12550

SUNY—College of Agriculture and Life Sciences at Cornell University
410 Thurston Avenue
Ithaca, NY 14853

SUNY—College at New Paltz
75 South Manheim Boulevard
New Paltz, NY 12561

Syracuse University
200 Administration Building
Syracuse, NY 13244

Utica College of Syracuse University
Burrstone Road
Utica, NY 13502

NORTH CAROLINA

Appalachian State University
Boone, NC 28608

Bennett College
900 East Washington Street
Greensboro, NC 27401

Campbell University
P.O. Box 546
Buies Creek, NC 27506

Mars Hill College
124 Cascade Street
Mars Hill, NC 28754

North Carolina Agricultural and Technical State University
1601 East Market Street
Greensboro, NC 27411

Pembroke State University
Pembroke, NC 28372

Salem College
P.O. Box 10548
Winston-Salem, NC 27108

Wingate College
Wingate, NC 28174

NORTH DAKOTA

University of North Dakota
Grand Forks, ND 58202

OHIO

Capital University
2199 East Main Street
Columbus, OH 43209

Findlay College
1000 North Main Street
Findlay, OH 45840

Heidelberg College
310 East Market Street
Tiffin, OH 44883

Kent State University
P.O. Box 5190
Kent, OH 44242

Marietta College
Fifth Street
Marietta, OH 45750

Miami University
Oxford, OH 45056

Ohio Dominican College
1216 Sunbury Road
Columbus, OH 43219

Ohio Northern University
Main Street
Ada, OH 45810

Ohio University
120 Chubb Hall
Athens, OH 45701

Otterbein College
Westerville, OH 43081

The Defiance College
701 North Clinton Street
Defiance, OH 43512

University of Dayton
300 College Park Avenue
Dayton, OH 45469

University of Rio Grande
P.O. Box 909
Rio Grande, OH 45674

University of Toledo
2801 West Bancroft Street
Toledo, OH 43606

Ursuline College
2550 Lander Road
Pepper Pike, OH 44124

Xavier University
3800 Victory Parkway
Cincinnati, OH 45207

Youngstown State University
Youngstown, OH 44555

OKLAHOMA

Northwestern Oklahoma State University
709 Oklahoma Boulevard
Alva, OK 73717

Oklahoma Baptist University
500 West University
Shawnee, OK 74801

Oklahoma Christian University of Science and Arts
P.O. Box 11000
Oklahoma City, OK 73136

University of Central Oklahoma
Edmond, OK 73034

University of Oklahoma—Norman
100 Asp Avenue
Norman, OK 73019

University of Tulsa
600 South College Avenue
Tulsa, OK 74104

OREGON

University of Oregon
240 Oregon Hall
Eugene, OR 97403

PENNSYLVANIA

Cabrini College
610 King of Prussia Road
Radnor, PA 19087

Duquesne University
600 Forbes Avenue
Pittsburgh, PA 15282

Elizabethtown College
One Alpha Drive
Elizabethtown, PA 17022

La Salle University of Pennsylvania
Alumni Hall
Mansfield, PA 16933

Mansfield University of Pennsylvania
Alumni Hall
Mansfield, PA 16933

Marywood College
2300 Adams Avenue
Scranton, PA 18509

Millersville University of Pennsylvania
P.O. Box 1002
Millersville, PA 17551

Point Park College
201 Wood Street
Pittsburgh, PA 15222

Seton Hill College
Greensburg, PA 15601

St. Francis College
P.O. Box 600
Loretto, PA 15940

Temple University
Philadelphia, PA 19122

University of Pittsburgh-Bradford
300 Campus Drive
Bradford, PA 16701

University of Scranton
800 Linden Street
Scranton, PA 18510

Westminster College
New Wilmington, PA 16172

RHODE ISLAND

Rhode Island College
Providence, RI 02908

SOUTH CAROLINA

Bob Jones University
Wade Hampton Boulevard
Greenville, SC 29614

University of South Carolina
Columbia, SC 29208

SOUTH DAKOTA

Huron College
Huron, SD 57350

TENNESSEE

East Tennessee State University
Campus Box 24430-A
Johnson City, TN 37614

Freed-Hardeman College
158 East Main Street
Henderson, TN 38340

Memphis State University
Memphis, TN 38152

**Southern College of Seventh-Day
   Adventists**
Box 370
Collegedale, TN 37315

University of Tennessee-Chattanooga
129 Hooper Hall
McCallie Avenue
Chattanooga, TN 37402

University of Tennessee-Knoxville
320 Student Services Building
Knoxville, TN 37996

TEXAS

Abilene Christian University
Box 7988
ACU Station
Abilene, TX 79699

University of North Texas
Box 13797
Denton, TX 76203

Southern Methodist University
P.O. Box 296
Dallas, TX 75275

Texas Christian University
Box 7988
ACU Station
Abilene, TX 79699

Texas Tech University
P.O. Box 4350
Lubbock, TX 79409

UTAH

Brigham Young University
A-153 ASB
Provo, UT 84602

Southern Utah State College
351 West Center
Cedar City, UT 84720

Weber State College
Box 1015
3750 Harrison Boulevard
Ogden, UT 84408

VIRGINIA

James Madison University
Harrisonburg, VA 22807

Liberty University
3765 Candlers Mountain Road
Lynchburg, VA 24506

Mary Baldwin College
Staunton, VA 24401

Radford University
Radford, VA 24142

Virginia Commonwealth University
P.O. Box 2526
821 West Franklin Street
Richmond, VA 23284

WASHINGTON

Central Washington University
Mitchell Hall
Ellensburg, WA 98926

Gonzaga University
Spokane, WA 99258

Pacific Lutheran University
Tacoma, WA 98447

Seattle University
12th and East Columbia
Seattle, WA 98122

Washington State University
342 French Administration
Pullman, WA 99164

WEST VIRGINIA

Bethany College
Bethany, WV 26032

Marshall University
400 Hal Greer Boulevard
Huntington, WV 25705

West Virginia University
P.O. Box 6009
Morgantown, WV 26506

West Virginia Wesleyan College
College Avenue
Buckhannon, WV 26201

WISCONSIN

Marquette University
1217 West Wisconsin Avenue
Milwaukee, WI 53233

Mount Mary College
2900 North Menomonee River Parkway
Milwaukee, WI 53222

D. FOUR-YEAR COLLEGES AND UNIVERSITIES OFFERING MAJORS IN ADVERTISING

A degree or background in advertising is helpful in many jobs in the retail industry. Continued education may give an applicant an edge in marketability and advancement prospects, as well as providing experience not otherwise available.

The following is a list of four-year schools that offer majors in advertising, grouped by state. More colleges are beginning to grant degrees in this area every year. Check the newest copy of *Lovejoy's* (found in the reference section of libraries, in guidance or counseling centers, and in bookstores) for additional schools giving degrees in this field.

ALABAMA

University of Alabama
Box 870132
Tuscaloosa, AL 35487

ARIZONA

Northern Arizona University
Box 4084
Flagstaff, AZ 86011

ARKANSAS

Arkansas State University
P.O. Box 1630
State University, AR 72467

Harding University
Box 762 Station A
Searcy, AR 72143

University of Arkansas—Little Rock
33rd and University Avenues
Little Rock, AR 72204

CALIFORNIA

Academy of Art College
540 Powell Street
San Francisco, CA 94108

Art Center College of Design
1700 Lida Street
Pasadena, CA 91103

California Lutheran University
60 Olsen Road
Thousand Oaks, CA 91360

California State University—Fresno
Shaw and Cedar Avenues
Fresno, CA 93740

California State University—Fullerton
Fullerton, CA 92634

Chapman University
333 North Glassell Street
Orange, CA 92666

Pepperdine University
24255 Pacific Coast Highway
Malibu, CA 90265

San Diego State University
5300 Campanile Drive
San Diego, CA 92182

San Jose State University
One Washington Square
San Jose, CA 95192

COLORADO

Adams State College
Alamosa, CO 81102

University of Colorado—Boulder
Campus Box B-7
Boulder, CO 80309

University of Northern Colorado
Greeley, CO 80639

University of Southern Colorado
2200 Bonforte Boulevard
Pueblo, CO 81001

CONNECTICUT

University of Bridgeport
126 Park Avenue
Wahlstrom Library
Bridgeport, CT 06601

FLORIDA

Florida International University
University Park
Miami, FL 33199

Florida Southern College
111 Lake Hollingsworth Drive
Lakeland, FL 33801

Florida State University
Tallahassee, FL 32306

University of Florida
135 Tigert Hall
Gainesville, FL 32611

University of Miami
P.O. Box 248025
Coral Gables, FL 33124

University of West Florida
11000 University Parkway
Pensacola, FL 32514

GEORGIA

Georgia Southern University
Box 8024
Statesboro, GA 30458

University of Georgia
114 Academic Building
Athens, GA 30602

ILLINOIS

Bradley University
1501 West Bradley
Peoria, IL 61625

Columbia College
600 South Michigan
Chicago, IL 60605

Northern Illinois University
De Kalb, IL 60115

Roosevelt University
430 South Michigan Avenue
Chicago, IL 60605

Southern Illinois University—Carbondale
Woody Hall
Carbondale, IL 62901

University of Illinois at Urbana-Champaign
506 South Wright Street
Urbana, IL 61801

INDIANA

Ball State University
2000 University Avenue
Muncie, IN 47306

Franklin College
Monroe Street
Franklin, IN 46131

Purdue University
Hovde Hall
West Lafayette, IN 47907

University of Evansville
1800 Lincoln Avenue
Evansville, IN 47722

IOWA

Briar Cliff College
3303 Rebecca Street
Sioux City, IA 51104

Clarke College
1550 Clarke Drive
Dubuque, IA 52001

Drake University
25th and University Streets
Des Moines, IA 50311

St. Ambrose College
518 West Locust Street
Davenport, IA 52803

KANSAS

Pittsburg State University
1701 South Broadway
Pittsburg, KS 66762

University of Kansas
126 Strong Hall
Lawrence, KS 66045

Wichita State University
1845 Fairmount Street
Wichita, KS 67208

KENTUCKY

Kentucky Wesleyan College
3000 Frederica Street
Owensboro, KY 42301

Morehead State University
Morehead, KY 40351

Murray State University
Murray, KY 42071

University of Kentucky
100 Funkhouser Building
Lexington, KY 40506

Western Kentucky University
Wetherby Administration Building
Room 209
Bowling Green, KY 42101

LOUISIANA

Louisiana Tech University
P.O. Box 3168
Tech Station
Ruston, LA 71272

Louisiana State University and Agricultural and Mechanical College
110 Thomas Boyd Hall
Baton Rouge, LA 70803

McNeese State University
Lake Charles, LA 70609

MAINE

Saint Joseph's College
Windham, ME 04062

MARYLAND

University of Maryland—College Park
College Park, MD 20742

MASSACHUSETTS

Boston University
121 Bay State Road
Boston, MA 02215

Emerson College
100 Beacon Street
Boston, MA 02116

Salem State College
352 Lafayette Street
Salem, MA 01970

Simmons College
300 The Fenway
Boston, MA 02115

MICHIGAN

Eastern Michigan University
400 Pierce Hall
Ypsilanti, MI 48197

Ferris State College
Big Rapids, MI 49307

Grand Valley State University
1 Seidman House
Allendale, MI 49401

Kendall College of Art and Design
111 Division North
Grand Rapids, MI 49503

Michigan State University
Administration Building—Room 250
East Lansing, MI 48824

Western Michigan University
Administration Building
Kalamazoo, MI 49008

MINNESOTA

Concordia College
Moorhead, MN 56560

Moorhead State University
1104 7th Avenue South
Moorhead, MN 56560

University of St. Thomas
2115 Summit Avenue
St. Paul, MN 55105

Winona State University
Winona, MN 55987

MISSISSIPPI

Jackson State University
1325 J.R. Lynch Street
Jackson, MS 39217

University of Mississippi
Lyceum Building
University, MS 38677

University of Southern Mississippi
Box 5011
Southern Station
Hattiesburg, MS 39406

MISSOURI

University of Missouri—Columbia
130 Jesse Hall
Columbia, MO 65211

NEBRASKA

Creighton University
California at 24th Street
Omaha, NE 68178

Hastings College
7th and Turner Avenues
Hastings, NE 68901

University of Nebraska at Kearney
905 West 25th Street
Kearney, NE 68849

University of Nebraska—Lincoln
14th and R Streets
Lincoln, NE 68508

NEVADA

University of Nevada—Las Vegas
4505 Maryland Parkway
Las Vegas, NV 89154

NEW HAMPSHIRE

Franklin Pierce College
Rindge, NH 03461

New England College
Henniker, NH 03242

NEW JERSEY

Rider College
2083 Lawrenceville Road
Lawrenceville, NJ 08648

Rowan College of New Jersey
201 Mullica Hill Road
Glassboro, NJ 08028

Seton Hall University
400 South Orange Avenue
South Orange, NJ 07079

NEW MEXICO

New Mexico State University
Box 30001
Department 3A
Las Cruces, NM 88003

NEW YORK

Baruch College
17 Lexington Avenue
New York, NY 10010

College of New Rochelle
School of Arts & Sciences
and School of Nursing
Castle Place
New Rochelle, NY 10805

Iona College
715 North Avenue
New Rochelle, NY 10801

Long Island University—Southampton Campus
Montauk Highway
Southampton, NY 11968

Manhattan College
Manhattan College Parkway
Riverdale, NY 10471

Marist College
North Road
Poughkeepsie, NY 12601

Medaille College
18 Agassiz Circle
Buffalo, NY 14214

School of Visual Arts
209 East 23rd Street
New York, NY 10010

Syracuse University
200 Administration Building
Syracuse, NY 13210

NORTH CAROLINA

Appalachian State University
Boone, NC 28608

Salem College
P.O. Box 10548
Winston-Salem, NC 27108

University of North Carolina—
   Chapel Hill
Campus Box 2200
Chapel Hill, NC 27599

NORTH DAKOTA

University of North Dakota
Grand Forks, ND 58202

OHIO

Columbus College of Art and Design
107 North Ninth Street
Columbus, OH 43215

Kent State University
P.O. Box 5190
Kent, OH 44242

Marietta College
Fifth Street
Marietta, OH 45750

Ohio University
120 Chubb Hall
Athens, OH 45701

The Defiance College
701 North Clinton Street
Defiance, OH 43512

University of Findlay
1000 North Main Street
Findlay, OH 45840

Xavier University
3800 Victory Parkway
Cincinnati, OH 45207

Youngstown State University
Youngstown, OH 44555

OKLAHOMA

Oklahoma Christian University of
   Science and Arts
P.O. Box 11000
Oklahoma City, OK 73136

University of Central Oklahoma
Edmond, OK 73034

University of Oklahoma—Norman
100 Asp Avenue
Norman, OK 73019

OREGON

University of Oregon
240 Oregon Hall
Eugene, OR 97403

PENNSYLVANIA

Cabrini College
610 King of Prussia Road
Radnor, PA 19087

Duquesne University
600 Forbes Avenue
Pittsburgh, PA 15282

Marywood College
2300 Adams Avenue
Scranton, PA 18509

Penn State—University Park
201 Shields Building
University Park, PA 16802

Point Park College
201 Wood Street
Pittsburgh, PA 15222

Seton Hill College
Greensburg, PA 15601

Temple University
Philadelphia, PA 19122

University of Scranton
800 Linden Street
Scranton, PA 18510

RHODE ISLAND

Johnson & Wales University
Abbott Park Place
Providence, RI 02903

SOUTH CAROLINA

University of South Carolina
Columbia, SC 29208

SOUTH DAKOTA

South Dakota State University
Box 2201-Administration Building
Room 200
Brookings, SD 57007

University of South Dakota
414 East Clark
Vermillion, SD 57069

TENNESSEE

Austin Peay State University
601 College Street
Clarksville, TN 37040

David Lipscomb College
Nashville, TN 37203

East Tennessee State University
Campus Box 24430-A
Johnson City, TN 37614

Memphis State University
Memphis, TN 38152

University of Tennessee—Chattanooga
129 Hooper Hall
McCallie Avenue
Chattanooga, TN 37402

University of Tennessee—Knoxville
320 Student Services Building
Knoxville, TN 37996

TEXAS

Abilene Christian University
Box 7988
ACU Station
Abilene, TX 79699

Lamar University
P.O. Box 10009
Beaumont, TX 77710

University of North Texas
Box 13797
Denton, TX 76203

Southern Methodist University
P.O. Box 296
Dallas, TX 75275

Texas Christian University
2800 South University Drive
Fort Worth, TX 76129

Texas Tech University
P.O. Box 42017
Lubbock, TX 79409

Texas Women's University
P.O. Box 22909
TWU Station
Denton, TX 76204

University of Texas-Austin
Austin, TX 78212

UTAH

Brigham Young University
A-153 ASB
Provo, UT 84602

Southern Utah State College
351 West Center
Cedar City, UT 84720

VIRGINIA

Mary Baldwin College
Staunton, VA 24401

Virginia Commonwealth University
P.O. Box 2526
821 West Franklin Street
Richmond, VA 23284

WASHINGTON

University of Washington
Seattle, WA 98195

Washington State University
342 French Administration
Pullman, WA 99164

WEST VIRGINIA

Bethany College
Bethany, WV 26032

Marshall University
400 Hal Greer Boulevard
Huntington, WV 25755

West Virginia University
P.O. Box 6009
Morgantown, WV 26506

WISCONSIN

Marquette University
1217 West Wisconsin Avenue
Milwaukee, WI 53233

APPENDIX II
TRADE ASSOCIATIONS, UNIONS, & OTHER ORGANIZATIONS

The following is a list of trade associations, unions, and organizations discussed in this book. There are also a number of other associations listed that might be useful to you.

The names, addresses, phone numbers, fax numbers, web addresses, and email addresses are included (when available) to help you easily get in touch with any of the organizations.

Many of the associations have branch offices located throughout the country. Organization headquarters can get you the phone number and address of your local branch.

Advertising Research Foundation (ARF)
641 Lexington Avenue
New York, NY 10022
phone: 212-751-5656
fax: 212-319-5265
email: email@arfsite.org
www.arfsite.org

Advertising Women of New York (AWNY)
153 East 57th Street
New York, NY 10022
phone: 212-593-1950
fax: 212-759-2865
email: awny85@aol.com

Affiliated Advertising Agencies International (AAAI)
2289 South Xanadu Way
Aurora, CO 80014
phone: 303-671-8551

African-American Beverage and Grocers Association
16200 Ventura Boulevard, Suite 208
Encino, CA 91436-4642

American Advertising Federation (AAF)
1101 Vermont Avenue NW, Suite 500
Washington, DC 20005
phone: 202-898-0089
fax: 202-898-0159
email: aaf@aaf.org

American Artists Professional League (AAPL)
47 5th Avenue
New York, NY 10003
phone: 212-645-1345

American Assembly of Collegiate Schools of Business (AACSB)
AACSB-The International Association for Management Education
600 Emerson Road, Suite 300
St. Louis, MO 63141-6762
phone: 314-872-8481
fax: 314-872-8495
www.aacsb.edu

American Association of Advertising Agencies (AAAA)
405 Lexington Avenue, 18th Floor
New York, NY 10174-1801
phone: 212-682-2500
fax: 212-682-8391
www.commercepark.com/AAAA/index.html

American Association of Mom and Pop Retail Food Stores
c/o Oscar J. Coffey Jr.
117 Broadway
Oakland, CA 94607-3715

American Association of Retired Persons (AARP)
601 E Street NW
Washington, DC 20049
phone: 202-434-2277
toll-free: 800-424-3410
fax: 202-434-2320
www.aarp.org

American Automotive Leasing Association (AALA)
700 13th Street NW, Suite 950
Washington, DC 20005
phone: 202-393-7292
fax: 202-393-7293
email: amautolsg@aol.com

American Booksellers Association (ABA)
828 S. Broadway
Tarrytown, NY 10591
phone: 914-591-2665
toll-free: 800-637-0037
fax: 914-591-2720
email: info@bookweb.org
www.bookweb.org

American Collegiate Retailing Association (ACRA)
c/o Dr. Michael M. Pearson
Department of Marketing
Georgia Southern University
P.O. Box 8154
Statesboro, GA 30460-8454
phone: 912-681-5336
fax: 912-871-1523

American Compensation Association (ACA)
14040 New Northsight Boulevard
Scottsdale, AZ 85260
phone: 480-951-9191
fax: 480-483-8352
toll-free: 877-951-9191
email: aca@acaonline.org
www.acaonline.org

American Institute of Certified Public Accountants (AICPA)
1211 Avenue of the Americas
New York, NY 10036-8775
phone: 212-596-6200
toll-free: 800-862-4272
fax: 212-596-6213
www.aicpa.org

**American Institute of Graphic Arts
(AIGA)**
164 5th Avenue
New York, NY 10010
phone: 212-807-1990
toll-free: 800-548-1634
fax: 212-807-1799
www.aiga.org

**American Management Association
(AMA)**
1601 Broadway
New York, NY 10019-7420
phone: 212-586-8100
fax: 212-903-8168
www.amanet.org

**American Marketing Association
(AMA)**
311 S. Wacker Drive, Suite 5800
Chicago, IL 60606
phone: 312-542-9000
toll-free: 800-262-1150
fax: 312-542-9001
email: info@ama.org
www.ama.org

American Purchasing Society (APS)
P.O. Box 256
Aurora, IL 60506
phone: 630-859-0250
fax: 630-859-0270
email: propurch@aol.com
www.american-purchasing.com

**American Society for Training and
Development (ASTD)**
Box 1443
1640 King Street
Alexandria, VA 22313
phone: 703-683-8100
fax: 703-683-8103

American Society of Artists (ASA)
P.O. Box 1326
Palatine, IL 60078 USA
phone: 312-751-2500

**American Specialty Toy Retailing
Association (ASTRA)**
c/o Janet Koerner
206 6th Avenue, Suite 900, Midland
  Building
Des Moines, IA 50309-4018
phone: 515-282-8192
fax: 515-282-9117
email: astra@astratoy.org
www.astratoy.org

**American Truck Stop Owners
Association (ATSOA)**
P.O. Box 4949
Winston-Salem, NC 27115-4949
phone: 910-744-5555
fax: 910-744-1184

**American Wholesale Marketers
Association (AWMA)**
1128 16th Street
Washington, DC 20036
phone: 202-463-2124
toll-free: 800-482-2962
fax: 202-463-6456
email: davids@awmanet.org
www.awmanet.org

Apparel Guild (AG)
2655 Park Circle
East Meadow, NY 11554
phone: 516-735-1595
fax: 516-735-1595

Art Directors Club (ADC)
104 West 29th Street
New York, NY 10001
phone: 212-643-1440
fax: 212-643-4266
email: adcny@interport.net
www.adcny.org

**Association for Business
Communication (ABC)**
Baruch College
17 Lexington Avenue
New York, NY 10010
phone: 212-387-1620
fax: 212-387-1655

**Association for Retail Technology
Standards (ARTS)**
P.O. Box 15066
Reading, PA 19612-5066
phone: 610-929-7393
fax: 610-929-7336

Association of Book Travelers (ABT)
c/o Jay Bruff
P.O. Box 1795
New York, NY 10185
phone: 914-353-6180
primary contact: Paul Drougas, President

**Association of Coupon Professionals
(ACP)**
35 E. Wacker Drive, Suite 500
Chicago, IL 60601
phone: 312-782-5252
fax: 312-782-1140
email: service@couponpros.org
www.couponpros.org

**Association of Direct Marketing
Agencies (ADMA)**
P.O. Box 3139
New York, NY 10163-3139
phone: 212-644-8085
fax: 212-644-0296
email: JWPgroup@aol.org

**Association of Promotion Marketing
Agencies Worldwide (APMA)**
750 Summer St.
Stamford, CT 06901
phone: 860-325-3911
fax: 860-969-1499
email: mccapma@aol.com
www.apmaw.org

**Association of Retail Marketing
Services (ARMS)**
244 Broad Street
Red Bank, NJ 07701-2003
phone: 732-842-5070
fax: 732-219-1938
email: Gerhop@aol.com

**Association of Sales Administration
Managers (ASAM)**
c/o Bill Martin
Box 1356
Laurence Harbor, NJ 08879
phone: 732-264-7722
fax: 732-264-0232

**Association for Women in
Communications**
1244 Ritchie Highway, Suite 6
Arnold, MD 21012-1887
phone: 410-544-7442
fax: 410-544-4640
email: pat@womcom.org

**Association of Sales and Marketing
Companies**
2100 Reston Parkway, Suite 400
Reston, VA 20191-1218
phone: 703-758-7790
fax: 703-758-7787
email: info@asmc.org
www.asmc.org

**Building Owners and Managers
Association International (BOMA)**
1201 New York Avenue NW, Suite 300
Washington, DC 20005
phone: 202-408-2662
fax: 202-371-0181
email: soppen@boma.org
www.boma.org

Business Marketing Association
400 North Michigan Avenue, 15th Floor
Chicago, IL 60611
phone: 312-409-4262
fax: 312-409-4266
email: bma@marketing.org
www.marketing.org

California Retailers Association (CRA)
980 9th Street, Suite 2100
Sacramento, CA 95814-2741
phone: 916-443-1975
fax: 916-441-4218

Canadian Booksellers Association (CBA)
789 Don Mills Road, Suite 700
Toronto, ON
Canada 3CC 1T5
phone: 416-467-7883
fax: 416-467-7886
email: smckean@cbabook.org
www.cbabook.org

Canadian Federation of Independent Grocers (CFIG)
La Federation Canadienne des Epiciers Independants (FCEI)
2235 Sheppard Avenue E, Suite 902
Willowdale, ON
Canada M2J 5B5
phone: 416-492-2311
fax: 416-492-2347

Christian Booksellers Association
P.O. Box 200
Colorado Springs, CO 80901
phone: 719-576-7880
toll-free: 800-252-1950
fax: 719-576-9240
email: info@cba-intl.org
www.cbaonline.org

CIES, Food Business Forum
5549 Lee Highway
Arlington, VA 22207
phone: 703-534-8880
fax: 703-534-9080
www.ciesnet.com

Clothing Manufacturers Association of the U.S.A. (CMA)
730 Broadway, 9th Floor
New York, NY 10003
phone: 212-529-0823

College Enterprises
c/o Nancy S. Nash
P.O. Box 8795
Williamsburg, VA 23187-8795

Commercial Street Market
c/o Marlee Yant
224 E. Commercial Street
Springfield, MO 65803-2940

Custom Tailors and Designers Association of America (CTDA)
P.O. Box 53052
Washington, DC 20009-9052
phone: 202-387-7220
fax: 202-387-7713
www.ctda.com

Direct Marketing Association (DMA)
1120 Avenue of the Americas
New York, NY 10036-6700
phone: 212-768-7277
fax: 212-302-6714
email: webmaster@the-dma.org
www.the-dma.org

Direct Marketing Association Catalog Council (DMACC)
1120 Avenue of the Americas
New York, NY 10036
phone: 212-768-7277
fax: 212-768-4576

Direct Marketing Club of New York (DMCNY)
224 Seventh Street
Garden City, NY 11530
phone: 516-746-6700
fax: 516-294-8141
email: info@dmcny.org
www.dmcny.org

Direct Marketing Educational Foundation (DMEF)
1120 Avenue of the Americas
New York, NY 10036-6700
phone: 212-768-7277
fax: 212-302-6714
www.the-dma.org/dmef

Direct Marketing Insurance and Financial Services Council (IFSC)
c/o Direct Marketing Association
1120 Avenue of the Americas, 13th Floor
New York, NY 10036-6700
phone: 212-768-7277
fax: 212-302-6714
www.the-dma.org

Discovery Shoppe League
c/o Peggy Sever
315 Flume Street
Chico, CA 95928-5428

Distribution Research and Education Foundation (DREF)
1725 K Street NW
Washington, DC 20006
phone: 202-872-0885
fax: 202-785-0586
email: dref@nawd.org

Electronic Funds Transfer Association (EFTA)
950 Herndon Parkway, Suite 390
Herndon, VA 20170
phone: 703-435-9800
fax: 703-435-7157
www.efta.org

Electronic Retailing Association (ERA)
2101 Wilson Boulevard, Suite 1002
Arlington, VA 22201
phone: 202-289-6462
toll-free: 800-987-6462
fax: 202-682-0603
www.retailing.org

Floor Covering Council
403 Axminister Drive
Fenton, MO 63026
phone: 314-326-2636
fax: 314-326-1823

Food Marketing Institute (FMI)
800 Connecticut Avenue NW
Washington, DC 20006
phone: 202-452-8444
fax: 202-429-4519
email: fmi@fmi.org
www.fm.org

General Merchandise Distributors Council (GMDC)
1275 Lake Plaza Drive
Suite C
Colorado Springs, CO 80906
phone: 719-576-4260
fax: 719-576-2661

Graphic Artists Guild (GAG)
90 John Street, Suite 403
New York, NY 10038
phone: 212-791-3400
toll-free: 800-500-2627
fax: 212-791-0333
email: pr@gag.org
www.gag.org

Greater Wilmington Merchants Association
208 Dock Street
P.O. Box 1035
Wilmington, NC 28402
phone: 910-762-7397
fax: 910-762-3247

Grocers Home Center Institute (HCI)
5822 West 74th Street
Indianapolis, IN 46278
phone: 317-299-0339
fax: 317-328-4354
email: nrha@iquest.net
www.nrha.org

Home Furnishings International Association (HFIA)
110 World Trade Center
P.O. Box 420807
Dallas, TX 75342-0807
phone: 214-741-7632
fax: 214-742-9103
email: hfia@dallas.net
www.hfia.com

Idaho Retailers Association
4980 West State, Suite B
Boise, ID 83703
phone: 208-853-2874
fax: 208-853-0696
email: shopalot@micron.net

INCODA
2 Forest Avenue
Oradell, NJ 07649
phone: 201-261-8884
fax: 201-261-8887

Independent Insurance Agents of America (IIAA)
127 South Peyton
Alexandria, VA 22314
phone: 703-683-4422
toll-free: 800-221-7917
fax: 703-683-7556

Institute of Internal Auditors (IIA)
249 Maitland Avenue
Altamonte Springs, FL 32701-4201
phone: 407-830-7600
fax: 407-831-5171
email: iia@theiia.org
www.theiia.org

Institute of Real Estate Management (IREM)
430 North Michigan Avenue
Chicago, IL 60611-4090
phone: 312-329-6000
toll-free: 800-837-0706
fax: 312-410-7960
email: rvukas@irem.org
www.irem.org

Indiana Retail Council
1 North Capitol, Suite 430
Indianapolis, IN 46204

phone: 317-632-7391
fax: 317-632-7399

Institute of Store Planners (ISP)
25 North Broadway
Tarrytown, NY 10591
phone: 914-332-1806
toll-free: 800-379-9912
fax: 914-332-1541
email: adminisp@ispo.org

International Association of Airport Duty Free (IAADFS)
1200 19th Street NW, Suite 300
Washington, DC 20036
phone: 202-857-1184
fax: 202-429-5154
email: iaadfs@dc.sba.com
www.iaadfs.org

International Association of Business Communicators (IABC)
1 Hallidie Plaza, Suite 600
San Francisco, CA 94102
phone: 415-433-3400
fax: 415-362-8762
email: leader-centre@iabc.com
www.iabc.com

International Association of Ice Cream Vendors (IAICV)
c/o Charlene Mayfield
1900 Arch Street
Philadelphia, PA 19103-1498
phone: 215-564-3484
fax: 215-564-9785
email: assnhqy@hetaxs.com

International Council of Shopping Centers (ICSC)
1221 Avenue of the Americas
New York, NY 10020
phone: 646-728-3800
fax: 212-589-5555
email: icsc@icsc.org
www.icsc.org

International Foundation of Employee Benefit Plans
18700 W. Bluemound Road
P.O. Box 69
Brookfield, WI 53008
phone: 262-786-6700
fax: 262-786-8670
toll-free: 888-334-3327
email: pr@ifebp.org
www.ifebp.org

International Mass Retail Association (IMRA)
1700 North Moore Street, Suite 2250
Arlington, VA 22209
phone: 703-841-2300
fax: 703-841-1184
www.imra.org

Internet Professionals Association (IPA)
P.O. Box 92
Passumpsic, VT 05861

Ironwood Retail Merchants Association
100 East Aurora Street
Ironwood, MI 49938
phone: 906-932-1122
fax: 906-932-2078

Joint Labor Management Committee of the Retail Food Industry (JLMC)
2120 L Street NW, Suite 245
Washington, DC 20037
phone: 202-331-0950
fax: 202-331-0952

Kansas Association of Store Operators
503 Adair Circle
Hutchinson, KS 67502-2034

Kentucky Retail Federation
512 Capitol Avenue
Frankfort, KY 40601
phone: 502-875-1444
fax: 502-875-1444
www.kyretfed.com

Louisiana Association of College Stores
c/o University of New Orleans Bookstore
New Orleans, LA 70148

Louisiana Retailers Association
343 Third Street, Suite 303
Baton Rouge, LA 70801-1309
phone: 224-344-9481
toll-free: 880-572-2378
fax: 225-383-4145
email: laretail@communique.com

Mail Advertising Service Association International (MASA)
1421 Prince Street
Alexandria, VA 22314
phone: 703-836-9200
toll-free: 800-333-6272
fax: 703-548-8204
email: masa-mail@masa.org
www.masa.org

Mail Order Association of America (MOAA)
1877 Bourne Court
Wantagh, NY 11793
phone: 516-221-8257
fax: 516-221-5697

Maine Merchants Association
5 Wade Street
P.O. Box 5060
Augusta, ME 04332
phone: 207-623-1149
fax: 207-623-8377

Manufacturers' Agents National Association (MANA)
23016 Mill Creek Road
P.O. Box 3467
Laguna Hills, CA 92654
phone: 949-859-4040
fax: 949-855-2973
email: mana@manaonline.org
www.manaonline.org

Manufacturers Representatives Educational Research Foundation (MRERF)
P.O. Box 247
Geneva, IL 60134
phone: 630-208-1466
fax: 630-208-1475
email: info@mrerf.org
www.mrerf.org

Marketing Research Association (MRA)
1344 Silas Deane Highway, Suite 306
Rocky Hill, CT 06067-0230
phone: 860-257-4008
fax: 860-257-3990
email: email@mra-net.org

Maryland Retailers Association
171 Conduit Street
Annapolis, MD 21401
phone: 410-269-1440
toll-free: 800-669-1445
fax: 410-269-0325
email: mdretail@aol.org

Memento Shop Council
c/o Cindy L. Downing
5323 East McKinley Avenue
Fresno, CA 93722-9050

Merchants Association of Florida
P.O. Box 972
Tampa, FL 33601
phone: 813-273-7702

Michigan Association of College Stores (MACS)
c/o John Belco
Western Michigan University Bookstore
Bernhard Center
Kalamazoo, MI 49008
phone: 616-387-3930
fax: 616-387-3941
www.wmich.edu/bookstore

Michigan Association of Convenience Stores
1900 Michigan National Tower
Lansing, MI 48933
phone: 517-487-9139
toll-free:
fax: 517-487-0702
email: griffin@voyager.net

Michigan Department Stores Association (MDSA)
221 North Pine Street
Lansing, MI 48933
phone: 517-372-5656
fax: 517-372-1303

Michigan Grocers Association
221 North Walnut Street
Lansing, MI 48933
phone: 517-372-6800
toll-free: 800-947-6237
fax: 517-372-3002

Michigan Retailers Association (MRA)
221 North Pine Street
Lansing, MI 48933
phone: 517-372-5656
toll-free: 800-366-3699
fax: 517-372-1303
email: lmeyer@retailers.com
www.retailers.com

Minnesota Retail Merchants Association
50 East 5th Street, Suite 208
St. Paul, MN 55101
phone: 651-227-6631
fax: 651-297-6260
email: mrma@mnretail.org

Mississippi Association of Convenience Stores
P.O. Box Drawer 3859
Jackson, MS 39207
phone: 601-354-4077
fax: 601-353-5561

Missouri Retailers Association
618 E. Capitol
P.O. Box 1336
Jefferson City, MO 65102
phone: 573-636-5128
fax: 573-636-6846
email: moretailer@aol.com

Montana Food Distributors Association (MFDA)
2697 Airport Way, Unit A
P.O. Box 5775
Helena, MT 59604
phone: 406-449-6394
fax: 406-449-0647

Montana Retail Association
1537 Avenue D, Suite 320
Billings, MT 59102
phone: 406-256-1005
email: mtretail@wtp.net

Museum Store Association (MSA)
501 South Cherry Street, #460
Denver, CO 80222-1325

National Advisory Group, Convenience Stores/Petroleum Marketers Association (NAG)
2063 Oak Street
Jacksonville, FL 32204-4492
phone: 904-384-1010
fax: 904-387-3362
email: hhowton@bellsouth.com
www.nag-net.com

National Alliance of Supermarket Shoppers (NASS)
c/o Martin Sloane
300 SE 5th Avenue Apartment 2120
Boca Raton, FL 33432-5059

National Association of Business and Industrial Saleswomen (NABIS)
5107 North Mesa Drive
Castle Rock, CO 80104
phone: 303-660-3696
email: nabis@juno.com

National Association of Catalog Showroom Merchandisers (NACSM)
186 Birch Hill Road
Locust Valley, NY 11560-1832
toll-free: 800-334-4711

National Association of College Stores (NACS)
500 East Lorain Street
Oberlin, OH 44074
phone: 440-775-7777

toll-free: 800-622-7498
fax: 216-775-4769
email: info@nacs.org
www.nacs.org

**National Association of Convenience
    Stores (NACS)**
1605 King Street
Alexandria, VA 22314-2792
phone: 703-684-3600
fax: 703-836-4564
email: nacs@cstorecentral.com
www.cstorecentral.com

**National Association of Home Based
    Businesses (NAHBB)**
P.O. Box 30220
Baltimore, MD 21270
phone: 410-363-3698
www.usahomebusiness.com

**National Association of Professional
    Insurance Agents (NAPIA)**
400 North Washington Street
Alexandria, VA 22314
phone: 703-836-9340
fax: 703-836-1279
email: piaweb@pianet.org
www.pianet.com

National Association of Realtors (NAR)
430 North Michigan Avenue
Chicago, IL 60611
toll-free: 800-874-6500
fax: 312-329-5962
www.realtor.com

**National Association of Resale and
    Thrift Shops (NARTS)**
P.O. Box 80707
St. Clair Shores, MI 48080
phone: 810-294-6700
toll-free: 800-544-0751
fax: 810-294-6776
email: webmaster@narts.org
www.narts.org

**National Association of Retail
    Collection Attorneys (NARCA)**
1515 North Warson, Suite 109
St. Louis, MO 63132
toll-free: 800-633-6069
fax: 314-428-6190
email: narca@primary.net
www.narca.com

**National Association of Schools of Art
    and Design (NASAD)**
11250 Roger Bacon Drive, Suite 21
Reston, VA 20190

phone: 703-437-0700
fax: 703-437-6312
email: info@arts-accredit.org
www.arts-accredit.org

**National Association of Webmasters
    (NAW)**
9580 Oak Parkway, Suite 7-177
Folsom, CA 95630
phone: 916-608-1597
fax: 916-987-3022
email: info@joinwow.org
www.naw.org

**National Automobile Dealers
    Association (NADA)**
8400 Westpark Drive
McLean, VA 22102
phone: 703-821-7000
fax: 703-821-7075
email: nada@nada.org
www.nada.org

**National Confectionery Sales
    Association of America/Propress
    (NCSA)**
10225 Berea Road, Suite C
Cleveland, OH 44102
phone: 216-631-8200
fax: 216-631-8210

National Grocers Association (NGA)
1825 Samuel Morse Drive
Reston, VA 20190
phone: 703-437-5300
fax: 703-437-7768
www.nationalgrocers.org

**National Independent Automobile
    Dealers Association (NIADA)**
2521 Brown Boulevard
Arlington, TX 76006-5203
phone: 817-640-3838
fax: 817-649-5866
email: rb@niada.com
www.niada.com

**National Independent Flag Dealers
    Association (NIFDA)**
136 South Keowee Street
Dayton, OH 45402
phone: 513-222-1345
toll-free: 800-240-7449
fax: 513-222-5794
email: nifda@erinet.com
www.flaginfo.com

**National Nutritional Foods Association
    (NNFA)**
3931 MacArthur Boulevard, #101
Newport Beach, CA 92660-3021

phone: 949-622-6272
fax: 949-622-6266
email: nnfa@aol.com

**National Piggly Wiggly Operators
    Association (NPWOA)**
P.O. Box 1719
Memphis, TN 38101
phone: 901-395-8215
toll-free: 800-800-8215
fax: 901-395-8475
email: mr.pig@pigglywiggly.com
www.pigglywiggly.com

National Retail Federation (NRF)
325 7th Street NW, Suite 1100
Washington, DC 20004
phone: 202-783-7971
toll-free: 800-NRF-HOW2
fax: 202-737-2849
email: nrf@nrf.com
www.nrf.com

National Safety Council (NSC)
1121 Spring Lake Drive
Itasca, IL 60143-3201
phone: 630-285-1121
fax: 630-285-1315
www.nsc.org

**National Society of Public Accountants
    (NSPA)**
1010 North Fairfax Street
Alexandria, VA 22314-1574
phone: (703)-549-6400
toll-free: 800-966-6679
fax: 703-549-2984
email: nsa@wizard.net
www.nsa.org

**National Supply Distributors
    Association (NSDA)**
P.O. Box 31248-45437
5134 Bower Avenue
Dayton, OH 45431
toll-free: 800-922-8645

**NATSO, Representing the Travel Plaza
    and Truckstop Industry**
1199 North Fairfax Street Suite 801
Alexandria, VA 22314
phone: 703-549-2100
fax: 703-684-4525
email: feedback@natso.com
www.natso.com

**Natural Product Broker Association
    (NPBA)**
13045 SW 107th Court
Tigard, OR 97223
phone: 310-559-8267
fax: 503-639-3620

Nebraska Retail Federation
1303 H Street
Lincoln, NE 68508
phone: 402-474-5255

**New England Booksellers Association
(NEBA)**
847 Massachusetts Avenue
Cambridge, MA 02139
phone: 617-576-3070
fax: 617-576-3091
email: neba@neba.org

**New Jersey Retail Merchants
Association (NJRMA)**
332 West State Street
Trenton, NJ 08618
phone: 609-393-8006
toll-free: 800-87-NJRMA
fax: 609-393-8463
email: retailnj@aol.com

**New Orleans/Gulf South Bookseller's
Association**
P.O. Box 750043
New Orleans, LA 70175
phone: 504-895-2663

NIMA International
1225 New York Avenue NW, Suite 1200
Washington, DC 20005-6156
phone: 202-289-6462
toll-free: 800-987-6462
fax: 202-682-0603
www.nima.com

**Noe Valley Merchants and
Professionals Association (NUMPA)**
P.O. Box 460574
San Francisco, CA 94114
phone: 415-641-8687
toll-free: 800-641-8687
fax: 415-641-4737
email: noelaw@aol.com

Ohio Council of Retail Merchants
50 West Broad Street, Suite 2020
Columbus, OH 43215
phone: 614-221-7833
fax: 614-221-7020

Oklahoma Retail Merchants Association
2519 NW 23rd, Suite 101
Oklahoma City, OK 73107
phone: 405-947-5503

Oregon Retail Council
1149 Court Street NE
Salem, OR 97309

phone: 503-588-0050
toll-free: 800-452-7862
fax: 503-588-0052
www.aoi.org

**Pacific Coast Farmers' Market
Association**
4725 First Street, Suite 200
Pleasanton, CA 94566-7366

**Pacific Northwest Hardware and
Implement Association**
P.O. Box 17819
Salem, OR 97305-7819
phone: 503-226-1641
fax: 503-223-7611

**Petroleum Marketers Association of
Wisconsin/Wisconsin Association of
Convenience Stores (PMAW/WACS)**
121 South Pinkney Street, Suite 210
Madison, WI 53703-3338
phone: 608-256-7555
fax: 608-256-7666

**Pike Place Merchants Association
(PPMA)**
93 Pike Street, Room 312
Seattle, WA 98101
phone: 206-587-0351
fax: 206-447-9995

Professional Secretaries International
10502 NW Ambassador Drive
P.O. Box 20404
Kansas City, MO 64195-0404
phone: 816-891-6600
fax: 816-891-9118
www.main.org/psi

**Promotion Marketing Association of
America (PMAA)**
257 Park Avenue South, 11th Floor
New York, NY 10010-7304
phone: 212-420-1100
fax: 212-533-7622
email: pmaa@pmaalink.org
www.pmaalink.org

**Public Relations Society of America
(PRSA)**
33 Irving Place, 3rd Floor
New York, NY 10003-2376
phone: 212-995-2230
email: hq@prsa.org
www.prsa.org

Radio Advertising Bureau (RAB)
261 Madison Avenue, 23rd Floor
New York, NY 10016

phone: 212-681-7200
toll-free: 800-232-3131
fax: 212-681-7223
www.rab.com

**Retail Loss Prevention Association
(RLPA)**
222 Middle Country Road, #209
Smithtown, NY 11787
phone: 516-366-4290
fax: 516-366-4294
email: nlpb@aol.com

**Robotics International of the Society of
Manufacturing**
Engineers (RI/SME)
One SME Drive
P.O. Box 930
Dearborn, MI 48121-0930
phone: 313-271-1500
fax: 313-271-2861
www.sme.org/ri

Sales and Marketing Executives
5500 Interstate North Parkway, #545
Atlanta, GA 30328
phone: 770-661-8500
fax: 770-661-8512
email: smeihq@smei.org
www.smei.org

**Shelly Field Organization Career
Opportunity Seminars**
P.O. Box 711
Monticello, NY 12701
phone: 845-794-7312
www.shellyfield.com

Small Business Administration (SBA)
1441 L Street NW
Washington, DC 20416
phone: 202-653-6832
www.sba.gov

**Society for Human Resource
Management (SHRM)**
1800 Duke Street
Alexandria, VA 22314
phone: 703-548-3440
fax: 703-535-6490
email: shrm@shrm.org
www.shrm.org

**Society for Technical Communication
(STC)**
901 North Stuart Street, Suite 904
Arlington, VA 22203-1854
phone: 703-522-4114
fax: 703-522-2075
email: stc@stc-va.org
www.stc-va.org

Society of American Florists (SAF)
1601 Duke Street
Alexandria, VA 22314-3406
phone: 703-836-8700
toll-free: 800-336-4743
fax: 703-836-8705

Society of Illustrators (SI)
128 East 63rd Street
New York, NY 10021
phone: 212-838-2560
fax: 212-838-2561
email: society@societyillustrators.org
www.societyillustrators.org

The One Club
32 East 21st Street
New York, NY 10010
www.oneclub.com

United Food and Commercial Workers International Union (UFCW)
1775 K Street NW
Washington, DC 20006
phone: 202-223-3111
fax: 202-466-1562
www.ufcw.org

United States Department of Agriculture—Forest Service (USDA-FSVP)
P.O. Box 96090
Washington, DC 20090
phone: 203-235-8855
www.usda.gov

United States Department of Labor
200 Constitution Avenue NW
    Room S-1032
Washington, DC 20210
phone: 202-693-4650
www.dol.gov

U.S. Office of Personnel Management
1900 E Street NW
Washington, DC 20415-0001
phone: 202-606-1800
www.opm.gov/veterans/index.htm

Veterans Administration
810 Vermont Avenue
Washington, DC 20420
phone: 202-233-2741
www.va.gov

Women in Direct Marketing International (WDMI)
224 7th Street
Garden City, NY 11530
phone: 516-746-6700
fax: 516-294-8141
www.wdmi.org

Writers Guild of America, East (WGAE)
555 West 57th Street
New York, NY 10019
phone: 212-767-7800
fax: 212-582-1909
email: info@wgaeast.org
www.wgaeast.org

Writers Guild of America, West (WGA)
7000 West Third Street
Los Angeles, CA 90048-4329
phone: 213-550-1000
fax: 213-782-4800
www.wga.org

APPENDIX III
BIBLIOGRAPHY

A. BOOKS

There are thousands of books on all aspects of the retail and wholesale industries. The books listed below are separated into general categories, but subjects often overlap.

These books can be found in bookstores or libraries. If your local library does not have the ones you want, ask your librarian to order them for you through the interlibrary loan system.

This list is meant as a starting point. For other books that might interest you look in the business section of bookstores and libraries. You can also check *Books in Print* (found in the reference section of libraries) for other books on the subject.

ADVERTISING

Field, Shelly. *Career Opportunities in Advertising and Public Relations.* New York: Facts On File, 2001.

Katz, Ron. *Advertising and Marketing Checklists: One Hundred Seven Proven Checklists to Save Time & Boost Advertising Effectiveness.* Lincolnwood, IL: NTC Publishing, 1994.

Levenson, J. C. *Guerrilla Advertising: Cost Effective Tactics for Small Business Success.* Boston, MA: Houghton Mifflin Company, 1994.

Minsky, Laurence and Emily Calvo-Thornton. *How to Succeed in Advertising When All You Have Is Talent: Today's Top Creatives Show You How.* Lincolnwood, IL: VGM Career Horizons, 1996.

O'Barr, Will M. *Culture and The Ad: Exploring Otherness in The World Of Advertising.* Boulder, CO: Westview Press, 1994.

Ogden, James, R. *Essentials of Advertising.* Piscataway City, NJ: Research & Education Association, 1994.

Ramacitti, David F. *Do It Yourself Advertising.* New York: AMACOM, 1992.

BUYING AND PURCHASING

Banning, Kent B. *Opportunities in Purchasing Careers.* Lincolnwood, IL: VGM Career Horizons, 1998.

Clodfelter, Richard. *Retail Buying from Staples to Fashion to Fads.* Albany, NY: Delmar Publishers, 1993.

Friedlander, Joseph. *Management of Retail Buying.* New York: John Wiley & Sons, 1995.

National Retail Federation. *Buyer's Manual.* Washington, DC: National Retail Federation, 1999.

BUSINESS AND ECONOMICS OF RETAILING

Benson. *Retailing Industry.* I. B. Tauris & Company, 2000.

Coltman, Michael M. *Start and Run a Profitable Retail Business.* Bellingham, WA: Self-Counsel Press, 1993.

Randall, Dave and Richard Harper. *Organizational Change & Retail Finance.* New York: Routledge, 1999.

Richards, Kristen. *Retail and Restaurant Spaces: Portfolios of 40 Interior Designers.* Rockport, MA: Rockport Publishers, 1999.

Rutter, Baumgarten and Barksdale. *Retail User's Book.* New York: Intrepid Traveller Publications, 1999.

Simmons, Jim. *The Retail Environment.* New York: Routledge, 1990.

Stevenson, Lawrence N. *Power Retail.* New York: McGraw-Hill, 1999.

CONVENIENCE STORES

Toth, Adrienne. *Directory of Convenience Stores,* Trade Dimensions, 1994.

CUSTOMER SERVICE

Barlow, Janelle and Claus Moller. *A Complaint Is a Gift: Using Customer Feedback as a Strategic Tool.* San Francisco, CA: Berrett-Koeler Publishing, 1996.

Dutka, Alan. *AMA Handbook for Customer Satisfaction: A Complete Guide to Research, Planning and Implementations.* Lincolnwood, IL: NTC Publishing, 1995.

Peppers, Don & Martha Rogers. *The One to One Future: Building Relationships One Customer at a Time.* New York: Doubleday, 1997.

Varva, Terry G. *Aftermarketing: How to Keep Customers for Life Through Relationship Marketing.* Homewood, IL: Irwin Professional Publishing, 1995.

Wing, Michael J. & Arthur Andersen, *The Arthur Andersen Guide to Talking with Your Customers: What They Will Tell You About Your Business . . . When You Ask the Right Questions.* Dover, NJ: Upstart Publishing, 1997.

DIRECT MARKETING

Bodian, Nat G. *Direct Marketing Rules of Thumb: 1000 Practical and Profitable Ideas to Help You Improve.* New York: McGraw-Hill, 1994.

National Retail Federation. *Increasing Retail via the Telephone.* Washington, DC: National Retail Federation.

DIRECTORIES

Fairchild's Retail Stores Financial Directory. 1996. New York: Fairchild Books, 1995.

Retail Trade International 2000. London: Euromonitor PLC, 1999.

Toth, Adrienne. *Directory of Convenience Stores.* Trade Dimensions, 1994

ELECTRONIC RETAILING

Magdelena, Yesil. *Creating the Virtual Store:* New York: John Wiley & Sons, 1996.

National Retail Federation. *Telecommunications Survival Guide for Retailers.* Washington, DC: National Retail Federation, 1985.

Packaged Facts, Inc. *The Electronic Retailing Market.* New York: John Wiley & Sons, 1996.

Wolhandler, Harry. *Real Numbers Behind the Online Retail Industry.* ActivMedia Research, 1999.

————. *Top 100 Retail E-Commerce Websites.* ActivMedia Research, 1999.

FRANCHISING

Banning, Kent B. *Opportunities in Franchising Careers.* Lincolnwood, IL: VGM Career Horizons, 1995.

Bond, Robert E. *Bond's Top 50 Retail Franchises.* Sobo Visual Arts Inc., 1999.

————. *Bond's Top 50 Home-Based Franchises.* Naperville, IL: Source Book Publications, 1999.

Dixon, Ted. *The Franchise Annual Directory 2000.* Info Franchise News, 2000.

Franchise Opportunities Guide. International Franchise Association, 1999.

Menelsohn, Martin. *The Guide to Franchising.* New York: Cassell Academic, 1999.

Patel, Jay. *Franchising: Is It Fair? How to Negotiate an Equitable Franchise Agreement.* WeWrite Corporation, 1999.

Renn, Leslie D. *How to Start & Manage a Franchised Business: Step by Step Guide to Starting & Managing Your Own Business.* Lewis & Renn Associates, 1999.

Seid, Michael. *Franchising for Dummies.* Chicago, IL: IDG Books Worldwide, 2000.

HUMAN RESOURCES

Williams, Margaret. *The Employee Appreciation Program.* Bemidji, MN: Williams Publishing, 1998.

INTERNATIONAL RETAILING

Sternquist, Brenda. *International Retailing.* New York: Fairchild Books, 1998.

INTERNSHIPS

Retailing Merchandising Internship Manual. Prentice Hall, 1992.

LEASING

Stafford, Cliff. *Retail Spaces.* Rockport, MA: Rockport Publishers, 1999.

LOSS PREVENTION

Abramson, Susan and Marcie, Stuchin. *Shops and Boutiques 2000: Designer Stores and Brand Imagery.* PBC International, 2000.

Copeland, Bill. *Absolutely Complete Retail Loss Prevention Guide.* Absolutely Zero Loss, 2000.

————. *Investigations in Retail.* Absolutely Zero Loss, 1999.

————. *Private Investigation Trilogy.* Absolutely Zero Loss, 1999.

International Loss Control Institute, Inc. *Retail Audit.* International Loss Control Institute.

Shiller, Alice. *Store Shrinkage: Employee Pilferage and Customer Theft.* New York: Fairchild Books, 1992.

MANAGEMENT

National Retail Merchants Association. *Productivity.* Washington, DC: National Retail Merchants Association, 1988.

————. *Productivity In General Merchandise Retailing.* Washington, DC: National Retail Merchants Association, 1985.

————. *Perspectives on Retail Strategic Decision Making.* Washington, DC: National Retail Merchants Association, 1988.

————. *Retail Credit Operating Results.* Washington, DC: National Retail Merchants Association, 1985.

————. *Unique & Successful Selling Techniques.* Washington, DC: National Retail Merchants Association, 1988.

————. *Productivity.* Washington, DC: National Retail Merchants Association, 1988.

————. *Retail Credit Operating Results.* Washington, DC: National Retail Merchants Association, 1988.

————. *Productivity in General Merchandise Retailing.* Washington, DC: National Retail Merchants Association, 1985.

————. *Perspectives on Retail Strategic Decision Making.* Washington, DC: National Retail Merchants Association, 1988.

MANUFACTURING

Icon Group International. *Retail Electronic Equipment in Mexico: A Strategic Entry Report, 1995.* Icon Group International, 1999.

Retail Trade International, 1998. London: Euromonitor, 1998.

Weil, David. *A Stitch in Time: Lean Retailing & the Transformation of Manufacturing.* New York: Oxford University Press, 1999.

MERCHANDISING

Field, Katherine. *Stores: Retail Display & Design.* PBC International, 1999.

Rosenberg, Jerry M. *Dictionary of Retailing and Merchandising.* New York: John Wiley & Sons, 1995.

White, Frank. *Integrated Display and Visual Merchandising.* Saint Francis Press, 1994.

POINT OF PURCHASE RETAILING

Retail Reporting. *5 Points of Purchase.* New York: Morrow/Avon, 1997.

———. *Point of Purchase Retail.* New York: Morrow/Avon, 1999.

RETAILING

Allen, Debbie. *Trade Secrets of Retail Stars.* Image Dynamics, 1996.

Anderson, Carol H. *Retailing.* St. Paul, MN: West Publishing Company, 1992.

Bernstein, Jack. *Resume Writing, Interviewing and Roleplaying Skills for Salespeople Looking for New Jobs.* Manhattan Beach, CA: JB & Me, 1993.

Burns, David. *Retailing.* Houston: Dame Publications, 1998.

Burstiner, Irving. *Basic Retailing.* New York: McGraw-Hill Higher Education, 1990.

———. *How to Start and Run Your Own Retail Business.* Secaucus, NJ: Carol Publishing Group, 1998.

Guide to Retail and Service Businesses: Practitioners Publishing, 1998.

National Retail Federation. *Point-of-Sale.* Washington, DC: National Retail Federation, 1986.

Sternquist, Brenda. *Retailing.* New York: Fairchild Books, 1998.

Stevenson, Lawrence N. *Power Retailing.* New York: McGraw-Hill, 1999.

Strongin, Harriet. *Modern Retailing.* Prentice Hall, 1995.

Wickliffe, Vanessa; et al. *International Retailing.* New York: Fairchild Books, 1998.

Wileman, Andrew. *Retail Power Plays.* New York University Press, 1997.

Wilkinson, J. B. *Modern Retailing.* New York: McGraw-Hill Higher Education, 1992.

RETAIL FINANCING

Wrigley, Neil. *Retailing, Consumption & Capital.* Addison, Wesley Longman, 1996.

RETAIL—GENERAL

Archer, Jeanne S. *Up Against the Wal-Marts.* New York: AMACOM, 1996.

Bond, Ronald. *Retail in Detail.* PSI Research, 1996.

Bortz, Lauri. *5 & 10.* Abaton Book Company, 2000.

Newman, Andrew, and Cullen, Peter. *Retailing.* New York: Thomson Learning, 2001.

Quinn, Bill. *How Wal-Mart Is Destroying America.* Berkeley, CA: Ten Speed Press, 1998.

Thornton, Lorraine. *Retailing.* New York: Sterling Press, 1996.

Youngman, Ian. *Marketing Financial Services Through Retail Outlets.* Woodhead Publishing, 2000.

RETAIL MARKETING AND PROMOTION

Alexander, Nicholas. *Retail Marketing.* Frank Cass Publishers, 1996.

Falk, Edgar. *One Thousand One Ideas to Create Retail Excitement.* Prentice Hall, 1994.

Gordon, Ian and Allen Gordon. *Relationship Marketing: New Strategies, Techniques, and Technologies to Win The Customers You Want and Keep Them Forever.* New York: John Wiley and Sons, 1998.

Newell, Frederick. *The New Rules of Marketing: How to Use One-To-One Relationship Marketing to Be the Leader in Your Industry.* Homewood, IL: Irwin Professional Publishing, 1997.

Randall, Geoffrey. *Trade Marketing Strategies.* Newton, MA: Butterworth-Heinemann, 1994.

Samli, A. Coskun. *Strategic Marketing for Success in Retailing.* Greenwich, CT: Greenwood Publishing Group, 1998.

Simmons, Ross. *The Retail Promotion Idea Book.* Prosperity Publishing, 1995.

Swanon, Kristen K. *Promotion in the Merchandising Environment.* New York: Fairchild Books, 2000.

White, Frank. *How to Compete with Chain Superstores and Win!* Saint Francis Press, 1995.

———. *Retail Sales Planning and Promotion.* Saint Francis Press, 1994.

Woolf, Prian P. *Customer Specific Marketing.* Teal Books, 1996.

RETAIL STORE DESIGN

Institute of Store Planners. *Stores and Retail Spaces 2.* New York: Watson-Guptill Publications, Inc., 2000.

Pegler, Martin M, editor. *The Power of Visual Presentation: Retail Design/Kiosks/Exhibit Design/Environmental Design.* Visual Reference Publications, 2000.

PVC International. *Stores: Retail Design.* William Morrow & Company, 1999.

Retail Reporting. *12 Stores of the Year.* New York: Morrow/Avon, 1999.

Retail Reporting. *Entertainment Places.* New York: Morrow/Avon, 1999.

RETAIL STORE OPERATION

Cridland, Arthur. *I'll Take It: A Down-to-Earth Guide to Running Fine Retail Stores.* Trafford Publishing USA Distribution, 1999.

RETAIL TRADE DIRECTORY

Plunkett, Jack W. *Plunkett's Retail Industry Almanac, 1999–2000: The Only Complete Guide to the Hottest Retail Companies and Hottest Retail Trends.* Plunkett Research, 1999.

Retail Trade International 2000, Vol. 5: Americas. London: Euromonitor, 1999.

World Retail Directory 1999/2000. London: Euromonitor, 1999.

RETAILING

Blackwell, Roger D. *From Mind to Market: Reinventing the Retail Supply Chain.* Blackstone Audio Books, Inc., 1999.

Reid, T.J. *More Retail Details Mother Forgot to Mention.* New York: Retail Resources Publications, 1999.

Retail Reporting. *Store Fronts.* New York: Morrow/Avon, 1994.

———. *Stores of the Year.* New York: Morrow/Avon, 1994.

Rogers, Dorothy. *Retailing.* San Diego, CA: Harcourt College Publishers, 1999.

Wardell, Paula. *Successful Retailing.* Dover, NH: Upstart Publishing Company, 1993.

Weitz, Baron. *Essentials of Retailing.* New York: Macmillan Publishing Group, 1995.

West, Allen. *Handbook of Retailing.* Gower Publishing Company, 1998.

Zimmerman, Donald. *Effective Retailing.* Boston, MA: Houghton Mifflin Company, 1986.

SALES

Friedman Group. *No Thanks, I'm Just Looking.* Dubuque, IA: Kendall/Hunt Publishing Company, 1995.

Weiner, Sue. *Shopping Bag Secrets.* New York: Universe Publishing 1999.

SPECIAL EVENTS

Ernst and Young. *The Complete Guide to Special Event Management: Business Insights, Financial Advice and Successful Strategies from Ernst & Young.* New York: John Wiley & Sons, 1992.

Getz, Donald. *Event Management and Event Tourism.* Elmsford, NY: Cognizant Communications Corp., 1997.

Goldblatt, Joe. *Special Events: Best Practices in Modern Event Management.* New York: John Wiley & Sons, 1997.

Malouf, Lena. *Behind the Scenes at Special Events: Flowers, Props and Design.* New York: John Wiley & Sons, 1999.

SHOPPING CENTERS

International Council of Shopping Centers. *The Best of the Retail Challenge.* New York: International Council of Shopping Centers, 1991.

National Retail Federation. *Retailer's Guide to Shopping Center Leasing.* Washington, DC: National Retail Federation.

White, John R. *Shopping Centers & Other Retail Properties.* New York: John Wiley & Sons, 1996.

SPECIALTY STORES

Jacobson, Ruth. *Your Own Shop.* New York: McGraw-Hill, 1990.

National Retail Federation. *Improving Apparel Shop Profits.* Washington, DC: National Retail Federation, 1986.

————. *The Independent Policy Manual.* Washington, DC: National Retail Federation.

PBC International. *Shops and Boutiques.* New York: William Morrow & Company, 1999.

Topping, Ted. *Start and Run a Profitable Retail Business.* Bellingham, WA: Self-Counsel Press, 1997.

Torella, John A. *A Guide to Retail Success.* New York: Fairchild Books, 1997.

WHOLESALE

Alampi, Gary. *Wholesale and Retail Trade U.S.A.* Detroit, MI: Gale Group, 1995.

Educational Productions. *Merchandise Sourcing in the Global Marketplace.* New York: Fairchild Books, 1996.

Roush, Chris. *Inside Home Depot.* New York: McGraw Hill, 1999.

Sabavalla, Darius. *Technology in Distribution & Merchandising.* Polytechnic Press, 1998.

Sehnert, Tim K. *Managing Supplier Quality.* Monochrome Press, 1994.

B. PERIODICALS

Magazines, newspapers, membership bulletins, and newsletters may be helpful in finding information about a specific job category, finding a job in a specific field, or giving you insight into what certain jobs entail.

As with the books in the previous section, this list should serve as a beginning. There are many periodicals that are not listed because of space limitations. Periodicals also tend to come and go. Look in your local library or in a newspaper/magazine shop for other periodicals that might interest you.

ADVERTISING— GENERAL INTEREST

Ad Business Report
411 Lafayette Street
New York, NY 10003

Advertising Age
220 East 42nd Street
New York, NY 10017

Adweek
BPI Publications
1515 Broadway
New York, NY 10036

ADVERTISING RESEARCH

Journal of Advertising Research
Advertising Research Foundation
641 Lexington Avenue
New York, NY 10022

CATALOGS

Hammacher Schlemmer Bulletin
Hammacher Schlemmer
Operations Center
9180 Le Sant Drive
Fairchild, OH 45014

Catalog Age
Internec Publishing
11 Riverbend Drive South
P.O. Box 4234
Stamford, CT 06907

CHAIN STORES

Chain Store Age
425 Park Avenue
New York, NY 10022

MMR-Mass Market Retailers
Racher Press, Inc.
220 5th Avenue
New York, NY 10001

CUSTOMER SERVICE

Customer Service Advantage
Progressive Business Publication
370 Technology Drive
Malvern, PA 19355

COLLEGE STORES

College Store
National Association of College Stores
500 East Lorain Street
Oberlin, OH 44074

College Store Executive
Executive Business Media
825 Old Country Road
P.O. Box 1500
Westbury, NY 11590

CREATIVE (ARTISTS, ART DIRECTORS, ETC.)

AIGA Journal
American Institute of Graphic Arts
1059 Third Avenue
New York, NY 10021

Art Direction
10 East 39th Street
New York, NY 10016

Creative
Magazines/Creative, Inc.
37 West 39th Street
New York, NY 10018

DEPARTMENT STORES

Department Store Sales by Region
Jean Talon Building 502
Holland Avenue
Tunney's Pasture
Ottawa, ON K1A 0T6
Canada

Department Store Sales and Stocks
Jean Talon Building 502
Holland Avenue
Tunney's Pasture
Ottawa, ON K1A 0T6
Canada

Department Store Workers' Union Local I-S News
AFL-CIO
140 West 31st Street
New York, NY 10001

Department Stores
Info USA
5711 South 86th Circle
P.O. Box 27347
Omaha, NE 68127

Directory of Department Stores & Mail Order Firms
3922 Coconut Palm Drive
Tampa, FL 33619

DIRECT MARKETING

AMMA Bulletin
The Advertising Mail Marketing Association
1901 North Fort Meyer Drive
Arlington, VA 22209

Direct Marketing
225 Seventh Street
Garden City, NY 11530

DISCOUNT STORES

Directory of Discount and General Merchandise Stores
3922 Coconut Palm Drive
Tampa, FL 33619

Discount Merchandiser
233 Park Avenue South
New York, NY 10003

Discount Store News
425 Park Avenue
New York, NY 10022

Off-Price Retail
Value Retail News
11701 Belcher Road S
Largo, FL 33773

E-TAILING

Direct
1 River Road Drive South
Box 4949
Stamford, CT 06907

I-Marketing News
100 Avenue of the Americas
New York, NY 10013

FRANCHISES

Directory of Franchising Organizations
3922 Coconut Palm Drive
Tampa, FL 33619

LOSS PREVENTION

Peter Belin Report on Shrinkage Control
380 North Broadway
Jericho, NY 11753

MARKETING

Journal of Marketing
American Management Association
250 South Wacker Drive
Chicago, IL 60606

Marketers Forum
Forum Publishing Co.
383 East Main Street
Centerport, NY 11721

Retailer and Marketing News
P.O. Box 191105
Dallas, TX 75219

MERCHANDISING

Merchandising & Operating Results of Department & Specialty Stores
National Retail Federation Enterprises, Inc.
325 7th Street NW
Washington, DC 20004

OUTLETS

Factory Outlets
Info USA
5711 South 86th Circle
P.O. Box 27347
Omaha, NE 68127

Outlet Bound
P.O. Box 1255
Orange, CT 06477

Outlet Malls USA
Old Dog Press
P.O. Box 255
Churchville, MD 21028

Outlet Project
Value Retail News
11701 Belcher Road South
Largo, FL 33773

Outlet Retail
Value Retail News
11701 Belcher Road South
Largo, FL 33773

Value Retail News
Value Retail News
11701 Belcher Road South
Largo, FL 33773

PUBLIC RELATIONS, PUBLICITY, COMMUNITY RELATIONS

Inside PR
235 West 48th Street
New York, NY 10036

O'Dwyer's PR Market Place
271 Madison Avenue
New York, NY 10016

O'Dwyer's PR Services Report
271 Madison Avenue
New York, NY 10016

PR Watch
Box 600
Exeter, NH 03833

Public Relations Journal
PRSA
33 Irving Place
New York, NY 10003

RETAIL—GENERAL

Georgia Retailing News
3966 West Hilda Circle
Decatur, GA 30035

Inside American Retailing
Lebhar-Friedman Inc.
425 Park Avenue
New York, NY 10022

Inside Retailing
Lebhar-Friedman Inc.
425 Park Avenue
New York, NY 10022

Journal of Retailing
JAI Press, Inc.
55 Old Post Road #2
P.O. Box 1678
Greenwich, CT 06836

Journal of Retailing and Consumer Service
Elsevier Science Inc.
655 6th Avenue
New York, NY 10010

Midwest Retailer
8258 Columbs Avenue
Bloomington, MN 55420

Monthly Retail Trade: Sales and Inventories
US Bureau of the Census-Department of Commerce
Customer Service
Washington, DC 20333

Ohio Valley Retailer
4707 Hayes Avenue
Sandusky, OH 44870

Oklahoma Retailer
4500 North Sewell Avenue
Oklahoma City, OK 73118

Point of Purchase Magazine
Shore-Varrone
6255 Barfield Road
Atlanta, GA 30328

RT
355 Park Avenue South
New York, NY 10010

Retail Observer
1442 Sierra Creek Way
San Jose, CA 95132

Retail Roundup
22 Juniper Road
Port Washington, NY 11050

Retail System Alert
P.O. Box 332
77 Oak Street
Newton Upper Falls, MA 02164

Retailing News
14652 Bear Valley Road, #288
Victorville, CA 92393

Retailing Today
P.O. Box 249
Lafayette, CA 95459

ShoTalk
34th Street Partnership
212 West 35th Street
New York, NY 10001

RETAIL MANAGEMENT

George Whalin's Retail Management Letter
Retail Management Consultants
1635 South Rancho Santa Fe Road, Suite 206
San Marcos, CA 92068

APPENDIX IV
DIRECTORY OF CHAIN STORES

The following is a directory of the corporate offices of selected chain stores. The classification of some chain stores may overlap with those in the department store or grocery/supermarket listing. Be sure to check all the appendixes when looking for specific stores.

Names, address, phone numbers, fax numbers, and Internet addresses are included when available. Stores are listed alphabetically by name.

Use this list to get you started on locating internships, training programs, summer employment, or to send your resume when you are ready to go job hunting.

This list is provided as a starting point. There are many more chain stores located throughout the country. Inclusion or exclusion does not constitute endorsement or the lack of it by the author.

7-Eleven Inc.
P.O. Box 711
Dallas, TX 75221-0711
phone: 214-828-7587
fax: 214-841-6799
www.7-eleven.com

Big A Auto Parts
A.P.S. Inc.
3838 N Sam Houston Parkway E
Houston, TX 77032
phone: 713-507-1100
fax: 713-507-1310

Altmeyer Home Stores
Central City Plaza
New Kensington, PA 15068
phone: 724-339-6628
toll-free: 800-394-6628
www.altmeyer.com

Amber's Stores Inc.
12092 Forestgate
Dallas, TX 75238
phone: 972-889-1199

Ames Department Stores
2418 Main St.
Rocky Hill, CT 06067
phone: 860-257-2000
toll-free: 800-758-5804
fax: 860-257-2168
www.AmesStores.com

Ann Taylor Stores
142 West 57th Street
New York, NY 10019
phone: 212-541-3300
fax: 212-541-3379

Arthur Drugstores Inc.
190 Farmington Ave.
Hartford, CT 06105
phone: 860-522-3275
fax: 860-493-1607

Athlete's Foot Stores
Athlete's Foot Group Inc.
1950 Vaughn Road
Kennesaw, GA 30144
phone: 770-514-4500
fax: 770-514-4903
www.theathletesfoot.com

Autoworks Inc.
415 West Main Street
Rochester, NY 14608
phone: 716-235-1595

AutoZone, Inc.
123 South Front Street
Memphis, TN 38103-3607
phone: 901-495-6500
fax: 901-495-8300
www.autozone.com

B. Dalton Bookseller Inc.
122 5th Avenue
New York, NY 10011
phone: 212-633-3300

B.C. Moore and Sons Inc.
P.O. Drawer 72
Wadesboro, NC 28170
phone: 704-694-2171
fax: 704-694-6748

Babbage's Inc.
2250 William D. Tate Avenue
Grapevine, TX 76051
phone: 817-424-2000
fax: 817-424-2002
www.gamelord.com

USA Baby
Baby's Room Inc.
847 North Larch Avenue
Elmhurst, IL 60126
phone: 630-832-9880
fax: 630-832-0139
www.usababy.com

Banana Republic
1 Harrison Street
San Francisco, CA 94105
phone: 415-777-0250
fax: 415-896-0322
www.bananarepublic.com

Barnes and Noble Superstores Inc.
122 5th Avenue
New York, NY 10011
phone: 212-633-3300
www.bn.com

Bartell Drug Co.
4727 Denver Avenue S
Seattle, WA 98134
phone: 206-763-2626
fax: 206-763-2062
www.bartelldrugs.com

Bee-Gee Shoe Corp.
3155 Elbee Road
Dayton, OH 45439-1919
phone: 937-643-7400

Ben Franklin Stores
Ben Franklin Retail Stores Inc.
P.O. Box 5938
Chicago, IL 60680-5938
phone: 630-462-6100
fax: 630-690-1356

Bentley's Luggage Corp.
3353 NW 74th Avenue
Miami, FL 33122
phone: 305-591-9700
fax: 305-477-4131
www.bentleys.com

Best Buy
Best Buy Company Inc.
P.O. Box 9312
Minneapolis, MN 55440-9312
phone: 612-947-2000
fax: 612-947-2422
www.bestbuy.com

Betsey Johnson
Betsey Johnson Inc.
498 7th Avenue
New York, NY 10018
phone: 212-244-0843
fax: 212-244-0855

Bill's Dollar Stores
P.O. Box 6019
Ridgeland, MS 39158
phone: 601-899-4800
fax: 601-899-4798
www.billsdollar.com

Blockbuster
1201 Elm Street
Dallas, TX 75270
phone: 214-854-3000
fax: 214-854-3241
www.blockbuster.com

Bob's Stores Inc.
160 Corporate Street
Meriden, CT 06450
phone: 203-235-5775
fax: 203-235-0431
www.bobstores.com

Body Shops of America Inc.
6225 Powes Avenue
Jacksonville, FL 32217
phone: 904-737-0811
fax: 904-731-0652
www.bodyshop.com

Books-A-Million
402 Industrial Lane
Birmingham, AL 35211
phone: 205-942-3737
fax: 205-945-1772
www.booksamillion.com

Borders Inc.
100 Phoenix Drive
Ann Arbor, MI 48108
phone: 734-913-1100
fax: 734-973-4533
www.borders.com

Brookstone Inc.
17 Riverside Street
Nashua, NH 03062-1310
phone: 603-880-9500
www.brookstone.com

Burlington Coat Factory
1830 Route 130 North
Burlington, NJ 08016
phone: 609-387-7800
fax: 609-387-7071
www.coat.com

Cache
1460 Broadway
New York, NY 10036
phone: 212-575-3200
fax: 212-575-3225

Calico Corners
681 East Main Street
Mount Kisco, NY 10549
phone: 914-666-4486
www.calicocorners.com

Camelot Music Inc.
8000 Freedom Avenue NW
North Canton, OH 44720
phone: 330-494-2282
fax: 330-494-0394
www.camelotmusic.com

Casual Male Inc.
437 Turnpike Street
Canton, MA 02021-2720
phone: 617-361-2000

Channel Home Centers
945 Route 10
Whippany, NJ 07981
phone: 908-668-7000
fax: 973-887-1594

Fashion Bug
450 Winks Lane
Bensalem, PA 19020
phone: 215-245-9100
fax: 215-638-6759

Children's Place
1 Dodge Drive
West Caldwell, NJ 07006
phone: 973-227-8900
fax: 973-227-0321
www.childrensplace.com

CompUSA Inc.
14951 North Dallas Parkway
Dallas, TX 75240
phone: 972-982-4000
fax: 972-484-4276
www.compusa.com

Crown Books Corp.
3300 75th Avenue
Landover, MD 20785
phone: 301-731-1200
fax: 301-731-1838
www.crownbooks.com

CVS
CVS Drive
Woonsocket, RI 02895
phone: 401-765-1500
fax: 401-766-2917
www.cvs.com

Dick's Clothing and Sporting Goods Inc.
R.D. 2, Box 34-B
Verona, NY 13478
phone: 607-773-0165
fax: 607-773-0205
www.sports.com

Discount Drug Mart
211 Commerce Drive
Medina, OH 44256
phone: 330-725-2340
fax: 330-722-2990

Disney Stores
101 North Brand Boulevard, Suite 1000
Glendale, CA 91203
phone: 818-265-3435
www.disney.com

Egghead Software
1350 Willow Road
Menlo Park, CA 94025
phone: 650-470-2400
www.egghead.com

Dollar Tree
P.O. Box 2500
Norfolk, VA 23501-2500
phone: 757-321-5000
fax: 757-321-5111

Dress Barn
30 Dunnigan Drive
Suffern, NY 10901
phone: 914-369-4500
fax: 914-369-4829
www.dress-barn.com

Drug Emporium
155 Hidden Ravines Drive
Powell, OH 43065
phone: 740-548-7080
fax: 740-548-6541
www.drugemporium.com

Drug World Inc.
12201 Larchmere Boulevard
Cleveland, OH 44120
phone: 216-229-6223
fax: 216-229-3528

Eckerd Drugs
P.O. Box 4689
Clearwater, FL 33758
phone: 727-395-6000
fax: 727-395-7934
www.eckerd.com

Ethan Allen Interiors Inc.
Ethan Allen Drive
Bethel, CT 06801
phone: 203-743-8000
fax: 203-743-8298
www.ethanallen.com

Family Bargain Centers
4000 Ruffin Road
San Diego, CA 92123
phone: 858-627-1800
www.family-bargain.com

Family Dollar Stores
P.O. Box 1017
Charlotte, NC 28201
phone: 704-847-6961
fax: 704-847-5534
www.familydollar.com

Filene's Basement Corp.
40 Walnut Street
Wellesley, MA 02181
phone: 617-348-7000

Fine's
Azalea Garden Road
Norfolk, VA 23502
phone: 757-857-6013
fax: 757-857-4603

**Fortunoff Fine Jewelry
   and Silverware Inc.**
70 Charles Lindbergh Boulevard
Uniondale, NY 11553
phone: 516-832-9000
fax: 516-832-9361

The Gap
1 Harrison Street
San Francisco, CA 94105
phone: 415-427-2000
fax: 650-874-7815
toll free: 800-333-7899
www.gap.com

GapKids
1 Harrison Street
San Francisco, CA 94105
phone: 415-427-2000
www.gapkid.com

General Nutrition Companies Inc.
300 6th Avenue
Pittsburgh, PA 15222
phone: 412-288-4600
fax: 412-288-4764
www.gnc.com

Hit or Miss
100 Campanelli Parkway
Stoughton, MA 02072
phone: 781-344-0800
fax: 617-344-6766

Home Depot
2727 Paces Ferry Road
Atlanta, GA 30339-4024
phone: 770-433-8211
fax: 404-431-2739
www.homedepot.com

IKEA U.S. Inc.
Plymouth Commons
Plymouth Meeting, PA 19462
phone: 610-834-0180
fax: 610-834-0872
www.ikea.com

K-B Toys
100 West Street
Pittsfield, MA 01201
phone: 413-496-3000

Kaufmann's
400 5th Avenue
Pittsburgh, PA 15219-1704
phone: 412-232-2000
fax: 412-232-2965

Lerner Stores
460 West 33rd Street
New York, NY 10001
phone: 212-736-1222
www.lerner.com

Michaels Craft and Floral Warehouse
304 Constitution Drive
Virginia Beach, VA 23462
phone: 757-552-0772

OfficeMax Inc.
P.O. Box 22500
Cleveland, OH 44122-0500
phone: 216-921-6900
fax: 216-491-4040
www.officemax.com

Old Navy
345 Spear Street
San Francisco, CA 94105
fax: 415-427-5488
toll free: 800-333-7899

Paul Harris Stores
6003 Guion Road
Indianapolis, IN 46254-1299
phone: 317-293-3900
fax: 317-298-6940
www.paulharrisstores.com

Perfumania
11701 NW 101 Street Road
Miami, FL 33178
phone: 305-889-1600
fax: 305-592-5774
toll free: 800-927-1777
www.perfumania.com

Pergament Home Centers
101 Marcus Drive
Melville, NY 11747
phone: 516-694-9300
fax: 516-694-2411

Petsmart
19601 North 27th Avenue
Phoenix, AZ 85027
phone: 602-580-6100
fax: 602-580-6502
www.petsmart.com

Pier 1 Imports
301 Commerce Street, Suite 600
Fort Worth, TX 76102
phone: 817-252-8000
fax: 827-878-7883
toll free: 888-807-4371
www.pier1.com

Rag Shops Inc.
111 Wagaraw Road
Hawthorne, NJ 07506-2711
phone: 973-423-1303
fax: 973-427-6568

Rite Aid
P.O. Box 3165
Harrisburg, PA 17101
phone: 717-761-2633
fax: 717-975-5871
toll free: 800-916-7788
www.riteaid.com

Ritz Camera Centers Inc.
6711 Ritz Way
Beltsville, MD 20705
phone: 301-419-0000
www.ritzcamera.com

Saks Fifth Avenue
750 Lakeshore Parkway
Birmingham, AL 35211
phone: 205-940-4000
fax: 205-940-4987
www.saksincorporated.com

Sally Beauty
P.O. Box 490
Denton, TX 76202
phone: 940-898-7500
fax: 940-898-7501

www.sallybeauty.com

Sam's Club
608 S.W. 8th Street
Bentonville, AR 72712-6297
phone: 501-277-7000
fax: 501-273-4053
www.samsclub.com

Sav-on Drugs
21118 Bridge Street
Southfield, MI 48034-4032
phone: 248-851-7596
fax: 248-357-2332

Save-A-Stop Inc.
P.O. Box 82337
Oklahoma City, OK 73148
phone: 405-677-3371
fax: 405-677-5246

Service Merchandise
P.O. Box 24600
Nashville, TN 37202-4600
phone: 615-660-6000
fax: 615-660-3319
www.servicemerchandise.com

Spiegel Inc.
3500 Lacey Road
Downers Grove, IL 60515-5432
phone: 630-986-8800
fax: 630-769-2012
toll free: 800-345-4500
www.spiegel.com

Sports Authority Inc.
3383 North State Road 7
Fort Lauderdale, FL 33319
phone: 954-735-1701
fax: 954-484-0837
www.sportsauthority.com

Stanley Stores Inc.
P.O. Box 998
Vidor, TX 77670-0098
phone: 409-783-9134
fax: 409-783-9048

Staples Inc.
P.O. Box 9328
Westborough, MA 01581
phone: 508-370-8500
fax: 508-370-8989
toll free: 800-813-1588
www.staples.com

Stern's
Route 4, Bergen Mall
Paramus, NJ 07652
phone: 201-845-5500
fax: 201-845-2495
toll-free: 800-678-3767
www.federated.com

Stride Rite Corp
P.O. Box 9191
Lexington, MA 0242
phone: 617-824-6000
fax: 617-864-1372
www.strideritecorp.com

T.J. Maxx
770 Cochituate Road
Framingham, MA 01701
phone: 508-390-3000
toll-free: 800-926-6299
www.tjmaxx.com

Tandy
P.O. Box 17180
Fort Worth, TX 76102
phone: 817-390-3700
fax: 817-415-3500
www.tandy.com

Target Stores
P.O. Box 1392
Minneapolis, MN 55440
phone: 612-304-6073
fax: 612-304-5660
www.target.com

Today's Man Inc.
835 Lancer Drive
Moorestown, NJ 08057
phone: 609-235-5656
fax: 609-235-9323

U.S. Vision Inc
P.O. Box 124
Glendora, NJ 08029
phone: 609-228-1000

Value City Department Stores Inc.
3241 Westerville Road
Columbus, OH 43224
phone: 614-471-4722
fax: 614-443-9011
www.valuecity.com

Victoria's Secret
4 Limited Parkway E
Reynoldsburg, OH 43068
phone: 614-577-7000

Waldenbooks
100 Phoenix Drive
Ann Arbor, MI 48108
phone: 734-913-1100

Walgreen
200 Wilmot Road
Deerfield, IL 60015
phone: 708-940-2500
fax: 708-940-3566
www.walgreens.com

Wal-Mart
608 S.W. 8th Street
Bentonville, AR 72712-6297
phone: 501-277-7000
fax: 501-273-4053
www.walmart.com

Warner Bros. Consumer Products
4000 Warner Boulevard
Burbank, CA 91522
phone: 818-954-6000

Western Auto Supply
9680 Marion Ridge Drive
Kansas City, MO 64137
phone: 818-346-4000
fax: 818-346-4363
www.westernauto.com

Wolverine World Wide Inc.
9341 Courtland Drive NE
Rockford, MI 49351
phone: 616-866-5500
fax: 616-866-0257
toll free: 800-635-4536
wwwinc.com

Zale Corp.
901 W. Walnut Hill Lane
Irving, TX 75038-1003
phone: 972-580-4000
fax: 972-580-5336
www.zalecorp.com

APPENDIX V
DIRECTORY OF DEPARTMENT STORES

The following is a directory of the corporate offices of selected department stores. The classification of some department stores may overlap with those in the chain store listing. Be sure to check all the appendixes when looking for specific stores.

Names, address, phone numbers, fax numbers, and Internet addresses are included when available. Stores are listed alphabetically by name.

Use this list to get started on locating internships, training programs, summer employment, or to send your resume when you are ready to go job hunting.

This list is provided as a starting point. There are many more department stores located throughout the country. Inclusion or exclusion does not constitute endorsement or the lack of it by the author.

Abraham & Straus/Jordan Marsh Co.
420 Fulton Street
Brooklyn, NY 11201
phone: 718-875-7200
fax: 718-802-8877

Ames Department Stores
2418 Main Street
Rocky Hill, CT 06067
phone: 860-257-2000
fax: 860-257-2168
toll-free: 800-758-5804
www.AmesStores.com

B.C. Moore and Sons Inc.
P.O. Drawer 72
Wadesboro, NC 28170
phone: 704-694-2171
fax: 704-694-6748

Belk Brothers Co.
P.O. Box 31660
Charlotte, NC 28231
phone: 704-377-4251
fax: 704-342-4320

Bergdorf Goodman
754 5th Avenue
New York, NY 10019
phone: 212-753-7300
fax: 212-872-8677

Bloomingdale's
1000 3rd Avenue
New York, NY 10022
phone: 212-705-2000
fax: 212-705-2502
www.bloomingdales.com

Bon
1601 3rd Avenue
Seattle, WA 98181
phone: 206-344-2121
fax: 206-506-7722
toll-free: 800-552-7288

Bon-Ton Department Stores
P.O. Box 2821
York, PA 17405
phone: 717-757-7660
fax: 717-751-3198
www.bonton.com

Boscov's Department Stores
4500 Perkiomen Avenue
Reading, PA 19606
phone: 610-779-2000
fax: 610-370-3495
www.boscovs.com

Burdines
22 E. Flagler Street
Miami, FL 33131
phone: 305-835-5151
fax: 305-577-2234

Hudson's
700 Nicollet Mall
Minneapolis, MN 55402
phone: 612-375-2200
fax: 612-375-2687
www.dhc.com

Dillard's
Little Rock, AR 72203-0486
phone: 501-376-5200
fax: 501-376-5917
www.dillard's.com

Dunlap
200 Greenleaf Street
Fort Worth, TX 76107-1471
phone: 817-336-4985
fax: 817-877-1302
www.dunlaps.com

Famous-Barr
601 Olive Street
St. Louis, MO 63101
phone: 314-444-3111

Filene's
426 Washington Street
Boston, MA 02108
phone: 617-357-2100
fax: 617-357-2921

Hills Department Store Co.
15 Dan Road
Canton, MA 02021-2847
phone: 781-821-1000
fax: 781-821-6965
www.hills.com

J.C. Penney
6501 Legacy Drive
Plano, TX 75024-3698
phone: 972-431-1000
fax: 972-431-1977
www.jcpenney.com

Kaufmann's
400 5th Avenue
Pittsburgh, PA 15219-1704
phone: 412-232-2000
fax: 412-232-2965

Kmart
3100 W. Big Beaver Road
Troy, MI 48084
phone: 248-643-1000
fax: 248-643-5636
toll-free: 800-635-6278
www.kmart.com

Kohl's
N.56 W.17000 Ridgewood Drive
Menomonee Falls, WI 53051
phone: 414-703-7000
fax: 414-703-6143
www.kohls.com

Lord & Taylor
424 5th Avenue
New York, NY 10018
phone: 212-391-3344
fax: 212-944-1347
toll-free: 800-223-7440

Macy's East Inc.
151 W. 34th Street, 7th Floor
New York, NY 10001
phone: 212-695-4400
fax: 516-573-2957
www.macys.com

Macys California Inc.
170 O'Farrel Street, 11th Floor
San Francisco, CA 94102
phone: 415-397-3333
www.macys.com

Montgomery Ward
1 Montgomery Ward Plaza
Chicago, IL 60671
phone: 312-467-2000
fax: 312-467-3975
www.wards.com

Neiman-Marcus
1618 Main Street
Dallas, TX 75201
phone: 214-741-6911
fax: 214-742-4904
toll free: 800-937-4146
www.neimanmarcus.com

Nordstrom Inc.
1617 Sixth Avenue
Seattle, WA 98101
phone: 206-626-2111
fax: 206-626-1795
www.nordstrom.com

Saks Fifth Avenue
750 Lakeshore Parkway
Birmingham, AL 35211
phone: 205-940-4000
fax: 205-940-4987
www.saksincorporated.com

Sears
333 Beverly Road
Hoffman Estates, IL 60179
phone: 312-875-2500
www.sears.com

Stern's
Route 4, Bergen Mall
Paramus, NJ 07652
phone: 201-845-5500
fax: 201-845-2495
toll-free: 800-678-3767
www.federated.com

Strawbridge & Clothier
Market E. at 8th Street
Philadelphia, PA 19107
phone: 215-629-6000
fax: 215-629-684

Target Stores
P.O. Box 1392
Minneapolis, MN 55440
phone: 612-304-6073
fax: 612-304-5660
www.target.com

Value City Department Stores Inc.
3241 Westerville Road
Columbus, OH 43224
phone: 614-471-4722
fax: 614-443-9011
www.valuecity.com

Wal-Mart
608 S.W. 8th Street
Bentonville, AR 72712-6297
phone: 501-277-7000
fax: 501-273-4053
www.walmart.com

APPENDIX VI
DIRECTORY OF
SUPERMARKETS/GROCERIES

The following is a directory of the corporate offices of selected supermarkets and groceries. The classification of some supermarkets and grocery stores may overlap with those in the chain store listing. Be sure to check all the appendixes when looking for specific stores.

Names, address, phone numbers, fax numbers, and Internet addresses are included when available. Stores are listed alphabetically by name.

Use this list to get started on locating internships, training programs, summer employment, or to send your resume when you are ready to go job hunting.

This list is provided as a starting point. There are many more supermarkets and groceries located throughout the country. Inclusion or exclusion does not constitute endorsement or the lack of it by the author.

ABCO Markets
3001 W. Indian School Avenue
Phoenix, AZ 85017
phone: 602-222-1600
fax: 602-222-1684

Acme Markets
75 Valley Stream Parkway
Malvern, PA 19355
phone: 610-889-4000
fax: 610-889-3039
www.acmemarkets.com

Acme Markets of Virginia Inc.
P.O. Box 246
North Tazewell, VA 24630
phone: 703-988-2561

Ahold USA Inc.
950 E. Paces Ferry Road
Suite 2575
Atlanta, GA 30326
phone: 404-262-6050
www.aholdusa.com

Arden-Mayfair Inc.
P.O. Box 2256
Los Angeles, CA 90051
phone: 310-638-2842
fax: 310-631-0950

Albertson's
P.O. Box 13000
Spokane, WA 99213
phone: 509-921-5300
fax: 609-921-5300

American Consumers Inc.
P.O. Box 2328
Fort Oglethorpe, GA 30742
phone: 706-861-3347
fax: 706-861-3364

Ashcraft's Market Inc.
260 Oak Street
Harrison, MI 48625
phone: 517-539-6001

Bashas' Inc.
P.O. Box 488
Chandler, AZ 85248
phone: 602-895-9350
fax: 602-895-1206
www.bashas.com

Bel Air Markets
500 W. Capital Avenue
West Sacramento, CA 95605
phone: 916-373-3333
fax: 916-373-6391

Better Val-U Supermarkets Inc.
543 Wauregan Road
Danielson, CT 06239
phone: 860-779-0771

Bi-Lo
P.O. Drawer 99
Mauldin, SC 29662
phone: 864-234-1600
www.bi-lo.com

Big Y Foods
P.O. Box 7840
Springfield, MA 01102-7840

phone: 413-784-0600
fax: 413-731-8135
toll-free: 800-280-2449

Bonnie Be-Lo Markets
1157 Production Road
Norfolk, VA 23501
phone: 757-855-3371
fax: 757-853-7405

Buehler Food Markets Inc.
P.O. Box 196
Wooster, OH 44691
phone: 330-264-4355
fax: 330-264-0874

Buttrey Food and Drug Co.
P.O. Box 5008
Great Falls, MT 59403-5008
phone: 406-761-3401

Camellia Food Stores Coop
P.O. Box 2320
Norfolk, VA 23501
phone: 757-855-3371
toll-free: 800-368-3752
fax: 757-853-7405

Carr-Gottstein Foods
6411 A Street
Anchorage, AK 99518
phone: 907-561-1944
fax: 907-564-2580

City Market Inc.
P.O. Box 729
Grand Junction, CO 81502
phone: 970-241-0751
fax: 970-244-1052

Clemens Markets
155 Bustard Road
Kulpsville, PA 19443
phone: 215-361-9000
fax: 215-361-8777

D'Agostino Supermarkets Inc.
1385 Boston Post Road
Larchmont, NY 10538-3904
phone: 914-833-4000
fax: 914-833-4060

Food Emporium
1400 Food Center Drive
Bronx, NY 10474
phone: 718-862-7000
fax: 718-862-7050

Food Giant Supermarkets
120 Industrial Drive
Sikeston, MO 63801
phone: 573-471-3500
fax: 573-472-3135

Grand Union Company
201 Willowbrook Boulevard
Wayne, NJ 07470
phone: 973-890-6000
fax: 973-890-6671

King Kullen Grocery Company Inc.
1194 Prospect Avenue
Westbury, NY 11590
phone: 516-333-7100
fax: 516-33-7929
www.kingkullen.com

Pathmark Stores Inc.
200 Milik Street
Carteret, NJ 07008
phone: 732-499-3000
fax: 732-499-3072
www.pathmark.com

Pay and Save
1804 Hall Avenue
Littlefield, TX 79339
phone: 806-385-3366
fax: 806-385-5438

Pay Less Supermarkets
33 W. 10th Street
Anderson, IN 46016
phone: 765-649-3526
fax: 765-640-2495

Ralph's Grocery
1100 W. Artesia Boulevard
Compton, CA 90220
phone: 310-884-9000

Redner's Markets
3 Quarry Road
Reading, PA 19605
phone: 610-926-3700
fax: 610-926-6327

Safeway Stores Inc.
5918 Stoneridge Mall Road
Pleasanton, CA 94588-3229
phone: 925-467-3000
fax: 925-467-3321
www.safeway.com

Sam's Club
608 S.W. 8th Street
Bentonville, AR 72712-6297
phone: 501-277-7000
fax: 501-273-4053
www.samsclub.com

Shopper's Food Warehouse
4600 Forbes Boulevard
Lanham, MD 20706
phone: 301-306-8600
fax: 301-306-8885
www.shoppersfood.com

Shoprite
600 York Street
Elizabeth, NJ 07207
phone: 908-527-3300
fax: 908-527-3397
www.shoprite.com

Stop and Shop Supermarket Co.
P.O. Box 1942
Boston, MA 02105
phone: 781-380-8000
fax: 781-770-6033

Super Pride Markets
2936 Remington Avenue
Baltimore, MD 21211
phone: 410-235-9800
fax: 410-235-9819

Tom Thumb Food Markets Inc.
110 E. 17th Street
Hastings, MN 55033
phone: 651-437-9023
toll-free: 800-322-9023
fax: 651-438-2638

Trader Joe's
P.O. Box 3270
South Pasadena, CA 91031
phone: 626-441-1177
fax: 626-441-9573
toll-free: 800-746-7857
www.traderjoes.com

Wegman's Food Markets Inc.
1500 Brooks Avenue
Rochester, NY 14692
phone: 716-328-2550
fax: 716-464-4664
www.wegmans.com

APPENDIX VII
DIRECTORY OF CATALOG COMPANIES

The following is a directory of the corporate offices of selected catalog companies. The classification of some catalog companies may overlap with those in the chain or department store listing. Be sure to check all the appendixes when looking for specific companies.

Names, address, phone numbers, fax numbers, and Internet addresses are included when available. Catalogs are listed alphabetically by name.

Use this list to get started on locating internships, training programs, summer employment, or to send your resume when you are ready to go job hunting.

This list is provided as a starting point. There are many more catalog companies located throughout the country. Inclusion or exclusion does not constitute endorsement or the lack of it by the author.

Barnes and Noble
122 5th Avenue
New York, NY 10011
phone: 212-633-3300
fax: 212-675-0413
www.barnesandnoble.com

Bedford Fair Apparel
51 Weaver Street, Suite 2
Greenwich, CT 06831
phone: 860-629-2020
fax: 860-629-1035

Blair Corp.
220 Hickory Street
Warren, PA 16366-0001
phone: 814-723-3600

Book-of-the-Month Club
1271 Avenue of the Americas
New York, NY 10020
phone: 212-522-4200
fax: 212-522-7125
www.bomc.com

Bradford Publishing Co.
P.O. Box 448
Denver, CO 80201
phone: 303-292-2500
fax: 303-298-5014
www.bradfordpub.com

Brookstone Inc.
17 Riverside Street
Nashua, NH 03062-1310
phone: 603-880-9500
www.brookstone.com

Cabela's
One Cabela Drive
Sidney, NE 69160

phone: 308-254-5505
toll-free: 800-237-4444
fax: 308-254-6669

Calyx & Corolla
185 Berry Street, Suite 6200
San Francisco, CA 94107-1750
phone: 415-626-5511
toll-free: 800-877-0998
fax: 415-626-3781
www.calyxandcorolla.com

Camping World Inc.
P.O. Box 90018
Bowling Green, KY 42102
phone: 502-781-2718
toll-free: 800-626-6189
fax: 502-781-2775
www.campingworld.com

CDW Computer Centers Inc.
200 N. Milwaukee Avenue
Vernon Hills, IL 60061
phone: 708-465-6000
fax: 708-465-6800
www.cdw.com

Chadwick's of Boston
35 United Drive
West Bridgewater, MA 02379
phone: 508-583-8110
fax: 508-583-8110

Charles Keath Ltd.
1265 Oakbrook Drive
Norcross, GA 30093
phone: 770-449-3100
toll-free: 800-388-8565
fax: 561-241-1055

Claire's
3 S.W. 129th Avenue
Pembroke Pines, FL 33027
phone: 954-433-3900
toll-free: 800-253-6973
www.claires.com

Coldwater Creek Inc.
1 Coldwater Creek Drive
Sandpoint, ID 83864
phone: 208-263-2266
toll-free: 800-262-0040
fax: 208-263-1582
www.coldwater-creek.com

Company Store
P.O. Box 2167
La Crosse, WI 54602
phone: 608-785-1400
fax: 608-791-5790

CompUSA Inc.
14951 N. Dallas Parkway
Dallas, TX 75240
phone: 972-982-4000
fax: 972-484-4276
www.compusa.com

Computerware
605 W. California Avenue
Sunnyvale, CA 94086-5020
phone: 408-328-1000
toll-free: 800-326-0092
www.computerware.com

Crest Fruit Co.
100 N. Tower Road
Alamo, TX 78516
phone: 956-787-9971
fax: 956-787-7161

Damark International
7101 Winnetka Avenue N
Brooklyn Park, MN 55428
phone: 612-531-4500
fax: 612-531-0180
www.damark.com

Dell Computer Corp.
1 Dell Way
Round Rock, TX 78682
phone: 512-338-4400
toll free: 800-289-3355
fax: 512-338-8700
www.dell.com

Donna Salyers Fabulous Furs
20 W. Pike Street
Covington, KY 41011
phone: 606-291-3300
toll-free: 800-848-4650
fax: 606-291-9687
www.fabulousfurs.com

Doubleday Book & Music Clubs
401 Franklin Avenue
Garden City, NY 11530
phone: 516-873-4561
fax: 516-873-4714

Eddie Bauer
P.O. Box 97000
Redmond, WA 98073
phone: 425-882-6100
toll-free: 800-414-6110
fax: 425-882-6383
www.eddiebauer.com

EDUCORP
Pre12B W. Main Street
Elmsford, NY 10523
phone: 914-347-2955
toll-free: 800-843-9497
fax: 914-347-0217
www.educorp.com

Egghead Discount
22705 E. Mission
Liberty Lake, WA 99019
phone: 509-922-7031
www.egghead.com

Federated Department Stores Inc.
7 West 7th Street
Cincinnati, OH 45202
phone: 513-579-7000
toll-free: 800-261-5385
fax: 513-579-7555
www.federated-fds.com

Figi's Inc.
3200 S. Maple Avenue
Marshfield, WI 54449
phone: 715-387-1771
fax: 715-384-1261

Fingerhut
4400 Baker Road
Hopkins, MN 55343
phone: 612-932-3100
fax: 612-932-3292
www.fingerhut.com

Frederick's of Hollywood
6608 Hollywood Boulevard
Los Angeles, CA 90028
phone: 323-466-5151
fax: 323-962-9935
www.fredericks.com

Gateway 2000 Inc.
610 Gateway Drive North
Sioux City, SD 57049
phone: 605-232-2000
toll-free: 800-846-2000
fax: 605-232-2023

Gateway
4545 Towne Centre Drive
San Diego, CA 92121
phone: 858-799-3401
toll-free: 800-846-2000
fax: 605-232-2023
www.gateway.com

Green Mountain Coffee
33 Coffee Lane
Waterbury, VT 05676
phone: 802-244-5621
toll-free: 800-223-6768
fax: 802-244-5436
www.gmcr.com

Hammacher Schlemmer
303 W Erie Street
Chicago, IL 60610
phone: 312-664-8170
fax: 312-664-8618
www.hammacher.com

Hanover Direct
1500 Harbor Boulevard
Weehawken, NJ 07087
phone: 201-863-7300
fax: 201-272-3465
www.hanoverdirect.com

Harry and David
P.O. Box 299
Medford, OR 97501
phone: 541-776-2121
toll-free: 800-345-5655
fax: 541-864-2194
www.harryanddavid.com

Hello Direct
5893 Rue Ferrari
San Jose, CA 95138
phone: 408-972-1990
www.hellodirect.com

Hold Everything
100 N. Point Street
San Francisco, CA 94133
phone: 415-421-7900

Home Shopping Network
1 HSN Drive
St. Petersburg, FL 33729-9090
phone: 727-572-858
fax: 727-572-6362
www.hsn.com

J. Crew Group Inc.
770 Broadway
New York, NY 10013
phone: 212-209-2500
fax: 212-209-2666
www.jcrew.com

J.C. Penney
6501 Legacy Drive
Plano, TX 75024-3698
phone: 972-431-1000
fax: 972-431-1977
www.jcpenney.com

J. Jill Group Inc.
25 Recreation Park Drive
Hingham, MA 02043
phone: 781-740-2718
www.jjill.com

King Arthur Flour
P.O. Box 1010
Norwich, VT 05055
phone: 802-649-3881
toll-free: 800-343-3002
fax: 802-649-3323
www.kingarthurflour.com

L.L. Bean Inc.
1 Casco Street
Freeport, ME 04033
phone: 207-865-4761
toll-free: 800-341-4341
fax: 207-552-6821
www.llbean.com

Lands' End
5 Lands End Lane
Dodgeville, WI 53595
phone: 608-935-4835
toll-free: 800-356-4444
fax: 608-935-4260
www.landsend.com

Levenger Co.
420 S Congress Avenue
Delray Beach, FL 33445
phone: 561-276-2436
toll-free: 800-544-0880
fax: 561-276-1643
www.levenger.com

Lillian Vernon Corp.
One Theall Road
Rye, NY 10580
phone: 914-925-1200
fax: 914-925-1444
www.lillianvernon.com

Limited Inc.
P.O. Box 16000
Columbus, OH 43216
phone: 614-415-7000
fax: 614-415-7080

Magellan Group
P.O. Box 452
Louisiana, MO 63353
toll-free: 800-644-8100

Mary Maxim Inc.
P.O. Box 5019
Port Huron, MI 48061
phone: 810-987-2000
toll free: 800-962-9504
fax: 313-987-5056
www.marymaxim.com

Miles Kimball
41 W. 8th Avenue
Oshkosh, WI 54901
phone: 920-231-3800
fax: 920-231-6775

MotherNature.com Inc.
1 Concord Farms
Concord, MA 01742
phone: 978-929-2000
toll-free: 800-517-9020
fax: 978-929-2001
www.mothernature.com

National Business Services Inc.
1601 Magoffin Avenue
El Paso, TX 79901
phone: 915-544-1271
fax: 915-544-0325

Newport News
711 3rd Avenue, 4th Floor
New York, NY 10017
phone: 212-986-2585
fax: 212-916-8281

New York & Company
460 W. 33rd Street
New York, NY 10001
phone: 212-736-1222
www.lerner.com

NordicTrack
105 Peavy Road
Chaska, MN 55318
phone: 612-368-2500
toll-free: 800-328-5888
fax: 612-368-2539
www.nordictrack.com

OfficeMax Inc.
P.O. Box 22500
Cleveland, OH 44122-0500
phone: 216-921-6900
fax: 216-491-4040
www.officemax.com

Patagonia
259 W. Santa Clara Street
Ventura, CA 93001
phone: 805-643-8616
fax: 805-653-6355
www.patagonia.com

PlanetRx Inc.
349 Oyster Point Boulevard, Suite 201
South San Francisco, CA 94080
phone: 650-616-1500
toll-free: 888-840-7979
fax: 650-616-1585
www.planetrx.com

Plow and Hearth
P.O. Box 5000
Madison, VA 22727
phone: 540-948-2272
toll free: 800-627-1712
fax: 540-948-5369
www.plowhearth.com

Popcorn Factory
13970 W. Laurel Drive
Lake Forest, IL 60045
phone: 847-362-0028
www.thepopcornfactory.com

QVC
1200 Wilson Drive
West Chester, PA 19380
phone: 610-701-1000
www.iqvc.com

Rexall/Sundown Vitamins Inc.
6111 Broken Sound Parkway NW
Boca Raton, FL 33487
phone: 561-241-9400
fax: 561-995-0197
www.rexallsundown.com

Ross-Simons Jewelers
136 Route 5
Warwick, RI 02886
phone: 401-463-3100
toll-free: 800-344-6011
fax: 401-463-8639
www.ross-simons.com

Sears
333 Beverly Road
Hoffman Estates, IL 60179
phone: 312-875-2500
www.sears.com

Service Merchandise
P.O. Box 24600
Nashville, TN 37202
phone: 615-660-6000
fax: 615-660-3319
www.servicemerchandise.com

Sharper Image
650 Davis Street
San Francisco, CA 94111
phone: 415-445-6000
toll-free: 800-344-4444
fax: 415-445-1574
www.sharperimage.com

Shop at Home Inc.
P.O. Box 12600
Knoxville, TN 37912
phone: 423-688-0300
fax: 423-689-5069

Sid Tool Company Inc.
151 Sunnyside Boulevard
Plainview, NY 11803
phone: 516-349-7100
fax: 516-349-0265

SkyMall
1520 East Pima Street
Phoenix, AZ 85034
phone: 602-254-9777
toll-free: 800-759-6255
fax: 602-254-6075
www.skymall.com

Spiegel
3500 Lacey Road
Downers Grove, IL 60515-5432
phone: 630-986-8800
toll-free: 800-345-4500
www.spiegel.com

SunExpress
5 Omni Way
Chelmsford, MA 01824
phone: 978-442-3000

Surplus Direct
521 SE Chkalov Drive
Vancouver, WA 98683-5231
phone: 541-387-6000
fax: 541-386-5384
www.surplusdirect.com

Swiss Colony
1112 7th Avenue
Monroe, WI 53566
phone: 608-328-8400
fax: 608-328-8457

Talbots
175 Beal Street
Hingham, MA 02043
phone: 781-749-7600
fax: 781-741-7734
www.talbots.com

Time Warner Inc.
75 Rockefeller Plaza
New York, NY 10019
phone: 212-484-8000
fax: 212-956-2847
www.timewarner.com

Time-Life Music
20000 Duke
St. Alexandria, VA 22314
phone: 703-838-7000
www.timelife.com

Value Vision International
6740 Shady Oak Road
Minneapolis, MN 55401
phone: 612-947-5200
fax: 612-947-0188
www.vvtv.com

Williams-Sonoma
3250 Van Ness Avenue
San Francisco, CA 94109
phone: 415-421-7900
toll-free: 800-541-1262
fax: 415-983-9887
www.williams-sonoma.com

Wisconsin Cheeseman Inc.
P.O. Box 89
Sun Prairie, WI 53590
phone: 608-837-5166
fax: 608-837-5493

Woodcraft Supply
P.O. Box 1686
Parkersburg, WV 26102
phone: 304-422-5412
fax: 304-422-5417

World of Science
900 Jefferson Road, Building 4
Rochester, NY 14623
phone: 716-475-0100
fax: 716-475-1370
www.roccplex.com/wos

Young Pecan Shelling Company Inc.
P.O. Box 5779
Florence, SC 29502
phone: 843-662-2452
toll-free: 800-729-8004
fax: 843-666-2338
www.youngpecanplantations.com

APPENDIX VIII
TELEVISION SHOPPING CHANNELS

The following is a listing of the corporate offices of selected television shopping channels. Names, address, phone numbers, fax numbers, and Internet addresses are included when available.

Use this list to get started on locating internships, training programs, summer employment, or to send your resume when you are ready to go job hunting.

This list is provided as a beginning. Inclusion or exclusion does not constitute endorsement or the lack of it by the author.

Home Shopping Network
1 HSN Drive
St. Petersburg, FL 33729-9090
phone: 727-572-858
fax: 727-572-6362
www.hsn.com

Shop at Home Inc.
P.O. Box 12600
Knoxville, TN 37912

phone: 423-688-0300
fax: 423-689-5069

Shop at Home Inc.
P.O. Box 305249
Nashville, TN 37230-0524
phone: 615-263-8000
fax: 423-689-5069
www.ishopathome.com

QVC Network Inc.
1200 Wilson Drive
West Chester, PA 19380
phone: 610-701-1000
www.iqvc.com

APPENDIX IX
DIRECTORY OF MANUFACTURERS
AND OTHER COMPANIES

The following is a directory of the corporate offices of selected U.S. companies and manufacturers. The classification may overlap with those in other appendixes. This listing may be valuable to those seeking careers in the wholesale as well as retail trade.

Names, addresses, phone numbers, fax numbers, and Internet addresses are included when available. Companies are listed alphabetically by name.

Use this list to get started on locating internships, training programs, summer employment, or to send your resume when you are ready to go job hunting.

This list is provided as a starting point. There are many more manufacturers and other companies located throughout the country. Inclusion or exclusion does not constitute endorsement or the lack of it by the author.

A

AAMCO Transmissions, Inc.
One Presidential Boulevard
Bala Cynwyd, PA 19004-1034
610-668-2900
toll free: 800-523-0401
fax: 610-664-5897

ABC, Inc.
77 West 66th Street
New York, NY 10023
212-456-7477
www.abc.com

ACCO Brands Inc. Fortune Brands
300 Tower Parkway
Lincolnshire, IL 60069
847-541-9500
toll free: 800-989-4923
fax: 800-247-1317
www.acco.com

Ace Hardware Corporation
2200 Kensington Court
Oak Brook, IL 60523
630-990-6600
fax: 630-990-6856
www.acehardware.com

ACE USA Companies
1601 Chestnut Street
P.O. Box 41484
Philadelphia, PA 19101-1484
215-640-4555
fax: 215-640-2489
www.ace-ina.com

Adaptec
691 South Milpitas Boulevard
Milpitas, CA 95035
toll free: 800-959-7274
fax: 408-957-2546
www.adaptec.com

Adidas America
9605 SW Nimbus Avenue
P.O. Box 4015
Beaverton, OR 97076
503-972-2300
toll free: 800-448-1796
fax: 503-906-4515
www.adidas.com

Admiral-Maytag Appliance Sales Co.
240 Edwards Street
Cleveland, TN 37311
toll free: 800-688-9920
TDD toll free: 800-688-2080

Adobe Systems
345 Park Avenue
San Jose, CA 95110
408-536-6000
206-470-7000 (Seattle, WA)
toll free: 800-685-3507
toll free: 800-833-6687
toll free: 800-879-3219
www.adobe.com

Aetna, Inc.
151 Farmington Avenue
Hartford, CT 06156
860-273-0123
toll free outside CT: 1-800-US-AETNA
TDD/TTY: 860-273-3081
www.aetna.com

AFC Enterprises
America's Favorite Chicken Co.
6 Concourse Parkway, Suite 1700
Atlanta, GA 30328-5352
770-391-9500
toll free: 800-222-5857
fax: 770-353-3280
www.afc-online.com

Alamo Rent A Car
P.O. Box 22776
Ft. Lauderdale, FL 33335
954-522-0000
toll free: 800-445-5664
www.goalamo.com

Alberto Culver Co.
2525 Armitage Avenue
Melrose Park, IL 60160
708-450-3163
fax: 708-450-3435
www.alberto.com

Albertson's Inc.
250 Parkcenter Boulevard
Boise, ID 83706
208-395-6392
fax: 208-395-6773
albertson's.com

Albertsons Inc.
P.O. Box 5008
San Leandro, CA 94577
510-678-5444
fax: 510-678-5410

Alcon Laboratories, Inc.
6201 South Freeway
Fort Worth, TX 76134-2099

817-551-8298
fax: 817-551-3092

Allegheny Pharmacal Corp.
277 Northern Boulevard
Great Neck, NY 11021
516-466-0660
toll free: 800-645-6190

Allied Van Lines
P.O. Box 4403
Chicago, IL 60680
630-717-3590
toll free: 800-470-2851
fax: 630-717-3123
www.alliedvan.com

Allstate Insurance Co.
2775 Sanders Road
Northbrook, IL 60062
847-402-5448
fax: 847-402-0169
www.allstate.com

Almaden Vinyards
12667 Road 24
Madera, CA 93639
toll free: 800-726-9977

Amana Appliances
2800 220th Trail
Amana, IA 52204
toll free: 800-843-0304
www.amana.com

American Airlines, Inc.
P.O. Box 619612 MD 2400
Fort Worth, TX 75261-9612
817-967-2000
817-967-4162
fax: 817-967-4162

American Automobile Association
Mailspace 61
1000 AAA Drive
Heathrow, FL 32746

American Express Co.
777 American Express Way
Ft. Lauderdale, FL 33333
www.americanexpress.com

American Family Publishers
P.O. Box 62000
Tampa, FL 33662-2000
toll free: 800-AFP-2400

American Greetings Corp.
One American Road
Cleveland, OH 44144

216-252-7300, ext. 1281
toll free: 800-777-4891
www.corporate.americangreetings.com

American Home Products Corp.
5 Giralda Farms
Madison, NJ 07940
973-660-5000
toll free: 800-322-3129
www.ahp.com

American Standard, Inc.
P.O. Box 6820
Piscataway, NJ 08855-6820
toll free: 800-223-0068
fax: 732-980-6170

Ameritech
225 West Randolph Street, Room 30-D
Chicago, IL 60606
312-722-9411
toll free: 800-451-2761
www.ameritech.com

Amway Corporation
North American Business Region
7575 East Fulton Road
Ada, MI 49355
toll free: 800-544-7167
www.amway.com

Andersen Windows, Inc.
Window Care Call Center
100 Fourth Avenue North
Bayport, MN 55003
651-430-5150
toll free: 888-888-7020
fax: 651-430-5827
www.andersenwindows.com

Anheuser-Busch, Inc.
One Busch Place
St. Louis, MO 63118
314-552-1305
314-552-1311
toll free: 800-342-5283
fax: 314-552-1311
www.budweiser.com

AON Corporation
123 North Wacker Drive
Chicago, IL 60606
312-701-3000
312-701-3983
fax: 312-701-3793
www.aon.com

Apple Computer, Inc.
One Infinite Loop
Cupertino, CA 95014

toll free: 800-538-9696
www.apple.com

Appleseeps
30 Tozer Road
Beverly, MA 01915
978-922-2040
toll free: 800-767-6666
www.appleseeps.com

Arizona Mail Order
3740 East 34th Street
Tucson, AZ 85713
520-748-8600
fax: 520-750-6755
www.oldpueblotraders.com

Armour Swift Eckrich
2001 Butterfield Road
Downers Grove, IL 60515
630-512-1000
toll free: 800-325-7424
fax: 630-512-1124

Armstrong World Industries, Inc.
P.O. Box 3001
Lancaster, PA 17604
717-396-3040
toll free: 800-233-3823
fax: 717-396-4270
www.armstrongfloors.com

Artisoft, Inc.
Communications Software Group
One South Church Avenue
Suite 2200
Tucson, AZ 85701
520-670-7000
toll free: 800-846-9726
fax: 520-670-7101
www.artisoft.com

Asante Technologies
821 Fox Lane
San Jose, CA 95131
408-435-8388
toll free: 800-622-7464
fax: 408-432-1117
www.asante.com

The Associates, Texaco Portfolio
330 Barker Cypress Road
Houston, TX 77094
281-754-1728
fax: 281-754-1702

AT&T
295 North Maple Avenue
Basking Ridge, NJ 07920

908-221-2000
908-221-5942
toll free: 800-222-0300
TDD/TTY: 1-800-522-2880
fax: 908-221-1211
www.att.com

Atlantic Richfield Co.,
    ARCO Products Co.
4 Center Point Drive
La Palma, CA 90623
213-486-3511
toll free: 800-322-2726
www.arco.com

Atlas Van Lines, Inc.
P.O. Box 509
Evansville, IN 47703-0509
812-424-2222
toll free: 800-252-8885
fax: 812-421-7129
www.atlasvanlines.com

Aventis Corp.
P.O. Box 9627
Kansas City, MO 64134-0627
816-966-4000
toll free: 800-552-3656
fax: 816-966-3860
www.hmri.com

Avis Rent-A-Car System
4500 South 129th East Avenue
Suite 100
Tulsa, OK 74134-3802
toll free: 800-352-7900
fax: 918-621-4819
www.avis.com

Avon Products, Inc.
1251 Avenue of the Americas
New York, NY 10020
212-282-7571
toll free: 800-367-2866
toll free: 800-FOR-AVON
www.avon.com

B

Bacardi USA, Inc.
2100 Biscayne Boulevard
Miami, FL 33137
305-573-8511
toll free: 800-BACARDI
fax: 305-573-2730
www.Bacardi.com

Bali (Division of Sara Lee Corp.)
3330 Healy Drive
P.O. Box 5100 (27113)
Winston-Salem, NC 27113
336-519-6053
toll free: 800-225-4872
www.balinet.com

Ball Park Brands
P.O. Box 19170
Detroit, MI 48219
248-355-1100
toll free: 800-317-5867
fax: 248-355-3436
www.ballparkfranks.com

Bally Entertainment
8700 West Bryn Mawr Avenue
Chicago, IL 60631
773-399-1300

Bayer
36 Columbia Road
P.O. Box 1910
Morristown, NJ 07962-1910
973-331-4536
toll free: 800-331-4536
fax: 973-408-8000

Bear Creek Corp.
2518 South Pacific Highway
P.O. Box 299
Medford, OR 97501
toll free: 800-345-5655 (Harry and David)
toll free: 800-872-7673 (Jackson
    and Perkins)
fax: 541-776-2194
www.harryanddavid.com

Beatrice Cheese, Inc.
770 North Springdale Road
Waukesha, WI 53186
414-782-2750
toll free: 800-444-6101
fax: 414-782-0760
www.beatricecheese.com

Becton Dickinson and Co.
One Becton Drive
Franklin Lakes, NJ 07417
201-847-6658
fax: 201-884-5487

Beiersdorf, Inc.
Wilton Corporate Center
187 Danbury Road
Wilton, CT 06897
203-563-5800
toll free outside CT: 1-800-233-2340
fax: 203-563-5895

BellSouth Telecommunications, Inc.
37D57 BellSouth Center
675 West Peachtree Street, NW
Atlanta, GA 30375
404-927-7400
fax: 404-584-6545
www.bellsouth.com

Benckiser Consumer Products
Five American Drive
Greenwich, CT 06831
toll free: 800-284-2023

Best Foods
700 Silven Avenue
Englewood Cliffs, NJ 07632-9976
201-894-4000
toll free: 800-338-8831
fax: 201-894-2126
www.bestfoods.com

BF Goodrich Tires
P.O. Box 19001
Greenville, SC 29602-9001
864-458-5000
toll free: 800-521-9796
fax: 864-458-6650
www.michelin.com

BIC Corp.
500 Bic Drive
Milford, CT 06460
203-783-2000
www.bicworld.com

Binney & Smith Inc.
100 Church Lane
Easton, PA 18042
610-253-6272
toll free: 800-CRAYOLA
www.crayola.com

Bissell
P.O. Box 1888
2345 Walker Avenue, NW
Grand Rapids, MI 49544-2597
toll free: 800-237-7691
www.bissell.com

Black and Decker Power Tools
626 Hanover Pike
Hampstead, MD 21074
410-239-5300
toll free: 800-762-6672
www.blackanddecker.com

Block Drug Company, Inc.
257 Cornelison Avenue
Jersey City, NJ 07302-9988
201-434-3000
toll free outside NJ: 1-800-365-6500
fax: 201-434-4186
www.blockdrug.com

Bob Evans Farms, Inc.
3776 South High Street
Columbus, OH 43207
614-491-2225
toll free: 800-272-7675
fax: 614-497-4330
www.bobevans.com

Boca Research, Inc.
1601 Clint Moore Road
Boca Raton, FL 33487
fax: 561-997-2163
www.bocaresearch.com

Bojangles
P.O. Box 240239
Charlotte, NC 28224
704-527-2675
toll free: 800-366-9921
fax: 704-522-8677
www.bojangles.com

Borden, Inc.
180 East Broad Street
Columbus, OH 43215
614-225-4511
toll free: 800-727-8260
fax: 614-225-7680
www.bordenfamily.com

Borland
100 Enterprise Way
Scotts Valley, CA 95066
831-431-1000
toll free: 800-523-7070
fax: 408-431-4353
www.borland.com

BP/Amoco Oil Co.
Richard Smith, Manager
28341 Ferry Road
Warrenville, IL 60555
toll free: 800-333-3991
fax: 630-836-4530

Braun
1 Gillette Park
Boston, MA 02127
toll free: 800-BRAUN11
    (1-800-272-8611)
www.braun.com

Bridgestone/Firestone, Inc.
P.O. Box 7988
Chicago, IL 60680-9534
toll free: 800-367-3872
fax: 800-760-7859

Bristol-Myers Squibb Pharmaceutical Group
P.O. Box 4000
Princeton, NJ 08543-4000
609-252-4000
www.bms.com

British Airways
75-20 Astoria Boulevard
Jackson Heights, NY 11370
718-397-4000
toll free: 800-247-9297
fax: 718-397-4395
www.british-airways.com

Brown Shoe
8300 Maryland Avenue
Clayton, MO 63105
314-854-4000
toll free: 800-766-6465
fax: 314-854-4274
www.brownshoe.com

Brown-Forman Beverages Worldwide
Dianne Hall, Consumer Services Specialist
P.O. Box 1080
Louisville, KY 40201
502-585-1100
toll free: 800-753-4567 (Canadian Mist)

Budget Gourmet
P.O. Box 10
Boise, ID 83707
toll free: 800-488-0050
fax: 208-383-6309

Budget Rent-A-Car Corp.
P.O. Box 111580
Carrollton, TX 75011-1580
toll free: 800-621-2844
fax: 972-404-7869

Bull & Bear Group, Inc.
11 Hanover Square
New York, NY 10005
212-363-1100
toll free: 800-847-4200
fax: 212-363-1103
www.mutualfunds.net

Bulova Watch Co.
26-15 Brooklyn Queens Expressway
Woodside, NY 11377
718-204-3300

Burlington Coat Factory Warehouse Corp.
1830 Route 130 North
Burlington, NJ 08016
609-387-7800
fax: 609-387-7071

Burlington Industries, Inc.
3330 West Friendly Avenue
Greensboro, NC 27410
336-379-2472
fax: 336-379-4504
www.burlington.com

C

Cabela's, Inc.
One Cabela Drive
Sidney, NE 69160
308-254-5505 x1190
toll free: 800-242-1596
TDD/TTY: 1-800-695-5000
fax: 308-254-6680
www.cabelas.com

Caere Corporation
100 Cooper Court
Los Gatos, CA 95032
408-395-8319
toll free: 800-654-1187
fax: 408-395-8319
www.caere.com

Calvin Klein
Emily Stone, Vice President
205 West 39th Street
10th Floor
New York, NY 10018
212-719-2600

Campbell Soup Co.
Campbell Place
P.O. Box 26B
Camden, NJ 08103-1799
856-342-6111
toll free: 800-257-8443
fax: 856-342-6449
www.campbellsoup.com

Canandaigua Wine Co.
116 Buffalo Street
Canandaigua, NY 14424
716-394-7900
toll free: 888-659-7900
fax: 716-393-6950

Canon Computer Systems
15955 Alton Parkway
Irvine, CA 92618
949-753-4000
toll free: 800-423-2366
toll free: 800-848-4123
fax: 949-753-4239
www.ccsi.canon.com

Canon U.S.A., Inc.
One Canon Plaza
Lake Success, NY 11042
516-488-6700
toll free: 800-828-4040

Carfax Inc.
10304 Eaton Place Suite 500
Fairfax, VA 22030
toll free: 800-274-2277
fax: 703-218-2853
www.carfax.com

Carrier Air Conditioning Co.
P.O. Box 4808
Syracuse, NY 13221
315-432-7885
toll free: 800-227-7437
www.carrier.utc.com

Carter-Wallace, Inc.
1345 Avenue of the Americas
New York, NY 10105
212-339-5000
toll free: 800-833-9532
fax: 212-339-5100

Carvel Corp.
20 Batterson Park Road
Farmington, CT 06032-2502
860-677-6811
toll free: 800-322-4848
www.carvel.com

Casio, Inc.
570 Mt. Pleasant Avenue
Dover, NJ 07801
973-361-5400
toll free: 800-962-2746
fax: 973-361-3819
www.casio.com

CEC Entertainment, Inc.
4441 West Airport Freeway
Irving, TX 75062
972-258-8507
fax: 972-258-8545
www.chuckecheese.com

Celestial Seasonings
4600 Sleepytime Drive
Boulder, CO 80301-3292
303-530-5300
toll free: 800-351-8175
www.celestialseasonings.com

Ceridian Corp.
8100 34th Avenue South
Bloomington, MN 55425
612-853-8100

C.F. Hathaway
10 Water Street
Waterville, ME 04901
207-873-4241
toll free: 800-341-1003
fax: 207-873-8390

Chanel, Inc.
9 West 57th Street
44th Floor
New York, NY 10019-2790
212-688-5055
fax: 212-752-1851

Chase Manhattan Bank
270 Park Avenue
New York, NY 10017
212-270-9300
toll free: 800-AT-CHASE
fax: 212-270-1882
www.chase.com

Chattem, Inc.
1715 West 38th Street
Chattanooga, TN 37409
423-821-4571
toll free outside TN: 1-800-745-2429

Chesebrough-Ponds, USA
Consumer Services
800 Sylvan Avenue
Englewood Cliffs, NJ 07632
toll free: 800-743-8640
toll free: 800-786-5135
www.unilever.com

Chevron Products Co.
P.O. Box H
Concord, CA 94524
toll free: 800-962-1223
fax: 510-827-6820
www.chevron.com

Chicken of the Sea International
4510 Executive Drive, Suite 300
San Diego, CA 92121
858-597-4242
fax: 858-597-4566

Church & Dwight Company, Inc.
469 North Harrison Street
Princeton, NJ 08543-5297
609-683-5900
toll free: 800-524-1328
www.armhammer.com

CIBA Vision
11460 Johns Creek Parkway
Duluth, GA 30045
770-418-5117
toll free: 800-875-3001
www.cibavision.com

CIE America
2701 Dow Avenue
Tustin, CA 92780
714-753-2942
toll free: 800-877-1421
fax: 714-368-4880
www.citoh.com

CIGNA Property and Casualty Companies
Mark Whiter, Director
1601 Chestnut Street
Philadelphia, PA 19101-1484
215-761-4555
215-761-2489

Circuit City Stores, Inc.
9950 Mayland Drive
Richmond, VA 23233
804-527-4000
toll free: 800-627-2274
fax: 804-342-6481

Citizen Watch Company of America
8506 Osage Avenue
Los Angeles, CA 90045
310-649-0991
toll free: 800-321-1023

Clopay Building Products Co.
312 Walnut Street, Suite 1600
Cincinnati, OH 45202-4036
toll free: 800-225-6729
fax: 513-762-3519
www.paydoor.com

Clorox Co.
1221 Broadway
Oakland, CA 94612-1888
510-271-7571
www.clorox.com

Coats & Clark Inc
P.O. Box 12229
Greenville, SC 29612-0229
864-877-8985
toll free: 800-648-1479
www.coatsandclark.com

The Coca-Cola Co.
P.O. Box 1734
Atlanta, GA 30301
404-676-2121
toll free: 800-438-2653
TDD toll free: 800-262-2653
fax: 404-676-4903
www.thecocacolacompany.com

Coldwell Banker Corp
339 Jefferson Road
P.O. Box 3257
Parsippany, NJ 07054-3259
973-912-4000
toll free: 800-732-5867
fax: 973-912-4005

The Colgate-Palmolive Company
300 Park Avenue
New York, NY 10022
212-310-2000
toll free: 800-468-6502
toll free: 800-763-0246
fax: 212-310-3243
www.colgate.com

Collins & Aikman Products Co.
P.O. Box 32665
Charlotte, NC 28232
704-547-8500
fax: 704-548-2172

Colonial Penn Group, Inc.
399 Market Street
5th Floor
Philadelphia, PA 19181
215-928-8000

Columbia Gas of Ohio
P.O. Box 117
Columbus, OH 43216-0117
toll free: 800-344-4077
TDD/TTY: 1-977-460-2443
fax: 614-450-5502
www.columbiagasohio.com

The Columbia House Company
1400 N. Fruitridge Avenue
Terre Haute, IN 47811
www.columbiahouse.com

Combe Incorporated
1101 Westchester Avenue
White Plains, NY 10604-3503
914-694-5454
toll free: 800-431-2610

Compaq Computer Corporation
P.O. Box 692000
Houston, TX 77269
281-370-0670
fax: 970-282-9225
www.compaq.com

Computer Associates
P.O. Box 3391
Tulsa, OK 74101-3391
918-838-7638
405-947-5600 (Oklahoma City)
toll free: 800-722-9095
fax: 918-836-5918
www.dreyersoftware.com

ConAgra Frozen Foods
P.O. Box 3768
Omaha, NE 68103-0768
402-595-6000
toll free: 800-722-1344
fax: 402-595-7880
www.conagra.com

ConAgra Grocery Products Company
P.O. Box 4800
Fullerton, CA 92833
714-680-1431

Congoleum Corp.
3705 Quakerbridge Rd, Suite 211
Mercerville, NJ 08619
609-584-3610
toll free: 800-274-3266
fax: 609-584-3521
www.congoleum.com

Consolidated Stores Corp.
300 Phillipi Road
P.O. Box 28512
Columbus, OH 43228-0512
614-278-6800
toll free: 800-877-1253
www.cnstores.com

Continental Airlines, Inc.
P.O. Box 4607-HQ SCR
Houston, TX 77210-4607
toll free: 800-932-2732
email: custo@coair.com

Continental/General Tire, Inc.
1800 Continental Boulevard
Charlotte, NC 28273
toll free: 800-847-3349
fax: 1-888-TIREFAX (847-3329)
www.contigentire.com

Converse, Inc.
One Fordham Road
North Reading, MA 01864-2680
toll free: 800-428-CONS (2667)
fax: 508-664-7440
www.converse.com

Conwood Company, L.P.
813 Ridge Lake Boulevard
Memphis, TN 38120
901-761-2050
901-767-1302
toll free: 800-238-5990

Coors Brewing Co.
Consumer Relations
311 10th Street - NH475
Golden, CO 80401
303-279-6565
toll free: 800-642-6116
fax: 303-277-5415

Corel Corporation
1600 Carling Avenue
Ottawa
Canada ON KIZ 8R7
toll free: 800-772-6735 (Buffalo, NY)
toll free: 877-422-6735

Craftmatic Organization, Inc.
2500 Interplex Drive
Trevose, PA 19053-6998
215-639-1310
fax: 215-639-9941

Creative Labs
1523 Cimarron Plaza
Stillwater, OK 74075
405-742-6622 or 6655
toll free: 800-998-5227
www.creativelabs.com

Crown Books
3300 75th Avenue
Landover, MD 20785
toll free: 800-831-7400
www.crownbooks.com

Cuisinart (Division of Conair Co.)
One Cummings Point Road
Stamford, CT 06904
203-975-4600
609-426-1300 (in NJ)
toll free outside NJ: 1-800-726-0190
www.cuisinart.com

Culligan International Co.
One Culligan Parkway
Northbrook, IL 60062
toll free: 800-CULLIGAN
www.culligan.com

Cumberland Packing Corporation
Sweet'N Low
Two Cumberland Street
Brooklyn, NY 11205
718-858-4200
fax: 718-260-9017
www.sweetnlow.com

Current, Inc.
1005 East Woodmen Road
Colorado Springs, CO 80920
719-531-2717
719-594-4100
toll free: 800-525-7170
fax: 719-531-6510
www.currentcatalog.com

CVS/pharmacy
One CVS Drive
Woonsocket, RI 02895
401-765-1500
toll free: 800-666-0500
fax: 401-762-6949
www.cvs.com

Cyrix
2703 North Central Expressway
Richardson, TX 75080
972-968-8387
toll free: 800-462-9749
fax: 972-679-9857
www.cyrix.com

D

Dairy Queen
P.O. Box 39286
7505 Metro Boulevard
Minneapolis, MN 55439-0286
612-830-0200
fax: 612-830-0480
www.dairyqueen.com

The Dannon Co., Inc.
P.O. Box 90296
Allentown, PA 18109-0296
toll free: 877-DANNON US
fax: 610-231-8597

Danskin
P.O. Box 15016
York, PA 17405-7016
717-840-5817
toll free: 800-288-6749
fax: 717-840-5855

DAP Products, Inc
2400 Boston Street, Suite 200
Baltimore, MD 21224
410-675-2100
toll free: 800-543-3840
fax: 410-558-1097
www.dap.com

Deere & Company
1 John Deere Place
Moline, IL 61265
309-765-8000
www.deere.com

Del Laboratories, Inc.
565 Broad Hollow Road
Farmingdale, NY 11735
516-844-2020
toll free: 800-952-5080
toll free: 800-953-5080
fax: 516-293-1515
www.dellabs.com

Del Monte Foods
P.O. Box 193575
San Francisco, CA 94119-3575
415-247-3000
toll free: 800-543-3090
fax: 415-247-3080

Delta Air Lines, Inc.
P.O. Box 20980
Atlanta, GA 30320-2980
404-715-1450
fax: 888-286-3163
www.delta-air.com

Delta Faucets Company
55 East 111th Street
P.O. Box 40980
Indianapolis, IN 46280
317-848-1812
317-574-5555
toll free: 800-345-3358
www.deltafaucet.com

Deneba Software
1150 NW 72nd Avenue
Miami, FL 33126
305-596-5644
toll free: 800-622-6827
fax: 305-273-9069
www.deneba.com

Dep Corp.
2101 East Via Arado
Rancho Dominguez, CA 90220-6189
310-604-0777
fax: 310-537-3679

The Dial Corp.
15101 North Scottsdale Road
Scottsdale, AZ 85254
toll free: 800-258-DIAL (3425)
toll free: 1-800-528-0849
www.dialcorp.com

Diamond Multimedia
835 Sinclair Frontage Road
Milpitas, CA 95035
541-967-2450
toll free: 800-727-8772
fax: 408-325-7070
www.diamondmm.com

Diamond of California
1050 South Diamond Street
Stockton, CA 95201
209-467-6260
fax: 209-467-6205
www.diamondofcalifornia.com

Diet Center Worldwide, Inc.
395 Springside Drive
Akron, OH 44333
330-665-5861
fax: 330-666-2197

Digital Equipment Corp.
20555 State Highway 249
Houston, TX 77070
toll free: 800-332-4636
www.digital.com

Dillard's, Inc.
1600 Cantrell Road
Little Rock, AR 72201
501-376-5200
fax: 501-376-5917
www.dillards.com

Diners Club
183 Inverness Drive West
Englewood, CO 80111
303-799-9000
toll free: 800-234-6377
fax: 303-649-2891
www.dinerclubus.com

Dlink Systems
53 Discovery Drive
Irvine, CA 92618
949-788-0805
toll free: 800-326-1688
fax: 949-753-7033
www.dlink.com

Dole Food Company, Inc.
One Dole Drive
Westlake Village, CA 91362-7300
818-874-4000
toll free: 800-232-8888
fax: 818-874-4997
www.dole.com

Dollar Rent A Car Systems, Inc.
CIMS 7082, 5330 East 31st Street
P.O. Box 33167
Tulsa, OK 74153-1167
918-669-3000
918-669-8596
toll free: 800-800-5252
toll free: 800-800-6080
918-669-8596
www.dollar.com

Domino's Pizza, Inc.
P.O. Box 997
30 Frank Lloyd Wright Drive
Ann Arbor, MI 48106
313-930-3030
toll free: 888-DOMINOS
www.dominos.com

Doubleday Direct, Inc
401 Franklin Avenue
Garden City, NY 11530
516-873-4628
fax: 516-873-4384
www.booksonline.com

DowBrands
P.O. Box 68511
Indianapolis, IN 46268-0511
317-260-2000
toll free: 800-428-4795
fax: 317-873-8564
www.dowclean.com

Dr Pepper/Seven Up, Inc.
5301 Legacy Drive
P.O. Box 869077
Plano, TX 75024
972-673-7000
toll free: 800-527-7096
fax: 972-673-7171
www.drpepper.com

Drug Emporium, Inc.
155 Hidden Ravines Drive
Powell, OH 43065
740-548-7080, ext. 104
fax: 740-548-6651
www.drugemporium.com

Dunkin Donuts of America/Baskin Robbins
P.O. Box 317
Randolph, MA 02368
781-961-4000

Dunlop Tire Corp.
P.O. Box 1109
Buffalo, NY 14240-1109
716-639-5439
toll free: 800-548-4714
fax: 800-253-6702
www.dunloptire.com

DuPont Co.
Barley Mill Plaza
Reeves Mill Building
Wilmington, DE 19880-0010
302-774-1000
toll free: 800-441-7515

Duracell North America (Division of Gillette, Inc.)
Duracell Drive
Bethel, CT 06801
203-796-4304
toll free: 800-551-2355
fax: 203-796-4565
www.duracell.com

E

Eastman Kodak Co.
343 State Street
Rochester, NY 14650-3103
716-724-4000
toll free: 800-242-2424
www.kodak.com

Eckerd Corporation
8333 Bryan Dairy Road
P.O. Box 4689
Clearwater, FL 33758
813-395-6000
toll free: 800-325-3737
TDD/TTY toll free: 800-760-4833
fax: 813-395-7063
www.eckerd.com

Eddie Bauer, Inc.
P.O. Box 9700
Redmond, WA 98073-9700

425-882-6100
toll free: 800-426-6253
fax: 425-882-6383
www.eddiebauer.com

Edmund Scientific Co.
101 East Gloucester Pike
Barrington, NJ 08007-1380
856-547-3488
toll free: 800-728-6999
fax: 856-547-3292

Eizo Nanao Technologies
5710 Warland Drive
Cypress, CA 90630
toll free: 800-800-5202
fax: 562-431-4811
www.eizo.com

Electrolux Corporation
300 East Valley Drive
Bristol, VA 24201
toll free: 800-243-9078
fax: 540-645-2863
www.elux.com

Eli Lilly & Co.
Lilly Corporate Center
Indianapolis, IN 46285
317-276-2000
toll free: 800-545-5979
www.lilly.com

E-Machines
1211 Alderwood Avenue
Sunnyvale, CA 94089
408-541-1720

Emery Worldwide (A CNF Company)
One Lagoon Drive
Redwood City, CA 94065
650-596-9600
toll free: 800-227-1981
fax: 650-596-7983
www.emeryworld.com

Encore Marketing International, Inc.
4501 Forbes Boulevard
Lanham, MD 20706
301-459-8020
toll free: 800-638-0930
fax: 301-731-0525

Encyclopedia Britannica, Inc.
310 South Michigan Avenue
Chicago, IL 60604-4293
312-347-7000
fax: 312-347-7399
www.eb.com

Epson
3840 Kilroy Airport Way
Long Beach, CA 90806
310-782-0770
toll free: 800-GO-EPSON
    (1-800-463-7766)
www.epson.com

The Equitable Co., Inc.
1290 Avenue of the Americas
12th Floor
New York, NY 10104
212-554-1234

Ernest & Julio Gallo Winery
P.O. Box 1130
Modesto, CA 95353
209-341-3161
fax: 209-341-6600
www.gallo.com

Esprit de Corps
900 Minnesota Street
San Francisco, CA 94107-3000
415-648-6900
toll free: 800-4ESPRIT
fax: 415-550-3960

The Estee Lauder Companies, Inc
767 Fifth Avenue
New York, NY 10153
212-756-4801
fax: 212-756-4810
www.elcompanies.com

The Eureka Co.
307 North Main Street
Bloomington, IL 61701
309-823-5735

Experian
P.O. Box 949
Allen, TX 75013-0949
toll free: 888-EXPERIAN (397-3742)
www.experian.com

Exxon
436 Creamery Way, Suite 300
Exton, PA 19341
toll free: 800-243-9966
www.exxonmobil.com

F

Farallon Communications, Inc.
3089 Teagarden Street
San Leandro, CA 94577
510-346-8001
www.farallon.com

Family Circle Magazine
375 Lexington Avenue
New York, NY 10017-5514
212-499-2000

Faultless Starch/Bon Ami Co.
Consumer Affairs Department
1025 West Eighth Street
Kansas City, MO 64101-1200
816-842-1230
fax: 816-842-4328

Federal Express Corp.
P.O. Box 727
Department 1845
Memphis, TN 38194-1845
901-369-3600
toll free: 800-238-5355
fax: 901-395-4511
www.fedex.com

Federated Department Stores
7 West Seventh Street
Cincinnati, OH 45202
513-579-7000
fax: 513-579-7185
www.federated-fds.com

First Union National Bank
1525 West W.T. Harris Blvd.
Charlotte, NC 28212
toll free: 800-733-3862
www.firstunion.com

Fisher-Price
Consumer Affairs Manager
636 Girard Avenue
East Aurora, NY 14052
716-687-3000
toll free: 800-432-5437
TDD toll free: 800-382-7470
fax: 716-687-3494
www.fisher-price.com

**Florist Transworld Delivery Associates
    (FTD)**
3113 Woodcreek Drive
Downers Grove, IL 60515
630-719-7800
toll free: 800-669-1000

Flowers Industries, Inc.
Marta Turner, Vice President
P.O. Box 1338
1919 Flowers Circle
Thomasville, GA 31757
912-226-9110
fax: 912-226-1318
www.flowersindustries.com

Fort James Corp
P.O. Box 6000
Norwalk, CT 06856-6000
203-854-2458
toll free: 800-243-5384

Foster & Gallagher, Inc.
6523 North Galena Road
Peoria, IL 61632
309-691-4610 (Mon.–Fri., 8:30 A.M.–
    5 P.M.)
309-691-3633 (Mon.–Fri. after 5:15 P.M.)
toll free: 800-447-0878
309-589-2017

The Franklin Mint
U.S. Route One
Franklin Center, PA 19091
610-459-6000
toll free: 800-523-7622
fax: 610-459-6040

Frigidaire Home Products
P.O. Box 212378
Augusta, GA 30917
706-860-4110
toll free: 800-451-7007
fax: 614-792-4092
www.frigidaire.com

Frito-Lay
Cathy Dial, Group Manager
7701 Legacy Drive IA-70
Plano, TX 75024
972-334-5022
toll free: 800-352-4477
fax: 972-334-5071
www.fritolay.com

Fruit of the Loom, Inc.
One Fruit of the Loom Drive
Bowling Green, KY 42102-9015
270-781-6400
fax: 270-781-6400
www.fruit.com

Fuji Photo Film U.S.A., Inc.
1100 King George Post
Edison, NJ 08837
toll free: 800-800-FUJI (3854)
fax: 732-857-3487
www.fujifilm.com

Fujitsu Computer Products of America
2904 Orchard Parkway
San Jose, CA 95134
408-432-6333
fax: 408-894-1709
www.fcpa.com

Fuller Brush Co.
P.O. Box 1247
Great Bend, KS 67530-0729
316-792-1711
toll free: 800-523-3794
fax: 316-793-4523
www.fullerbrush.com

FWB Software
2722 Gough Street
San Francisco, CA 94123
415-345-4300
fax: 415-345-4358
www.fwb.com

G

Galoob Toys, Inc.
Manager
500 Forbes Boulevard
South San Francisco, CA 94080
415-508-2400
toll free: 800-934-8697
fax: 650-952-7084
www.galoob.com

G.D. Searle and Co. Pharmaceuticals
P.O. Box 5110
Chicago, IL 60680
847-982-7000
fax: 847-470-6633
www.monsanto.com

General Mills, Inc.
P.O. Box 1113
Minneapolis, MN 55440-1113
fax: 763-764-8330
www.generalmills.com

General Motors Acceptance Corp.
3044 West Grand Boulevard
Room AX348
Detroit, MI 48202
toll free: 800-441-9234
TDD toll free: 800-TDD-GMAC
www.gmacfs.com

The Generra Company
3920 North 34th Street #300
Seattle, WA 98103
206-728-6888
fax: 206-467-9326
www.generra.com

Genesee Brewing Co., Inc.
445 St. Paul Street
Rochester, NY 14605

716-546-1030
toll free: 800-SAY-GENNY (1-800-
    729-4366)
fax: 716-546-5011
www.highfalls.com

Georgia-Pacific Corp.
2300 Windy Ridge Parkway
Atlanta, GA 30339
404-652-4000
toll free: 800-BUILD-GP
    (1-800-284-5347)
www.gp.com

Gerber Products Co.
445 State Street
Fremont, MI 49413-1056
toll free: 800-4-GERBER
fax: 231-928-2423

Giant Food Inc.
P.O. Box 1804
Department 597
Washington, DC 20013
301-341-4365
TDD: 301-341-4327
fax: 301-618-4968
www.giantfood.com

Gillette Co.
P.O. Box 61
Boston, MA 02199
617-421-7000
toll free: 800-872-7202
fax: 617-463-3410

The Glidden Co.
925 Euclid Avenue
Cleveland, OH 44115
216-344-8000
fax: 216-344-8900

Global Village
1377 Clint Moore Road
Boca Raton, FL 33487
561-997-6227
toll free: 800-336-2009
fax: 561-523-2546

Golden Grain Co.
4576 Willow Road
Pleasanton, CA 94588
toll free: 800-421-2444

Goldstar (L.G. Electronics)
P.O. Box 6126
Huntsville, AL 35824
256-772-8860
toll free: 800-243-0000
fax: 800-448-4026

Gordon's Jewelers
A Subsidiary of Zale Corporation
901 West Walnut Hill Lane
Irving, TX 75038-1003
972-580-4924
fax: 972-580-5286

Greyhound Lines, Inc.
P.O. Box 660362
Dallas, TX 75266-0362
214-849-8000

GTCO Calcomp
14555 North 82nd Street
Scottsdale, AZ 85260
480-948-6540
toll free: 800-458-5888
fax: 480-443-2254
www.calcomp.com

GTE Corp.
One Stamford Forum
Stamford, CT 06904
toll free: 800-643-0997
www.gte.com

Guess? Inc.
1444 South Alameda Street
Los Angeles, CA 90021
213-765-3100
toll free: 800-394-8377
fax: 213-744-0855
www.guess.com

Guinness Import Co.
Six Landmark Square
Stamford, CT 06901-2704
203-323-3311
toll free: 800-521-1591
fax: 203-359-7209

H

H&R Block, Inc.
4400 Main Street
Kansas City, MO 64111-9986
816-753-6900
toll free: 800-829-7733
fax: 816-932-1800
www.hrblock.com

Hain Food Group
16007 Camino del Rey Cantera
Irwindall, CA 91706-7811
toll free: 800-265-6453

Hallmark Cards, Inc.
P.O. Box 419580
2501 McGee Avenue
Kansas City, MO 64141-9580

816-274-5111
toll free: 800-425-6275
toll free: 800-425-5627
www.hallmark.com

Hanes Hosiery (Division of Sara Lee Corp.)
P.O. Box 225
401 Hanes Mill Road
Winston-Salem, NC 27105
toll free: 800-342-7070
fax: 336-519-2154
www.haneshosiery.com

Hartz Mountain Corp.
400 Plaza Drive
Secaucus, NJ 07094
201-271-4800

Hasbro, Inc.
Consumer Affairs Department
P.O. Box 200
Pawtucket, RI 02862
toll free: 800-242-7276 (headquarters)
toll free: 800-255-5516
fax: 401-431-8082
www.hasbro.com

Heinz Frozen Foods
P.O. Box 10
Boise, ID 83707
toll free: 800-892-2401
www.oreida.com

Heinz U.S.A.
P.O. Box 57
Pittsburgh, PA 15230
412-237-5740
fax: 412-237-4230

Helene Curtis
800 Sylvan Avenue
Englewood Cliffs, NJ 07632
toll free: 800-621-2013
toll free: 800-782-8301
www.unilever.com

Hershey Food Corp.
100 Crystal A Drive
Hershey, PA 17033
717-534-6799
www.hersheys.com

Hertz Corp.
225 Brae Boulevard
Park Ridge, NJ 07656
201-307-2000

toll free: 800-654-3131
fax: 201-307-2928
www.hertz.com

Hewlett-Packard Co.
P.O. Box 10301
Palo Alto, CA 94303
650-857-1501
fax: 650-813-3254
www.hp.com

Hillshire Farm & Kahn's
3241 Spring Grove Avenue
P.O. Box 25111
Cincinnati, OH 45225
toll free: 800-328-2426
fax: 513-853-1626
www.hillshirefarm.com

Hilton Hotels Corp.
9336 Civic Center Drive
Beverly Hills, CA 90210
310-278-4321
fax: 310-205-4437
www.hilton.com

Home Depot, Inc.
2455 Paces Ferry Road, NW
Atlanta, GA 30339
770-433-8211
toll free: 800-553-3199
fax: 770-384-3440
www.homedepot.com

Home Shopping Network
One HSN Drive
St. Petersburg, FL 33729
727-872-1000
toll free: 800-284-3900
fax: 727-572-8854

Hometouch Mortgage
333 W. Wacker Drive, Suite 1410
Chicago, IL 60606
312-263-4663
toll free: 888-824-4663
fax: 877-325-4663
www.hometouchmortgage.com

Hoover Co.
101 East Maple
North Canton, OH 44720
330-499-9499
toll free: 800-944-9200
fax: 330-497-5065

Hormel Foods Co.
One Hormel Place
Austin, MN 55912-9989

507-437-5032
toll free: 800-523-4635
fax: 507-437-9852
www.hormel.com

Howard Johnson, Inc.
3400 NW Grand Avenue
Phoenix, AZ 85017
602-264-9164
fax: 602-264-7633

Huffy Bicycle Co.
401 Pleasant Valley Drive
Springboro, OH 45060
toll free: 800-872-2453
fax: 513-704-5980
www.huffy.com

Humana Inc.
500 West Main Street
P.O. Box 1438
Louisville, KY 40201-1438
502-580-1000
toll free: 800-664-4140
www.humana.com

Hyatt Hotels & Resorts
200 West Madison Street
30th Floor
Chicago, IL 60606
312-750-1234
toll free: 800-228-3336
fax: 402-593-5151
www.hyatt.com

I

IBM Computers
1500 Riveredge Parkway
Atlanta, GA 30328
919-517-2480
770-858-5980
fax: 770-644-5530
www.ibm.com

IBM International Support Center
New Orchard Road
Armonk, NY 10504
toll free: 800-IBM-4YOU (1-800-426-4968)
TDD/TTY toll free: 800-426-4832
fax: 520-799-4541
www.ibm.com

Improvements (Division of Hanover Direct, Inc.)
23297 Commerce Park
Beachwood, OH 44122
fax: 513-704-5980

Inglenook Vinyards
12667 Road 24
Madera, CA 93639
toll free: 800-726-4422

Intel
1900 Prairie City Road
Folsom, CA 95630
916-377-7000 (switchboard)
916-356-8080
www.intel.com

International Dairy Queen, Inc.
P.O. Box 39286
7505 Metro Boulevard
Minneapolis, MN 55439-0286
612-830-0200
fax: 612-830-0480
www.dairyqueen.com

Iomega
1821 West Iomega Way
Roy, UT 84067
801-778-1000 (headquarters)
toll free: 800-450-5522
fax: 801-779-5632
www.iomega.com

J

J. Baker, Inc.
555 Turnpike Street
Canton, MA 02021
781-828-9300
fax: 781-821-0614

Jackson & Perkins Nursery Stock
2518 South Pacific Highway
Medford, OR 97501
toll free: 800-872-7673
fax: 800-242-0329

Jameson Hospitality, LLC
Jameson Inns & Signature Inns
8 Perimetse Center East
Suite 8050
Atlanta, GA 30346
770-901-9020
fax: 770-901-9550
www.jamesoninns.com

J.C. Penney Co., Inc.
P.O. Box 10001
Dallas, TX 75301-7303
972-431-1000
fax: 972-431-9140
www.jcpenney.com

Jenn Air-Maytag Appliance Sales Company
240 Edwards Street
Cleveland, TN 37311
toll free: 800-688-1100
TDD toll free: 800-688-2080
www.jennair.com

Jenny Craig International
11355 North Torrey Pines Road
La Jolla, CA 92037
858-812-7000
fax: 858-812-2700
www.jennycraig.com

Jockey International, Inc.
2300 60th Street
P.O. Box 1417
Kenosha, WI 53140
260-658-8111
fax: 260-658-1812
www.jockey.com

John Hancock Mutual Insurance Co.
P.O. Box 111
Boston, MA 02117
617-572-6385
toll free: 800-732-5543
TDD toll free: 800-832-5282
fax: 617-572-8707
www.jhancock.com

Johnny Appleseed's, Inc.
30 Tozar Road
Beverly, MA 01915
978-922-2040
toll free: 800-767-6666
fax: 800-755-7557

Johns-Manville Corporation
P.O. Box 5108
Denver, CO 80217-5108
303-978-2000
toll free: 800-654-3103
www.jm.com

Johnson & Johnson Consumer Products, Inc.
199 Grandview Road
Skillman, NJ 08558
908-874-1000

Johnson Publishing Co., Inc.
820 South Michigan Avenue
Chicago, IL 60605
312-322-9200

Jordache Enterprises, Inc.
1411 Broadway
New York, NY 10018
212-944-1330

Joseph E. Seagram & Sons, Inc.
800 3rd Avenue
New York, NY 10022
212-572-1282
fax: 212-572-1264

Jostens
148 E. Broadway
Owatonna, MN 55060
507-455-6100
toll free: 800-854-7464
www.jostens.com

Just Born, Inc
1300 Stefko Boulevard
Bethlehem, PA 18017
610-867-7568
toll free: 800-445-5787
fax: 1-800-543-4981

Just My Size Clothing Co. (Sara Lee Corp)
Hanes Hosiery
P.O. Box 1938
401 Hanes Mill Rd
Winston-Salem, NC 27105
toll free: 888-567-3487

JVC Company of America
1700 Valley Road
Wayne, NJ 07494
973-315-5000
toll free: 800-252-5722
fax: 973-315-5042
www.jvcservice.com

K

K-III Magazines
745 Fifth Avenue
New York, NY 10151
212-745-0100

Kawasaki Motor Corp., U.S.A.
P.O. Box 25252
Santa Ana, CA 92799-5252
949-770-0400
fax: 949-460-5629
www.kawasaki.com

Keebler Company
Consumer Affairs
P.O. Box 1037
Elmhurst, IL 60126
630-833-2900
fax: 630-833-6961
www.keebler.com

Kellogg Company
P.O. Box CAMB
Battle Creek, MI 49016-1986
616-961-2000
toll free: 800-962-1413
toll free: 800-962-1516
fax: 616-961-9033
www.kelloggs.com

Kelly Springfield Tire Co.
12501 Willow Brook Road, SE
Cumberland, MD 21502-2599
301-777-6000
fax: 301-777-6008

Kemper Insurance Companies
1 Kemper Drive
C-3
Long Grove, IL 60049
847-320-3237
toll free: 800-833-0355
www.kemperinsurance.com

Kenner Products
P.O. Box 200
Pawtucket, RI 02862
toll free: 800-242-7276
fax: 401-431-8082
www.hasbro.com

Kensington Technology Group
2855 Campus Drive
San Mateo, CA 94403
650-572-2700
toll free: 800-535-4242
fax: 650-572-9675
www.kensington.com

Keytronic Corporation
P.O. Box 14687
Spokane, WA 99214
509-928-8000
fax: 509-927-5224
www.keytronic.com

Kimberly-Clark Corporation
401 North Lake
Neenah, WI 54956
920-721-8000
toll free: 800-544-1847
fax: 920-721-4766
www.kimberly-clark.com

Kinetico Incorporated
10845 Kinsman Road
P.O. Box 193
Newbury, OH 44065

440-564-9111
toll free: 800-944-WATER
fax: 440-564-9541
www.kinetico.com

The Kirby Company
1920 West 114th Street
Cleveland, OH 44212
216-228-2400
216-228-2403
toll free: 800-494-8586
fax: 216-529-6164
www.kirby.com

K-mart Corp.
3100 West Big Beaver Road
Troy, MI 48084
248-643-1000
toll free: 800-635-6278
fax: 248-614-1970

Kohl's Corp
N. 56 W 17000 Ridgewood Drive
Menomonee Falls, WI 53051
262-703-7000
toll free: 800-694-2674
fax: 262-703-6198
www.kohls.com

Kohler Co.
444 Highland Drive
Mail Stop 10
Kohler, WI 53044
920-457-4441
toll free: 800-456-4537
fax: 920-459-1611

Kraft Foods, Inc.
1 Kraft Court
Glenview, IL 60025
toll free: 800-323-0768
fax: 847-646-7853
www.kraftfoods.com

Kroger Co.
1014 Vine Street
Cincinnati, OH 45202
513-762-1589
toll free: 800-632-6900

Kyocera Optics, Inc.
2301-200 Cottontail Lane
Somerset, NJ 08873
732-560-0060
toll free: 800-526-0266
fax: 732-560-9221
www.yasmica.com

L

Land O'Lakes, Inc.
P.O. Box 64101
St. Paul, MN 55164-0101
651-481-2128
toll free: 800-328-4155
fax: 651-481-2959
www.landolakes.com

Land's End
P.O. Box 64101
Dodgeville, WI 53595
608-935-9341
toll free: 800-332-4700
toll free: 800-356-4444
TDD/TTY toll free: 800-541-3459
fax: 608-935-6254
www.landsend.com

Lane Furniture
701 Fifth Street
P.O. Box 151
Altavista, VA 24517
804-369-5641
fax: 804-369-3677
www.lanefurniture.com

La-Z-Boy Inc.
1284 North Telegraph Road
Monroe, MI 48162-3309
734-242-1444
www.la-z-boy.com

Lee Apparel
9001 West 67th Street
Merriam, KS 66202
913-384-4000

L'eggs Products
    (Division of Sara Lee Corp.)
P.O. Box 450
401 Hanes Mill Road
Winston-Salem, NC 27105
toll free: 800-925-3447
fax: 336-519-2154
www.leggs.com

LEGO Systems Inc
555 Taylor Road
P.O. Box 1600
Enfield, CT 06083-1600
toll free: 800-422-5346
fax: 860-763-7754
www.lego.com

Leichtung Workshops, Inc.
5604 Alameda Place, NE
Albuquerque, NM 87113

216-831-6191
toll free: 800-321-6840
fax: 505-821-7331

Lennox Industries, Inc.
P.O. Box 799900
Dallas, TX 75379-9900
972-497-5000
fax: 972-497-5299
www.davelennox.com

Lever Brothers Co.
800 Sylvan Avenue
Englewood Cliffs, NJ 07632
toll free: 800-598-1223
toll free: 800-598-5005
www.unilever.com

Levi Strauss & Co.
1155 Battery Street
San Francisco, CA 94111
toll free: 800-USA-LEVI

Levolor Home Fashion
4110 Premier Drive
High Point, NC 27265
336-812-8181
toll free: 800-LEVOLOR
www.lev.com

Lexmark International
740 New Circle Road
Building 004-2
Lexington, KY 40550
606-232-3000
fax: 606-232-2873
www.lexmark.com

Liberty Mutual Insurance Group
175 Berkeley Street
Boston, MA 02117-0140
617-357-9500
toll free: 800-344-0197 ext. 41015
fax: 617-574-6688
www.libertymutual.com

Lillian Vernon Corp.
2600 International Parkway
Virginia Beach, VA 23452
757-430-1500
fax: 757-430-1010
www.lillianvernon.com

The Limited, Inc.
Three Limited Parkway
Columbus, OH 43230
614-415-7000

Lincoln Electric Co.
Machine and Consumables

22801 St. Claire Avenue
Cleveland, OH 44117
216-383-2519
toll free: 800-833-7353
fax: 216-481-2309
www.lincolnelectric.com

L.L. Bean, Inc.
Casco Street
Freeport, ME 04033-0001
207-865-4761
toll free: 800-341-4341
TDD toll free: 800-545-0090
www.llbean.com

Long John Silver's Restaurants Inc.
P.O. Box 11988
101 Yorkshire Drive
Lexington, KY 40579-1988
859-543-6000
www.ljsilvers.com

L'Oreal Cosmetics
Division of Cosmair, Inc.
P.O. Box 98
Westfield, NJ 07091-9987
toll free: 800-332-2036
fax: 732-499-2599

Lotus Development Corp.
55 Cambridge Parkway
Cambridge, MA 02142
617-577-8500
www.lotus.com

M

Macromedia, Inc.
600 Townsend Street
San Francisco, CA 94103
415-252-2000
toll free: 800-470-7211
fax: 415-703-0924
www.macromedia.com

Macy's East
151 West 34th Street
New York, NY 10001
212-695-4400
toll free: 800-526-1202
www.macys.com

Macy's West
50 O'Farrell Street
San Francisco, CA 94102
toll free: 800-877-2655
www.macys.com

Magic Chef-Maytag Appliance Sales Company
240 Edwards Street
Cleveland, TN 37311
toll free: 800-688-1120
TDD toll free: 800-688-2080

Mannington Mills, Inc.
P.O. Box 30
Salem, NJ 08079
856-935-3000 ext. 5864
toll free: 800-356-6787
fax: 856-339-6099
www.mannington.com

Marine Midland Bank, N.A.
95 Washington Street
Atrium 3 North
Buffalo, NY 14273
716-841-1000
fax: 716-841-2547

Marriott Corp.
One Marriott Drive
Washington, DC 20058
fax: 402-390-1698
www.marriott.com

Massachusetts Mutual Insurance Co.
1295 State Street
Springfield, MA 01111
413-744-6165
413-744-3143
toll free: 800-487-7844
toll free: 800-767-1000
fax: 413-744-8545
www.massmutual.com

MasterCard International
P.O. Box 28468-0968
St. Louis, MO 63146-0968
toll free: 800-300-3069
fax: 314-542-3724
www.mastercard.com

Matsushita Services Co. of America
1 Panasonic Way
Secaucus, NJ 07094
201-348-7000
toll free: 800-211-7262

Mattel, Inc.
333 Continental Boulevard
El Segundo, CA 90245-5012
310-252-2000
toll free: 800-524-TOYS (8697)
fax: 310-252-4190

Maxicare Health Plans, Inc.
1149 South Broadway
Los Angeles, CA 90015
213-742-0900
fax: 213-365-3499
www.maxicare.com

Maxis
2121 North California Boulevard, #600
Walnut Creek, CA 94596
925-933-5630
toll free: 800-245-4525
fax: 925-927-3736
www.maxis.com

Maxtor
2191 Zanker Road
San Jose, CA 95131
toll free: 800-262-9867
fax: 408-922-2085
www.maxtor.com

May Department Stores Co.
611 Olive Street
St. Louis, MO 63101
314-342-6300
fax: 314-342-3038
www.maycompany.com

Maybelline, Inc.
Division of Cosmair Inc
P.O. Box 1010
Clark, NJ 07066-1010
toll free: 800-944-0730

Mayflower Transit, Inc.
P.O. Box 26150
Fenton, MO 63026-1350
636-326-3100
toll free: 800-428-1234

Maytag Appliance Sales Company
240 Edwards Street
Cleveland, TN 37311
toll free: 800-688-9900
TDD toll free: 800-688-2080
www.maytag.com

McCormick & Co., Inc.
211 Schilling Circle
Hunt Valley, MD 21031
410-527-8753
toll free: 800-632-5847
fax: 410-527-6005
www.mccormick.com

McDonald's Corp.
Kroc Drive
Oak Brook, IL 60523
630-623-6198
www.McDonalds.com

McGraw-Hill, Inc.
1221 Avenue of the Americas
New York, NY 10020
toll free: 800-262-4729
fax: 614-759-3641
www.books.mcgraw-hill.com

MCI WorldCom
1200 South Hayes Street
11th Floor
Arlington, VA 22202
toll free: 800-677-6580
www.mci.com

McKee Foods Corp.
P.O. Box 750
Collegedale, TN 37315
toll free: 800-522-4499
fax: 423-238-7150

McKesson Water Products Co.
3280 East Foothill Boulevard, #400
Pasadena, CA 91109
818-585-1000
toll free: 800-4WATERS
fax: 818-585-8553

Mercruiser
3003 North Perkins Road
Stillwater, OK 74075
405-377-1200
fax: 405-743-6560

Melitta USA, Inc.
13925 58th Street North
Clearwater, FL 34624
727-535-2111
toll free: 888-635-4882
fax: 727-530-7870

Mellon Financial Corp.
One Mellon Bank Center
Room 5135
Pittsburgh, PA 15258-0001
412-234-8552
fax: 412-236-1818

The Mentholatum Co., Inc.
707 Sterling Drive
Orchard Park, NY 14127
716-882-7660
toll free: 800-688-7660
fax: 716-677-9531
www.mentholatum.com

Merrill Lynch, Pierce, Fenner & Smith
P.O. Box 9084
Princeton, NJ 08543-9084
609-282-6920

Mervyn's
22301 Industrial Boulevard
Hayward, CA 94541
510-727-5208

Metropolitan Life Insurance Co.
One Madison Avenue
New York, NY 10010
212-578-5044
toll free: 800-638-5000
fax: 212-685-8042
www.metlife.com

Michelin North America, Inc.
P.O. Box 19001
Greenville, SC 29602
toll free: 800-847-3435
www.michelin.com

Michigan Bulb Co.
1950 Waldorf NW
Grand Rapids, MI 49550
616-453-5401
fax: 616-735-2628

Microsoft Corp.
One Microsoft Way
Redmond, WA 98052-6399
425-882-8080
www.microsoft.com

Mid-Michigan Surgical Supply
595 North Avenue
Battle Creek, MI 49017
616-962-9541
toll free: 800-445-5820
fax: 616-926-9650

Midas International Corp.
1300 Arlington Heights Road
Itasca, IL 60143
toll free: 800-621-0144
fax: 800-450-2207

Miles Kimball Co.
41 West 8th Avenue
Oshkosh, WI 54906-0002
920-231-1992
TDD: 920-231-5506
fax: 920-231-6915

The Milnot Company
100 South Fourth Street
St. Louis, MO 63102
314-655-2100
toll free: 877-MILNOT1

toll free: 877-BEECH-NUT
fax: 314-655-2201
www.milnot.com

Milton Bradley
P.O. Box 200
Pawtucket, RI 02862
413-525-6411 (headquarters)
toll free: 888-836-7025
fax: 401-431-8082
www.hasbro.com

Minolta Corp.
101 Williams Drive
Ramsey, NJ 07446
201-825-4000
www.minoltausa.com

Minwax/Sherwin-Williams
10 Mountain View Road
Upper Saddle River, NJ 07458-1934
toll free: 800-526-0495
fax: 201-818-7605
www.minwax.com

Mitsubishi Electronics America, Inc.
9351 Jeronimo Road
Irvine, CA 92618
toll free: 800-332-2119
fax: 949-465-6147
www.mitsubishi-tv.com

M&M/Mars, Inc.
800 High Street
Hackettstown, NJ 07840
908-852-1000
toll free: 800-222-0293
www.m-ms.com

Mobil
436 Creamery Way, Suite 300
Exton, PA 19341
toll free: 800-243-9966
www.exxonmobil.com

Mobil Oil Credit Corp.
11300 Corporate Avenue
Lenexa, KS 66219-1385
toll free: 800-225-9547
fax: 703-846-6002

**Monet Group Inc. Crystal Brand
   Jewelry Group**
3400 Pawtucket Avenue
East Providence, RI 02860
401-434-4500

Monsanto Co.
800 North Lindbergh Boulevard
St. Louis, MO 63167
314-694-1000
www.monsanto.com

Montgomery Ward
535 West Chicago Avenue
Chicago, IL 60671
312-467-2000
fax: 312-467-2175

**Morgan Stanley, Dean Witter, Discover
   & Co.**
2 World Trade Center
66th Floor
New York, NY 10048
toll free: 800-733-2307

Morton International
100 North Riverside Plaza
Chicago, IL 60606
312-807-2693
fax: 312-807-2899
www.morton.com

Motts, Inc.
P.O. Box 3800
Stamford, CT 06905
203-968-7500
toll free: 800-426-4891
www.motts.com

Movado Group, Inc.
Holly Russo, Director
125 Chubb Avenue
Lyndhurst, NJ 07071
201-460-4800
fax: 201-460-3832

**Mutual Life Insurance Company of
   New York (MONY)**
1740 Broadway
New York, NY 10019
212-708-2000
www.mony.com

Mutual of Omaha Insurance Co.
Mutual of Omaha Plaza
Omaha, NE 68175
402-351-5625
toll free: 800-775-6000
fax: 402-351-3768
www.mutualofomaha.com

N

Nabisco Foods Group
100 DeForest Avenue
East Hanover, NJ 07936
toll free: 800-NABISCO
fax: 973-503-2202
www.nabiscoworld.com

National Amusements, Inc.
200 Elm Street
Dedham, MA 02026

781-461-1600
fax: 781-326-6899

National Car Rental System, Inc.
7700 France Avenue South
Minneapolis, MN 55435
612-893-6480
toll free: 800-468-3334
fax: 612-830-2936

National Presto Industries, Inc.
3925 North Hastings Way
Eau Claire, WI 54703-3703
715-839-2121
fax: 715-839-2122

National Fuel Gas Company
10 Lafayette Square
Buffalo, NY 14203
toll free: 800-453-3513
fax: 716-857-7061
www.nationalfuelgas.com

NBC
30 Rockefeller Plaza
New York, NY 10112
212-664-2333

NCE Computer Group
1975 Friendship Drive, Suite C
El Cajon, CA 92020
619-212-3000
toll free: 800-458-0300

**Near East Food Products (Division of
   Quaker Oats)**
321 N. Clark Street
Leominster, MA 01453
312-222-7111
www.quakeroats.com

Neiman-Marcus
P.O. Box 729080
Dallas, TX 75372
214-761-2660
toll free: 800-685-6695
fax: 214-761-2650
www.neimanmarcus.com

Nestlé USA
800 North Brand Boulevard
Glendale, CA 91203
toll free: 800-225-2270
fax: 818-549-6330
www.nestleusa.com

Netopia, Inc.
2470 Mariner Square Loop
Alameda, CA 94501
510-814-5100
fax: 510-814-5020
www.netopia.com

Neutrogena Corp.
Consumer Information Center
5760 West 96th Street
Los Angeles, CA 90045
toll free: 800-582-4048
fax: 310-337-5564
www.neutrogena.com

Nevada Bell
645 East Plumb Lane
Reno, NV 89502
775-333-4339
fax: 775-333-2364

Newport News, Inc.
5000 City Line Road
Hampton, VA 23661
757-827-7010
fax: 757-825-4106

Nexxus Products Co.
P.O. Box 1274
Santa Barbara, CA 93116-9976
805-968-6900
toll free: 800-444-6399
fax: 805-968-6540
www.nexxusproducts.com

Niagara Mohawk Power Corp.
Dey's Centennial Plaza
P.O. Box 5300
Syracuse, NY 13250-5300
315-460-7015
fax: 315-460-7147
www.nimo.com

Nike, Inc.
Nike/World Campus
1 Bowerman Drive
Beaverton, OR 97005-6453
503-671-6453
toll free: 800-344-6453
email: www.nike.com

Nine West Group Inc.
9 West Plaza
1129 Westchester Avenue
White Plains, NY 10604-3529
914-640-6400
fax: 914-640-6069
www.ninewest.com

Norelco Consumer Products Co.
   (Division of Philips Electronics
   North America Corp.)
1010 Washington Boulevard
P.O. Box 120015
Stamford, CT 06912-0015
toll free: 800-243-7884
fax: 860-975-1812

Northwest Airlines
C6590
5101 Northwest Drive
St. Paul, MN 55111-3034
612-726-2046
toll free: 800-225-2525
www.nwa.com

Northwestern Mutual Life
   Insurance Co.
720 East Wisconsin Avenue
Milwaukee, WI 53202
414-299-7179
fax: 414-299-2463
www.northwesternmutual.com

Norwegian Cruise Lines
7665 Corporate Center Drive
Miami, FL 33126
305-436-4000
toll free: 800-327-7030

Novartis Consumer Health, Inc.
560 Morris Avenue
Building F
Summit, NJ 07901-1312
toll free: 800-452-0051 (Over-the-counter
   products)
fax: 908-598-7583
www.novartis.com

Novartis Crop Protection
410 Swing Road
Greensboro, NC 27409
336-632-6000
toll free: 800-334-9481
www.novartis.com

Novartis Pharmaceuticals
59 Route 10
East Hanover, NJ 07936
toll free: 800-742-2422
www.novartis.com

Novell, Inc.
1555 North Technology Way
Orem, UT 84097
toll free: 800-638-9273
fax: 801-228-5176

Nu Tone, Inc.
Madison and Redbank Roads
Cincinnati, OH 45227
513-527-5231
fax: 513-527-5122
www.nutone.com

The NutraSweet/Equal Co.
P.O. Box 2986
Chicago, IL 60654-0986
www.equal.com; www.nutrasweet.com

O

Olan Mills, Inc.
4325 Amnicola Highway
P.O. Box 23456
Chattanooga, TN 37422-3456
423-622-5141
toll free: 800-251-6320
fax: 423-499-3864
www.olanmills.com

Olympus America
2 Corporate Center Drive
Melville, NY 11747
516-844-5000
toll free: 800-622-6372
fax: 516-844-5262

Ontrack Computer Systems
9023 Colombine Road
Eden Prairie, MN 55347
612-937-2121

Orkin
2170 Piedmont Road NE
Atlanta, GA 30324
404-329-7400
toll free: 800-346-7546
fax: 404-633-2315

Ortho, Roundup and Greensweep
14111 Scottslawn Road
Marysville, OH 43041
toll free: 800-225-2883
www.ortho.com

Orville Redenbacher
P.O. Box 4800
Fullerton, CA 92834
714-680-1431

OSCO Drugs, Subsidiary of American
   Stores
P.O. Box 27447
Salt Lake City, UT 84127-0447
801-961-5600
toll free: 800-541-2863
fax: 801-531-0768

Outboard Marine Corp.
100 Sea Horse Drive
Waukegan, IL 60085
847-689-6200
fax: 847-689-5489
www.omc-online.com

Owens Corning World Headquarters
One Owens Corning Parkway
Toledo, OH 43659-0001
419-248-8000
www.owenscorning.com

P

Pac-Fab, Inc.
1620 Hawkins Avenue
Sanford, NC 27330
919-774-4151
919-775-4206
fax: 919-775-1127
www.pacfab.com

Pacific Bell
140 New Montgomery Street
San Francisco, CA 94015
toll free in CA: 1-800-791-6661
toll free: 800-697-6500 (nationwide)

PaineWebber Inc.
1000 Harbor Boulevard
7th Floor
Weehawken, NJ 07087
201-902-4936
toll free: 800-354-9103
fax: 201-902-5795

Paramount Cards Inc.
400 Pine Street
Pawtucket, RI 02860
410-726-0800
toll free: 800-343-2239
fax: 401-726-0920
www.paramountcards.com

Pella Corp.
102 Main Street
Pella, IA 50219
515-628-1000
fax: 515-628-6070

Pennzoil-Quaker State Company
P.O. Box 2967
Houston, TX 77252-2967
713-546-4000
toll free: 800-990-9811
fax: 713-546-4325
www.pennzoil-quakerstate.com

Pepsi-Cola Co.
1 Pepsi Way
Somers, NY 10589-2201
toll free: 800-433-2652
fax: 914-767-6177
www.pepsico.com

Perdue Farms
P.O. Box 1537
Salisbury, MD 21802
410-543-3000
toll free: 800-473-7383
www.perdue.com

The Perrier Group
777 West Putnam Avenue
Greenwich, CT 06830
203-531-4100
fax: 203-863-0256

Pfizer Inc.
235 East 42nd Street
New York, NY 100175755
(212) 573-2323
www.pfizer.com

Pharmacia and UpJohn Corp.
7000 Portage Road
Kalamazoo, MI 49001
toll free: 800-253-8600
www.pnu.com

Pharmavite Corporation
15451 San Fernando Mission Boulevard
Mission Hills, CA 91346
toll free: 800-276-2878
toll free: 800-314-HERB
fax: 818-837-8609
www.vitamin.com

Philip Morris USA
120 Park Avenue
New York, NY 10017
917-663-2883
toll free: 800-343-0975
fax: 917-663-5362
www.philipmorris.com

Philips Lighting Company
200 Franklin Square Drive
Somerset, NJ 08875-6800
732-563-3081
toll free: 800-555-0050
fax: 732-563-3116
www.lighting.philips.com/nam

Phillips Petroleum Co.
16 Phillips Building
Bartlesville, OK 74004
918-661-1215
fax: 918-662-2075
www.phillips66.com

Phillips-Van Heusen Corp.
1001 Frontier Road, Suite 100
Bridgewater, NJ 08807
908-685-0050
fax: 908-704-8045

The Pillsbury Company
MS 2866
200 South 6th Street
Minneapolis, MN 55402
612-330-4966
toll free: 800-767-4466
www.pillsbury.com

Pioneer Electronics Service, Inc.
P.O. Box 1760
Long Beach, CA 90810
310-952-2561
toll free: 800-421-1404
fax: 310-952-2821
www.pioneerelectronics.com

Pirelli Tire Corporation
300 George Street
New Haven, CT 06511
203-784-2200
fax: 203-784-2408

Playskool (Division of Hasbro)
P.O. Box 200
Pawtucket, RI 02862
800-242-7276
fax: 401-431-8082
www.hasbro.com

Playtex Apparel, Inc.
P.O. Box 631
MS 1526
Dover, DE 19903-0631
302-674-6000
302-674-6381
toll free: 800-537-9955
fax: 302-674-6022

Polaroid Corp.
201 Burlington Road
Bedford, MA 01730
781-386-2000 (collect calls accepted
    within MA)
toll free outside MA: 1-800-343-5000
fax: 781-386-5605
www.polaroid.com

Polo/Ralph Lauren Corp.
4100 Beachwood Drive
Greensboro, NC 27410
toll free: 800-775-7656
fax: 910-632-9097

Price Chopper Supermarkets
501 Duanesburg Road
Schenectady, NY 12306
518-356-9480
518-355-5000
toll free: 800-666-7667
fax: 518-356-9595
www.pricechopper.com

Procom Technology
1821 East Dyer Road
Santa Ana, CA 92705
714-852-1000
toll free: 800-800-8600
fax: 714-852-1221

Procter & Gamble Co.
P.O. Box 599
Cincinnati, OH 45201-0599
513-945-8787
www.pg.com

Provident Mutual Life Insurance
1000 Chesterbrook Boulevard
Berwyn, PA 19312-1181
610-407-1717
toll free: 800-523-4681
fax: 610-407-1379

**Prudential Insurance Company
    of America**
Prudential Plaza, 24th Floor
751 Broad Street
Newark, NJ 07102
201-802-6000
toll free: 800-837-3645
fax: 201-622-4729

**Prudential Property & Casualty
    Company**
23 Main Street
P.O. Box 500
Holmdel, NJ 07733
908-946-6000
toll free: 800-437-5556
fax: 908-946-6245

Prudential Securities Inc.
One New York Plaza
New York, NY 10292
toll free: 800-367-8701
fax: 212-778-2899

Publishers Clearinghouse
382 Channel Drive
Port Washington, NY 11050
516-883-5432
toll free: 800-337-4724
fax: 516-883-5769

Q

Quaker Oats Company
P.O. Box 049001
Chicago, IL 60604-9001
www.quakeroats.com

Quantum Corp.
525 Sycamore Street
Milpitas, CA 95035
toll free: 800-826-8022

Quark, Inc.
1800 Grant Street
Denver, CO 80203
toll free: 800-676-4575
fax: 303-894-3398

QVC Incorporated
Goshen Corporate Park
1200 Wilson Drive
West Chester, PA 19380
610-701-1000
fax: 610-701-1138
www.qvc.com

R

Ralston Purina Company
Checkerboard Square
St. Louis, MO 63164
toll free: 800-778-7462
fax: 314-982-4580
www.purina.com

RDS Computers
2801 Yale Street
Santa Ana, CA 92704
714-751-2008
toll free: 800-827-3998
fax: 714-751-5522
www.maginnovision.com

Reader's Digest Association, Inc.
Reader's Digest Road
Pleasantville, NY 10570-7000
914-238-1000
toll free: 800-234-9000
toll free: 800-846-2100
TDD toll free: 800-735-4327
fax: 914-238-4559
www.readersdigest.com

**The Regina Corporation, Division of
    Ventura**
P.O. Box 638
Long Beach, MS 39560
toll free: 228-867-8507
fax: 800-235-8750

Reliance Insurance Company
Three Parkway
Philadelphia, PA 19102-1376
215-864-4445
toll free: 800-441-1652
fax: 215-864-4640

**Remington Arms (Division of DuPont
    Co.)**
870 Remington Drive
P.O. Box 700
Madison, NC 27025-0700
toll free: 800-243-9700
www.remington.com

Remington Products Company
60 Main Street
Bridgeport, CT 06004
203-367-4400
toll free: 800-736-4648
www.remington-products.com

**Rhone-Poulenc Rorer Pharmaceuticals
    Inc.**
500 Arcola Road
Collegeville, PA 19426
610-454-8000
www.rpr.rpna.com

Rich-Seapak Corporation
P.O. Box 20670
McKinnon Airport Road
St. Simons Island, GA 31522
912-638-5000
toll free: 888-732-7251
www.seapak.com

Rodale Press Inc.
33 East Minor Street
Emmaus, PA 18098
toll free: 800-848-4735
fax: 610-967-8964

Rolex Watch U.S.A. Inc.
665 Fifth Avenue
5th Floor
New York, NY 10022
212-758-7700
fax: 212-980-2166

Roto-Rooter Corp.
300 Ashworth Road
West Des Moines, IA 50265
515-223-1343
fax: 515-223-6109
www.roto-rooter.com

Royal Oak Sales, Inc.
1 Royal Oak Avenue
Roswell, GA 30076
678-461-3200
toll free: 800-241-3955
fax: 678-461-3233

Royal Silk
Office Manager
800 31st Street
Union City, NJ 07087
toll free: 800-962-6262

Rubbermaid
1147 Akron Road
Wooster, OH 44691-6000
330-264-6464, ext. 2505
fax: 330-202-5445
www.rubbermaid.com

Ryder Truck Rental
P.O. Box 020816
Miami, FL 33102-0816
toll free: 800-327-7777
fax: 305-593-4463

S

Safeway, Inc.
5918 Stoneridge Mall Road
Pleasanton, CA 94588-3229
925-467-3000
www.safeway.com

Saks Fifth Avenue
12 East 49th Street
3rd Floor
New York, NY 10021
212-940-5027
toll free: 800-239-3089
fax: 212-940-5031

Salomon Smith Barney
388 Greenwich Street
20th Floor
New York, NY 10013
212-816-6000
fax: 212-723-2184

Samsung Electronics America
1 Samsung Place
Ledgewood, NJ 07852
973-691-6200
toll free: 800-SAMSUNG
toll free: 800-726-7864
fax: 973-691-6201
www.sosimple.com

Sanyo Fisher Co.
1411 West 190th St., #700
Gardena, CA 90248
toll free: 800-421-5013
www.sanyoservice.com

Sara Lee Corp.
L'eggs Products, Inc.
P.O. Box 450
401 Hanes Mill Rd
Winston-Salem, NC 27105
toll free: 800-925-3447
fax: 336-519-2207
www.leggs.com

Sargento Foods Inc.
One Persnickety Place
Plymouth, WI 53073
920-893-8484
toll free: 800-243-3737
fax: 920-893-8399
www.sargento.com

S.C. Johnson and Son, Inc.
1525 Howe Street
Racine, WI 53403
414-260-2000
toll free: 800-558-5252
fax: 414-260-4805
www.scjohnsonwax.com

Schering-Plough HealthCare Products, Inc.
3030 Jackson Avenue
Memphis, TN 38151-0001
901-320-2998
toll free: 800-842-4090
fax: 901-320-2954

The Scotts Company
14111 Scottslawn Road
Marysville, OH 43041
toll free: 800-543-8783

Scotts Miracle-Gro Products, Inc.
800 Port Washington Boulevard
Port Washington, NY 11050
516-883-6550
toll free: 800-645-8166
fax: 516-883-6563
www.miracle-gro.com

Scudder Kemper Investments, Inc.
345 Park Avenue
New York, NY 10154
toll free: 800-225-5163

Seagate Technology, Inc.
920 Disc Drive
Scotts Valley, CA 95066
fax: 405-429-6356
www.seagate.com

Sealy Mattress Manufacturing Company
1 Office Parkway
Trinity, NC 27370
336-861-3500

Sears Merchandise Group
3333 Beverly Road
731-CR
Hoffman Estates, IL 60179
847-286-2500
toll free: 800-549-4505
fax: 800-427-3049
www.sears.com

SEIKO Corporation of America
1111 MacArthur Boulevard
Mahwah, NJ 07430
201-529-5730
201-529-3316 (service & repair)
fax: 201-529-1548
www.seiko.com

Seiko Instruments USA
1130 Ringwood Court
San Jose, CA 95131
408-922-1917
fax: 408-922-1959

Sempra Energy
101 Ash Street
San Diego, CA 92101-3017
toll free: 877-273-6772
www.sempra.com

Serta, Inc.
325 Spring Lake Drive
Itasca, IL 60143
630-285-9300
toll free: 800-426-0371
fax: 630-285-9330
www.serta.com

Sharp Electronics Corp.
Dorothy Scott, National Manager
1300 Naperville Drive
Romeoville, IL 60446
toll free: 800-237-4277
www.sharp-usa.com

The Sharper Image
650 Davis Street
San Francisco, CA 94111
toll free: 800-344-5555
fax: 415-391-1584
www.sharperimage.com

Shell Oil Co.
P.O. Box 2463
Department 210
Houston, TX 77252-2463
toll free: 800-248-4257
fax: 713-241-0581
www.shellus.com

Sherwin-Williams Company
Paint Stores Group
101 Prospect Avenue, NW
Cleveland, OH 44115-1075
216-566-2151
toll free: 800-4SHERWIN (474-3794)
fax: 216-566-1660
www.sherwin-williams.com

Shoney's, Inc.
1717 Elm Hill Pike
Nashville, TN 37210
615-391-5201
toll free: 800-522-9200
fax: 615-231-1604

Simmons Company
P.O. Box 2768
Norcross, GA 30091-2768
770-798-9660
fax: 770-613-5539

The Singer Corporation
4500 Singer Road
Murfreesboro, TN 37129
toll free: 800-474-6437
www.singerco.com

Slim-Fast Foods Company
777 South Flagler Drive
West Tower, Suite 1400
West Palm Beach, FL 33401
561-833-9920
fax: 561-223-1248

Snapper, Inc.
535 Macon Road
McDonough, GA 30253
770-954-2500
770-957-9141
fax: 770-957-7981
www.snapper.com

Sonesta International Hotels Corp.
200 Clarendon Street
Boston, MA 02116
617-421-5451
toll free: 800-SONESTA (reservations)
fax: 617-927-7649
www.sonesta.com

Sony Corp. of America
Sony-CISC
12451 Gateway Boulevard
Fort Myers, FL 33913
941-768-7600
toll free: 800-222-7669
fax: 941-768-7790
www.sel.sony.com

Southwest Airlines
Love Field
P.O. Box 36647
Dallas, TX 75235-1647
214-792-4223
fax: 214-792-5099
www.southwest.com

**Spalding Sports Worldwide/Top Flite
   Professional Golf**
425 Meadow Street
P.O. Box 901
Chicopee, MA 01021-0901
413-536-1200
toll free: 800-225-6601
fax: 413-322-2673
www.sports@spalding.com

Spiegel Catalog, Inc.
3500 Lacey Road
Downers Grove, IL 60515-5432
630-769-2311
fax: 630-769-2490
www.spiegel.com

Spencer Gifts, Inc.
6826 Black Horse Pike
Egg Harbor Township, NJ 08234
609-645-3300
toll free: 800-762-0419

**Springs Industries Inc.
   Springmaid/Performance**
787 7th Avenue
New York, NY 10019
212-903-2100
toll free: 800-537-0115
fax: 212-903-2115

Sprint
1603 LBJ Freeway, Suite 300
Dallas, TX 75234
972-405-6100
toll free: 800-347-8988
fax: 972-405-6114

**Stanley Hardware (Division of the
   Stanley Works)**
480 Myrtle Street
New Britain, CT 06050

860-225-5111
toll free: 800-622-4393

**State Fair Foods, Inc.
   (Division of Sara Lee)**
3900 Meacham Boulevard
Haltom City, TX 76117
817-427-7700
toll free: 800-294-3247
fax: 817-427-7777
www.consumer@statefairfoods.com

**State Farm Mutual Automobile
   Insurance Company**
One State Farm Plaza
Bloomington, IL 61710
309-766-7870
www.statefarm.com

Stokley USA, Inc.
250 East 5th Street
Cinncinati, OH 43202
toll free: 800-872-1110
fax: 414-569-3760

Stop & Shop Supermarket Co., Inc.
P.O. Box 1942
Boston, MA 02105
toll free: 800-767-7772
fax: 617-770-6033
www.virtual-valley.com/stopandshop

Storage Dimensions
1656 MacArthur Boulevard
Milpitas, CA 95035
408-954-0710
fax: 408-944-1200

Sunbeam/Oster Household Products
P.O. Box 948389
Orlando, FL 32794-8389
toll free: 800-597-5978
fax: 1-800-478-6737
www.sunbeam.com

Sunset Magazine
P.O. Box 56656
Boulder, CO 80322
toll free: 800-777-0117
fax: 303-661-1994

Swatch Watch USA
1817 William Penn Way
Lancaster, PA 17604
717-394-7161
fax: 717-399-2211

The Swiss Colony, Inc.
1112 Seventh Avenue
Monroe, WI 53566

608-324-4000
toll free: 800-544-9036
fax: 608-242-1001
www.swisscolony.com

Symantec Corporation
20330 Stephens Creek Boulevard
Cupertino, CA 95014
408-253-9600
toll free: 800-441-7234
www.symantec.com

T

Talbots
175 Beal Street
Hingham, MA 02043
781-749-7600
toll free: 800-992-9010
toll free: 800-TALBOTS
toll free: 800-533-3201
TDD toll free: 800-624-9179
fax: 781-741-4136

Tampax, Procter & Gamble
P.O. Box 599
Cincinnati, OH 45301
www.tampax.com

Tandy Corp./Radio Shack
600 One Tandy Center
Fort Worth, TX 76102
toll free: 800-843-7422
fax: 817-390-3292
www.tandy.com

Target Stores
33 South 6th Street
P.O. Box 1392 CC-48C
Minneapolis, MN 55440
612-304-6000
TDD/TTY toll free: 800-347-5842
fax: 612-304-4996
www.target.com

Teac America
7733 Telegraph Road
Montebello, CA 90640
323-726-0303
fax: 323-727-7621
www.teac.com

Teledyne Water Pik
1730 East Prospect Road
Fort Collins, CO 80553-0001
970-484-1352
toll free: 800-525-2774
fax: 970-221-8298
www.waterpik.com

Teleflora
11444 West Olympic
4th Floor
Los Angeles, CA 90064
310-231-9199
toll free: 800-421-2815
fax: 800-232-3811

Tenneco, Inc.
500 North Field Drive
Lake Forest, IL 60045
203-863-1000
fax: 203-862-1914
www.tenneco.com

Tetley USA, Inc.
P.O. Box 856
100 Commerce Drive
Shelton, CT 06484-0856
203-929-9200
toll free: 800-728-0084
toll free: 800-732-3027
fax: 203-926-0876

Texas Instruments, Inc.
Consumer Relations
7839 Churchill Way MS3962
Dallas, TX 75251
972-917-8324 (technical support)
toll free: 800-842-2737
fax: 972-917-0747
www.ti.com

Thermo Quest
P.O. Box 649
Nillcreek Road
Marietta, OH 45750
740-373-4763
toll free: 800-848-3080
fax: 740-568-5712
www.forma.com

Thompson's Co. (Division of Sherwin-Williams)
Midland Building
101 Prospect Avenue NW
P.O. Box 647
Cleveland, OH 44115
www.thompson.waterseal.com

3M
3M Center
Building 225-1S-15
St. Paul, MN 55144-1000
651-737-6501
toll free: 800-364-3577 (3M HELP)
toll free: 800-713-6329 (Fax)
fax: 651-737-7117
www.3m.com

Time Warner Inc.
75 Rockefeller Plaza
New York, NY 10019
212-484-8000
www.timewarner.com

Timex Corp.
P.O. Box 2740
Little Rock, AR 72203-2740
501-370-5781
toll free: 800-448-4639
fax: 501-370-5747
www.timex.com

TJX Companies (T.J. Maxx)
770 Cochituate Road
Framingham, MA 01701
508-390-1000
toll free: 800-926-6299

Tonka Products (Division of Hasbro, Inc.)
P.O. Box 200
Pawtucket, RI 02861-0200
toll free: 800-255-5516
fax: 401-727-5901
www.hasbro.com

Tops Friendly Market, Ohio Division
17000 Rockside Road
Maple Heights, OH 44137-4390
216-518-6720
fax: 216-518-6022

The Toro Company
8111 Lyndale Avenue South
Bloomington, MN 55420
612-888-8801
toll free: 800-348-2424 x4001
www.toro.com

Toshiba America
82 Totowa Road
Wayne, NJ 07470
toll free: 800-631-3811
www.toshiba.com

Totes/Isotoner
9655 International Boulevard
Cincinnati, OH 45246-5658
513-682-8200
fax: 513-682-8606
www.totes.com

Tourneau, Inc.
3 East 54th Street
3rd Floor
New York, NY 10022
212-758-3265
toll free outside NY: 1-800-223-1288

Toys "R" Us
461 From Road
Paramus, NJ 07652
201-262-7800
toll free: 888-243-6337
fax: 201-599-8992
www.toysrus.com

Trans World Airlines, Inc.
1415 Olive Street, Suite 100
St. Louis, MO 63103
314-589-3600
TDD toll free: 800-421-8480 (reservations)
fax: 314-589-3626
www.twa.com

The Travelers Companies
One Tower Square 4GS
Hartford, CT 06183-9079
860-277-0111
fax: 860-954-3956
www.travelers.com

Tripp Lite
111 W. 35th Street
Chicago, IL 60609
773-869 1234
fax: 773-869-1351
www.triplite.com

TruServ Corporation
8600 West Bryn Mawr
Chicago, IL 60631-3505
773-695-5000
fax: 773-695-5184
www.truserv.com

Tupperware
P.O. Box 2353
Orlando, FL 32802-2353
fax: 407-847-1897

Turtle Wax, Inc.
5655 West 73rd Street
Chicago, IL 60638-6211
708-563-3600
toll free: 800-805-7695
fax: 708-563-4302
www.turtlewax.com

TXU
TXU Electric and Gas Company
1601 Bryan Street
Dallas, TX 75201-3401
972-791-2888
www.txu.com

Tyson Foods
P.O. Box 2020
Springdale, AR 72765-2020
501-290-4714

toll free: 800-233-6332
fax: 501-290-7930
www.tyson.com

U

U-Haul International
P.O. Box 21502
Phoenix, AZ 85036-1502
602-263-6771
toll free: 800-528-0463
fax: 602-263-6984
www.u-haul.com

Umax Technologies
3561 Gateway Boulevard
Freemont, CA 94538

Unilever Cosmetics International
Calvin Klein Cosmetics Company
350 Clark Drive
Mt. Olive, NJ 07828
toll free: 800-715-4023
fax: 973-691-7764

Uniroyal Tires
P.O. Box 19001
Greenville, SC 29602-9001
864-458-5000
toll free: 800-521-9796
fax: 864-458-6650
www.michelin.com

UNISYS Corp.
Unisys Walk
Blue Bell, PA 19424-0001
215-986-4011
toll free: 800-328-0440
toll free: 800-874-8647
fax: 215-986-5669
www.unisys.com

United Airlines
P.O. Box 66100
Chicago, IL 60666
847-700-4000
fax: 847-700-2214
www.ual.com

United States Fidelity & Guarantee Co.
   (USF&G)
5801 Smith Avenue
Baltimore, MD 21209
410-205-3000
www.usfg.com

United Van Lines, Inc.
One United Drive
Fenton, MO 63026
314-326-3100

toll free: 800-948-4885
fax: 314-326-3111
www.unitedvanlines.com

US Airways
P.O. Box 1501
Winston-Salem, NC 27102
336-661-8126
fax: 336-661-8187
www.usairways.com

V

ValueStar
360 22nd Street, 4th Floor
Oakland, CA 94612
510-808-1311
510-808-1300
toll free: 800-310-6661
fax: 510-808-1440
www.valuestar.com

The Valvoline Company
P.O. Box 14000
Lexington, KY 40512
606-357-7847
toll free: 800-354-9061
fax: 606-357-7918 or 800-682-6994
www.valvoline.com

Verizon
1095 Avenue of the Americas
New York, NY 10036
212-395-2121 (main switchboard)
toll free: 800-721-2300
toll free: 800-621-9900
TTY toll free: 800-974-6006
www.bellatlantic.com

Viacom, Inc.
Karen Zatorski, Vice President
1515 Broadway
52nd Floor
New York, NY 10036
212-258-6346
www.viacom.com

Visa USA, Inc.
P.O. Box 8999
San Francisco, CA 94128-8999
650-432-3200
www.visa.com

Vons Companies, Inc.
618 Michillinda Avenue
Arcadia, CA 91007
626-821-7000
fax: 626-821-3654
www.supermarkets.com

W

Wagner Spray Tech Corp.
1770 Fernbrook Lane
Plymouth, MN 55447
612-553-7000
toll free: 800-328-8251
fax: 612-509-7555

Walgreen Company
Consumer Relations
200 Wilmot Road
Deerfield, IL 60015
847-914-2704
toll free: 800-289-2273
fax: 847-914-3105
www.walgreens.com

Wal-Mart Stores, Inc.
702 SW Eighth Street
Bentonville, AR 72716-0117
501-273-4000
toll free: 800-WAL-MART
fax: 501-621-2063
www.wal-mart.com

Walter Drake, Inc.
4519 Edison Avenue
Colorado Springs, CO 80915
719-596-3140
toll free: 800-525-9291
fax: 719-637-4984

Wang Laboratories, Inc.
290 Concord Road
Billerica, MA 01821-4130
978-967-5000
toll free: 800-639-9264
fax: 978-967-0829

Warner-Lambert Consumer Group
182 Tabor Road
Morris Plains, NJ 07950
973-385-2000
fax: 973-385-6667
www.prodhelp.com

Weider Health and Fitness
21100 Erwin Street
Woodland Hills, CA 91367
818-884-6800
fax: 818-704-5734

Weight Watchers Gourmet Food Company
P.O. Box 10
Boise, ID 83707
www.weightwatchers.com

The West Bend Company
400 Washington Street
West Bend, WI 53095
262-334-2311
fax: 262-334-6800
www.westbend.com

WestPoint Stores
P.O. Box 609
West Point, GA 31833-0609
toll free: 800-533-8229
fax: 706-645-7783
www.martex.com

Wet Seal Inc.
26972 Borbank Road
Foothill Ranch, CA 92610
714-699-3900
fax: 714-583-0715

Whirlpool Corporation
2303 Pipestone Road
Benton Harbor, MI 49022-2427
616-923-7700
toll free: 800-253-1301
fax: 616-923-7829
www.whirlpool.com

Williams-Sonoma
10000 Covington Cross Drive
Las Vegas, NV 89144
702-360-7000
toll free: 800-541-1262
fax: 702-360-7091

Winn-Dixie Stores, Inc.
Box B
Jacksonville, FL 32203
904-783-5000
www.winn-dixie.com

Winnebago Industries
605 W. Crystal Lake Road
P.O. Box 152
Forest City, IA 50436-0152
641-585-6252
toll free: 800-537-1885
fax: 641-585-6704
www.winnebagoind.com

Wrangler
P.O. Box 21488
Greensboro, NC 27420
336-332-3564
fax: 336-332-3223
www.wrangler.com

Wm. Wrigley Jr. Company
410 North Michigan Avenue
Chicago, IL 60611
312-644-2121
fax: 312-644-0015
www.wrigley.com

WUIP International
5200 Keller Springs Road, Suite 1131
Dallas, TX 75248
972-233-0966

Wyse Technology
3471 North First Street
San Jose, CA 95134
408-473-1200
408-435-2770 (service and parts)
fax: 408-473-1222

X

Xerox Corporation
P.O. Box 1600
800 Long Ridge Road
Stamford, CT 06904
203-968-3000
toll free: 800-275-9376
www.xerox.com

Xircom USA
2300 Corporate Center Drive
Thousand Oaks, CA 91320
805-376-9200
fax: 805-376-9100
www.xircom.com/tech

Y

Yamaha Motor Corporation
Lindsey Foster, Division Manager
6555 Katella Avenue
Cypress, CA 90630-5101
714-761-7435
toll free: 800-962-7926
fax: 714-761-7559
www.yamaha-motor.com

Z

Zenith Electronics Corp.
1000 Milwaukee Ave.
Glenview, IL 60025
256-772-1515
toll free: 888-3 ZENITH
www.zenith.com

Zenith Packard Bell
8285 West 3500 South
Magna, UT 84044
toll free: 800-227-3360
www.packardbell.com

APPENDIX X
GLOSSARY

The following is a list of abbreviations, acronyms, and terms that should prove helpful to individuals interested in working in the retail and wholesale industries.

accounts receivable   Monies due for merchandise which has been sold

add-on merchandise   Additional merchandise which may be sold to a customer

advertised item   Products featured in ads, flyers, or commercials

advertising   Promoting a product through paid ads, commercials, or other media

all sales final   No refunds, credits, or exchanges after the sale of a product or merchandise

approval code   A special code given by a credit card company when a transaction for a sale is approved and authorized

authorization code   A series of numbers or letters given by a credit card company when a transaction is authorized

automated   A process that is completed by a computer or other machine

B2B   Business to Business; a wholesaler is generally a business-to-business retailer

B2C   Business to consumer; a retailer generally is a business-to-consumer company

back order   Merchandise that is not currently in stock, but is on order and will be available at a later date

bar code   A set of encoded lines and spaces that can be scanned to identify merchandise

benchmark   Achievement standards in the industry

bins   Boxes, containers, or enclosed shelving used to display store merchandise

Black Friday   A retail term referring to the day after Thanksgiving in the United States. It is the start of the Christmas holiday shopping season, and for many retailers, the biggest shopping day of the year.

brackets   The fixtures that hold up the displays on a store's wall

building a display   Arranging merchandise samples in a visually pleasing manner in the store

C.O.D.   Cash On Delivery; see below

cash discount   The retail price of a product less a percentage if a customer pays cash

Cash On Delivery   Customer pays on delivery of merchandise

cash refund   Monies received for returned merchandise

cash register tape   Paper tape in the cash register on which transactions are recorded

cash register   The machine that records transactions

comparison shopping   Shopping at competing retailers to compare their merchandise, prices, and service

competition   Similar retailers targeting the same customers

computerized inventory system   A computer program which tracks a retailer's or wholesaler's inventory

consumer   Customer

cost   The price of merchandise

CRM   Customer relationship management; focuses on customer relationships instead of transactions

customer satisfaction   How pleased and satisfied customers are with a company; providing good service in a pleasant manner and meeting the customer's expectations

customer service   The art of providing good service that meets or exceeds customers' expectations

daily sales audit   A review of daily sales journals against the receipt of funds

date of invoice   The date a credit period begins

demographics   The breakdown of an area into statistical categories; demographics are often used to determine placement of stores

distressed goods   Merchandise that has been damaged or soiled

distributor   Individual or company that moves merchandise from a manufacturer to retail outlets

DOI   Date of invoice

EAS   Electronic article surveillance; electronic device utilized to help control shoplifting

E-Commerce   Buying and selling merchandise through the Internet

electronic scanner   a machine or computer that reads bar codes

expenses   The cost of operating a business

forecasting   Predicting future sales or trends in sales

freestanding store   A retail store which is not in a mall or shopping center

gross margin   The profit a business has before it deducts the expenses of operations

hypermart/hypermarket   A retail outlet with a warehouse appearance such as Sam's or BJ's

impulse purchase   A purchase made without prior planning by a customer

initial markup   The first or original price markup on merchandise

inventory   A method of checking the value and amount of merchandise on hand by taking a physical count of stock

journal roll   The cash register tape on which transactions are recorded. These are kept by the store for records.

kiosk   A leased booth, car, or area inside of a store or mall

loss leader   Merchandise sold at an extremely low or attractive price to entice customers to come into the store or make a purchase from a retailer

mail order retailing   Sale of merchandise through the mail from items such as catalogs or direct mail

manufacturer   Producer of products

markdown   A reduction of the selling price

markup   Used in retail; the difference between the selling price of merchandise and the cost of that merchandise

merchandising   The buying and selling of merchandise

percentage-of-sales method   Method of developing the advertising budget based on a percentage of past or anticipated sales

One-Stop   Wholesale distributor of specialty merchandise

promotional advertising   Advertising by a retailer used to attract customers

rack jobber   A wholesaler allowed by a store to stock and replenish merchandise on display racks; many department stores have rack jobbers handle their CD or book stock

receipt   Paper from the cash register or credit card machine given to a customer

referral premium   Gift or cash reimbursement awarded to current customers who refer potential new customers; car salespeople and dealers often utilize referral premiums

register   Machine that records customer transactions

retail price   The price a consumer pays for merchandise

retailer   Company that sells merchandise to a consumer

retailing   Selling goods and services to customers

ROG   Receipt of goods

sales per square foot   Refers to the net sales of a retailer divided by the square feet of selling space of the store

search the net   Going on-line to visit various sites on the Internet

shrinkage   The loss of merchandise as a result of shoplifting, internal theft, and damage

SKU   See Stock Keeping Unit

standards   The brackets used to hold up wall displays

stock   A store's supply of goods and merchandise

stock Keeping Unit   The identification number given to each item by the retailer

stuffers   A promotional piece or advertisement accompanying a billing or credit card statement or placed in customers' shopping bags

tearsheet   Copy of an advertisement from the newspaper or magazine; most companies will not pay for ads without a tearsheet

trades   Newspapers and magazines that are geared to a specific industry

turnover   Determines how quickly merchandise is sold; may also refer to employee retention rates

unit-of-sales method   Means by which an advertising budget is established based on the number or projected number of sales of an item, instead of the dollar amount

union card   A card that is used to identify members of a specific union

universal Product Code   A set of encoded lines and spaces which can be scanned to identify a product

UPC   See Universal Product Code

visual merchandising   The arrangement of items in a pleasing manner for display

web   The World Wide Web

website   A place on the World Wide Web

WWW   World Wide Web

ABOUT THE AUTHOR

Shelly Field is a nationally recognized motivational speaker, career expert, stress specialist, and author of over 25 best-selling books in the business and career fields.

Her books instruct people on how to obtain jobs in a wide variety of areas including the hospitality, music, sports and communications industries, casinos and casino hotels, advertising, public relations, theater, the performing arts, entertainment, animal rights, health care, writing and art; and how to choose the best career for the new century.

She is a frequent guest on local, regional, and national radio, cable, and television talk, information, and news shows and also does numerous print interviews and personal appearances.

Field is a featured speaker at conventions, expos, casinos, corporate functions, employee training and development sessions, career fairs, spouse programs and events nation-wide. She speaks on empowerment, motivation, careers, gaming, human resources; attracting, retaining and motivating employees; customer service, and stress reduction. Her popular seminars, *"STRESS BUSTERS: Beating the Stress in Your Work and Your Life"* and *"The De-Stress Express"* are favorites around the country.

Field is a career consultant as well as a life and career coach to businesses, educational institutions, employment agencies, women's groups, and individuals. She is a corporate consultant to businesses throughout the country, appearing at job fairs and providing assistance with human resources issues such as attracting, retaining, and motivating employees, customer service training and stress management in the workplace.

As president and CEO of The Shelly Field Organization, a public relations and management firm handling national clients, she also does corporate consulting and has represented celebrities in the sports, music, and entertainment industries as well as authors, businesses, and corporations.

For information about personal appearances or seminars, contact **The Shelly Field Organization** at P.O. Box 711, Monticello, NY 12701 or log on to www.shellyfield.com.

INDEX